AF352611

MYTHOLOGY AND
FOLKLORE OF THE HUI,
A MUSLIM CHINESE PEOPLE

MYTHOLOGY AND FOLKLORE OF THE HUI, A MUSLIM CHINESE PEOPLE

Shujiang Li
Karl W. Luckert

Translations by Fenglan Yu, Zhilin Hou, and Ganhui Wang

Chinese Editorial Assistance, Zongqi Yu
Assistance with Arabic, Mahmoud Abu Saud

State University of New York Press

Published by
State University of New York Press, Albany

For information, address State University of New York Press,
State University Plaza, Albany, N.Y., 12246

Production by Marilyn P. Semerad
Marketing by Bernadette LaManna

Library of Congress Cataloging-in-Publication Data

Li, Shujiang, 1946–
    Mythology and Folklore of the Hui, a Muslim Chinese people /
Shujiang Li, Karl W. Luckert ; translations by Fenglan Yu, Zhilin
Hou, and Ganhui Wang ; Chinese editorial assistance Zongqi Yu;
assistance with Arabic Mahmoud Abu Saud.
        p.   cm.
    Translated from Chinese.
    Includes bibliographical references and index.
    ISBN 0-7914-1823-5. — ISBN 0-7914-1824-3 (pbk.)
        1. Muslims—China—Folklore. 2. Mythology, Chinese. I. Luckert,
Karl W., 1934–   . II. Title.
GR335.L47475 1994
398.2'0951—dc20
                                                        93-21529
                                                        CIP

To the Memory

of

Martha M. Metz (1896–1986)

and

Mahmoud Abu Saud (1914–1993)

CONTENTS

5. Islam and Other Religions

6. Muslims Under the Emperor

7. Origins of the Hui Nationality

8. Hui Leaders With and Against the Empire

Preface

Mythology and Folklore of the Hui is placed into the hands of English readers for the first time. A small number of the stories that are included were written down in dynastic times. A few more in this collection were recorded in the decades before the disastrous Cultural Revolution (1966–1976) that erased most of the humanities, and much of China's historiography and culture, from her system of education. While early dynastic stories were written primarily to explain the Hui or Muslim presence over against the Han majority, some samples from the early 1960s show the restless Hui minority more or less in accord with contemporary revolutionary goals and with nation building. A trace of this sentiment has also shown up, here and there, after the Cultural Revolution, during the late 1970s and early 1980s. During the 1980s and into the 1990s Professor Li Shujiang, as director of the Nationalities Literature Center at the University of Ningxia, has, in collaboration with colleagues and graduate students, organized a team effort for collecting Hui mythology and folklore. Most of the stories in this collection were recorded by this group during the 1980s. Some stories were previously published by various institutions in China.

Meanwhile, during the 1970s and 1980s, the American co-author, Karl W. Luckert, had developed his own love for ethnology and folklore. He has recorded and published a number of Navajo Indian oral traditions. In collaboration with the Museum of Northern Arizona Press and the University of Nebraska Press he has published the American Tribal Religions book series. As an historian of religions he felt obliged to look beyond his American Indian area of emphasis. When China again opened its doors to foreign scholars he began traveling there since 1987, in search of folklore.

We thank professors Chen Yongling, Wei Cuiyi, Li Zengxiang, Hu Zhenhua, and others at the Central Institute for Nationalities, in Beijing, for their assistance and mediation. When Li Shujiang and Karl W. Luckert finally met at the University of Ningxia, in 1988, with the assistance of Mahmoud Abu Saud, they benefited from the goodwill and wise counsel of professors Zhang Kuei and Wang Shiyi.

Foremost appreciation for the existence of this volume is expressed, of course, to all the Hui people who have shared their stories with the world and with us. We also thank our friend, Chuma Wang Zhengwei, for his cooperation and for his many suggestions while the authors planned this collection. A special word of thanks is offered to Ningxia governmental as well as Hui religious leaders who have permitted our work and helped it along. In addition, field assistance to the authors was rendered by Chuma Wang Zhengwei, Wang Ganhui, Yu Fenglan, Hou Zhilin, Li Zengxiang, Zhou Pengqi, Li Shuanzhu, and Zhao Hui.

Translation of *Mythology and Folklore of the Hui* into English was first done in two parts, in Ningxia. Yu Fenglan has translated the first half, and Hou Zhilin and Wang Ganhui together have done the second half. Their translations were then revised by Luckert with the help of Yu Zongqi, who worked under a graduate assistant stipend provided by Southwest Missouri State University. The translators, in continual dialogue with Li and Luckert, have in turn reexamined the revisions.

Commentary was initially provided by Li and Luckert in approximately equal portions. Chinese introductory materials were translated by Yu Fenglan and adapted by Luckert to accommodate Western modes of curiosity and limitations. The extent to which the Chinese author's original contributions were omitted, neglected, or distorted in the Preface, Introduction, and the texts, should be considered the fault of the American co-author. Mahmoud Abu Saud has provided information and suggestions about Arabic roots and nuances; Jeffrey T. Kenney and Christopher Melchert have helped solve Arabic puzzles as well. Heidi Luckert helped with a round of proofreading. We thank Gregory D. Alles, Gary L. Ebersole, Wei Cuiyi, Dru C. Gladney, and Thomas J. Barfield, as well as some readers who remain anonymous, for having read the manuscript and having offered helpful suggestions. All mistakes that have survived in spite of the good advice of these people remain the burden of the American co-author.

Supplementary travel support was contributed by the Institute of International Islamic Thought, the Zakat and Research Foundation, the Nada Institute, Mahmoud Abu Saud, Southwest Missouri State University, and the University of Ningxia.

MYTHOLOGY AND FOLKLORE OF THE HUI, A MUSLIM CHINESE PEOPLE

Introduction

Hui people in China officially have been classified by their government as a nationality *(minzu)*. By and large they still abide within the spiritual beam of light, the religion of Islam, that has been radiating from Arabia since the seventh century. They live at many places throughout China, and beyond—from the Tianshan Mountains in Xinjiang, to both sides of the Taiwan Strait, from the Changbai Mountains and the Heilongjiang River to the southeastern hills on the Loess Plateau, to the Yungui tableland, to the Tibetan highlands, and to the grasslands of Inner Mongolia.

According to the most recent official census, of 1989/90, the Hui population in China now numbers over eight and a half million.[1] Private estimates by Muslim leaders vary and are usually higher. While the census figures represent reasonably accurate counts of people who registered as Hui, the actual number could indeed be higher. In the aftermath of persecution during the Cultural Revolution (1966–1976) many Muslims, dispersed throughout China, preferred to remain invisible during the 1982 census. It is possible that still in 1989 some of these have insisted on their accustomed veil of anonymity.

Since the founding of the People's Republic of China, in 1949, special autonomous "Hui" regions were established—prefectures and counties in which these people can live together in communities and follow their own traditions. This is the case in places like Ningxia, Gansu, Xinjiang, Hebei, Qinghai, Yunnan, and Guizhou. Some large

---

[1]Among China's fifty officially recognized nationalities, ten more or less adhere to the religion of Islam. Their total number of 17,592,370 divides, according to the 1989/90 census, as follows. (Population figures of the 1982 census are given in parentheses.) Hui—8,602,978 (7,219,352); Uighur—7,214,431 (5,957,112); Kazakh—1,111,718 (907,582); Dongxiang—373,872 (279,397); Kirgiz—141,549 (113,999); Salar—82,697 (69,102); Tadjik—33,538 (26,503); Uzbek—14,502 (12,453); Baoan—12,212 (9,027); Tatar—4,873 (4,127).

Figure 1. Distribution of the Hui population (8,602,978), according to the 1989/90 census, by provinces and municipalities: Beijing 207,006; Tianjin 159,349; Hebei 492,022; Shanxi 57,761; Inner Mongolia 192,808; Liaoning 263,422; Jilin 122,777; Heilongjiang 139,078; Shanghai 49,709; Jiangsu 121,120; Zhejiang 17,186; Anhui 300,294; Fujian 92,124; Jiangxi 9,331; Shandong 459,597; Henan 868,865; Hubei 77,625; Hunan 93,205; Guangdong 8,845; Guangxi 28,190; Hainan 5,695; Sichuan 108,638; Guizhou 126,500; Yunnan 522,046; Tibet 2,987; Shaanxi 130,899; Gansu 1,094,354; Qinghai 638,847; Ningxia 1,524,448; Xinjiang 681,527.

cities have special sections or "ghettos" designated for Hui people. In all these places the name "Hui" identifies, nowadays, one of ten officially recognized Muslim nationalities—of which the Hui, Dongxiang, Salar, and Baoan for the most part speak Chinese and the six others use non-Chinese languages.

Historians of religions traditionally have ignored Islam in China because, from a distance, it appeared "sinicized" or assimilated to Chinese culture. Its syncretism confounded the purity of core-Islam as it was thought to exist in the Near East. Moreover, throughout the centuries Chinese converts to Islam have continued to communicate with one another in Mandarin, and that fact was taken as primary evidence to prove their assimilation. General Sinologists, in turn, have ignored Muslims in China because Confucianism, Daoism, Buddhism, and recently Maoism, have seemed infinitely more important. The void in English academic literature about Chinese Muslims appears to have been disturbed by the Protestant missionary Marshall Broomhall who, in 1910, published a book with the plaintive title *Islam in China: A Neglected Problem.*

After it was possible again, during the 1980s, for Westerners to study and do research in China, a number of scholars—Aubin, Fletcher, Forbes, Gladney, Israeli, Leslie, Lipman, Pillsbury, and others—began publishing significant information concerning the political, social, and cultural dimensions of the Muslim existence in China. *Mythology and Folklore of the Hui* is presented here neither as an addition nor as a challenge to their thoughtful conclusions. Our presentation is no more and no less than an independent expansion into the still-neglected field of Chinese Muslim mythology and folklore. Chinese Muslim people are hereby given an opportunity to introduce themselves to the world, to speak for themselves while retelling some of the stories which they already have told their children and grandchildren. Listening together with them to these Hui stories, while sitting upon the knees of the parents and grandparents, is the fastest way of getting to know these people better.

Of course, the authors realize that in the political milieu which envelops East and West no innocently intended collection of folklore can hope to be appreciated apolitically. The very mentioning of the Hui, as in "Hui nationality" *(Hui minzu)* or "Hui folklore," may be misunderstood as an affront to friends and scholars who for a decade or so have tried to enlighten us about how diverse and ethnologically undefinable this "Hui nationality" really is. In deference to them it would be easier to abandon the label "Hui" and refer instead to "Chinese Muslims" or to "Muslim Chinese." A number of reasons block for us this road of escape.

Mythology and Folklore of the Hui is only one of several volumes of mythology and folklore presently being prepared for publication by the American co-author. "Kazakh Traditions" and "Uighur Stories" already have been translated into English and are being edited to be released soon. At this point in time, Kazakhs and Uighurs can be classified as "Chinese Muslims" or as "Muslim Chinese" as well. Books require titles, and titles must distinguish books from other books. It is at this practical precipice that theoretical considerations about "Hui-ness," or about the unreasonableness of the Chinese *minzu* sooner or later will come to grief.

There are other facts that extend beyond the simple ambition of bookmaking. Western scholars tend to dislike the government that has classified and counted some of its people as being Hui—and in the process has redefined their self-designation "Hui" (Muslim) to boot. Like it or not, the fact remains that everywhere in China "Hui" now is the name of the people whose folklore we present. There is a prehistory to the present policies of the Chinese government that should be of some interest to Western readers.

Sun Yatsen distinguished five groups of Chinese peoples—Han, Manchu, Mongolian, Tibetan, and Hui; his "Hui" group still included Uighurs and Kazakhs. Chiang Kaishek espoused a single nation of Chinese people and acknowledged only the presence of certain regional and religious differences.[2] The subsequent recognition of the Chinese-speaking Hui people as a distinct nationality resulted in part from the conflict that ensued between Communist leaders and the Koumintang. It also came about in part because of the Hui people's entanglements with the political fortunes of the Socialist state in Ningxia and Gansu, during the 1930s and 1940s.

In the decade following the "Long March" of 1935, the Red Army under Mao Tsedong sought refuge and survived in territories settled mostly by Hui Muslims—in Ningxia and in Gansu. As a gesture of distinguishing himself from Chiang Kaishek, it seems, and as a sign of goodwill toward his hosts in Ningxia and Gansu, Mao

---

[2]Dru C. Gladney, *Muslim Chinese—Ethnic Nationalism in the People's Republic* (Cambridge: Harvard University Press, 1991), pp. 83–84.

Tsedong recognized the Hui people as a distinct "nationality," along with Mongol and Miao peoples, in a speech on November 6, 1938, during the Sixth Central Committee session, and then again in an official document of the Communist Party in 1941. When the Red Army prevailed against the Koumintang forces, in the late 1940s, a measure of appreciation toward their Hui hosts endured.

By our estimate, the Hui people were not passive victims upon whose pristine innocence some arbitrary Marxist-Stalinist-Maoist category of *minzu* was somehow imposed. The number of people who nowadays wish to be counted as Hui continues to grow, and the people so categorized and counted have learned to ride within this Trojan horse. Being a nationality, they have learned how to turn a minority stigma into privileges and advantages over against the Han majority. Of course, judging from the general history of majority backlashes and holocausts, this trend will surely boomerang some day against the minorities if all of presentday China stays together. For the moment however, under pressures which have been released by the recent breakup of the Soviet Union, the advantages that come with belonging to a northwestern minority *minzu* will continue to multiply well into the forseeable future. For that same forseeable future the name "Hui" will be used politically by Chinese leaders as well as by those whom they have so named.

While Western readers of folklore cannot be expected to embrace the Marxist-Stalinist-Maoist theory of nationalities more or less in stride, a measure of sympathy and historical understanding is nevertheless called for. After all, the Chinese ideological complication was generated by fellow Westerners, by Marx and Engels who happen to have been countrymen of the German-born co-author who is responsible for this Introduction. Receptive Socialist revolutionaries were obliged, by Marxist theory, to discount religion wherever they found it—because it was opium that hitherto was administered by feudalistic oppressors to exploit the poor. Because the religion of Chinese Muslims could not be officially acknowledged as being something rational, legitimate or honorable, the official meaning of "Hui-ness"—and never forget that the people who demanded *minzu* status and privileges kept knocking at the door—had to be upgraded and secularized to become rational in the Marxist sense by which the government felt obliged to rule. The name "Hui," therefore, was used no longer to mean "Muslim" but to designate a culturally distinct ethnic minority. Cultural and historical factors, rather than religious ones, were utilized in defining the Hui nationality.[3] From this point arises our next methodological difficulty.

Unlike their Chinese colleagues who are still not in the habit of thinking positively about religions, most Western scholars would prefer to collect Hui folklore based upon some implied religious "Hui-ness." Indeed, if seen from a Western perspective it is the Islamic religious inheritance of the Hui that most distinguishes them from the vast Han majority. Thus, in light of this Western predilection it would seem reasonable for us to select Hui stories on the basis of whether or not they conform to the values or faith of Islam.

It is indeed a fact that numerous religious Hui myths and legends unambiguously reflect, and even extol, Islamic tradition and values. Inasmuch as we are publishing Hui stories for Western readers, we have eagerly included many of that variety. But there is another angle to consider. Nowhere in the world can folklore be neatly classified under the rubric of a universalistic world religion. That is to say, Hui folklore carries within itself many traces of pre-Islamic notions. And not every member of the Hui nationality subscribes to or even knows the five pillars of Islam, and not everyone attends Friday prayers at the mosque. Many participate in public prayers only once or twice a year, perhaps to celebrate the end of Ramadan, or Qurban. Most never darken the door of a mosque. That is to say, their thinking has gotten atuned to post-Islamic secular modernity or atheism.

It is practically impossible, and would be arbitrary at best, to come up with an assortment of Hui stories chosen in conformity with an Islamic norm—as, for example, it would be equally impossible to assemble a canon of Christian folklore. How Christian in predominantly Christian lands are "Cinderella," "Red Ridinghood," or "Sleeping Beauty"? Not even all the Hui stories that overtly subscribe

---

[3]In the case of the Hui people, the argument for *minzu* status cannot be made on the basis of language. Four Islamically influenced nationalities, the Hui, Dongxiang, Salar, and Baoan, speak Mandarin Chinese and the six others use non-Chinese languages. Moreover, the presence of converts to "Hui-ness" who still speak Tibetan (as in Qinghai) or Bai (as in Yunnan) languages—languages which were deemed basic for recognizing the Tibetan and Bai nationalities—confounds even the negative fact of Hui Muslims having no language of their own. The only objective criterion for delimiting the *Hui minzu*, aside from the people's own desire for more autonomy, remains the religion of Islam. In accordance with Marxist ideology, *minzu* status could only be given after religious facts were transposed into a broader context of cultural, societal, and economic realities.

to Islamic values, or that have been told by an ahong, would delight every sincere Muslim in the world. The authors of this book, working as an intercultural inter-university team, have chosen—and we think wisely—to subscribe to the current Chinese official definition. We use the name "Hui" as the secular designation of a Chinese nationality. With this publication we are trying to assemble neither a Chinese echo to "Thousand and One Nights," nor are we trying to produce a Chinese "Hadith."

In order to transcend the cloud of political and ideological problems that are evoked by the presence of Chinese nationalities, with which recent Western scholarship has been much preoccupied, we must provide an outline of the larger evolutionary context within which we can move. Of course, the original Lewis Henry Morgan-style stage evolutionism, which informed Marx and Engels, need not be resurrected for this purpose; but neither can the process of evolution be dismissed out of hand. Mythology and folklore, their adjustments in human space and through linear time, cannot be understood by continuing to focus exclusively on political, social, or economic phenomena. The theory of evolution is solidly established in physics and biology, as well as in anthropology; it is with us to stay. Human, cultural, and religious evolution is a process that has left obvious traces in mythology and folklore—as it has left imprints on everything that the human mind has ever grasped. And what harm will be done if our evolutionistic categories or phases resonate favorably in the minds of people who over decades have been exercised in Marxist ideology? If their nineteenth-century evolutionism can no longer be deemed rational by Western scholars, neither can our disregard for evolutionary reality be considered rational anymore—not after what in recent decades we have learned about human evolution.

Real life in general, and real Hui life in particular, is not encapsuled in eternal static structure. Like all human cultures in this world, so also theirs has been ever changing. But the hallmark of human minds is to have long memories, and folk traditions contain many tenacious traces of collective memory about very ancient ways and living conditions. While the Hui stories in this collection can all be enjoyed for their overt plots, they will come even more alive for the historically astute reader if they are approached with an eye focused on historical and evolutionary points of transition.

We must alert our readers to four important moments in the evolution of what has become the Hui folklore tradition. Specific themes and motifs can be traced to distinct evolutionary culture strata or moments in time. First we shall consider traces of mythology from "hunter-gatherer culture," then adjustments to "domesticator culture." Thereafter we contemplate Hui traditions in relation to "grand domestication" and Chinese religious "universalisms." Traces of influence from the most recent worldwide stratum, "secular democratization," we shall mention only as far as it is necessary to put our corpus of Hui stories in perspective.[4]

The *hunter-gatherer* phase in human evolution is marked by humans controlling the end of plant and animal life cycles. *Domestication*, later, extended this control to embrace the beginnings and durations of life cycles as well. *Grand domestication* means that some domesticators advanced beyond the mere control of plants and animals to also take control, or to overdomesticate, human groups and their gods. *Universal salvation religions*, such as Buddhism, Christianity and Islam, have begun by ignoring the boundaries of existing empires or grand domestication systems. Eventually, here and there, all these universalistic movements have relapsed into earlier modes of over-domestication. *Secular democratic revolts* are universalistic reactions to re-overdomesticated religious universalisms.

In any case, by viewing Hui life situations through the conceptual windows of evolutionary strata, we expect to achieve a better understanding of Hui life in the larger Chinese and worldwide scheme of things.[5]

---

[4]For a more complete delineation of evolutionary sequences, and of religion over against culture, see Karl W. Luckert, *Egyptian Light and Hebrew Fire* (Albany: SUNY Press, 1991), chapter 1.

[5]In reaction to nineteenth-century progress-oriented social theories of evolution, evolutionary thinking has gone out of fashion in many Western anthropological circles. Nevertheless, a project such as this—accomplished in close collaboration between an American and a Chinese scholar—we believe, requires at this point in time a fresh focus on evolution. Must the West continue to dislike evolutionistic thinking simply because Marx and Engels have based their ideology on a now outdated version of nineteenth-century evolutionary theory?

From Hunting to Domestication

An exhaustive commentary on traces of evolutionary phases in Hui mythology would require several volumes. Only a few sample stories can actually be alluded to in this Introduction. It is nevertheless assumed that, with the help of these sketchy allusions and with the evolutionary schema that is implied, a reader can more easily blaze his or her own trail through the remainder of Hui folklore.

It goes without saying that when the Hui Muslim identity began developing in China, hunting and gathering by itself was no longer a viable economy. Nevertheless, human memory expressed as folklore outlasts concrete modes of making a living. Motifs in folklore are not simply replaced by new motifs; rather, they accumulate and they conglomerate like sedimentary geological and archeological strata. In this manner the transition from hunting to domestication is still clearly distinguishable in Hui stories.

The Shamans' Quest. Viewed in evolutionary perspective, in a time when our ancestors were still hunters of wild animals the earliest shamans used to be the intelligentsia. Trickery and pursuit are the primary "scientific" or "cultural" ambitions of hunter folk everywhere. Ordinary hunting requires that huntsmen go in pursuit of animal victims whom in one way or other they hope to conquer, if not by superiority of sheer power then by superiority of wit. Being able to invent weapons, that is, substitutional teeth and claws that can bite from a distance, has been the singlemost important trick in the cultural repertoire of our humanoid ancestral hunters. Hunting is trickery, good hunting is trickery well done. Shamans, who constituted the intelligentsia among hunter bands, had to be, therefore, supreme tricksters first of all. Such shamans knew how to deal, and how to intervene, not only between humankind and their targeted animals, but between humankind and their hunter gods as well. Traditionally the greater-than-human hunter deities have themselves been hunters. Most of them have originally roamed as natural and superior predators. Some animal masters began their divine careers roaming as lead animals in herds.

Ordinary huntsmen, by the advice of shamans, have wandered in conquest of meat that was the substance of their life; but ancient shamans have ventured beyond this basic quest for meat. They have also struggled to secure health and well-being in general, from a realm beyond the limits where the hunters' weapon trickery was effective. While all hunters went on journeys in quest of food, their shamanic heroes went on journeys in quest of broader blessings from the gods, in pursuit of greater knowledge and life, of powers to heal. Adan and Haowa, and Shisi, who is added in "Adan and Haierma" (though already safely within the culture stratum of horticultural domesticators) echo in Hui mythology still as the primeval shamanic questers who obtained, and ate, the basic elements that support human life. Some unknown shamanic hero among archaic hunters has gone in search of fire, and that ancient quest echoes in the Hui domesticator version of "Adang Brings Fire"—as it also echoes in the hunter versions of some American Indian stories about Coyote and in the Greek grand domesticator myth which tells about Prometheus.

Successors of shamans in post-hunting cultures, members of the domesticator intelligentsia, continued their explorations and their travel pursuits in search of livestock, land, seeds, and rain. The hunters' quest, which formerly was intensified to the level of shamanic visionary journeys, was subsequently, at the domesticator level, democratized and depreciated to journeys of ordinary craftsmen apprentices. All the while, the larger goals of the ancient shamanic quests have remained visible in these later craftsmen journeys, about which we are told in "Straw Rope Valley" and "In Search of the Golden Sparrow."

Later grand domesticators, imperialists, have elaborated on this archaic travel tradition and have added the quest for kingdoms, as in "The Serpent Grandfather's Treasure Chest." Then, in other parts of the world, under conditions where the grand domestication quest for kingdoms could no longer be justified, a more noble pilgrimage in search of objects like a "holy grail" could be substituted.

The still more democratized search for lesser treasures ranks next in line. Many Hui myths, legends, and tales attest to this general evolutionary adaptive "deterioration" of the shamanic quest among post-hunting culture strata. Our collection contains samples from the entire spectrum of possibilities.

Hunter Tricksters in Prehuman Flux. Hunting is trickery and aggression. But every posture of aggression at any level of cultural achievement also has its counterpart, or finds its foil, in religious retreat behavior and in guilt-laden retreat-oriented thinking.

Retreat from "trickster" mythology is expressed by way of sub-scribing to a mythology of "prehuman flux." Among ancient and primitive hunter traditions, anywhere in the world, one finds a recurring religious theme describing prehuman times and conditions: At the beginning of the present world order of hunting, the animals and the gods were still indistinguishable from humankind. They still were all the same kind of "people" in a primeval state of flux. Back in primeval times they could alter their appearances and exchange their skin clothing, and, consequently, could appear as members of any species of humans, animals, or gods, they wished. In those primordial times the "people" still spoke a common language and understood one another. In those paradisical times, they were not yet hunting and killing each other for food.[6]

An allusion to this form of nostalgia, to prehuman flux and a primordial language, can still be found in Hui tales like "Why People Do Not Understand Animals" and "A Soldier Understood the Sky-larks." The latter tale brings religious prehuman flux nostalgia all the way into the advanced evolutionary stratum of grand domestication and militarism.

The notion of a prehuman condition of physical changeability and paradisical flux, of shared "clothes" and a harmonious coexistence, stands in sharp contrast with another genre of hunters' storytel-ling—their trickster tales. Trickster stories comprise the scientifically hypothetical and aggressive dimension in the activities of primitive hunters. By contrast, prehuman flux mythology represents the human conscience with its hunter nostalgia for equality and harmony. It represents religious surrender and identification with the greater world of living relatives.[7] A world filled with all kinds of animal people—as opposed to only human people—is not exactly suited to justify a lifestyle of hunting and killing. Such a mythology of

---

[6]For a discussion of prehuman flux mythology, in a hunter context, see Karl W. Luckert, *The Navajo Hunter Tradition* (Tucson: University of Arizona Press, 1975), pp. 133ff.

[7]Of course, trickster tales of the type which expose would-be tricksters as bunglers defeat the motif of aggression. They heap laughter and ridicule on over-ambitious aggressive tricksters. Bungler tales turn the corner and prepare the way for common-sense religious "retreat" thinking, and thereby for religious behavior.

creaturely egalitarianism is maintained for contemplating repentance from hunting.

Themes of religious nostalgia, in folklore, generally outlast the corresponding themes of science or trickery. This is so because all achievements and tricks of culture require continual balancing with common-sense religious retreat behavior. In the general process of cultural evolution the ways of retreat generally do lag behind the ways of progress. Retreat is called for, is recalled and reenacted, to balance momentary modes of excessive aggression.

Then, inasmuch as the living space of creatures is finite, all conquests by individuals do ultimately reach an end. Religious retreat behavior will necessarily remain relevant to the very end, because death and the end can be rationalized most easily as retreat. Of course, a radical religious repentance from the entire quest for food is impractical for as long as the penitent, and his kind, wish to eat and to survive. Thus, to substitute for limitations in the dimension of space, human aggression is conveniently deflected, translated, and sublimated, in the dimension of time—where memories of the past become folklore in the present. All this is accomplished with the same rationality and intellect that also has made aggression in space reasonable and possible.

A remembered retreat along the dimension of time may mean regression to an older and simpler level of cultural aggression—as hunting nowadays is being reduced, or sublimated, to some kind of recreation or sport. Retreat into memories of the past sometimes calls for regression to an older lifestyle—the kind of regression that overdomesticated "civilized" humankind expresses as it sings and dreams of an idyllic landscape, and a simpler world for domesticators "where sheep may safely graze."

Obviously, with weak religious retreat-oriented memories of this sort an aggressive culture cannot be balanced safely. Humanistically speaking, and for the sake of human survival, it is nevertheless better for a society to cultivate some such weak balances—some ancient stories and rites—than try to get along with no means of balancing at all. Without religious limits or balances a human society cannot maintain equilibrium and survive. Its people will destroy others, and themselves in the process.

"Luguma Reverts to Hunting" is a Hui story that reflects the typical transition from hunter-gatherer to domesticator ways of thinking. The principal animals in this story are the wolf, tiger, and hawk. All three of these are formidable predators. For our primitive ancestral hunters these natural predators still roamed as greater-than-human and therefore "divine" role models. During the early 1970s, in Navajoland, I personally became acquainted with an old hunter who still hunted in accordance with that ancient Stone Age mythology and religion. He identified mystically with a divine Wolf.

In our present Hui story the wolf retains its ability to do genuine prehuman flux transformations; nevertheless, as a potential divine hunter tutelary who now roams among domesticator folk, this ancient wolf has become a thoroughly defamed and evil being.

At the same time, the tiger and the hawk still are acknowledged as being friends of our human hero. But even these friendly potential hunter tutelaries no longer are freely roaming hunter gods. Their status has been reduced by human domesticator ambitions. They are domesticated and controlled after the manner of friendly hunting dogs. All the same, this story reflects the identity crisis of males caught up in the transition from a lifestyle of hunting to domestication. Possibly, this story reflects as well an earlier Chinese matrilocal domesticator situation according to which a son had to leave the parental estate where he had been laboring during his youth, and according to which he had to surrender his property claims to a sister. Some such sibling rivalry seems implied by the general plot of this story.

In any case, this disowned farmer's son regresses along the dimension of evolutionary time—to a life of romanticized hunting with a pet tiger and a pet hawk. True to the ancient hunter context, these predators together are still better hunters than their human master. Together they destroy the evil wolf and save their man. In a hunter-gatherer culture these predators would, on that account, still have qualified to function as divine hunter tutelaries. But this farmer's son no longer is destined to be a full-time hunter. By way of his romanticized temporary regressions from domestication into hunting (which in the dimension of evolutionary time signify religious retreat) he eventually returns to save the village of domesticators from his defamed wolf sister.

Fortunately, the wolf confesses to not being the hero's real sister and is, therefore, annihilated without an encumbrance of guilt. It is hunters' logic of "prehuman flux" and metamorphosis that makes the plot of this transitional narrative possible. In the end the son's honor is vindicated and he regains his rightful place as leader in a village of domesticators. He, a male, has thereby become the legitimate heir of the family estate.

In the narrative "Horse Brother" we find similar transitional hunter mythology that is called upon to rationalize and to support a program of domestication—including the cultivation of the soil and the operation of a farm dominated by males. The man goes in search of arable land. The sibling rivalry which in "Luguma Reverts to Hunting" has been directed against matrilocality, and against a sister, is here replaced with a process of first liberating, and then banning again, the hero's "brothers" who mythologically represent the obsolete hunter era. All this liberating and banning still happens in hunter fashion, in conformity to the logic of prehuman flux transformationalism.

A measure of prehuman flux identity with horses is implied for the hero himself, by the fact that a horse has brought him to his foster grandmother. But the prehuman flux details concerning his own person are left unexplained.[8] In any case, his Stone Brother and his Elm Brother are prehuman flux transformations, of a stone person and a tree person, respectively. The human hunter's creative arrow has transformed them into his own kind. Weapons were the tools by which hunters have tried to "create"—and by which progressive warriors have feigned creativity ever since.

Wives fly in as pigeons and transform themselves into marriageable housekeepers at a point in time when the farm already has been well established by the men. Thus the men could claim ownership of the entire domestication enterprise. Wives are expected to obey their men, and when they disobey in as small a point as failing to drive away a mischievous cat, disaster strikes. The women become vulnerable to a Nine-headed Master whose specialty is to suck blood out of women.[9]

---

[8]The Mongolian counterparts to this story, "Der Sohn des Rappen" and "Der Sohn der Stute," acknowledge the hero as being a real offspring of horses. See Lorincz, *Mongolische Märchentypen* (Budapest, 1979), pp. 77f.

[9]In the Mongolian version the three brothers marry three swan maidens. These wives try to retrieve fire, as in the Hui version, but a demoness sucks their blood. A masculine demon who sucks blood appears, however, in a somewhat different context. See Laszlo Lorincz, *Mongolische Märchentypen*, pp. 77, 259.

Fortunately the Horse Brother is an able match for this Nine-headed Master. He outwits and defeats him. But then, the victorious hero is temporarily banned by the intrigue of his own brothers. In the end he survives and dispatches his hostile brothers back into their prehuman condition. As a determined domesticator—as the totemic brother of a mighty domestic animal—the Horse Brother need no longer acknowledge his kinship to stones and trees. He now controls them. He utilizes these things to build houses and storage sheds. The wives of the two brothers revert to the shape and status of pigeons, and these animals are henceforth tolerated at farmers' homesteads.

A Comparative Sidestep. It is necessary to scrutinize the primary antagonist of Horse Brother, namely, the Nine-headed Master. A comparison with neighboring traditions will reveal how in this mythical figure there has survived an interesting relic from ancient Asiatic hunter traditions. In the Hui story this monster has nine heads of which only the middle one can see. Who is he? Is he only a figment of a creative Hui storyteller's imagination? The fact that the forementioned Mongolian parallel exists (see footnotes 8 and 9) speaks against this possibility. The story obviously has not originated with the Hui. It can be traced back to an older stratum of hunter culture.

The threat to masculine deer-hunter egos, by stags, is confessed to in the "Deer Woman" story of the Navajo Indian hunter tradition. There the sister of hunters has mated with a stag. She bore him fawns, which were killed by one of her brothers.[10] Obviously, in that story is expressed a hunters' guilt of killing kindred deer, combined with the men's jealousy for a woman. They participate in prehuman flux ways of transformation while stalking deer; they hunt disguised in buck skins. Back home the woman of the hunters conceivably could—or just might—put on doe skins to play her feminine role and mate with actual deer bucks. Such behavior could reasonably be expected of a human female if she, too, were to participate in the male hunters' mythological world of prehuman flux transformationalism. Within a hunters' realm that is filled with divine people, with animal people, and with human people—a realm which already has

---

[10]Luckert, *Navajo Hunter Tradition*, pp. 70ff.

ruptured between male human killers and female nourishers—a semblance of justice could be achieved by contemplating the participation of all persons in prehuman flux.

The Ostyaks in western Siberia tell the story of a hunter who went out to hunt deer...(elk and reindeer). While he was gone his sister back home flirted with a seven-headed forest spirit. Thereafter that forest spirit pursued the deer hunter. The latter barely escaped with his life when, fortunately, he was being helped by smaller animal tricksters—Hare, Otter, Sparrow, Crow—who managed to alert the hunter's already domesticated tutelary helpers, Wolf and Bear. After three years of struggle the seven-headed forest monster was killed and burned. The hunter was rewarded for his deed by a grand domesticator, a king, who gave him his youngest daughter in marriage. The deer hunter's own "sister," however, avenged the death of the seven-headed forest spirit who had been her lover. As a result the hunter died. But he was resurrected again with the help of his animal friends.[11]

Who is this seven-headed forest spirit? Clearly, in this Ostyak version he is the avenger of deer whom the hunter was in the habit of killing. He is a defamed Animal Elder, a divine Master of Animals in the form of deer. The hunter's conscience has seen him as a many-headed bugaboo, with a deer head in the middle, one which sees, and an even number of extra heads or antler points above each side. By mentioning such a forest demon, as a revelation received by the deer hunters' own guilty conscience, the hunters could in turn surely frighten their women and their children.

The bogy complex of multiple deer antlers, the negative version of a many-headed monster who appears in the dusk forests of northern Asia as an enemy of the hunters, has produced mythological offspring in subsequent agricultural civilizations unto which the descendants of northern deer hunters—who meanwhile turned herders—have descended. In the grand domestication scenario of the famous Indian epic "Ramayana," by Valmiki who wrote perhaps in the second century B.C.E., the archaic hunters' abduction-and-

---

[11]See Janos Gulya, *Sibirische Märchen—Wogulen and Ostjaken* (Düsseldorf: Diedrichs Verlag, 1968), pp. 139ff.

revenge theme is still kept very much intact. The deer and his many-headed ghostly manifestation still appear together as well.[12]

Adaptations to Domestication

The Hui Genesis. Hui stories about Adam and Eve subscribe to Near Eastern prototypes which here and there are alluded to in the Quran. But then, Islamic meanings that trickled in from Arabia and Central Asia were planted into the deep soil of Chinese culture. The combined experiences of Hui men, women, and children, grew fresh native roots to nourish and help assimilate imported meanings.

Already in the Hebrew book of Genesis, with which many Quranic ideas about creation have remained aligned, one finds a distinction between general cosmogony (Genesis 1–2:3) and an earthy anthropogenesis (Genesis 2:4–25). A similar duality can be noticed between the first two Hui versions about Adam and Eve and the third version.

According to the first two versions the angelic Adam and Eve were expelled from heaven as punishment for sin. And by contrast, the third version rather concretely narrates the creation of Adam from five colors of earth. This earthward orientation links up nicely with other Near Eastern traditions, as well as with traditional Chinese Panku mythology. Both elements of Hui creation mythology rationalize and support a world order of domesticators. Moreover, in contrast with the well defined Semitic horticultural garden paradise, the Hui notion of paradise accommodates their own experience in marginal agriculture.

From an evolutionary perspective it should be noted that an awareness of the "sin of eating" exists virtually everywhere; it is already in primitive hunter-gatherer consciousness. Of course, at the economic level of hunters the divinely forbidden fruits were still the bodies of fellow animal persons. Primitive hunter religiosity has for the most part been developed to atone for the sin of killing and of eating kindred animal people. Share offerings given to divine hunter tutelaries, food tabus, ritualized vomiting, and fasting are therefore among the means of hunter-gatherer salvation. Horticulturists and

---

[12]See Makhan Lal Sen, trans., *The Ramayana of Valmiki* (New Delhi: Munshiram Manoharlal Publishers, 1978).

orchard gardeners, later, substituted arboreal fruits for what formerly used to be forbidden guilt-precipitating animal bodies. Marginal Hui cereal cultivators have transferred, quite logically, this primeval guilt of eating to "grain-fruits." All the while, any kind of fruit would have satisfied the logic of the Hui narrative, because according to that mythology all foods were forbidden to the angelic ancestors of humankind.

Adam and Eve, who as angelic beings in heaven have sinned by way of eating, were relegated to the dark earth. Their Islamic atonement consisted of reciting scripture and praying five times a day. Their sin of eating has transformed them not only into hungry killer beings with alimentary ducts, but also has given them their sexuality. Adam was able to swallow his fruit only a little ways before it got stuck, whereas Eve swallowed hers all the way down—deep enough to afflict her with menses. These natural consequences of sin were immediately balanced and neutralized with redemptive ceremonial measures. Men and women would henceforth be fulfilled by doing their prayers, by kneeling and squatting respectively. Ice-cold knees and buttocks are constant reminders of the people's proper roles during life on earth. These posture-specific afflictions of males and females define their relationship and behavior toward one another and, in prayer, toward Allah.

After thirty-six male and female pairs of twins, the son Shisi was the first single birth given by Eve. He became a first great culture hero for the lifeways of domestication. Riding on a thousand-foot-long serpent who happened to be a heavenly messenger, Shisi traveled back to God's heaven to request more paradisical fruits—for nourishment as well as for fertility.

This story plot is definitely not an attempt to upstage Muhammad's nocturnal flight on a winged steed which, at some point, he continued on a rug (see "The Festival of Ascent"). Rather, in the old China of agricultural domesticators, flying serpents were familiar divine beings. Some serpentine dragons were identified with rain-bearing clouds and were as such, by ancient Chinese reckoning, well suited for travel in the new Islamically revealed upward direction of Allah's heaven.

As might be expected from a trip sponsored by an Islamically redeemed ancient dragon deity of Chinese cultivators, the God in heaven who went through the trouble of utilizing the dragon as one of his angels did the human domesticator families on earth a good turn. First he scattered humankind abroad to give them more space, and then he dropped down on them the five Chinese domestic cereals as well as the six domestic animals.[13]

Han mothers have contributed their share to the Hui oral legacy, and it need not surprise anyone to find in this instance that ancient Chinese cosmogonic themes have intruded as well. Our third creation story, especially, displays a wonderful Near Eastern/Chinese collage of ideas. It begins within the Near Eastern frame of reference and, perhaps unawares, muses about how a supreme creator would have acted toward a Mediterranean "Mother Earth." How might God have created humankind upon such a varicolored earth?

Similar deliberations about the creation of Adam can be found in Hebrew mythology. There the earth refused to give up her soil for the creation of Adam—on account that she might be cursed by humankind. In the Hui version the soil varieties do the refusing. The concept of "God," according to Islamic understanding, disallowed the possibility of an Earth resisting God's will as an independent personage. Different types of ingredient soils, of different colors, were therefore recognized analytically.[14]

The Near Eastern story of an Adam, a First Man, naturally invited a comparison with stories about China's First Man, Panku. Near Eastern traditions do not elaborate on the cosmic significance of the death of Adam, at least not after the manner of paleo-planters' *dema* theology, as this is the case with the Chinese myth about Panku.[15] But this did not stop Chinese Muslims from improvising a "near death" situation for that very process of Adam's creation.

---

[13]The five domestic cereals of the Han Chinese are rice, two kinds of millet, wheat, and beans. The six Chinese domestic animals were pig, bovine, goat, horse, fowl, and dog. If he were asked for specifics, a Muslim storyteller would be hard put to acknowledge the pig as one of the bonafide God-given six domestic animals. Undoubtedly, he would have named the camel instead.

[14]See Louis Ginzberg, *Legends of the Jews* (New York, 1961 [1909]), p. 28.

[15]For a commentary on the *dema* concept among paleo-planters see Adolf E. Jensen, *Myth and Cult among Primitive Peoples* (Chicago, 1963). *Dema* deities, in primordial times, have created by dying as sacrificial victims. By their deaths they have contributed living and self-propagating matter, foremostly edible plants, which have become food for humankind. The Chinese primordial being, Panku, may be understood in terms of *dema* theology.

As in the Hebrew Genesis, the Hui Adam was created by God in potter's fashion. It therefore seemed reasonable that he should have been given his primary soft shape while lying down. However, this first human creature disobeyed God's command and tried to sit up before his material had sufficiently hardened. His still-soft skull broke open and some of his soul-essence escaped. The diffusion of his powers happened in the same manner in which life energies were said to have escaped from the dying Panku, according to ancient Chinese mythology. Instead of becoming an immortal, Adam's energies spread forth to create mountains, metals, land animals, and sea animals.

In our third Hui version the origin of Eve is nicely rationalized, in near egalitarian planter fashion, to match typical *dema* ontology. Eve budded from Adam's rib cage, as a large lump at first—and after the manner in which tubers are propagated. The two became sexually differentiated only by eating the forbidden fruit, differently. Sexual feelings for one another necessitated their painful awareness of experiencing separation for the sake of contrast.[16] They searched and groped in the dark and found each other again. They found themselves on ice. Together they slipped, and together they have continued to slip ever since. They were obligated by God to maintain differential constancy in their prayer postures while showing love toward one another and respect toward Allah. The danger of committing marital idolatry requires a religious check and balance—requires mutual surrender to Allah in gender-specific postures.

The Old Dragon Religion. If only one conspicuous pre-Islamic deity were to be mentioned here, as being still alive in Hui mythology, it would have to be the Dragon as a bringer of rain. We have seen earlier how this Dragon deity has been intruding as a positive agent already into the third Hui story of "Adan and Haierma." There this ancient Chinese serpentine being is not an epitome of evil; rather, it functions positively as a messenger or carrier angel of Allah.

After the fashion of live thunderclouds, the ancient Dragon deity also provides fire, as in "Adang Brings Fire." In numerous other stories the Dragon gives treasures and sometimes even adds his own

---

[16]The separation of Adam from Eve is also a theme in Judaism—as a separation of penance. See Reinhold Mayer, *Der Babylonische Talmud* (München: Wilhelm Goldmann Verlag, 1963), p. 82.

daughter as a bride for the human hero. Traditionally the Dragon's primary function has been to provide water for domesticators, for planters foremostly, but also for Chinese herders. That is the very reason why, as Dragon King, this rain god nowadays still lives in pools of water and in the ocean.

A cult of the Dragon also has flourished in South Asia since prehistoric times. In the civilization of pre-Aryan India, which has flourished along the Indus River, the Dragon has been a divine power who provided life and rain for agriculture. The Aryans, who invaded the Indus Valley around 1500 B.C.E., have villainized and demonized this native agricultural deity as Vrtra, the "Obstacle" or "Resister." According to the Rig-Veda, that "Obstacle" was said to have held back the waters which subsequently were released by Indra, the Aryan war god. Indra was given credit for having killed this Resister, and also for the fact that the monsoon rain waters began to flow again in India. However, it may safely be assumed that the Rain Serpent of the pre-Aryan Dasyus used to release its water for Indian planters without first being clubbed to death by an Aryan war god.

The Vrtra of the Indus civilization and the Chinese Rain Dragon functioned as one and the same Asiatic deity.[17] On average that Dragon was a superior and benevolent deity of agricultural folk and, understandably, when nomadic herders invaded and overran native planters along the Indus, this defeated divine Resister was made to stand proxy for its equally defeated agricultural devotees. The Aryan god Indra had conquered—his devotees had overdomesticated—the Dasyu people, whereby the people and their rain deity were reduced together to the status of losers.

Nomadic pastoralists on horseback cherished games of conquest, and they dreamt of crowns and kingdoms that could be won. Herders who were already skilled in controlling animal herds were easily tempted to go a step farther. They became grand domesticators and as such began to control human herds, that is, they controlled domesticator folk together with their gods. The acclaimed killing of Vrtra by their god Indra must therefore be understood in relation to

---

[17]The same rain deity and cloud serpent can also be found in ancient Middle American civilization, as well as in the serpent cult of maize-planting Pueblo Indians in the American Southwest. See Karl W. Luckert, *Olmec Religion* (Norman: University of Oklahoma Press, 1976).

the larger Aryan need to justify their conquest, their reorganization of agriculture, and their subjugation of Dasyu planter folk.

Pre-Islamic (yes, even pre-Confucian) mythology has survived in China, amazingly obvious, embedded in Hui folklore and with certain adjustments to cultural progress. Whereas in worldwide hunter mythology the ancient shamanic heroes still went on trance journeys to visit some type of Master of Animals, the later Hui domesticator Yisima traveled to the home of Sun in pursuit of knowledge about agriculture and herding. There is even more continuity. Ancient hunter shamans often ended their human careers with joining the families of the gods with whom they had become acquainted during their trance journeys. Some of them are said to have married into the households of the gods. Here, however, in Hui domesticator culture (which more often than not had to survive under grand domesticator warlords or emperors who, in turn, usurped the roles of divine Dragons), the story is adjusted to where some lowly heroes married the princess daughter of the Dragon King, in an aristocratic manner.

Like their hunter-shaman predecessors, so these Hui heroic inlaws of the Dragon King were obligated to join eventually the family of their Dragoness and to conform to, and endorse, the rules of matrilocality. Of course, this theme in Hui mythology by itself does not prove matrilocality among the ancestors of presentday Hui. The basic Dragon mythology is of Han origin, and the Hui have based their Dragon stories on no more than what, at the time, seemed to be common-sense Chinese ontology. Moreover, it must have been obvious to most men who were questing for kingdoms, that it would be easier to win royal status, or a kingdom, by marrying a princess than by having to win it through actual strife and conquest.

Chinese imperial grand domesticators have subjugated not only peasants who worshipped the Dragon. Kings and emperors—acting as weather makers, or as rulers who liked to take credit for good weather for greater authority over planters—have usurped the role of this rain god. This much is reflected, indirectly, by the fact that the farmers' Dragon deity has increasingly been redefined in the terminology of imperial grand domestication. The Dragon has been titled "Dragon King" and he was thereby inducted into the ranks of Chinese superhuman royalty. As such the god resides underwater in a palace. There he sits on a throne, in a throne room, complete with body guards and all.

In a few Hui stories, as in "The Dragon Tablet" and in "The Story of Winding River," the mediation of rain by way of dealing with the Dragon deity seems to suggest traces of an ancient practice of human sacrifice; and the sacrifice of human victims, in turn, signified a grand domesticator's feeding of the Dragon deity in payment for ownership of land and people. In "The Dragon Tablet" the hero kills a bad Dragon King and usurps his place by transforming himself into a more benevolent Dragon.[18] All this sounds like the logic implicit in human sacrifice, whereby victims who are sacrificed to a hungry deity render that deity new, satisfied, and therefore more benevolent.[19]

All the while in the Islamic context, where in the holy presence of the supreme Allah even a benevolent Phoenix sister has shamed herself into banishment, it would occasionally seem reasonable rather to dispose of an ancient Dragon deity than to appease it. The hero in "The Dragon Tablet," even though in the end he becomes a victim himself, cuts an evil Dragon King to pieces with a divinely fortified copper tablet. Quranic words of God, "He sends down...," are inscribed on the tablet and inject Allah's very own command into the human quest for rain. The presence of a copper tablet, on which Sura 42, 29 is inscribed in Arabic, testifies to an ahong's determined participation in the Islamic effort of conquering the ancient Dragon deity (see photograph 10). To the extent that the hero himself gets absorbed by Dragon reality, pre-Islamic Chinese agricultural religion and traditional ontology reassert themselves. By contrast, the story about "Sai Dianchi and the Dragons" features a more flawless conquest in the name of Islam, without leaving a trace of sacrificial logic. A non-sacrificial solution is also achieved in "Adang Brings

---

[18]Publication of this story, in China, has evoked objections on the part of a few Hui readers who asserted that Hui Muslims never used Dragon tablets. Therefore in Yunnan, during the summer of 1992, we examined and photographed such an object. See photograph 10.

[19]In Middle America, from the Olmecs to the Aztecs, human sacrifices to a rain deity have developed into fullfledged overdomestication schemes which required tens and hundreds of thousands of human victims. The Vedic formula, of Purusha energy being transformed into Prajapati energy (i.e. the victim eaten as food substantially becomes the eater), appears to express the logic for all of these ceremonial and mythical instances.

Fire." There the hero retained his humanity and the "fierce Dragon" was permitted to return to its cave as a reformed Dragon, alive.

In "The Story of Winding River" a human sacrifice for the purpose of obtaining water is no longer a sufficient reason. The human death is described like an accident, but in context it is immediately sublimated and rationalized to where it serves the general establishment of Islam in the Winding River area. In "The Dragon Dish" the rain-making rite is Islamicized in still greater detail. The rain Dragons have come under the control of a Muslim who has made his pilgrimage to Mecca. The ritual is connected with the holy month of Ramadan, with fasting, and prayer to Allah. The ritual proceeds from the mosque and requires the offering of rosary beads to fishes which are, presumably, related to Dragons. The Dragons themselves are symbolically controlled or "domesticated" by pious Muslims, in a ceramic dish.

In any case, in the Hui context it was the universalistic religion of Islam itself that has curtailed and revised the ancient notion of human sacrifice by way of placing the deaths of human victims, the Dragon Tablet, as well as the ceramic Dragon Dish, under the auspices of the mosque and in the service of Islam.

Relationship to Islam and Other Chinese Religions

Islamic *jihad* or "holy war" has not been among the means by which the religion founded by Muhammad has spread in China. This is not to say that Muslims in China were less warlike than their counterparts in Central Asia or in the Near East. Rather, it simply means that the *jihad* ethos of Islam, as occasionally it was activated during the spread of Islam around the globe, was filtered along its journey into China through variegated layers of other types of herder and warrior religiosity. All the while, their submission to Allah has not kept Muslims from also serving the otherwise deified Chinese emperor, the Son of Heaven.

Islam in China spread by conversions and by intermarriage with non-Muslims. The community of Muslims has regularly insisted that partners in marriage accept Islam rather than permit accommodations the other way around. The story of "Eunuch Sanbao at the Welcoming Pavilion" nicely reflects Muslim expectations regarding these arrangements, even in a situation where the incoming bride was the daughter of a prominent Han general. Cases where daughters of

Muslims have married non-Muslims, even if the latter promised to convert, are extremely rare.

Conversion to Islam on the part of a bride who, coming typically from a Buddhist or Daoist background, married a Muslim man, elicited some fresh personality traits—even some advantages. Interreligious marriages were almost never of the arranged type but necessarily had to be based on individual commitment and love. Thus, young people who joined the Muslim community naturally were more daring and claimed greater freedom. Moreover, to be in daily communication with the creator and sustainer of the whole universe could do a lot to furbish Hui egos. When a Han Chinese converts to Islam or dons the white cap, or more distinctly still, a turban and a coat that approximates the Near Eastern cloak, he sets himself apart from a billion other Chinese folk. By the same token, the lady who marries one of these radiantly optimistic men, by personal commitment and love, asserts herself as a special individual as well.

Of course, with all of these advantages has come also the burden of belonging to a minority. In "Eunuch Sanbao at the Welcoming Pavilion" that burden has been dealt with realistically and with diplomatic skill. In "Do Not Listen to the Hui" the stigma of ethnic otherness is being nicely joked aside.

In "A Temple Appears from Nowhere" we have the testimonial of a confident Muslim storyteller. This is not so much a tale about proper relations for Muslims with other religions in China, with Buddhism or Daoism, but is rather a boastful tale about a Muslim institutional founder, an ahong, who was able to perform greater miracles than his closest Buddhist competitor. The Muslim hero slighted the bodhisattvas, and he selected a warrior figure to accompany him instead, and, while he was at it, he preempted the founding of what appears to be a Daoist temple. Implicitly this type of story puts forth a claim of superiority for God and for the religion of Islam. It implies the inferiority of Buddhism and Daoism. As far as such ridicule and wit among Hui storytellers is concerned, surely, they enjoyed dishing it out more than taking it in.

A similar confrontation between Islam and traditional Chinese religion is developed in "Why Has the Phoenix Gone?" Allah and the arrogant ancient feminine bird of happiness engaged in a wager by which only she had something to lose. Expectedly, the Phoenix lost her bet with the almighty and all-wise Allah and, from the perspective of Muslims, that explains sufficiently why she need no longer show up or be taken seriously. Allah and his ahong together have won the wager and have brought two distant Muslim lovers together for a timely marriage. Allah has thereby demonstrated not only his ability to outwit antiquated deities, but also his caring about mundane human concerns, loves, and hopes. By contrast, the Phoenix has demonstrated the irrelevancy of her ancient kind of religion. Now she is remembered in Hui tales primarily for entertainment, it seems. All the while, and fortunately, she is left intact just enough to please Han neighbors who still might wish to regard her more in earnest.

The ancient Chinese god of wealth, an old-age fellow, still appears and does intervene in the lives of Hui Muslims. After lengthy journeys he still arranges the means and fortunes for better living. But in Hui stories this aged and ancient Chinese god has blended in, more or less, with the figure of an archetypal Muslim ahong. In "The Straw Rope Valley" the old man leads a Hui journeyman to a better land where he can learn the progressive craft of a blacksmith. In addition, the old man tutors him in the arts of reading and writing. In "Yinbolaxi" and "Why Has the Phoenix Gone?" the old man is specifically identified as an ahong, whereas in "Musa" his identity as an ahong is hinted at only by the presence of a copper kettle that sits by a spring in the old man's garden. Presumably this Tang kettle is being used for the prescribed Islamic ritual washings.

In "Colorful Stones" the old man is an ahong who teaches a practical lesson about the relative values of material treasures and filial piety. And in "The Stone Monkey" he teaches that same moral lesson after the fashion of an ahong. But having also inherited the role of the ancient Chinese god of wealth, the old ahong in that story remains in charge of a stone monkey which functions, intermittently, as an inexhaustible source of silver. A wise ahong replaces the ancient Chinese god of wealth in many other stories.

Mentionings of Jewish people in this volume of Hui Muslim stories are exceedingly rare. In "The Mule and the Horse" the Jews are mentioned only briefly, as a group of enemies with whom the early Muslims were at war. The setting of this story seems to harken back to the years at Medina (622–630 C.E.) when Muhammad had a falling out with the Jews, who were once his allies. Nevertheless, the story plot as such appears to be Asiatic.

Equally scarce in Hui folklore are statements concerning Hui relationships with Christians in China. The one negative statement about Catholics, in "Rhymed Couplets" of the Du Wenxiu cycle, is set in the context of rebellion. Quite obviously, the Catholic mission at Dali could only have been established with the express permission of the emperor. As a result it found itself too closely associated with the imperial dynasty. Relations with revolutionary governments produce difficult dilemmas for all foreign missionaries. By contrast, Islam in China had become indigenous some centuries earlier. It occasionally accepted, but never depended for its survival on, help from foreign missions. The Catholic dilemma was amplified and rendered practically unsolvable by the fact that Du Wenxiu, the Muslim leader of the rebellion in Yunnan, had targeted Dali to become the center for his revolution. In any case, during our visit to the Dali area, in 1992, we discovered a tolerant ambience of civility among Muslims, Buddhists, and Christians in the area (see photograph 9).

The Quest for Paradise. In Hui folklore the quest for paradise emerges as a natural extension from the ordinary quest for health, land, and a better livelihood. Occasionally, as in "The Straw Rope Valley," one resembling the ancient Chinese god of wealth appears to lead the way to a paradise. At other instances it is honesty and love that results in a marriage with the princess daughter of the Dragon King. Such happens to be the case in "Mansuer" and in the "Zither Master Hasang." A princess appears even in "The Dragon Tablet" where the human hero forthrightly kills the Dragon King and usurps his position. The trace of ancient sacrificial logic in the latter plot has already been suggested.

Sometimes, in direct contrast to heroic violence, the better life is found by way of domesticators' retreat into hunter-gatherer nostalgia, whereby animals who have been injured by violent hunters are bandaged and mended by a more compassionate type of non-hunter. The animals which are so rescued turn out to be divine beings with extraordinary resources. When they emerge from their prehuman flux animal disguises they reward their human saviors with some great treasure. "Saierdong's Stick" and "The Serpent Grandfather's Treasure Chest" are prime examples of this type. Even the hero in "Horse Brother," who distinguishes himself as a superior hunter, is one who is saved by a bird whose wing, injured by another hunter, he has mended. We have in this instance an idealization of hunting on one hand, and the rejection of hunting in the name of less violent behavior toward select types of animals on the other.

The story "In Search of the Golden Sparrow" features the most amazing Hui quest for paradise, by far. It would be nice to know how far in Hui society this story has actually spread. Three brothers are sent by their mother to look for the Golden Sparrow, who is known to bring happiness and prosperity. The only sure Islamic elements in this story are the mother's routine farewell wishes: "May Allah be with you!" But during most of the story the three sons are not only sent by their mother but also are guided in the right direction by an old and needy woman. The moral authority of a matriarchal order is implied. The third brother succeeds in finding the Golden Sparrow because he obeyed his mother and the old woman, and because he was kind to needy animals along the way. This means he abdicated the violence of ordinary hunting. He defeated wild beasts in the enchanted forest with sheer filial obedience, will power, and long-suffering. Finally, at the end of his road, the successful third brother found a paradisical garden into which he gained entrance only with the help of animals whom he had rescued along the way. This vindicates his nostalgic return to hunters' prehuman flux in harmony with animals. Aside from its crystal enclosure, this paradise described by a Hui storyteller holds another great surprise. Not Allah and his angels live therein, but instead the one and only Golden Sparrow who brings life, prosperity, and happiness. Who says that the Phoenix and her divine bird kindred have become irrelevant in Hui mythology!

In "Yaya and the Golden Sparrow" the Hui quest for land, for the good life, and paradise—yes, even the quest for the goodwill of a wonderful Golden Sparrow—has been translated into the experiential world appropriate for a Hui girl. A lesser, but nevertheless heavenly golden sparrow, has been sent to earth to atone for a wrong he committed in heaven. The love of the heroine redeems him from his predicament and, at the very moment when her devotion to her beloved is rewarded, they are both swept away to an idyllic garden in a mountain valley.

Recent Traces of Secularization

A few stories in this collection show significant traces of the past forty years of Chinese history. The task of discussing these, or identifying all of these, is best postponed until another time—for a number of non-academic reasons. Until that later time, the reader will be left to wonder about stories like "Breeding the Yanqi Horse," "The Phoenix and Her City," or "Xueda and Yinlin."

In "Lilang Subdues the Dragon" we are obviously faced with more recent, post-Islamic sentiments that attempt to demythologize the ancient Chinese Dragon deity far beyond what pious Muslims thought reasonable or necessary. Here it is no longer Allah or a devoted Muslim like Sai Dianchi who limits the Dragon's role, or who mediates rain. Here a hero, who abolishes sacrifices to the deity, and who proceeds to lead the god through the village as his prisoner, represents the common people. Model citizens now assert control over what China's ceremonial emperors have schemed to control all along—namely, the Dragon deity which through the ages has fascinated China's agricultural masses. The physical presence of the Dragon deity at the Lantern Festival is celebrated, unabashedly, as the people's victory and the god's humiliation. While he submits to the will of the people, the Dragon abdicates his role as a god.

The Islamic competition with China's ancient agricultural deity, epitomized Islamically by the fights of Sai Dianchi and by accommodating Dragon rituals in mosques, has contemporaneously been waged also by means of Han folk rituals. The physical symbolic appearance of any kind of god, during any kind of festival, signifies that human artistry has taken control. The struggle against China's Dragon deity has intensified during recent decades of secularization, under the influence of Western philosophical and scientific materialism. Whether this struggle will soon be over, or whether it will be won by someone human, is still too early to tell. New episodes of human encounters with this ancient God of Asia's farmers—dragon stories that will amuse people in the twentyfirst century—continue to be added to the Han Chinese folklore repertoire. It can safely be expected that creative Hui minds will participate in this development.

*   *   *

Our Introduction, with its lengthy detour of placing Hui folklore in the context of evolution, has come full circle. Our opening discussion pertained to "Hui-ness" and dealt with theoretical difficulties in the task of collecting stories of so-called "Hui" people. The lengthy detour into the subject of evolution itself contains our most inclusive answer. Folklore, wherever in the world we find it, is a conglomerate of existential pebbles and splinters of people's memory. The process of conglomeration began perhaps a million or more years ago among hominid hunter-gatherers when, for the first time, they were able to recall their experiences and express them with words. Human experiences in subsequent evolutionary strata of culture—in domestication, grand domestication, universal salvation religion, and in the stratum of secular revolutions—all have added their own fresh bulk to this conglomeration of inherited and bequeathed folklore.

Should, for the sake of Islamic purity, all traces of secular democratic/socialistic expressions be excluded? Should the folklore of the Hui Muslims have stopped evolving at the dawn of the twentiest century—perhaps to better match the European collections from the nineteenth century? All stories that seem to endorse social protest and recent revolutions—thus all stories that utilize Muslim rebels to endorse later secular revolutions—and that endorse nationbuilding, or all stories devoid of Islamic values, and all story characters of the "bad landlord" variety, would have to be purged from this collection.

A segment of readers, perhaps some university-educated Hui people in China, would like us to do to Islamicized Hui stories what Western anti-*minzu* readers might wish we do to secularized and socialistically tainted stories—namely, exlude them. These former are the people who for decades have learned how to appreciate and to praise the "cultural" contributions of Islam to China. In the Museum of Nationalities, in Urumqi, their teachers display an Uighur dictionary with Arabic script as evidence for the Muslims' importation of "literacy" into the region; copies of the Quran and of other Islamic books—the content of that literacy—are conspicuously absent.

If on the other hand we were to conform to the expectations of anti-*minzu* readers, and permit only religiously tinted Hui stories into our collection, we would first have to establish a satisfactory Islamic turn-of-the-century norm. The truth is, we are unable to define or to generate such a norm. If in addition we also were to conform to the purity standards of socialism, expected of us by some people in China, then preciously little would remain between the covers of this book. The authors will make no pretense at attempting any such measures. Allah can and probably will take care of his own folklore themes, and serious Western readers have no other choice but to apply their own evolutionary and historical scrutiny to the texts. Our readers and future scholars will have to ask their own historical questions of the texts, in their own time, as to which story motifs could have been added to the lore, which might have been altered, when, and under what historical pressures or circumstances.

We conclude this Introduction by offering to our readers no greater comfort than our conviction—that a serious evolutionary-historical approach to the texts will eventually bring into better focus for the individual reader any theme or motif that fascinates. Conversely, it will help relativize and diminish the significance of any theme that bothers.

PHOTOGRAPHIC GLIMPSES
OF HUI LIFE

1. An ancient tomb, in an ancient cemetery for Muslims in Guangzhou. The inscription reads "Wangesu Mu" (Wan Gars Tomb). Some Muslims believe that Wangesu is Wahb Abu Kabcha, the cousin of Muhammad. For alternatives compare Gladney (1991, pp. 8, 267). Photo: Luckert

2. The Beacon Tower Mosque is esteemed for being one of the four most ancient mosques in China. Photo: Li

3. The Feng Huang Mosque in Hangzhou, Zhejiang, viewed from the roof
of a nearby building. Islam was brought here during Song times (1127–
1179). Less than 3,000 Hui live now in Hangzhou. Photo: Luckert
4. The Niujie Street Mosque in Beijing is a place of central significance
for Muslims in China. Photo: Luckert

5. At Kun Yang, Yunnan, the monument of Zheng He (1371–1434), the famous navigator who reached the Near East and Africa. Photo: Luckert

6. The body of Du Wenxiu, leader of the Panthay Hui Rebellion in Yunnan (1855–1873), lies buried only a few kilometers from Dali. His head was carried about by Qing troops and finally discarded somewhere. Photo: Luckert

7. At the village mosque of Shi Pang, at the northern end of the Dali Plain, in Yunnan, men have gathered for afternoon prayers. Curious women and children, attracted by the presence of a foreigner, look on from the portico. Photo: Li

8. In conclusion the men request a group photograph with their guest. Photo: Li

9. Displayed on the wall of a Christian mission in Xia Guan, Yunnan, is a banner, presented to the Christian Patriotic Movement Committee: "Everyone's duty is to make the country prosper. We love religion and we love the country. Presented by the Xia Guan Islamic Association, April 11, 1982." The General Secretary of the Islamic Association subsequently explained: "For dedications of mosques, temples, and churches in our area all religious organizations exchange such banners. We congratulate each other because all religions have the same goal." Photo: Luckert

10. A "Dragon tablet" made of copper, displayed at the Museum of the Yunnan Nationalities Institute, in Kunming: "It is he who sends down rain for them when they have lost all hope, and spreads abroad his mercy. He is the guardian worthy of praise." (Sura 42, 29) Photo: Luckert, by courtesy of the Museum

11. The tomb of Qi Jingyi (1656–1719), founder of the Qadariyya *menhuan* ("saintly lineage" or "school"), in Linxia, Gansu. Photo: Li

12. The tomb of Ma Mingxin (1719–1781), founder of the Jahriyya *menhuan*, in Lanzhou, Gansu. Photo: Luckert

13. On Lotus Mountain, in Gansu, it is time for the annual pilgrimage. As the smoke of incense rises by the Buddhist temple, Buddhists, Daoists, and yes, Hui as well, climb the mountain in a steady stream. More recently added were the statues of three fairy maidens who slew a dangerous Dragon—one who threatened a Buddhist monk absorbed in meditation, or one who simply troubled the waters. Photo: Luckert
14. On a mountain in Lintan county, Gansu, two Hui generals now sit enthroned as gods. *Left*, Chang Yuchun. *Right*, Hu Dahai. They served the Ming emperor Zhu Yuanzhang (1368–1398) and defeated the Tibetans. Their temple, destroyed during the Cultural Revolution, is in the process of being rebuilt. Photo: Luckert

15. Near the top of Phoenix Mountain, at Xining, Qinghai, sits the tomb of Gutubu Hashimu Erpudunlehamani (grandson of Mu Sheng, son of Husaini) who came to southern Yunnan, from Bhagdad, during the reign of Ghengis Khan (ca. 1216). Photo: Luckert
16. The Nanshan Tomb Mosque at Xining, Qinghai. Photo: Luckert

17. The total number of Tibetan Hui now living in Qinghai and elsewhere—converts from Buddhism to Islam—was given to us as 16,000. Villages with a sizeable Hui population tend to lose their Tibetan (Buddhist) people through acculturation and exodus. This village scene, in Qunke township, featured only two lamas. Photo: Luckert

18. At the Qunke Mosque an ahong teaches approximately thirty students. He reads from the Quran in Arabic and translates spontaneously into Tibetan. Converted to Islam, a Tibetan no longer considers himself to be a "Tibetan"—which consequently means "Buddhist." A Hui is a Muslim who, by definition, has "come into the region from outside." Photo: Li

19. At the Great Shaanxi Mosque, in Changji, Xinjiang, one finds descendants of nineteenth century exiles from Shaanxi. Their people can also be found in Guyuan; see photograph 56. Photo: Luckert
20. This is the day of the Ashura festival at the Great Shaanxi Mosque. Everyone eats porridge prepared for this occasion in huge quantities and with many kinds of ingredients. Photo: Li

21. Islam is the dominant religion practiced in Ningxia. Forty-six percent of the total population, nearly one and a half million, are Hui Muslims. Many are actively practicing their religion—nowadays again under the benign sponsorship of the state. In recent years many mosques have been rebuilt, added, or expanded. At the South Mosque, in Yinchuan, scaffolding was present in 1988 for adding two minarets. Photo: Luckert
22. The finished South Mosque in summer of 1992. Photo: Luckert

23. It is a Friday morning and, inside the South Mosque, a few men and women leisurely await the call to collective prayer. Photo: Luckert
24. Muslim men are gathering also at another Yinchuan mosque. Photo: Luckert

25-26. The province of Ningxia lies along the upper reaches of the Yellow River. With the help of irrigation canals its territory has been wrested from the southern end of the Gobi Desert. Photos: Luckert

27. Close to a rural mosque, in the suburbs of Ningxia's capital city, Yinchuan, the wheat is ripening. Photo: Luckert
28. People have begun harvesting. Photo: Luckert

29. A school for Islamic instruction (jingxueyuan) has recently been built in Yinchuan. Photo: Luckert

30. In Najiahu Village this entrance leads to the courtyard of a mosque that was built around 1500 by the descendants of Sai Dianchi. The legend of this Dragon-fighting governor is included in this book. Photo: Luckert

31. Muslims have gathered here for collective prayer, on a Friday after-noon. In China the *mihrab*, which indicates the direction of Mecca, is situated at the center of the western wall. Photo: Zhou Pengqi

32. Plaques, on each side of the mihrab, display words of God from the Holy Quran in gold on green. 1. *Left*, "And hold fast, all together, by the rope which God extends for you and be not divided among your-selves" (3:103). 2. *Right*, "Persevere in your prayers, especially the middle prayer, and stand before God, devout in mind" (2:238). Translated by Mahmoud Abu Saud. Photo: Luckert

33. In Wuzhong City most people have already left the market. A food vendor still dishes out generous servings of dumplings. Photo: Luckert
34. As long as the author, Luckert, can remember, people at his home have been insisting that the standard press for making *Spätzle* (a speciality of Schwaben in southwest Germany) was invented there. Nevertheless, the contraption used here appears to be a prototype of all *Spätzles* machines in the world. Photo: Luckert

35. The Hui owner of an apple orchard, in Wuzhong, poses to help illustrate the story in our book titled "Asking Permission." Photo: Luckert

36. On an irrigated field, in central Ningxia, people are working. They almost blend in with the landscape. Photo: Luckert

37. An Islamic bookstore in Wuzhong City. Photo: Luckert
38. *Zakat*, the giving of alms, is one of the five pillars of Islam. Public posting of contributions, at the entrance of a mosque in Wuzhong, is intended to generate generosity. In China *zakat* is given mainly to support the mosque, because in a thoroughly socialized state it is often difficult to find someone significantly poorer than the rest to give to. Photo: Luckert

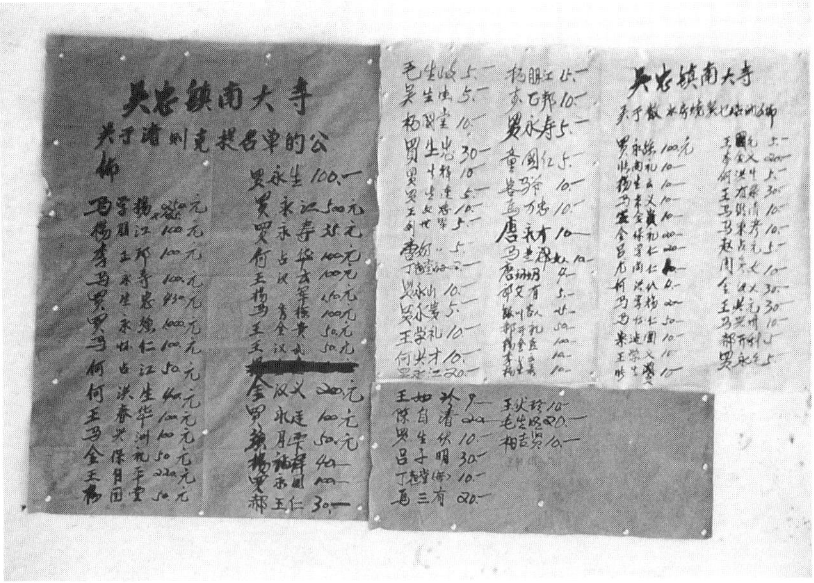

39. In a Wuzhong home, four elderly ladies have washed and dressed for prayer. Photo: Wang Ganhui
40. At another home a hostess demonstrates how she prays. A woman's prayer postures at home are identical with those of her husband. For public prayers in a mosque this posture is deemed inappropriate for females, and most Chinese mosques exlude women. Females are permitted to enter the Niujie Street Mosque, in Beijing, but must wear trousers. Photo: Luckert

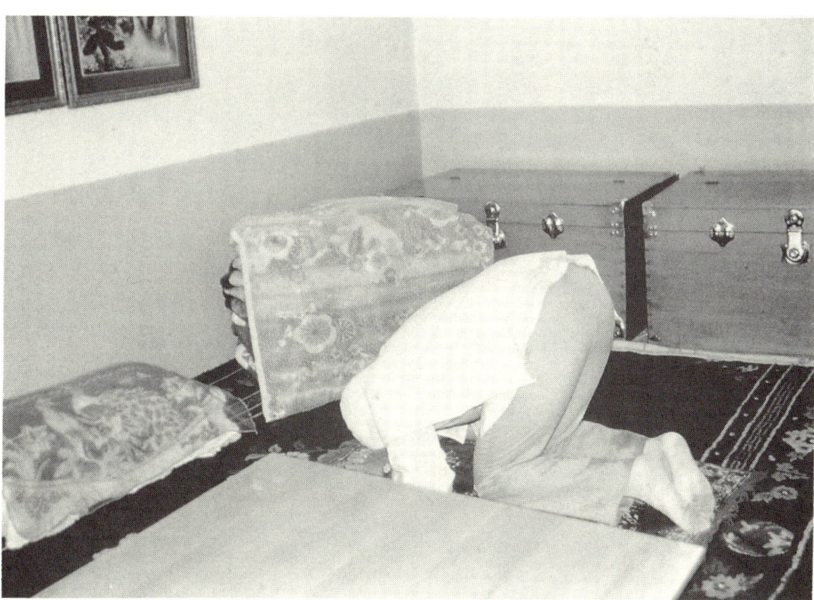

41. As is the custom everywhere, the lady of another home welcomes her guests with tea. This room serves as sitting room and as bedroom. The bed is oriented to the west, and the wallhanging depicts the Kaaba, in Mecca. The oldest generation lives in the western-most room—as they await heaven next in line, via Mecca. Photo: Luckert

42. Tongxin City is famous for its huge market where almost anything within the Ningxia economy is being bought or sold. Two-wheel tractors, teams of donkeys, or carts pulled by single animals, deliver goods—and just as easily haul them away. Photo: Luckert

43. From under a butcher's tent meat is sold in any quantity, fresh off the hook. Photo: Luckert

44. Wooden harrows are sold to farmers to prepare their fields for sowing. Photo: Luckert

45. A vendor weighs out his *woju* vegetables. Photo: Luckert

46. Two young ladies in the process of buying their fineries—perhaps in happy anticipation of their wedding day. Photo: Luckert

47. We are guests at the home of Ahong Li, head imam at the Grand Mosque, at Tongxin. Photo: Zhou Pengqi
48. The Grand Mosque at Tongxin. On a Friday afternoon the ahong invites us into the prayer hall with our cameras. Photo: Luckert

49. Ritual cleansing is prescribed for every Muslim who comes into the presence of God or enters the mosque to pray. A special washing hall is therefore provided. Photo: Zhou Pengqi

50. Before prayer the ahong preaches a sermon, offering encouragement and guidance for Muslims entrusted to his care. Photo: Zhou Pengqi

51. Quranic verses resound from mortal human lips: echoes of the heavenly Quran, recited in praise of God's glory. Photo: Zhou Pengqi
52. Typically an ahong teaches several apprentices, or *mullahs*. He tutors them in reading the Holy Quran. Photo: Zhou Pengqi

53. This is the tomb of Hu Denzhou, a revered ahong from Shaanxi province who died here while visiting some five centuries ago. Three bicycles stand outside the tomb. Inside, at this very moment, three young men burn incense and chant Quranic verses. Photo: Luckert

54. Inside the tomb of another teacher, who died "two or three centuries ago," we find rosaries to the left and the remains of incense sticks upon an altar in the back. These are evidence that Quranic prayers are regularly recited also in this tomb. Photo: Luckert

55. Back at Banqiao Daotang, near Wuzhong City, a member of the Jahriyya *menhuan* prays at the grave of Ma Jinxi, grandson of Ma Hualong. In a shrine before his master's tomb he burns incense and prays in alignment with his teacher's position of rest, due north. Photo: Zhou Pengqi
56. The Shaanxi Mosque at Guyuan counts approximately 2,000 members. Some of them, who had come to pray on a Sunday, line up for a group portrait. The ancestors of these Hui Muslims were expelled from Shaanxi Province around 1875, and exiled here, after having participated in a rebellion. Photo: Li

57. At a roadside village, in southern Ningxia, a husband and his wife hang up wild *juecai* plants for drying. These edibles will be sold as a cash crop, to a cannery, for processing. Photo: Zhou Pengqi
58. Their daughter demonstrates the resonance of her mouthharp. Photo: Zhou Pengqi

59. At the village of Xinglong it is a market day. The arrival of a foreign visitor has made a difference. People who earlier had been milling around aimlessly, suddenly become followers. Photo: Zhou Pengqi

60. In the city of Xiji, Ahong Ma Zhongxian, a seventy-three-year-old haji, tells us the legend about "Tomb of an Unknown Ahong at Twenty-li Place" which is included in this book. Photo: Zhou Pengqi

61. Hui as well as Han people go to Twenty-li Place on pilgrimages. Long ago a Han imperial officer scoffed the dead saint who lies buried there. He was instantly stricken with a twisted neck. For atonement the official donated a sum of money to enlarge the saint's tomb. History tends to repeat itself. Some decades ago Red Guards scoffed the sanctity of this place; the government, in 1990, paid for its restoration. Photo: Luckert

62. Progress is obvious, in 1992. Photo: Luckert

63. Some men at the Shanjiaji Village Mosque have prepared a meal for us—with meat. Proudly they watch whether and how we eat.
Photo: Luckert

64. A friendly host in Shanjiaji displays the shape of his Tang water kettle, to help illustrate the story "Wan Gars."
Photo: Luckert

65. Farmers are building a barn next to their homestead. Their primary
building material is adobe blocks. Photo: Zhou Pengqi
66. The ladies at the homestead welcome us into their kitchen where
steambread is being baked for the noon meal. Photo: Zhou Pengqi

67. While the bread bakes on the hearth the master of the house, in another part of the dwelling, lights three incense sticks—a custom he inherited from Buddhist ancestors. He prays by the *mihrab* in his home. Photo: Zhou Pengqi

68. The two most important Islamic festival days are Breaking the Fast after Ramadan, and the Feast of Sacrifice. Today is Qurban, the Feast of Sacrifice. On this special day, in a Khufia mosque in Yinchuan, a government representative offers friendly greetings to his Muslim citizens. Photo: Zhou Pengqi

69. Between rounds of prayer the ahong expounds divine words from the Holy Quran. His role as a mediator, between God and fellow humankind, is dramatized by the shepherd's staff which he holds in his hands. Photo: Zhou Pengqi

70. Under the exterior stairway two sheep are prepared for sacrifice. The ahong recites the Qurban prayer: "Allah is greatest! Allah is greatest! Praise be to Allah!" In patriarchal times, Abraham had so substituted a ram for his son Ishmael. Photo: Zhou Pengqi

71. Every culture has religious ways to justify a measure of killing. The ahong, on behalf of his people, praises God from whom he accepts these animals as food. God himself thereby assumes responsibility for their death. God so judges what is moderation and what is excess. Photo: Zhou Pengqi
72. Beyond the divinely set limit of sacrifice, in ritualized space—by Allah's grace and human stewardship—extend pastures where sheep may safely graze. Photo: Zhou Pengqi

1

The First Ancestors of Hui Muslims

Adan and Haowa
First Version

Place: Yinchuan, Ningxia
Narrator: Told in a mosque, by the Ahong Wang Fuchen
Recorder: Xie Rong (Hui), 1980[1]

It is said that long, long ago, the earth was wrapped in total darkness. There were no flowers yet, no songbirds, no humankind, or other living beings. Then suddenly, one day, a rumbling noise was heard, a red light flashed between heaven and earth. And from this red light slowly came forth a man and a woman. The man was Adan (Adam) and the woman was Haowa (Hawwa, Eve).

Adan formerly was one of Allah's angels (*tienxian*) and Haowa was a female angel. One day these two were walking together, some-

---

[1]Xie Rong (1932–1984) was a Hui scholar of Ningxia Hui folk literature. His role as a cadre occasionally inspired him to create brand-new "Hui stories," dedicated by him to the noble cause of nation building. We have included in this publication only a few stories which we are reasonably sure he obtained from Hui narrators. We alert the reader that stories by this recorder include also "Duoer Tea," "The North Pagoda," "Nuha and Suoli," "A Small Wooden Bowl," "Yaya and the Golden Sparrow," "Yimamu Questions a Stone," "Yimamu Examines a Corpse," "Yimamu Questions a Hen," "The Donkey Knows Its Way," and "Pushing the Millstone." How can the authors justify the risk that one or the other of these stories may mostly be Xie Rong's fabrication? Well, in that case, a broad-minded reader can still discern what kind of ideology it was that affected China and "Hui" intellectuals during the 1970s and 1980s.

where among deep rosy clouds, near the heavenly fruit orchard. From a hundred steps away they smelled a wonderful fragrance, and they became intoxicated by that scent. They crossed the rainbow bridge and came to a garden in which trees stood laden with deep red and bright yellow fruits. These fruits began to fascinate them.[2]

Adan was so excited that he then picked two grain-fruits (*maiguo*) and gave one to Haowa, who immediately put hers into her mouth. She was so eager that she swallowed it whole, without chewing. Adan took only a bite out of his—but, while his bite was swallowed only halfway down his throat, he was caught doing it. Heavenly beings are not permitted to eat anything. They will cease to be holy and pure if they do so. Because Adan and Haowa together transgressed against this heavenly rule, God decreed that henceforth they should live on earth.

The world was shrouded in utter darkness and the sea of misery had no bounds. Adan and Haowa survived only with great difficulty. While kneeling and squatting upon a frozen river they prayed to Allah by way of reciting Quranic verses, five times in the course of each day.

One hundred years passed, and five hundred more years followed these. Allah was moved by the sincerity and piety which Adan and Haowa displayed toward him. And the merciful God therefore commanded, and instantly the earth and the sky broke apart. Between earth and sky, in the east, dawn cracked forth and the radiant sun arose to shine. The bright moon and the twinkling stars appeared in the evening. The world was now illuminated so that Adan and Haowa could see and recognize each other. They threw themselves into each other's arms with boundless joy. But then, in her excitement Haowa slipped and ended up sitting upon the ice. Adan also slipped and dropped to his knees upon that primeval glacier. In that position they continued to pray every day. Each time before they prayed they cleansed their hands and their feet—namely, their hands which

---

[2]The story of Adam and Hawwa (Adan and Haowa) can be found in the Quran, mainly in 2:34–37, and in the Hebrew Genesis, whereby the Arabic "Hawwa" corresponds to the biblical "Eve" (Mahmoud Abu Saud). Nevertheless, the *tienxian* are here an adaptation to Chinese mythology: originally Adan was a masculine and Haowa was a female heavenly being. This story in its totality therefore presents a dual explanation concerning the origin of sexuality.

formerly touched the forbidden fruit. They rinsed their mouths because with these they had eaten the fruit.

Another five hundred years passed, and because they repented Allah agreed to forgive them. But some distinct characteristics remained associated with their bodies. Adan's throat was bulging a little on account of the half-swallowed fruit. His knees had become cold because he slipped and landed on his knees upon the ice. All the while, the belly of Haowa was enlarged because she had swallowed the fruit whole. Her buttocks became cold as a result of her initial fall upon that frozen river. Moreover, because both have expressed a desire to eat, Allah gave them a sensation of hunger.

Allah also let them become husband and wife, to help each other, and to live together day and night—to let them satisfy their needs by way of working. He let the earth reward them fairly, in proportion to their efforts.

Adan cut through mountains to channel in water. He cultivated wastelands and turned them into fruitful fields. He modified the earth in accordance with the model of heaven and paradise. Haowa reached out and picked a rose-colored cloud and cut it up into many kinds of little flowers, similar to those that bloomed in the garden of paradise. She scattered them all over the world. God also gave to them the grain-fruit that formerly they stole and ate. And so, by careful cultivation, grains became their stable food.[3] By their untiring hands the wilderness was transformed into a landscape of picturesque mountains and rivers.

Adan and Haowa gave birth to seventy-two twins—a boy and a girl for each set of twins. At the thirty-seventh birth, however, they received only a son, named Shisi. The family worried very much over the marriage prospects of this single boy; he had no wife. Moreover, many places on this vast earth were still uninhabited. Adan discussed this situation with his sons and daughters and resolved to send some of them to the heavenly paradise to obtain more fruits—so that by way of eating these his daughters, as well, would be enabled to bear

---

[3]The mythical *maiguo*, some kind of large "grain-fruit" from which big bites can be taken, stands in some kind of a relationship to wheat, which is the primary food grain in China's northwest. It is conceivable that pomegranates—full with seeds and marriage symbolism for Han people—were originally alluded to, in China, by this Near Eastern myth. In any case, Hui storytellers among whom we inquired did not know about a relationship with pomegranates.

children. He also wanted them to obtain Allah's further instructions. But all his children just stood and looked at each other and kept silent, all except Shisi. He was single and carefree, and he bravely volunteered.

"My dear Father and Mother, for the sake of my kind brothers and sisters I will go and bring back the heavenly fruits, and also receive Allah's further instructions—even though I may risk my life and barely escape death."

Shisi climbed mountains and waded across rivers; he endured severe cold and extreme heat; he suffered from hunger. For countless days and over a vast distance he trudged onward. Despite blisters on his feet and swelling in his legs, Shisi refused to abandon his goal of finding Allah. With each step forward he prayed.

One day he was so exhausted that he fell to the ground, and he fell asleep at the top of a high mountain. There he had a dream, and in this dream he saw a white serpent (a boa), the body of which was a hundred zhang (ca. 1,000 feet) long and as thick as a barrel. The serpent raised its head and wiggled its body, and then it spoke to Shisi: "Handsome Lad, do not be afraid. I am a heavenly messenger (*tienxian*), sent to you by Allah to bring you to paradise. Please, climb upon my back and prepare for a ride—but close your eyes!"

Shisi did as he was told, and with the speed of a gust of wind he arrived at the gate of paradise, carried by that serpent. By the gate stood the angel Haole. After having understood the request which Adan had sent, Haole prayed silently to Allah. He made a gesture while heaving and swaying his white beard. Instantly a howling whirlwind began blowing up dust. It darkened the sky and concealed everything. It swept Adan (and Haowa), including their seventy-two sons and daughters, up into the sky and dropped them onto every corner of the earth. Allah also dropped onto the earth the five cereals, together with the six domestic animals.[4] From that moment onward the earth enjoyed paradisical prosperity.

---

[4]In Islamic literature, outside China, the five cereals or six animals are not mentioned (Mahmoud Abu Saud). In Chinese tradition the five cereals are rice, two kinds of millet, wheat, and beans. The six domestic animals are pig, bovine, goat, horse, fowl, and dog. One can assume that Hui Muslims, if asked specifically, would exclude the pig and substitute the camel.

As for Shisi, having been brave and unselfish, he was invited by Allah to remain in the heavenly paradise as one of his angels.

Adan and Haowa
Second Version

Place: Southern Ningxia
Narrator: Wang Xueyi (Hui), Tongxin, Ningxia
Recorder: Wang Zhengwei (Hui), 1980, University of Ningxia

It is said that long, long ago, Allah created the first man, the holy man (*shengren*) Adan. Soon after that he also created a spouse for him, a woman made out of Adan's rib.[5] Her name was Haowa.

After the holy man Adan had come into being, God taught him the names of all things and beings; he even let Adan answer the questions which angels raised concerning these names, one by one. Soon thereafter God assigned Adan and Haowa to live in paradise in order to watch over it. They could live a life of pleasure there, well fed and well clad. They were, however, prohibited to eat of the grain-fruit in paradise.

At first Adan and Haowa obeyed Allah's command. They did not even look at this fruit. But then one day, when the holy man Adan had gone somewhere, the Devil (Yinbulisi) hastened into paradise and spoke to Haowa.

"The grain-fruit in paradise is the most fragrant, sweet, and delicious food. If you do not taste it, you will regret it as long as you live."

Haowa could not withstand this temptation and lost her resolve. She picked one with ease, and she ate it. When Adan came back she told him that the fruit tasted very good. And so Adan also went after

---

[5]The creation of Hawwa from Adam's rib is mentioned in alBukhari's Hadith (Mahmoud Abu Saud). It was recorded earlier in Genesis 2:21-24.

one and took a bite. When he was about to swallow that fruit an angel appeared, and he saw him do it. The angel grabbed Adan by his throat so that the fruit got stuck there. Ever since that moment, a man has had an "Adam's apple" in his throat. By the same token, women menstruate monthly, because Haowa swallowed the fruit all the way down.

*   *   *

Adan and Haowa disobeyed Allah's voice and ate the fruit. As a result they were driven out from paradise and made to live on the dark earth.

Adan and Haowa could not see anything on earth. They lived separate from each other and in darkness. After a long time, in that primeval darkness, they happened to meet each other on a frozen river, and they embraced each other. They laughed with joy and held on to each other to support themselves. That night, on the ice, Adan and Haowa joined. And from that time on a man's knees and a woman's buttocks have been cold.

*   *   *

After they had joined themselves, Adan and Haowa remained squatting upon the ice. Soon the sky brightened in the east. There was now light on earth. Adan and Haowa for the first time saw each others' faces and their naked bodies. Haowa felt ashamed, and she picked a leaf to cover the lower portion of her body. Adan tore a strip of bark from a tree to cover his as well.

Thereafter, Adan and Haowa never separated. They no longer lived together as carefree as they once had been in paradise. They now made a living by working with their own hands. Somewhat later Haowa became pregnant. The sage Adan prayed to Allah and asked him to forgive their sin of having eaten the grain-fruit. Allah then gave them another commandment, stipulating that they must wash four things—their faces, their foreheads, hands, and feet—so as to take the stains off their bodies and to atone for their sins.

They were required to wash their faces because with their eyes they saw the forbidden fruits; with their mouths they ate of them; and with their noses they smelled them. They were required to wash their foreheads because with these they touched the branches and the leaves of the fruit tree. They were required to wash their hands because with these they picked the fruits. And they were required to wash their feet because with these they walked up toward the tree.[6]

From that time onward there were human beings on earth. Also at that point in time the ablution ritual (*wuduyi*) was handed down to Muslims for them to prepare themselves for prayer.

Adan and Haierma
Third Version

First published in *Hei long jiang min jian wen xue (The Folk Literature of Heilongjiang)*, 1981.
Place: Heilongjiang
Recorder: Zhang Wenbing

It is said that at the time of creation there were no human beings in the world. There was only Allah. His four heavenly angels emerged from fire. They still had no definite form.

Allah considered it not much fun to exist like this, day in and day out. So he sent forth his first heavenly angel to fetch soil of five colors—red, yellow, blue, white, and black. But the five types of soil refused the request, and they said, "We are used to receiving all sorts of dirty things, such as feces, urine, and spittle. Being as dirty as we are, how can we have an audience with Allah! Please go back."

The heavenly messenger returned, and thereupon God sent the second heavenly angel to fetch the five colors of soil and instructed him before leaving, "Be sure to bring back the five. I am going to fashion a man out of these."

Upon being told about Allah's specific intentions, the five kinds of earth were even more reluctant. So, God had no other choice but

---

[6]The act of washing the mouth, hands, feet, and the face corresponds to the ablution which Muslims perform before offering their prayers. Nowhere in the Arabic texts are these washing rites traced back to Adam and Hawwa (Mahmoud Abu Saud).

to send his third heavenly messenger to fetch the five kinds of earth. His name was Abraham (Yinbolaxi).[7]

The five-colored earth told Abraham, "I am not worthy to see Allah, and I am even less worthy to be molded into a man. I cannot possibly come with you."

Then Abraham said, "I was sent by Allah. So you will have to come along to Allah and explain yourself." He tolerated no argument. Instead, he seized the five colors of earth and said, "Let us go!"

Allah was very pleased to see Abraham return with the soil of five colors. He added some water to the soil, and from these elements he fashioned a man, lying down. God called him "Adan," and he improved on him every day. He admonished him not to get up by himself. Nevertheless, as time passed Adan grew tired of just lying down. He felt strong enough to rise up by himself. Therefore, one day, while Allah was momentarily absent, Adan tried to sit up.

"Oh, now I did it!" Adan's skull cracked open and his vital energies leaked out. Some of his soul-essence reached the mountains and became minerals of all sorts—gold, silver, copper, iron, tin, and others. Some of it went up into the sky and became birds of all kinds. Some reached the ground and became various animals. Some went to the rivers and lakes and became various kinds of fishes, turtles, shrimps, and crabs. Adan realized the danger he was in. He knew that if all his soul-energy escaped he would die. With his left hand he hurriedly took some mud from the middle of the sole of his right foot, and he took some from the sole of his left foot with his right hand, to seal the crack on his head with mud.

That is why, nowadays still, man has a hollow arch at the bottom of both feet—because he took mud from there to seal the crack that opened on his skull.

It is said that man would be immortal if it were not for the fact that our first ancestor, Adan, let some of his soul-essence escape when first he started to sit up on his own. God knew that there was no use complaining about what had happened. He continued to improve on the shape of Adan to a point of completion. When at last God permitted him to rise, Adan wandered from place to place. He

---

[7]"Yinbolaxi" is the Chinese version of the Arabic "Ibrahim," which is the biblical Abraham (Mahmoud Abu Saud).

ate some fruits when he was hungry, and he drank from the river in paradise when he was thirsty.

After some time a mysterious lump appeared on Adan's third rib. It grew larger and larger. And no one knew how long it would be before the lump would erupt and a woman would come forth. And no one knew why Allah named her Haierma.[8]

Adan noticed that Haierma was different from himself, and a sexual passion overcame him. He implored Allah that he be given a wife—and God agreed to let Haierma be that wife. Adan and Haierma were appointed to watch over the grain-fruit garden of paradise.

And God enjoined them before they went: "You must not touch the fruit. If you do, I will punish you."

Adan and Haierma kept Allah's warnings in mind and guarded the garden conscientiously. Spring passed and autumn was approaching. The flowers withered and all the trees were heavily laden with fruits.

When the fruits were ripe Haierma spoke to Adan, and while she spoke water gathered in her mouth. "We have been cultivating these trees seven springs and eight autumns. Why should we not pick a fruit and taste it?"

Adan was afraid. He shook his head and said, "No, we must not touch what Allah has forbidden."

"There are plenty of fruits in the garden. And besides, we will eat only one—or a half. And surely, God will never notice if you and I keep quiet." Then, with ease, Haierma plucked a large one and broke it into halves. A sweet smell greeted her. It caused her taste buds to itch as if a little hand was reaching out to touch them. Haierma gave half of the fruit to Adan. She put the other half into her own mouth and swallowed. Adan accepted his half and put it into his mouth. He, too, was about to swallow when he heard Allah's voice. He became terribly frightened, so much so that the fruit got stuck in his throat.

Both were severely scolded by Allah. To punish them, God caused the fruit in Adan's throat to protrude, as a reminder of his sin. The fruit inside Haierma was transformed into menses. And then God

---

[8]Most probably the name "Haierma" is derived from the Arabic "Hurma," which means "wife" (Mahmoud Abu Saud).

separated them and placed Adan in the east and Haierma in the west. God made them miss each other, and they could not come together.

Adan had no idea where Haierma was, nor did Haierma know where Adan was. Every morning Haierma combed her hair by the sea. A swallow carried some of her loose hair to the place in the east where Adan was. Likewise, Adan washed his face every morning. The swallow carried the beard hair, which he had washed out, westward to Haierma. Observing the direction from which the swallow flew, Adan reasoned that Haierma must be in the west. Haierma, likewise, realized that Adan was in the east. So they started to seek each other in the direction of the swallow's path. Eventually they came together. As a result of their long separation they had developed a deep longing for one another.

Many years passed and together they had seventy-two children, resulting from thirty-six births. The older sons married their younger twin sisters, and in this manner they multiplied.

Adan and Haierma, and their offspring, lived together at one place. They made much noise chatting and laughing. Allah became greatly annoyed by their hubbub. He therefore drove them to a place south of Tianshan Mountain, in Xinjiang. These are the ones who became the ancestors of the Hui people.

2

Muhammad and His Companions

Origin of the Jujube Dates

Place: Southern mountain area, Ningxia
Narrator: Wang Yidi (Hui)
Recorder: Wang Zhengwei (Hui), 1981

People who have ever eaten a jujube date *(zao)* always ask about its origin. So it has been said that long, long ago, the Muslims once again had trouble with some pagans with whom they ended up fighting at close range. The chief of the pagans, with broadsword in hand, advanced toward Muhammad determined to kill him.

Seeing the man run after him with his sword, to slay him—and considering himself to be less strong—Muhammad kept running and turning right and left, to throw the pursuer off his track. At last he took off his blue gown—so as to be less recognizable—and sat down on a pile of dirt to rest, with his head bowed low.

After a while this pagan chief came running up to Muhammad, almost out of breath, and he asked, "Have yo-you seen a ta-tall fe-fellow just pa-pass by?"

Keeping his head low Muhammad calmly replied, "Yes, he was running southeast."

"Show me the way to him. Quick!" said the chief.

But Muhammad said, "Wait until I have eaten a date." And while speaking he tore a lump of cotton from the inside of his robe. He twisted and rolled it with his right hand and dug a hole in the ground. There he planted this lump of cotton.

The chief said, "You have just planted a seed. When will you have your date? Hurry! Do not dally!"

Muhammad smiled. "No need to rush. We shall have it immediately."

The chief did not believe it and said, "If I could eat your date that quickly, I would serve you as my master."

Muhammad said, "Let us see."

And no sooner had he finished these words when out from the ground sprouted a fresh jujube shoot.[1] Momentarily it grew a foot tall and brought forth two flowers. Before long these two blossoms bore two dates.

Muhammad said, "In the name of Allah," and began picking the dates off the little tree.[2] He ate one himself and gave the other to the chief.

Both dates were extraordinarily sweet and sticky. So, after having eaten, the pagan chief stared at Muhammad with amazement and thought to himself, "What an able man! He could make the jujube shoot bear two dates and share one with me! Hey-hey! Who might this be?"

Noticing the chief's bewilderment, Muhammad looked up and said, "I am the very Muhammad. In God's name! Kill me if you wish!"

The pagan chief looked him over, up and down. And after having thought again about having eaten the date, he dropped his sword. He stepped forward and grasped Muhammad's hands. "We should no longer be enemies. Henceforth I shall live in peace with Muslims."

From that moment on both were reconciled. The jujube tree that had been planted by Muhammad grew profusely, and all the people could eat delicious sweet dates. Muslims henceforth regarded these

---

[1]The Chinese date-like fruit, *zao shu miao* or jujube, grows on shrubs or trees. It belongs to the buckthorn family.

[2]*Taisimi* is a Hui transliteration from the Arabic *tasmiah*. Muslims usually start their activities, such as eating or putting on clothes, by way of saying *tasmiah*, that is, *"Bismi-Allah!,"* which means "In the name of God," (Mahmoud Abu Saud).

dates as very precious things. They also use the kernels of these dates as beads for their rosaries, to count prayers.

To Earn One's Livelihood

Place: Urumqi, Xinjiang
Narrator: Haidiche (Hui)
Recorder: Guo Xiumei (Hui), 1984

Long, long ago a young man named Musa left his home town.[3] He went idle and roamed about everywhere. He was unable to do large tasks and unwilling to do small ones, and he barely survived on the table scraps of others.

One day he begged from a family whose yard was filled with fresh flowers. Before he even knocked at the door the master of the house happened to emerge. He approached the young man Musa and looked him over, up and down. Then he asked with a smile, "Young man, what family property do you own?"

Musa felt embarrassed. "What property can I own? I only have an old felt pad for sleeping, a drinking bowl, and a rope for getting water."

"Ha hah!" laughed the host. "All right, young man, go and bring them here."

In a short time the young man came back with these three items. Then the master of the house and the young man together went to the market and sold these things. With the money they bought an axe. When they returned the host asked his worthy wife to provide a meal. He let the young man eat his fill and, in addition, wrap up some dry

---

[3]The name "Musa" is derived from the Arabic "Mousa," the biblical Moses. The story itself seems to be developed upon the basis of an alBukhari hadith: "It is better for one to earn his living by collecting firewood than to beg from others" (Mahmoud Abu Saud). Inasmuch as "Musa" in this story is the proper name of a person who is not the biblical Moses, it is left untranslated in its Chinese form.

provisions. After the meal the host wound a long hemp rope around the young man's waist and sent him to the mountain with his axe, to cut firewood. He expected to see him back again half a month later.

Having accepted the master's advice, Musa cut firewood sticks and sold them in the market. Soon he could not only eat his fill, but also put on new clothes, and still have some money left over in his pocket. Only then did he realize the host's intention, and from the bottom of his heart he began to feel grateful. It was he who taught him how to earn a living.

Half a month passed, and at the appointed time Musa returned to the master's house. The master was happy to receive him. After exchanging greetings the young man expressed his thanks and promised never to idle and to roam anymore.

Having heard this, the master spoke these memorable words, "Earning one's livelihood is better than begging."

The young man nodded and agreed. When his time had come to leave, he respectfully inquired about the name of his host.

Gently smiling the master replied, "My name is Muhammad."

Potato Story

Place: Qinghai
Narrator and Recorder: Ma Jinxiang (Hui), 1985

It has been said that, once upon a time, when Muhammad led a holy war campaign, his entire army was surrounded and bottled up in a barren mountain valley. Soldiers and horses were awfully hungry and worn out. No grain was available. It appeared that the soldiers and horses would die of hunger. The holy man Muhammad had to face west and pray to Huda (Allah) for help.

After his prayer was completed, Muhammad showed his warriors to a ridge and asked them to build an oven shaped like a Chinese hearth. They took lumps of clay and piled them up in the shape of a shock of wheat—of one that sits like a cone. Into this hearth they placed firewood and lit a fire. Nearby they gathered many stones, the size of a fist. Muhammad asked his men to fill the oven with these stones and to seal the opening with lumps of clay. Soon the lumps of clay were heated to a fiery red. The oven was tightly sealed with clay so that no air could escape; and the soldiers were baffled by all of this.

Two hours (a *shichen*) passed and Muhammad asked his men to remove the earth cover.[4] Immediately a sweet smell greeted everyone. And when they looked the stones had disappeared, and instead they saw some red- and brown-hued lumps. They broke them apart and tasted them. Wonderful! And so, in this manner, they cooked many more white stones for a big meal. The soldiers satisfied their hunger and afterward broke through the enemy lines.

Some time after the holy battle was over, a Muslim warrior came again to that place and smelled a pleasant fragrance. He found a leafy type of plant growing over a large area, of a kind he had never seen before.

Being curious he dug the ground with his fingers and discovered some things resembling those white stones which they had eaten earlier. He told other people to dig them out and to keep some for seed. These seeds have been passed down to us, year after year. They are the very potatoes we have today. In order to remember Muhammad's contribution, nowadays, Muslim children often roast potatoes in this manner to eat.

---

[4]Two hours: a *shichen*, or one of twelve equal periods in a day, each comprising two hours. Traditionally in China, a day and a night together were divided into twelve units.

The Mule and the Horse

Place: Qinghai
Narrator and Recorder: Han Changlin (Hui), 1980

Once, while on a mission journey, Muhammad was vigorously pursued by Jews. When he had nearly come to the end of his strength, he saw a mule grazing, just ahead of him. He implored the mule for help. Yet the mule continued eating and remained indifferent to his request.

Knowing that the Jews would soon catch up with him, Muhammad anxiously looked ahead and saw a horse standing in a plowed field. He ran up to it for help. With its hooves the horse dug a deep trench into the plowed field and Muhammad quickly lay down into it. The horse lay across the trench and pretended to be resting. After the Jews had run past, the animal stood up.

Then, to thank this horse, Muhammad promised that horses would be able to rest their hooves when they are tired. By the same token, as punishment, he did not permit the mule to give birth, not ever. Since that day, horses often lift up their hooves when they stop to rest; and mules have not been able to foal.

The Festival of Ascent

Place: Yinchuan, Ningxia (known also in Shaanxi)
Narrator and Recorder: Ahong Ma Guang Wen, 1990

According to Yiben Abasi, a follower of the "Sacred Gate," the angel Gabriel (Zhebolayile), and the other angel [probably Michael], told the holy man Muhammad that in ancient times lived a hero whose name was "Shemuernei."[5] He fought a thousand months for the Muslim people.

Shemuernei had the teeth of camels. When he was thirsty, sweet water would come forth through his teeth, and when he was hungry food would exude through them as well. With such teeth he was able to endure and to defeat many enemies, and no enemy was able to defeat him. Therefore his enemies solicited Shemuernei's non-Muslim wife to kill him. They promised that if she succeeded they would give her many treasures of gold and silver.

Once, while Shemuernei was resting she tied him up with the strongest rope available. When he awoke he wanted to know who tied him up. She said that she did it, because she wanted to know whether he could break this rope. Then Shemuernei tensed his muscles and the rope broke.

Another time she tied him up with iron rods. When Shemuernei woke up he wanted to know again who tied him up. She admitted that she had done it, and again he asked her for the reason. She said she wanted to know whether he had still greater strength.

Then Shemuernei divulged to his wife that he was the army general of Allah, "In this world no-one can defeat me, nor can anyone's strength match mine. Only my own strands of hair can bind me."

When his wife found out that only his own hair could bind him, she cut off his hair while he was asleep. And with it she tied him up. Then she invited his enemies into the house. The enemies tied him to a post, cut off his ears, dug out his eyes, cut out his tongue, and cut off his hands and feet.

After he had been tortured in this manner, Allah sent the angel Zhebolayile to see whether Shemuernei had any requests.

Shemuernei pleaded, "Allah, please help me move this pillar. Let this house fall down to kill my enemies and my wife."

So Allah gave him strength, and the house collapsed. His enemies and his evil wife were killed.

---

[5]"Yiben Abasi" is "Ibn Abbas," the first cousin of the Prophet. He is considered the most authoritative exegete of the Quran. "Zhebolayile" (Gabriel) is "Jibreel" in Arabic. (Mahmoud Abu Saud). This story obviously is a Hui variation of the "Samson" legend in the Hebrew Bible. See Judges 13–16.

Later Allah granted him again his ears, his eyes, his hands, and his feet. From that time on he continued fighting during daytime hours, and he prayed at night.

When holy man Muhammad heard this story, his admiration for Shemuernei was great. And he said, "Allah! My followers do not live long enough to do an adequate number of good deeds. How would it be possible for them to attain that higher level?"

Thereupon Allah granted to the holy man Muhammad the wonderful night, the Night of Ascent. And he told him:

"If your followers observe my expectations, tonight, they will attain the same level of perfection that this hero had achieved. They will even surpass him."

When he heard this, Muhammad was exceedingly glad, and he thanked Allah, endlessly.

It has been said that there was another reason for Muhammad's ascent. Earth and Sky quarrelled. The Earth said to Sky, "I am stronger than you, because Allah has bestowed on me seas, rivers, mountains, trees, flowers, and variously shaped things."

Sky was not convinced and said, "I am much stronger than you, because I am adorned with the sun, with the moon and the stars."

The Earth retorted, "But I have the Kaaba, which all the holy men and their followers come to visit the year-round."

Sky was speechless and then begged God, "Allah! You are the Lord who has promised to answer all prayers. Please have the holy man Muhammad ascend to me, so that by way of becoming associated with him I might receive the same honor as Earth."

Allah granted his request. He ordered Zhebolayile and the other angel to get the Burelai, a heavenly horse, to carry Muhammad to heaven.[6]

Zhebolayile put upon the horse a saddle inlaid with red gems, and a yellow jade bridle as well. He led this horse to the gate of the sage Muhammad, in Mecca. Thereupon the sage Muhammad was

---

[6]The heavenly being "Burelai" is "alBuraq" in Arabic. The other angel alluded to may be the one mentioned later as "Weicayilai" (Mahmoud Abu Saud). All angels in this story, and elsewhere in this collection, are thought of in Chinese fashion as *tienxian*, that is, as some kind of "heavenly beings." These are called *tienxian* in Han mythology.

awakened, and Zhebolayile said, "Sage, please get up. This is going to be a wonderful night for you. You are to these sincere people like the sun, and you are like the full moon on the fifteenth night."

Upon hearing these words, Muhammad got up quickly and opened the door. The angels Zhebolayile and Weicayilai stood by the door.[7] Zhebolayile told Weicayilai: "Go get some *zamzam* water and I will wash the heart of the holy man Muhammad."

He opened the chest of the sage and washed his heart three times and then led him to the Zamzam spring. There he told the guardian of that spring, "Get some *zamzam* water for the sage to wash himself."

After Muhammad had purified himself, Zhebolayile told him that now he would take him to Allah. Muhammad got on the horse and followed Zhebolayile and, in this manner, they arrived at the gate of heaven. Zhebolayile knocked at the gate, and the angel who guarded the gate asked, "Who are you?"

Zhebolayile answered, "I am Zhebolayile, the great angel. And this here is the holy man Muhammad."

The first person whom Muhammad met in the first heaven was the sage Adan (Adam). Muhammad said, "Peace!" to him. Adan answered back with, "Peace," and then offered his congratulations.

Muhammad was then led to the second heaven, the sky of which was of iron. Zhebolayile knocked at the gate. Again a guardian angel asked, "Who are you?"

Zhebolayile answered, "I am Zhebolayile, the great angel. And this here is the holy man Muhammad."

When the great angel opened the gate, Muhammad saw two handsome boys and asked, "Who are these boys?"

Zhebolayile answered, "They are Yehaiya and Ersa (Jesus) who have been waiting at the gate to welcome you, Muhammad."[8]

They greeted each other with... "Peace."

---

[7]One may assume that Weicayilai is Michael who in the Quran (2,98) is mentioned together with Gabriel (Mahmoud Abu Saud).

[8]"Yehaiya" may be the biblical Isaiah. "Ersa" is the prophet Jesus, founder of Christianity.

Then Muhammad was brought to the third heaven, which had a copper sky. They knocked at the door. The door opened, and the angel who guarded the gate asked, "Who are you?"

They identified themselves. The angel opened, and they entered. There Muhammad saw a boy who looked like the moon on the fifteenth night. He asked Zhebolayile who he was. He was told that it was the sage Younusi (Younus). They extended greetings to each other.

Then Muhammad came to the fourth heaven, which had a sky of gold. They knocked at the gate and a guardian angel asked, "Who are you?" and then invited them to enter. Muhammad stepped into a very bright courtyard. On the wall was written: "There is no Lord but Allah, and Muhammad is Allah's messenger." Zhebolayile explained to Muhammad that this was the courtyard of the sage Yidereisi (Idris), and he introduced him, "This is the sage Yidereisi." They shook hands and greeted each other with "Peace."

Then Muhammad came to the fifth heaven, which had a sky made of green emerald. After their introduction to the guardian angel there they were permitted to enter. Muhammad met the holy man Harennai (Harun). They said, "Peace," to each other, and Harennai congratulated him, shaking his hand.

Muhammad then went to the sixth heaven, which had a sky of pearls and jewels. They knocked at the gate and introduced themselves to the guardian angel there. Upon entering Muhammad met a man, and Zhebolayile told him that this was the holy man Musa (Moses). Muhammad greeted him, and Musa congratulated him for having come to heaven.

Muhammad and Zhebolayile then entered the seventh heaven. The sky was brightly lit. After introducing themselves to the guardian angel there they entered. Muhammad saw an old man sitting on an imperial dragon bed. Zhebolayile introduced him: "This is your grandfather, the holy man Abraham." Muhammad said, "Peace," to him, and Abraham also responded with, "Peace."

Abraham then asked Muhammad to pass on his peace to his Muslim followers: "Please tell them that in paradise the landscape is beautiful, that the water is sweet, that the ground is level, and that the seedlings of grain grow sturdy. Praise the Lord for his bright splendor! All worship belongs to Allah! There is no god but Allah! Allah is greatest! Unless we place our trust in the almighty Allah, our sins will not be forgiven and our efforts will be without strength!"

After that, Muhammad descended one heaven after another. He came again to the holy man Moses. The latter asked Muhammad what Allah had commanded that his followers should do. Muhammad told him that God expected his followers to prostrate themselves [fifty times a day]. Moses suggested that he should go back and ask Allah to reduce this requirement, because he himself had tried this, when he required Israel to do that many prostrations. They had failed. And neither would the followers of Muhammad be able to do them all. So Muhammad went to see Allah and implored that the number of pious prostrations be reduced for his followers. Allah readily took off five.

When Muhammad returned to Moses, the latter told him that these were still too many to accomplish and on that account Muhammad went back to Allah again. Then another five were taken off. But when Moses heard about this he told Muhammad that this many were still impossible to do. And in this manner Muhammad begged Allah nine times in succession. Altogether Allah took off forty-five prayers of prostration. Only five remained.

The holy man Moses still insisted that Muhammad's followers were unable to do that many. But then Muhammad told him that he felt ashamed to beg for more reduction. This is why Muslims prostrate themselves for prayer five times a day.

In memory of that special night, however, the Muslims celebrate one day in the year which they have named the Festival of Ascent, or the Night of Ascent. On that night all Muslims, men and women alike, approach Allah and prostrate themselves [fifty times], they do something charitable, and they recite verses from the Quran.

The Ashula Meal

Place: Ningxia
Narrator: Wang Yidi (Hui)
Recorder: Wang Zhengwei (Hui), 1979

One hundred days after breaking their fasting, during Ramadan, the Hui people have a communal meal called Ashula (Ashura). It consists of porridge cooked with a mixture that may include millet, rice, wheat, barley, hyacinth beans, peas, soybeans, mung beans, dates, walnut meats, onions, and/or other things.

Why do Hui people have the Ashula meal on that day?[9] A story explains it.

Long, long ago, the holy man Ali led his men into battle.[10] The fighting lasted three days. The men ran out of food and their horses out of forage. After the battle Ali's courtyard was thronged with a crowd of hungry soldiers. A cauldron of water was boiling, but Fatima, Ali's wife, had nothing to put into it. Ali was deeply worried. How could all these soldiers fight with empty stomachs?

He called his two sons, Hasai (Hussein) and Hasan (Hassan), and told them, "I have a good friend in town. He is a carpenter. Go and borrow some rice and flour from him." The two brothers went at once.

The soldiers were too hungry to endure much longer. Someone stuck his head through the door and asked, "Is the meal ready yet? We are dying from hunger!"

---

[9]"Ashula" is derived from the Arabic "Ashura" and refers to the tenth day of the month Moharram. It is customary among almost all Muslims in the world to celebrate this day by preparing a meal consisting mostly of cereals. These represent the bounties of God (Mahmoud Abu Saud). See photographs 19 and 20.

[10]The names mentioned in this legend are those of Ali's family. Ali was the first cousin of the Prophet Muhammad and the first male to embrace Islam. He married the youngest daughter of the Prophet, Fatima, and they had two sons, Hassan and Hussein. This story about Ali, the miracle worker, may hint at some remote Shiite influence or emphasis (Mahmoud Abu Saud).

To comfort the hungry crowd, Ali had to say again and again, "Please be patient. Please wait a little. The meal will be ready any moment now."

They waited and waited, but Hasai and his brother did not come back. Fatima could not wait any longer. She ran to the riverside and picked up many small stones; she brought them home and washed them clean. Then she put them into the cauldron.

A moment later Hasai and Hasan came back with two sacks. Fatima felt relieved. She asked, "Have you borrowed any grain?"

"Yes, we have. Come and have a look, Mother," whispered Hasai to his mother.

Fatima looked into the bags, only to find that they were filled with sawdust. She sighed with a heavy heart. The shouting outside became louder and louder. Fatima could do nothing about it. She had to put the sawdust into the cauldron, too.

Ali was conversing with the soldiers when he learned that his sons had come back. He hurried into the house and asked them, "Have you borrowed anything?"

"That good friend of yours turned a deaf ear on us," answered Hasai with a sigh.

Ali lifted the cauldron cover. Oh my Allah! It was full of sawdust and stones![11] The four of them looked at each other. No one had a better idea. Fatima continued adding wood to the fire.

After a while a smell of rice and beans leaked forth. Ali was greatly surprised. His wife took off the cover and saw the cauldron full of porridge. She took a spoon full and examined it carefully. The sawdust had become millet and rice. Various stones had turned into hyacinth beans, peas, soybeans, and mung beans. There were dates, walnut meats, and many other delicious things contained in the porridge. It smelled good. She tried some. It tasted like mutton soup.

Ali was overjoyed. He ran out to tell his men, "Muslims, the meal today is especially delicious. You may eat as much as you want."

The soldiers rushed into the house. Fatima and her two sons, each with a scoop in hand, filled their bowls. And surprisingly,

---

[11]The trick of boiling or baking stones while pretending to cook, as is demonstrated here and in the "Potato Story" earlier, can be found in old Arabic literature. It persisted during the early Islamic era (Mahmoud Abu Saud).

though the cauldron was not overly large, there seemed to be no end to the porridge. Some had three bowls of porridge, and some had five. Others exerted themselves to eat some more even after they had eaten their fill. One of the Muslims ate so much on that day that he died of overeating.

Ali announced in the presence of all, "Allah will not punish those who die of overeating today."

So, even nowadays, the Hui people eat their fill at the Ashula feast. They either invite people to eat at their homes, or they send meals to other people. Many will get together to eat until they are quite full. They also call the Ashula feast Grain Day, Mother's Day, or Fatima's Day.

3

The Quests
of Culture Heroes
and Saviors

Adang Brings Fire

First published in *Min jian wen xue (Folk Literature)*, (Beijing: Beijing Press), 1961.
Place: Guizhou
Recorders: Folk Literature Working Group of Guizhou

In very, very ancient times, no embers of fire or tinder were yet on earth.[1] All humankind ate raw and cold food. One day a volcano erupted. The fields became like a sea of fire, and everything in the forest burned until grasses and trees were reduced to ashes. Also, a lot of wolves, tigers, and leopards were burnt to death. People gathered up these burned wild beasts and ate them. They tasted rather delicious. From that time on humankind was acquainted with the usefulness of fire. But no one kept and maintained the glowing embers. After the burning of the forest, people continued as they did before and lived on raw cold food.

---

[1] This story, though it was told by a Hui about a Hui hero, shows almost no trace of Islamization. It is included in this collection primarily to indicate the range of Hui dragon mythology, as well as to account for a well-nigh universal motif. Surely, the quest for fire is a theme that can safely be projected back all the way to campfire conversations among cave men, during the Stone Age.

Since that time, whenever fire was mentioned, people would talk about it a lot. Some said that the embers had fallen from heaven; others insisted that they were brought by the wind, and the majority agreed with the latter. So they sent a young fellow named Adang to go in search of embers.

Adang vowed not to return until he found embers. But he had no idea where these might be. He believed that he would find them after having traveled to all the corners of the world. With that in mind he began traveling everywhere. Wandering onward he climbed seventy-seven huge mountains, crossed seventy-seven wide rivers, and passed through seventy-seven immense dark forests. Searching all the while, among mountains and alongside rivers, he failed nevertheless. Upon seeing a blood-red leaf he suspected it to be embers, and repeatedly he picked up such things with cheerful anticipation. But when they felt cold he threw them away. Sometimes he saw a flying bird with red feathers; he believed the feathers to be embers. He pursued one with all the energy he could muster. At long last he hit the bird with a stone and it fell to the ground. It did not feel hot, nor was it embers. Then again, he mistook a small red animal for embers. He did his utmost to chase after it. He caught it. Yet it too did not burn his hand, nor was it embers.

Such were his experiences a thousand times, and then ten thousand times. And each time he failed. But in spite of it all, he continued his search without ever stopping. When he felt tired he rested in the forest, and when he was hungry he picked wild fruits to be his food.

Then Adang thought, "How will it be possible for me to achieve all this by myself? I must try to find a better way." Among all the varieties of birds, the swallow can fly farthest. Perhaps it knows where the embers are. He asked a swallow, "Hello, Swallow, you fly non-stop all year round. Have you ever seen embers anywhere? I will give you gold, or silver if you prefer, if you tell me where they are."

"I want neither your gold nor your silver. Only permit me, in the future, when you build a house, to build my nest on your roof beam to enable us to avoid suffering in wind and rain. And do not get angry if my children dirty your house when they relieve themselves."

Adang replied, "I do not mind that at all, and you may live on our roof beam. Just tell me where the embers are!"

"Embers are in Flame Mountain, at the foot of the western sky. But it is too far from here for you to go there. On foot you will not be able to reach that place in your entire lifetime."

Then Adang said, "I most certainly will make it there."

And so Adang walked westward. He continued to journey for thirty-three days and nights. Yet, no flaming mountain could be seen. But he was not disheartened and continued walking.

The thoughtful Adang considered again how to solve his problem. He realized that if he merely continued on foot, it was unlikely that he would ever get to the embers. Wild horses run faster, and he concluded that it would be better to ask one of them to carry him there. Adang found a wild horse and explained to him his predicament.

The horse said, "You can ride on my back. But later you must mow grass to feed me and build a stable for me to live in, to prevent my being hurt by tigers."

Adang said, "Surely!"

So he rode on horseback to the foot of the western sky. Many days passed before they arrived at the river that separates heaven from earth. On the other side of this river was the bright-red Flame Mountain that made them feel hot even though they were still separated from it by the river. Adang reached into the water and it felt very hot. A lot of dead boiled fishes floated in the river. Adang snatched a few of them to eat—large ones and small ones, long ones and short ones, broad ones and flat ones, some red and some of other colors.

Oh, they tasted much more delicious than the meat of animals on land. Adang continued to grab fish and piled them up.

The wild horse said, "On account of snatching fish, do not forget to get the embers."

Adang said, "No, no! I only would like to take lots of these back home with me, to share."

After a while he asked the wild horse, "The water is very hot, how can I cross it?"

The wild horse told him, "There is a cave in the bank of this river, and inside that cave a thunder axe can be found. But, in the cave also lies a fierce Dragon who guards this axe. You will have to fight that Dragon first. If you win, the axe is yours. You can then point that axe toward the river, and the water will immediately become a wide road. In this manner you will be able to cross over on an even surface. If you fail, you will be eaten alive by that fierce Dragon."

Adang was not afraid of death—but how could he defeat this fierce Dragon? His own death, he thought, did not matter. But, it mattered greatly to him if, without embers, the people could not cook their meals. He contemplated this problem again and again, even to the point where he felt a headache coming on. Still, he could not come up with a solution. He asked the wild horse for a good method to defeat the fierce Dragon.

The horse said: "Why would you want to defeat it with your bare hands? You will have to find a way to lure it out and make it pursue you. You must then run circles around it. As its head pursues you, it will coil itself into a ball. Then you must head directly for the cave to fetch the axe. The moment you have the axe in your hands the Dragon will be defeated."

Adang understood this plot immediately. In accordance with what the wild horse said, Adang lured the fierce Dragon into the open and ran circles around it. Before long it had coiled itself into a ball and could not move anymore. Adang quickly ran into the cave, seized the axe, and came back out.

Seeing the axe, the fierce Dragon was so afraid that he begged for mercy and pleaded with Adang. "Clever Adang! Do not kill me. I will tell you how to take the embers back home; without that knowledge you will fail to obtain them and be unable to carry them. They are very hot."

Adang considered this to be a reasonable offer and said, "Tell me first the way."

The Dragon said, "There is a lid at the back of the axe. Open the lid and you will see an empty chamber. Put embers into it, and in that manner you will be able to carry them home."

Adang agreed that what the Dragon had said was true. Thus, inasmuch as the Dragon had made a contribution, he reasoned that he should not kill it. And so he permitted it to return to its cave.

Adang pointed his axe toward the river, and the flowing river —whaah! It crackled and transformed itself into a flat sheet of even road.

Then the wild horse shouted, "Adang, run over to fetch the embers quickly! The road will not wait for you long."

Adang ran across the flat stone road very fast. He took two embers from the foot of Flame Mountain. He put them into the hollow at the back of his axe. Then he closed the lid and ran back with great haste. No sooner had he reached again the river bank than the flat stone road disappeared. It cracked up, with heaven swaying and earth shaking. The gushing river flowed again.

"What is this all about?" Adang asked in surprise.

The wild horse said, "When the thunder axe is filled with embers it will thunder and will rain. Originally the flat stone road was water. Therefore, when thunderbolts flash it will once again melt back into water."

Now that he had obtained his embers, Adang rode home on the back of the horse. He also carried his cooked fish. The wild horse ran so fast that Adang saw nothing but mountains and forests speed backward on both sides. He heard the wind whistle past his ears. The horse was flying! In three days and three nights Adang reached his home.

Because Adang brought back the embers, people learned how to burn things and how to cook their meals. Also, that wild horse became a domestic one. Because of Adang's great contribution, later generations carried a "fire sickle (*huo lian*) bag" at their belts to commemorate him. It is said that the bag itself was the box in which Adang kept his embers. The sickle blade chips, made of firestone or flint, were the very embers which Adang had fetched. The farmers' flint stone sickle was the very thunder axe which Adang brought back.

Sai Dianchi and the Dragons

First published in *Yun nan shao shu Min Zu Zi Liao (Yunnan Minority Materials)*, Kunming, 1981.
Place: Yunnan
Recorder: Li Qingshen (Hui)

It has been said that one hundred dragons lived in Kunming, and they often caused trouble. They would turn fields into vast lakes of water. People in towns and cities had to row boats if they wanted to go somewhere. Crops were washed away and houses were destroyed. The people suffered a lot.

Then Sai Dianchi came to Kunming.[2] After he made his rounds of inspection, and some inquiries, he at last located the den of dragons. Soon after that he dispatched an army of Hui warriors to capture these dragons. But, no sooner than the dragons had received news about this campaign, they decided to flood and to drown the entire city.

One day, when Sai Dianchi had just finished sunrise morning prayer (*salat al-fajr*), one of the soldiers arrived to report, "All the dragons have gone up to Sunhua Mountain. Please give orders to capture them."

Sai Dianchi immediately mounted his horse to ride toward Sunhua Mountain. Then he reined in his horse and looked afar. Around the top of the mountain he saw dark clouds gathering and blotting out the sky. It would not be long before the floodwaters would come. Momentarily, he ordered the Hui army to surround the mountain with orders to capture the dragons. Within a minute, their battle drums set the earth atremble, and the Hui soldiers all rushed bravely up the mountain. When the one hundred dragons saw the soldiers running towards them, each of them changed into a human figure and fought them with weapons in hand. As they fought in this manner the

---

[2]Sai Dianchi was a provincial governor of Yunnan during the Yuan dynasty (1271–1368). Professor Dru C. Gladney kindly has alerted us to the fact that this Sai Dianchi was Sayyid Adjall, the Bukharan governor of Southwest China.

dragons could not withstand much longer. They slowly retreated to the mountain top. There they shouted to one another and resumed their original serpentine shapes. A blast of wind began to surge and to lift them upward, and with that the one hundred dragons escaped into black clouds.

Seated upon his horse Sai Dianchi shouted, "No!" He quickly raised his right hand and pulled off his turban and hurled it at the dragons with all his strength.

Suddenly, from that turban myriads of bright rays streaked across the sky and shot straight toward the dragons. The moment the Dragons perceived this bright light they hurried back into the clouds as fast as they could. But the bright rays moved faster than flashes of lightning.

A while later the dragons were tightly wrapped up in the turban cloth. And then, while Sai Dianchi motioned with his hand, the turban which contained all the captive dragons descended onto the mountain top. With one hand he grabbed an end of the turban cloth and thereby dragged the dragons to a crevice that led into the mountain. There he tied them down. With his other hand he inscribed an edict which he imposed upon the dragons—to the effect that they were forever forbidden to cause trouble.

After that he ordered his Hui soldiers to build a dam at the entrance of Sunhua Mountain, over thirty meters high. Ever since that time, the floods have ceased to come to Kunming.

Lilang Subdues the Dragon

Place: Linxi, Inner Mongolia
Recorder: Liu Dezhu, 1981

In ancient times there was a silver-horned old Dragon who was in charge of clouds and rain. The Dragon was lazy and greedy. People were obligated to lay out offerings for him when the rainy season came, every year. For more offerings he gave more rain; for less offerings he gave less rain; and when he received nothing the outcome was that not a single drop of rain would fall.

One year, during the rainy season, the people from East Village and from West Village, respectively, laid out their offerings for the silver-horned old Dragon who (for that occasion) changed himself into a tall man. In that form he came to enjoy the offerings. Having had much fat pork and wine given to him in (the non-Muslim) East Village, he went over to West Village and wagged his head. He was displeased with the offerings upon that altar, and he said, "Why not put out some fat pork for me?"

Seeing how the old Dragon found fault, Lilang the ceremonial leader, a young man of over twenty, approached and explained, "We Hui people do not touch pork. Please give some consideration to our ways and customs."

The old Dragon turned a deaf ear and flew into a rage. "All people worship me, because all the clouds and rain have always been under my command. How dare you talk arrogantly to me? To give consideration to you? Ridiculous! Well, well, just wait and see!" And the Dragon left in a huff.

As a result, that year, the East Village had good weather for its crops while the West Village received only two fingers' width of rain. Because of their bad harvest the people in West Village had to live on chaff and wild herbs all year.

The next year when the rainy season came, Lilang and the villagers were very angry. They decided not to offer the Dragon anything.

The silver-horned Dragon came to West Village only to find that nothing had been offered. Very much annoyed, he went so far as to allot to West Village not a single drop of rain. People who lived in West Village consequently got no harvest and were forced to go begging. Some even sold their children.

The third year came. Lilang's father said to Lilang: "We cannot go on defying the Dragon like this, my Son. You better lay out some offerings."

"That will not do! It would mean begging the old thing for mercy."

The father said with a sigh, "What else can we do but beg for mercy? If the Dragon gets angry again we will all die from starvation."

"Can we think of a way to subdue..."

His father hurriedly covered Lilang's mouth with his hand and pleaded, "Oh, please, stop talking nonsense! No one has ever subdued a dragon. Go and talk it over with others, but do arrange to have some offerings!"

Unable to persuade the old man, Lilang had to prepare some offerings for the silver-horned Dragon. But what was there left to lay upon the altar after several poor harvests? The villagers themselves were reduced to eating tree bark and grass roots. Having no better idea, Lilang gathered up a basketful of pebble stones and put them upon the altar.

The Dragon once again changed himself into a tall man and came in a haste. He was so hungry that he grabbed the pebble stones and swallowed them all. After a while he began to feel that something must have gone wrong with his stomach. He rolled on the ground with pain. Flames began coming forth from his head, and smoke rose from his tail. The joints of his body creaked and his mouth was spurting clouds. Upon a piece of cloud the Dragon rode up into the sky. He twisted and rolled in the sky, gulping down white clouds and tearing black clouds into pieces. People heard muffled thunder in the sky, then hailstones like large pebbles began pouring down. Roofs were broken. Cows and sheep were severely hurt, and people in both villages suffered a lot.

When the fourth "rainy season" drew near the people felt very sad because they had nothing to offer to the Dragon. "Do not worry," said Lilang, "inasmuch as Nuwa could mend the Heaven, and Jingwei could fill up the sea, we can subdue a dragon. Last year we made it swallow pebble stones; this time I have a better idea. I can surely subdue it!"

The people were not quite convinced. They indeed wondered how Lilang could subdue the Dragon.

Lilang sold his own thatched cottage. With the money he bought some flour and butter. He got up early the next morning and made some deep-fried dough cakes. Then he called all the villagers to help lay out these offerings. Hardly had they put the cakes on the altar when the old Dragon, again in the form of a tall man, came staggering along. Already half drunk, he took the cakes to be large pieces of pork fat. Outrageously delighted, the Dragon swallowed a basketful of cakes all at once.

"Ha, Ha!" he shouted with loud laughter. "People on earth live on grain. And crops of grain live on rain. Who dares not to worship me! I have finally won out over you! Ha, Ha!..."

"Ha, Ha!" Lilang cut in with even louder laughter. "It is too early for you to rejoice! All the people hate you to the bones. We will not let you bully us at your will. This time it is we who have conquered you!"

"How dare you!" The Dragon jumped with rage. And at the moment he jumped he felt great pain in the vicinity of his heart and liver.

Lilang laughed loudly. The old Dragon could not stand the pain any longer. He threw himself on the ground and kept rolling over and over. No matter what he did, he could no longer ascend into the sky.

While he had fried the cakes, Lilang had enclosed an iron ring in each cake. And when the cakes were ready he had linked them together in a chain. The old Dragon swallowed the cakes quickly, together with the iron chain, without really noticing. Now Lilang took hold of one end of the chain and yanked. The slip links tightened. The loop locked around the Dragon's heart and liver, and that made it impossible for him to get free.

Then, to teach the Dragon a lesson, Lilang continuously yanked at the chain. In great pain the old Dragon twisted on the ground and begged for mercy. Lilang did not desist before the Dragon was down to his last trace of a breath. The villagers clapped and cheered.

Lilang then lectured the Dragon: "For years you have been extorting huge payments from the people on the strength of your power to make it rain. Today your fate is in my hands. From now on you must allocate rain to every corner of the land. You must stop bartering. And do not be so selfish and bully us people ever again."

"Have mercy on me! Please!" The old Dragon begged with a nod of consent. "I was wrong to have done so many bad deeds. If you spare me, I will serve the people. I will make amends for my faults by doing good deeds. I promise to give you good weather for your crops, year after year."

Lilang said, "All right, I will spare you since you are willing to correct your wrongs. But it is not up to myself. You will have to go from door to door and ask the villagers for mercy."

The Dragon was forced to agree. And so, led by Lilang and accompanied by people, the Dragon went from door to door to beg forgiveness. By nightfall he had only been to a portion of the families. So Lilang lit a torch and they went on to finish the remaining households.

And sure enough, since that time the silver-horned old Dragon has given enough rain to that entire area every year.

And why do the people nowadays reenact such Dragon and lantern pageants? The dragons are actually begging the people for mercy. The people also use this occasion to celebrate their victory over the old Dragon and to express their joy about plentiful harvests.

The Sun Advises

First published in *Gan su min jian gu shi xuan (Folk Stories of Gansu)*. Lanzhou: Gansu People's Press, 1962.
Place: Linxia (Hezhou), Gansu
Recorder: Ke Yang

In ancient times lived an old man whose wife and son had died and whose daughter-in-law had remarried. Only his small grandson, Yisima, stayed with him.[3] Though quite young, Yisima was very intelligent and capable. He took good care of his old grandfather and showed proper filial respect toward him.

One year Yisima's grandfather fell ill. Offering him soup and medicine, Yisima waited on him from evening to midnight and from sunrise until the moon came up. He never left the old man alone, not even for a moment. He was always ready to help him. Because of his care the grandfather felt better by the time winter was over. In spring

---

[3] "Yisima" may be an alteration of the Arabic "Usama" (Mahmoud Abu Saud). It is doubtful whether a devout Muslim of Hezhou (Linxia)—of a most conservative Islamic region—would tell a myth that portrays the sun as a deity existing alongside Allah. But be that as it may, a collector of Hui myths must keep an open mind and admit pre- and post-Islamic Hui traditions. This type of story, of human heroes visiting a Sun Deity, can be found as far away as among Indians in the American Southwest. Its presence in the Hui repertoire conflicts with the status of Allah not any more than do numerous Hui stories about ancient Chinese dragon deities.

the old man felt better still. By summer he could sit up a while in bed. Yisima was very happy to see his grandfather's condition improve with each day that passed.

Having been confined to his bed by illness for a long time, the old man wanted very much to go outside and to absorb some sunshine. It was a fine day. Yisima helped him out of the room to sit upon a felt mat, in the sunshine.

"I am thirsty, I would like to have a fresh pear," the old man said to Yisima.

"Please stay where you are, Grandpa. I will go and buy it for you right away," answered Yisima.

After Yisima had left, the old man was sitting alone in the courtyard where during summer the heat of the sun was very strong. After his long illness, he was still very weak. He could not endure the scorching sun. By and by, he began to see starlets and fainted.

When Yisima came back with some pears he found that his grandfather had died of a sunstroke. He cried sadly and, with tears in his eyes, he carried his grandfather into the room and laid him on his bed.

He thought, "O Sun, how could you have killed my grandfather! I will go and have a word with your mother!"

Yisima took a bag of dried food with him and started traveling westward, in the direction of sunset. He had been told that Sun lived at the western boundary.

After many days of walking, one day, Yisima met some farmers. They stopped him and asked, "Where are you going in such a hurry, young man?"

"I am going to see Sun's mother."

"Well, we have been told that Sun's mother is truly kind-hearted. When you see her, please tell her that it is both difficult and slow to plow with a wooden plow, pulled by man. Ask her whether there might be a better way to plow."

"All right, I will remember to ask on your behalf."

Yisima went on his way. He had walked for a long time when he saw a shepherd coming towards him. "You are sweating all over, Young Man. Where are you going?"

"I am going to look for Sun's mother."

"Ah, that is very good! Will you do me a favor? The wool of my sheep is so long that they cannot walk fast. Please ask her what I should do with them."

"That is fine. I will ask for you."

"Thank you," said the shepherd. "But I hear that Sun's home is far away. Can you walk that far?"

"Never mind," Yisima said with resolve, "I am determined to find Sun's home, even though I may have to walk a hundred years."

Just then a woolly sheep suddenly began to speak to Yisima: "Let me help you, young man. Please hold on to my horns. I will carry you to see Sun's mother."

Yisima was surprised, and rather perplexedly he asked, "Do you think you are up to it?"

"Of course he is," said the shepherd. "This old sheep of mine is in fact very intelligent."

Yisima mounted the sheep and, all of a sudden, the woolly animal ascended toward the sky as if it had wings. Yisima could only hear the wind whistling past his ears. They covered millions of miles and finally arrived at the foot of a high mountain, by the sea. The woolly sheep landed accurately in front of a palace and then told Yisima, "This is Sun's home. Please go in. I will wait for you here."

Yisima knocked at the red-painted gate. A white-haired old granny opened the gate for him. She was surprised to see Yisima and asked, "Young Man, what are you here for?"

"Are you Sun's mother?"

"Yes. What can I do for you?"

"Your son has burnt my grandfather to death. I am here to reason things out with you."

"Oh, is it my son who is to blame? I will have to lecture him," said the old granny. "Young Man, please come in for a little rest. You must be very tired."

Yisima followed Sun's mother into the palace. The old granny took out many goodies to treat him. She told him, "Please be assured, Young Man, when my son returns I will ask him how to bring your grandfather back to life. Have you any other concerns?"

Yisima put forth the questions of the farmers and of the shepherd, and the old granny promised to ask Sun when he came back. Just at that moment it suddenly became bright with red light shining outside the room.

The old granny said, "My son has come back. Hide behind me, Young Man, otherwise you will be scorched."

The giant Sun entered the room, panting, and momentarily the room became burning hot.

"How are you today, Mother?"

"I am fine, my Son," said the old granny. "But I think that with your rays you are giving off too much heat, unto the earth, during summer. You make the crops wither, and the people suffer much."

"All right, Mom. From now on I will ask Sister Cloud to accompany me. In hot weather she will sprinkle rain onto the earth."

"That will be good! But now, if an old man died from heat because you kept shining down unto earth, what can one do to bring him back to life?"

"Mother, he is not really dead. He has just gone off and fainted. All you have to do is to cool his forehead with some cold spring water. He will soon come around again."

"Another thing. It happens to be the case that the farmers have been living a hard life, while suffering from constant drought. And because they also have to pull the wooden plow, life has been very difficult for them."

"It would be much easier if they were to attach an iron plowshare to the wooden plow and have it pulled by two oxen."

"The shepherds and their sheep are also suffering a lot. It is difficult for them to walk in the scorching heat, especially with their wool grown long."

"That is easy. Just shear the sheep twice a year. It will make them feel more comfortable. Besides, wool is very useful. People can twirl strings of wool to knit, make felt mats, wool sweaters, and blankets. And is there anything else you want me to do, Mother?"

"Nothing else, my Son. Do not be lazy. Send light and warmth to the earth on time."

"I will remember what you said, Mother." With these words the giant Sun took a large bath towel and went off to take a bath in the sea.

Yisima thanked the kindhearted old granny. He left and rode homeward on the woolly sheep. Along his way home he told the farmers and the shepherd what Sun had said. They were full of gratitude toward Yisima. The farmers attached an iron share to their plow and had it pulled by two oxen. The shepherds began to shear their sheep twice a year. These ways were then handed down to later generations.

Upon his arrival back home, Yisima brought his grandfather back to life by way of applying some clear spring water. The two began to live together happily again.

Horse Brother the Cultivator

Place: Changji, Xinjiang
Recorder: Sarding (Hui), 1981

Long, long ago, there was an old and poor grandma who lived alone, with no child, no property, but only an old horse. One day the old horse went out to graze and slowly came back at sunset. To her great delight, the grandma saw a boy riding on its back. Henceforth she began to regard the boy as her little grandson, and she raised him carefully. The boy grew up to be a clever and intelligent young man, of great strength. The boy gave presents to his grandmother and attended her with great care until she died. Because he had been brought in by the horse, and because nobody knew his parents, he was called Horse Brother.

Horse Brother was not only a strong man but also a good archer. In the area where they lived very little rain fell, and consequently the villagers lived very miserable lives. Horse Brother decided to find a better place to live. With bow and arrows he went on his journey.

He walked until he had passed eighteen horse stops.[4] When he saw the vast Gobi Desert ahead, he felt greatly disappointed. Just then he heard someone call his name: "Horse Brother, Horse Brother, help me!"

He turned but did not see anything but a large rock behind him. He turned again and continued walking. The voice called again, "Horse Brother, Horse Brother, help me!" He again turned but saw nothing but the rock. This time he raised his bow, put on an arrow, and let it fly at the rock. And blomm! The rock was split into halves and from it jumped forth a young fat fellow. He expressed his thanks to Horse Brother and asked him where he was going. Horse Brother told him what he was up to. The young man decided to take Horse Brother as his older brother and to follow him in search of a good place to live. Thereupon Horse Brother called him "Stone Brother."

------

[4]Posts to tie up horses for periods of rest were placed at regular intervals along the roadway.

The two brothers walked on and on and passed another eighteen horse stops. At last they came to a place full of elm trees. Horse Brother was not satisfied with that place either. He was just about to leave when someone behind him called, "Horse Brother, Horse Brother, help me!"

He turned to look. What he saw was actually an old elm tree. He took his bow and let an arrow fly at it. Blomm! The elm tree was split open at the middle, and out of it came a thin tall fellow. The fellow thanked Horse Brother and accepted him as his older brother. He, as well, was willing to go with him. Horse Brother regarded him as the third brother and called him Elm Brother. Together they continued their journey.

The three brothers walked on and on. They journeyed past another eighteen horse stops, and they arrived at the foot of Bogota Mountain. There was rich land with plenty of water, and lush grass. South of this place was the huge mountain, in the north flowed a river, in the east lay a lake, and in the west stood a large forest. They were all quite pleased to settle at this place. The next day Horse Brother and his two younger brothers made some tools and went to claim wasteland for cultivation.

The three brothers spared no pains to cultivate, to hunt, to herd, to build a house, and to erect a fence. Within a few years their lives became easier. They had grain, milk, meat, and everything. But they felt it a pity that there was no trace of human habitation all around, and that they could not have wives to do housework. Gradually Stone Brother and Elm Brother became regretful and complained about their having settled there. Horse Brother tried to persuade them by every means, and gradually they felt better about it.

One day after work, to their great surprise, they found a meal ready for them with meat, steamed bread, and tea with milk. This happened several days in a row. So the three brothers decided that one of them should stay at home to find out who had cooked the meals.

On the first day Elm Brother was left behind. He waited and waited, but no one came. Eventually he became tired and fell asleep. When he woke up the meal had already been cooked. Horse Brother held this against him and asked Stone Brother to remain in the house the next day. But he too fell asleep and found out nothing at all. On the third day Horse Brother himself remained at home.

In the house he waited and waited, but no one came. Gradually he began dozing off. Suddenly he thought about the experiences of his two brothers, and he stood up. He took the jar and carried in some water, then he cut firewood, and last he went into the shed to milk a cow. While milking he heard some noises outside and saw three pigeons descending from the sky. Horse Brother remained calm and finished milking silently.

The three pigeons descended into the yard and, in the twinkling of an eye, were transformed into three beautiful girls dressed in white clothes and scarfs. They looked as pure and clear as jade, dazzling and brilliant. Smiling broadly, the girls took off their outer clothes, washed their hands, and began to cook. When they saw the water jar full of water, firewood laid ready, and meat and milk in cans, they smiled at each other. With smiles on them, their faces were even more fascinating and beautiful.

In a short while they finished stewing meat, steaming bread, and boiling milk. Then they washed their hands, walked into the yard, and put on their dress clothes and their scarfs. But at the moment before they were about to turn back into pigeons, Horse Brother quickly ran out from the cowshed and blocked their way.

Contrary to his expectation, the girls were not at all surprised about his sudden appearance. They only smiled with closed lips, and they neither spoke nor moved. Horse Brother bolstered his courage and asked the three girls for marriage, on behalf of all three brothers. Still, the girls remained silent. Assuming that they had agreed, he asked them to change into pigeons again and hid them in the house.

In the evening, when the two brothers came back and it appeared that Horse Brother had discovered nobody, they were just about to laugh at him. But at this moment Horse Brother brought out the three pigeons and told the brothers what had happened. He let them choose wives for themselves, and each of the two selected his favorite one. The one that was left became Horse Brother's wife.

After that the three pigeons turned again into three beautiful girls. The one that was left for Horse Brother was the most beautiful. The three brothers married the three beautiful girls, and they lived together. They continued cultivating land and went hunting and herding, while their wives remained at home to do housework.

One day a cat came along, and no one knew from where. It was hungry and very thin. Horse Brother said that a cat naturally loves wealth and dislikes poverty. It also likes to be flattered. This cat should therefore be driven away. But the three wives thought it to be a pitiful thing, and so they kept it. Day by day the cat gradually became stronger and more mischievous. Once it scratched spun thread into a mess. The wives got so angry that they slapped it. In response the cat, taking the wives unawares, put out the fire in the hearth and ran away. When the wives were ready to cook they found the fire extinguished, and the cat gone. They were angry and anxious. They had to go out and borrow embers. But no other human habitations were nearby. Only in the distance, on Bogota Mountain, could they see black smoke. So they made their way toward that place of smoke.

They traveled quite a distance before they came into the mountain valley and found a young fellow herding sheep. The three wives asked him for embers. But the young fellow said that he dared not give it to them without his host's permission. His host was Nine-heads Master. The three wives had to walk along the valley toward the house of Nine-heads Master.

Having walked for a long time they came to a big cave, outside of which some lean and gaunt-looking women were working. The wives told these women about the reason for their coming and they, too, told them that this must be approved by Nine-heads Master. Guided by these women, they went into the cave. Many times they turned right and left before they reached Nine-heads Master's living quarters. There the three wives saw a curious looking man, with nine heads, lying on a bear skin. In each of his heads were two eyes, but only the eyes on the head in the middle could see. Seeing the strangers he glared at them, fiercely and maliciously, and shouted, "What do you come here for?"

"We want to borrow some embers, because the cat has put out our fire."

Looking at them, Nine-heads Master thought for a while and then replied, "All right, I will give you some embers. You must be hungry now. I will give you a bag of beans as well, so that you may have it on your way home." He asked someone to fetch some embers for them, and also to fill a bag of beans for them. The bag had a small hole in it. The three wives accepted the embers and the beans and left for home, happily.

Upon reaching their home they quickly prepared a meal. They did not tell the three brothers about what had happened—because they had not done as Horse Brother had told them, and because they caused this incident themselves.

The next day Nine-heads Master followed the trail of beans which had been scattered unintentionally along the road by the wives on their way home. He arrived while the brothers were working in the field. The three wives became exceedingly frightened. Nine-heads Master greedily sucked some blood from them, one after the other, and then left. Before that, although he had nine heads, none of the eyes could open except the two in the head at the middle. The others would not open until he had sucked some women's blood. The blood of his own female servants had been sucked dry, and now he came for the blood of these three wives. From that time on he came every day. The three wives were quite angry and afraid but dared not tell Horse Brother.

With the passing of time, Horse Brother noticed that the wives became increasingly more pale and got thinner and thinner. He asked what the matter was. So the wives had no choice but to tell him from the beginning what happened. When he heard, Horse Brother became furious. He swore to kill that nine-headed one.

The first day Elm Brother volunteered to hide in the house, waiting for Nine-heads Master. But when the fierce-looking Nine-heads Master appeared, Elm Brother was too frightened to come out. He quivered and nearly fainted. Nine-heads Master sucked the blood and then went off, leisurely. The second day, Stone Brother was left in the house and the same thing happened to him as to Elm Brother. The third day Horse Brother himself had to stay home.

Nine-heads Master entered, looked around, and then began to suck the blood of the three wives. Horse Brother suddenly jumped forth, shouting, "You cannot escape this time!"

At first the Nine-heads Master was shocked. He then threw himself in the direction of Horse Brother with his mouth wide open. Horse Brother took out an arrow, took aim, and shot at him. It was the man's left eye that the arrow struck. The Master let out a yell of pain and fled away.

Tracking the bloodstain, Horse Brother ran after him into the Bogota Mountain valley. He met a young shepherd who told him that Nine-heads Master was recuperating at home. During the daytime he asked the women servants to lap his eye; at night the shepherd himself had to do it. He vowed that when his eye was recovered he would go and devour Horse Brother. Upon hearing this, Horse Brother said that he would very much like to herd sheep for a time. For that span of time he encouraged the shepherd boy to leave the mountain and enjoy his freedom. The young man was so delighted that he put the whip into Horse Brother's hand and ran down the mountain, quickly.

At sunset Horse Brother drove the sheep into the nine-headed Master's cave. He told the women what he was going to do. They were all glad to hear it. He corralled the sheep, and he took the tongue which he had cut from the mouth of a sheep to the bed in which Nine-heads Master was lying.

"Why do you come back so early?" the Nine-heads Master asked.

"It is already dark, Master!"

"Any sheep lost?"

"No, Master!"

"Now come and lap my eye."

Horse Brother took the sheep tongue and started to lap his eye. Feeling a bit of pain, Nine-heads Master asked, "Why is your tongue so rough today?"

"Because of the cold weather, outside, my tongue was frozen."

"Then try your best. When my eye has recovered I will go and devour Horse Brother."

Horse Brother could bear it no longer. He drew out a knife and stabbed him with full strength. The middle head was cut off. He continued with several more cuts. Nine-heads Master screamed terribly, and died.

Horse Brother distributed all the property of Nine-heads Master to his servants and set them free. He himself began his journey home.

Meanwhile, back home, Stone Brother and Elm Brother had been hatching an evil plot as well: the two could possess all the property if Horse Brother were disposed of, and his wife could then serve them as well. So, while Horse Brother went to kill Nine-heads Master they plotted secretly for an opportunity to kill him.

One day, returning from hunting, the two brothers told Horse Brother that in Bogota Mountain they had found a large valley. It was too deep for its bottom to be seen. Inside this valley grew very white lotuses that greeted people with their pleasant fragrance. They invited Horse Brother to go and to have a look.

The next day Horse Brother followed them to Bogota Mountain, and they actually found that deep valley which was full of beautiful and fragrant lotus flowers.

While Horse Brother was looking down over the edge of the abyss, his Stone and Elm brothers gave him a sudden push from behind. Horse Brother felt himself falling down and down, and finally he felt himself supported by a patch of lotuses. He was not hurt at all. Yet, he had no means to climb back up. It was his luck that the bottom of the valley was filled with flowers and wild fruit trees, and so Horse Brother lived on these things.

One day a swan fell down to the bottom; one of its wings was wounded. Horse Brother took pity on it and picked some medicinal herbs for its wound. He put lotus roots on it. It was not very long before the swan recovered. In order to repay the kindness of Horse Brother, the swan let him sit on its back and flew up to the high ground in the course of three days and three nights.

Horse Brother said farewell to the swan, and then he made his way home. By then he had become very thin and black. His beard had become long and his clothes shabby. At the door he met his wife, also in shabby clothes, carrying a pack of firewood toward the room. He hurried to say politely, "Sister, please give me something to eat."

His wife looked at him, up and down, and did not recognize the poor man, and she said, "A moment please!"

Then she turned back to the house. A minute later she brought a kettle of tea and deep-fried cakes to him, "Greetings! Today is the anniversary of the death of my husband, Horse Brother. Please eat this food and pray for him." Tears were rolling down her face while she was speaking.

After eating, Horse Brother saw his bow hanging on the wall, in the yard. He walked over and took it down. When he was about to try it out, the Stone and Elm brothers came into the yard. They shouted at him, "Poor Beggar! What are you doing here? The bow belonged to Horse Brother. No one can touch it since he has slipped and fallen into the deep valley. You, a beggar, think you can do so? Get out!"

Horse Brother said to Stone Brother with a smile, "Look at the stone over there."

Stone Brother was just turning his body when Horse Brother shot at the stone. Blomm! The stone was broken into two halves and Stone Brother was drawn into the stone at once. Then Horse Brother said to Elm Brother, who was too frightened to remain calm, "Look at the elm tree by the gate." Another arrow whirred and the elm tree was split in the middle. Elm Brother was drawn into the tree as well.

So that is the reason why, nowadays, many Hui people have stepping stones by their gates for getting on a horse, and why the trunks of elm trees are always cracked open.

Not until this moment did the wives recognize the passerby as Horse Brother. They were very happy. Horse Brother went into the house, washed his face and changed his clothes. And now after Stone and Elm brothers had been returned to their places of origin, Horse Brother spoke to them. "What will you do? You may stay or leave, as you like."

His wife expressed her willingness to remain with him her whole life. The other two put on their white clothes and scarfs. They quickly turned into two pigeons and flew high up in the sky. But soon they returned and alighted on the roof, talking intimately with their older sister, murmuring from morning till evening. Consequently, Hui people of every family, who today live at the foot of Bogota Mountain, very much enjoy raising white pigeons.

After these events, Horse Brother and his beautiful wife lived together happily. Later, upon hearing this story, people came from afar and settled there one after another. Their offspring also became diligent, brave, and kind—like Horse Brother.

The Raising of Bogota Mountain

First published in *Bo ge da (Bogota Magazine)*. Changji: Xinjiang, 1983.
Narrator: Ma Shi (Hui)
Recorder: Ma Yuqing (Hui)

It is said that Bogota Mountain formerly was not as high as it is today. It used to be a very small hill, with grass on it. Many sheepherders' children drove their animals up on that hill to graze. Among them was a boy named Yisima. His mother died when he was only six years old, and his father died when he was seven. Yisima was an orphan, and the neighbors took pity on him. They would ask him to join them for dinner whenever there was a Muslim festival. They would let him eat his fill and also give him some fried cakes to take along. Their children were told not to take advantage of Yisima.

But the poor orphan was ill-treated by Toothless Wang, who was the richest man in the village. Wang was a miser who wished he could divide every penny into two. He gave Yisima and his farm workers little pay, and never enough to eat. Even during holidays and festivals he let them eat steamed sorghum bread with salted vegetables—not to mention what he offered them to eat on ordinary days. Yisima and the farm workers hated Toothless Wang to the very marrow of their bones. And oh, how they hoped for an early death of that old scoundrel!

One day Yisima lost a sheep. He was very worried and afraid because Toothless Wang would break his legs if he was unable to find the lost sheep. With the help of other boys he searched for it across hill and dale. By sunset Yisima was so hungry and thirsty that he could hardly move another step.

Suddenly, in the distance, a flash of light could be seen. Yisima quickened his steps and noticed two things shining. They turned out to be two bright golden objects. Yisima thought to himself, "Now I am saved. It will not matter now if I cannot find the lost sheep. I will give these two valuables to Toothless Wang. They are certainly much more precious than that small and lean sheep of his."

He was about to go when he noticed a white-bearded old man appear as if from nowhere. Frightened, like a thief stopped on the spot, Yisima quickly dropped the treasures.

"My Son, these treasures are for you. Pick them up!" the old man said with a smile.

When he saw that the old man meant no harm, Yisima bent over again to pick up the valuables. And he heard the old man explain, "They are two priceless treasures. The one in your left hand is called the Mountain-lifting Peach, and the one in your right hand is called the Mountain-propping Stone. No matter which mountain you go to, if you want to raise that mountain, all you need to do is place the Mountain-lifting Peach on its summit, and the mountain will rise. Then you put the Mountain-propping Stone at the bottom of the mountain, before you crawl in underneath. Inside you can then get whatever you want. But remember, you can only take what you really need. Never take anything you do not need."

With these words the white-bearded old man disappeared. Yisima went on his way back home with great delight. He would tell the shepherds what had happened to him and let them have a look at his treasures. With these he would provide the poor villagers with whatever they lacked, so that they would never again worry about food and clothes. Nobody would herd sheep for Toothless Wang anymore. The cruel landlord would die from anger.

All the shepherd children went with Yisima to Bogota Mountain, to test the treasures. They put the Mountain-lifting Peach at the summit of the mountain and thereupon the mountain rose slowly, as expected. It rose until it slowly left the ground at its base. They hurried down and put the Mountain-propping Stone at its base. And while at first the stone was very small, once it had been placed at the bottom of the mountain it grew and became larger. Inside (under the mountain) Yisima and his fellow shepherds saw a mill, larger than a wagon wheel. It was turning incessantly, and out from that mill came nothing but gold kernels and gold beans. The poor boys had never seen so much gold in their lives. They jumped with joy. Each of them got a handful of gold beans. Then they gathered up the two precious items and drove home their sheep.

Hearing that Yisima had lost a sheep, Toothless Wang flew into a rage as if someone had cut out a piece of flesh from his body. He gave Yisima three days to find the lost sheep, or else Yisima would have to pay a fat yearling in compensation. Now that Yisima had the treasures he was not at all afraid. He asked if he could pay for it with gold.

Toothless Wang replied with a sneer, "Of course you can. All right. I will ask for not more than a *qian* of gold. It will do."

"I can even give you a *liang* of gold!"[5] And, taking a gold bean from his pocket, Yisima held it before Toothless Wang. The latter, though quite accustomed to seeing silver and gold, was stupefied at the sight of so much gold.

Yisima put a gold bean into his hand and said, firmly, "I will not herd sheep for you, beginning tomorrow. You better find someone else."

---

[5]A *qian* is five grams, whereas a *liang* is fifty grams.

Toothless Wang, who had been making a long face, was all smiles. He rolled his eyes, indicating that he had an idea. He asked Yisima to help himself to some tea first, and after that to stay for dinner. Yisima would not listen to him. Toothless Wang tried to fool Yisima into telling the truth—and (eventually) he succeeded.

"I have obtained a Mountain-lifting Peach that can lift mountains. Those who go under the mountain can find gold." With these words he left Wang's house. Yisima deliberately held back some information—he said nothing about the Mountain-propping Stone.

Now that Toothless Wang knew that Yisima had valuables with magic power that could lift mountains, he sneaked into Yisima's room and stole the two golden treasures. He ran to Bogota Mountain without stopping and put both pieces on its summit. Seeing the mountain rise slowly, Toothless Wang turned wild with joy. He was so eager that he crept into the narrow opening right away. The gold mill kept turning and Toothless Wang kept carrying gold outside. After a while he had gathered a heap of gold as high as a man. But he was still not satisfied. He dragged out one sack after another. When he became too tired to carry he just lay on the ground, to rest and to continue later.

He said to himself, "Let this be the last time. After this I will carry forth no more gold."

Just then he heard a loud rumble which sounded like thunder. The trees bent in a fierce wind. The mountain suddenly began to settle down over Wang's head. In great haste he tried to run out. Unfortunately, the way out was blocked by his heap of gold. Gold beans and gold grains kept rolling down the heap, and Wang slid deeper and deeper under the base of the mountain. Only his head was still sticking out. His mouth and nostrils were filled with gold grains.

Once lifted, a mountain should be supported by the Mountain-propping Stone, otherwise it will drop. Toothless Wang knew only part of what is necessary about these powerful valuables. His ignorance cost him his life.

The next morning, when the villagers knew that Toothless Wang had died under Bogota Mountain, they all went to have a look. They praised Yisima because he had rid the people of a nuisance. Yisima climbed to the top of the mountain to retrieve his treasures.

Then, from among the small hills nearby he raised one after another, and he offered the villagers to take what they needed. The five types of seeds and domestic animals were found under some of the hills. Cloth and clothes, gold and silver, were found under others. The peasants took seeds of the five crops, took six domestic animals, cloth, and clothes. Nobody laid his hands on the gold and silver. The villagers regarded gold and silver as being useless.

Yisima stacked up all the small hills which he raised at the top of Mount Bogota. It became higher and higher until it was as high as it is today. All the people clapped and cheered, saying, "Toothless Wang will never move or be able to turn over under the weight of that high mountain."

Hundreds of years have since passed. The mill under Bogota Mountain is probably still turning. However, the Mountain-lifting Peach and the Mountain-propping Stone have gotten lost.

Luguma Reverts to Hunting

Place: Bogda, Xinjiang
Narrator: Han Shengyuan (Hui)
Recorder: Liu Xiying, 1984

Once upon a time, in a village, there lived a young man who was named Luguma. He had a young sister named Meinai. They were very rich and had many sheep and cows. Their mother loved them dearly. They lived a very happy life.

Not long thereafter things began to change.

Every day when the herd animals were driven home the number was correct. But when they were counted the next morning they always were one short—either a sheep, or a cow, or a horse, or a mule.

"What is the matter?" Luguma was wondering. He decided to stay up late and see what went on.

At midnight Luguma saw his own sister, Meinai, come down the stairs, look around, cover herself with a wolf skin, roll over on the ground three times, and finally turn into a black wolf. After that she went into the barn and pulled down a sheep to the ground and began to eat. After finishing off the sheep she went away.

Luguma could not believe his eyes, but it was true. He drew his bow and let an arrow fly at the black wolf. He hit only the left front leg. The black wolf let out a howl, ran toward the stairs, rolled again on the ground and changed back into Meinai. She hid the wolf skin under the stairway and hurriedly went upstairs.

Luguma lay down to sleep without saying anything. The next day Meinai did not come down at noon for lunch.

"What is wrong with you, my daughter?" her mother hurried upstairs and asked.

"Last night I got up to urinate; then my brother shot an arrow at me—Mom—I am in great pain," Meinai answered and cried.

Her mother looked at her arm and saw that it had been shot and fractured.

The mother immediately told their father, and the father became indignant: "This bad boy! So cruel! He would kill his own sister. We must drive him out and never let him come back."

"You may go wherever you want to go. You will not have me as your father, and neither will I have you as my son anymore. We do not need you. Be gone! Get out!" the father shouted. He gave him some money and a horse and drove him away. Whatever Luguma explained was unbelievable. He had to leave.

He walked and wandered and did not notice how far he had gone. He found himself in a wooded and hilly land. A large village was there. Not until night had fallen did he find a kindhearted villager who let him stay.

The villager's family was very kind to Luguma. From that time on he worked and managed their household affairs. With the passing of time the kindhearted old man saw that the young man was intelligent, diligent, and honest. He let his daughter marry him. And after marriage their life together improved and got better.

One day when Luguma was gathering firewood on the mountain he found a wounded young hawk. He brought it home and took good care of it. On another day, when he was hunting on the mountain he caught a young tiger and brought it home. He looked after it very carefully, also.

Before long the young hawk and the young tiger grew big. Luguma took them with him every time he hunted or when he gathered firewood.

Early one morning Luguma sat on the threshold, very upset. His wife wondered, "You have been looking happy every day. What is the matter with you today?"

He said, "I have been away from home two years. My father, my mother, and my sister are at home. I want to visit them. But I am afraid your father will be unhappy if I leave. So, I am worried."

"Oh, it does not matter. Just ride a horse to visit your father, your mother, and your sister, and come back soon."

"Yes, yes," he said happily.

Before he started on his journey Luguma told his wife, "Take good care of the tiger and the hawk. Feed some meat and food to them every day. Let them eat their fill. If the hawk does not continuously flutter or cry, and if the tiger does not scratch the door or growl, do not set them free. But do so if the hawk flutters about, and if the tiger jumps and growls. This means I will be coming back."

Luguma put everything in good order and went away. He reached his village on horseback, but there he found no signs of human habitation. It was just an empty village. What had happened? What was the matter? He went into a house and searched through the front and the back yards. Grass was growing everywhere. He went to go into another yard. Before he reached the front door his sister Meinai appeared to meet him. He looked around and saw human fingers, bones, and also animal bones everywhere. He remembered the black wolf which he saw two years ago, and he was overcome with fear.

"This is terrible. I must leave from here as soon as possible!" he thought.

"Brother, Brother, do you not recognize me? I am Meinai," said Meinai while running out of the yard ahead of Luguma. She caught one of his horse's legs and ate it. Then she ran back and asked, "Brother, why has your horse only three legs?"

"Yes, my horse has only three legs."

"I will go and have a look again." This time she ate another leg and came back, "Brother, I find that your horse has not three legs but two."

"Oh yes, it actually has only two legs," answered Luguma.

"What shall I do?" he thought, standing there worrying.

Momentarily he thought of a ruse, "My sister, I am feeling too hot. I want to sit on the roof for a while."

"All right, I will go and make a meal for you."

"Oh yes, I will sit on the roof, and please give me a *sanxian*."[6]

"But be sure to let your legs dangle down over the top window. If I cannot see you I will be anxious."

"All right."

Luguma took his *sanxian* and climbed to the top of the house. He took off his boots and hung them above the top window and began to play the *sanxian*. While he was playing, Meinai called him again: "Brother, do not leave me. I am preparing a meal for you."

"I am here. I will not leave you."

While Luguma was in a state of great anxiety, a yellow mouse and a white mouse crept out to him, from the roof. They spoke to him: "Boy, leave here as soon as possible. We will play the *sanxian* for you." Luguma thanked them and ran away barefooted.

When the water was boiling, Meinai was ready to ask Luguma to come down; she meant to cook and to eat him. She called him several times but no one answered.

She went upstairs and saw only a yellow mouse and a white mouse play the *sanxian* and boots hanging from the roof over the window. Being very upset, she clutched her forehead and in response another large eye appeared. Looking into the distance she saw Luguma running away barefooted.

Hastily Meinai covered herself with the wolf skin and rolled herself on the ground three times, and thereby she turned into a black wolf. She ran straight after him. The black wolf nearly had caught up with him when Laguma noticed some large trees ahead. He climbed up one of these trees.

The black wolf ran to the tree and said, "Where can you go? Do you know who I am? I am a black wolf who came from the mountain. Two years ago I saw your sister, Meinai, playing outside. I ate her up and wrapped myself into your sister's appearance. I ate your sheep, cows, horses, and mules every day. And hey! You shot an arrow at me. But now I have consumed all the people and animals in the village who did not run away. I was just ready to leave here, because I have nothing to eat anymore. It was good that you came on your own accord. You want to run away? I can chew down this tree; then I will see where you can go."

---

[6] A three-stringed instrument for plucking.

With these words the wolf began to gnaw at the tree with his teeth. He gnawed and gnawed. The tree almost fell when Luguma jumped across onto another tree. He continued doing so until in the end only one tree remained.

"Wait a while. My teeth are blunt now." The black wolf lowered its head and began to sharpen its teeth on a stone.

Meanwhile, back home, Luguma's wife was embroidering. She noticed that the hawk kept fluttering and that the tiger was growling and scratching continuously. She remembered what Luguma had told her, and accordingly she set them free. The hawk flapped its wings and flew off, and the tiger leapt away.

Now the black wolf's teeth were sharpened. When the wolf was just about ready to bite into the trunk of the last tree, the hawk alighted on that tree and the tiger also arrived. The hawk threw itself on the black wolf and scratched out its eyes. The tiger jumped upon the black wolf and bit into its head. Luguma was saved.

The villagers who had run away came back when they heard that the black wolf had been gotten rid of. They all asked Luguma to stay in their village.

Luguma said, "I will go and bring back my wife and remain here forever."

From then on the village became prosperous again.

Breeding the Yanqi Horse

Place: Yanqi Autonomous County
Recorder: Yao Jinhai (Hui), 1984

Ever since the Yanqi breed of horses had become famous, the small old town of Yanqi was considered to be a gem that was coveted by all the rulers of past feudalistic dynasties.[7] But as time passed there were fewer and fewer horses in Yanqi.

Before people really knew it, the Yanqi breed of horses had almost become extinct. Originally these fine horses had been the product of many years of careful breeding. Their disappearance brought much concern to the poor Mongol, Hui, Kazakh, and Uighur peoples at Yanqi. It would have been a small thing only to get paid a hundred yuan less per horse. But, when the imperial court would fight against foreigners, their cavalry would not have good battle steeds to ride on. That would have been a serious problem.

As the saying goes, there is no lack of courageous men among the Hui people. So, when news of the impeding extinction of the famous horse reached a Hui youth, named Yiha, he became deeply worried. He made up his mind to bring back again the famous Yanqi breed. Yiha was a clever young man.

To retrieve the fine breed of horses, Yiha modestly inquired of Mongol and Kazakh herdsmen who for generations had been raising horses. Seeing that Yiha was sincere with his effort at learning, the gallant Mongol horsemen and their brave Kazakh friends told him to drive a herd of fine strong mares to the uninhabited Bosten Lake area for grazing. The place was haunted by wild boars and bears. In the Bosten Lake area roamed a sturdy dragon stallion that could gallop as swiftly as the wind and as quickly as lightning. Only by letting the mares mate with this dragon stallion could the famous breed of horses be reclaimed.

To cause a fresh breed of Yanqi horses come forth more quickly, the brave Yiha left his native home for the Bosten Lake area with mares carefully chosen by his Mongol and Kazakh friends, and also with the blessings of Uighur singers. Along his way he killed seven times seven—forty and nine—fierce wild boars and eight times eight—sixty and four—strong bears. After nine times nine—eighty and one—days of trudging, he finally arrived in the Bosten Lake area where the dragon stallion was known to live.

The brave Yiha made his home there in a reed hut and survived by hunting wild ducks and by catching fish in the lake. He waited patiently for the dragon stallion to appear. Whenever he encountered difficulties he looked up to the bright moon and thought about his

---

[7]Yanqi is a county in Xinjiang.

loved ones back home, also about his friends among different nationalities who had given him help and their blessings. The very thought of them gave him courage and strength to overcome his difficulties.

At long last, during a night in late autumn, in the fifth year, large waves began to surge on Bosten Lake. Along with the neighing sound of a stallion, hoof beats could be heard approaching the mares.

Yiha could not help but shed tears of joy when he realized that finally the long-expected dragon stallion was coming. The dragon stallion was coming at last! The waves subsided as a result of its earthshaking neigh. The tall and sturdy dragon stallion appeared before Yiha's mares. His eyes were as bright as lamps; his hoofs were like jasper; his black mane was as wavy as willow trees.

Having never before seen the likes of the stallion, the mares were badly frightened at the sight of him. They all began to run away in terror, except the jade mare which had been selected by Mongol friends. She cast a bashful glance toward the stallion, and she stood there quietly with her head bent low. She appeared like a girl awaiting her lover. Now and then she emitted sounds as if she was singing a beautiful love song.

The dragon stallion gently approached the jade mare, strutting just like a handsome young prince. He looked at the jade mare for a long while. His soft eyes exuded tenderness and love. Then they slowly went off together into the reed marshes, one following the other, like two lovers who meet after a long separation.

The sun was already up on the next day when the jade mare came forth from the marsh reeds, subdued. Her face was blushed scarlet like that of a bride. Her beautiful eyes glistened with tears of happiness.

In an instant, beautiful swans and sweet-voiced larks arrived and flew around the jade mare, singing and skipping. After many years of tranquil sleep the Bosten Lake was active again with noise and excitement as if it were celebrating a great festival.

A year passed. The jade mare gave birth to a colt as red as fire. Yiha was afraid that the hard-won fine colt might be seized by robbers once it was driven away from the lake area. He decided not to return home until after it had grown up and after he had bred additional good ones.

Unfortunately, the colt refused to graze. It only drank water. Yiha was greatly worried to see it becoming thinner and thinner. But he could do nothing about it.

Seven months later the dragon colt died. Yiha cried in grief. His cry made the clouds tremble, and his tears deprived the sun and the moon of their brilliance.

A wild goose happened to pass by the lake and heard Yiha's bitter sobs. It flew off to tell the Mongol, the Hui, the Kazakh, and Uighur peoples of Yanqi that the dragon colt was dead.

Upon hearing the bad news, these peoples each chose from among their group an old man of high prestige, such a one as had a wide range of experience, to go to Bosten Lake to visit the brave Yiha. They carried with them many presents for Yiha, along with their people's sincere greetings.

The old man who was sent by the Hui people brought him greetings from his family. The Mongol elder told Yiha, in the event that the jade mare should mate again with the dragon stallion and give birth to another dragon colt, to give that colt some sheep blood to drink. The blood of sheep has the smell of grass. Once the colt had drunk the blood it would grow fond of tender grasses and reeds. He also told Yiha to make the colt lick cast iron, so that it would attain strong bones and muscles.

The Uighur elder brought for Yiha an elaborately made felt blanket. Because there was much wind in the Bosten Lake area, he told him that a newborn colt will easily catch cold. He told Yiha that in the event of wind he should cover the colt with the blanket. He should protect the young animal with this felt blanket against a variety of illnesses, and so enable it to grow up into a healthy valuable horse.

Then there was an old Kazakh man who brought with him a gold saddle blanket, paid for with money collected from among Kazakh people. He said that a person will appear more handsome if dressed in a decent suit and cap, and so will a horse with a good saddle blanket. He told Yiha to put the gold blanket upon the colt that was to be born the following year. It was the only colt deserving such a gold saddle blanket.

Yiha wiped away his tears. He thanked the old Hui man for bringing him greetings from home. He assured him that he would heed the Mongol elder's advice. Accepting the felt blanket and the gold saddle sent by Uighur and Kazakh people, he swore to the old men that he would not leave the Bosten Lake area until he had bred another precious colt.

Winter passed with its snows and cold wind. When spring came the leaves of reeds turned green again. After he had gone through severe cold and hardships, bearing the words of the elders in mind, Yiha remained to welcome still another spring in the Bosten Lake area—at the place haunted by wild boars and bears.

It had been said that the dragon stallion would appear once every ten years, but he reappeared that spring. Nobody knew whether it was Yiha's sincerity that had motivated the dragon stallion or whether it was simply Allah's will. The dragon stallion galloped on his jade-like hooves, he left the spray of lake water in his wake. He approached the jade mare in the quiet of the night.

At daybreak the jade mare sent the dragon stallion off, with sentiments of deep love. Then she raised her head and gave forth a joyous neigh in front of her master's hut—as if she understood Yiha's wishes very well.

Awakened by the neigh of the jade mare, Yiha emerged from his hut. From the manner of her complacency he could infer that the jade mare had met the dragon stallion again. From then on Yiha took still greater care of her. He would give her clear spring water to drink when she was thirsty and cover her with the felt blanket when she was cold. He often cut fresh tender reeds and grasses to feed her.

Under this amount of care by Yiha the jade mare never fell ill. She grew fat and strong. In about a year's time she gave birth to another colt as red as fire. Yiha did as the Mongolian elder had told him. He killed a sheep every now and then and gave the blood to the colt to drink. He also let the colt lick the piece of cast iron which had been left behind by the Mongolian. When it was cold at night, Yiha would take out the felt blanket to protect the little colt.

As the saying goes, "effort put forth steadfastly will not disappoint." Yiha looked after the little colt carefully. Gradually it began to eat grass. In less than half a year, this colt grew into a good stallion, worthy of that designation.

For three long years Yiha trained the young stallion. It was transformed into a priceless horse that could gallop at lightning speed. When it neighed it sounded like a tiger. It was so strong that it could carry a load of a thousand *jin*, and it could cover the distance of a thousand *li* in one day.[8]

To repay the kindness that was shown him by people of the various ethnic groups, Yiha decided to give to each group a few of his precious colts. He worked hard for another three years and propagated about a hundred superior horses from his stallion. He then put the gold saddle which the Kazakh man had given him upon the stallion. Riding him and driving a herd of second-generation Yanqi horses—the product of many years of dedicated labor by people from various ethnic groups—Yiha left the Bosten Lake area and returned to the home he had left long ago.

It has been said that on the day when brave Yiha arrived at his native place, bringing his valuable horses, he was given a warm welcome by his Hui elders and brothers, by the gallant Mongol horsemen, the hospitable Uighur young men, and the smart Kazakh herdsmen. They came from all directions to celebrate the triumphant return of the brave Yiha.

In memory of these joint efforts, put forth by various nationalities to re-establish a fine breed of horses, the peoples who live in the Yanqi area called their breed of horses the "Cooperative (Hezuo) Horse." But with the passage of time, the designation of these famous horses was gradually changed to "Heshuo Horse."[9] The horses were then named after the Heshuo county of the Bayingguoleng Mongol Autonomous Prefecture. Actually, the "Heshuo Horse" should be called "Hezuo Horse."

---

[8]One thousand *jin* equal five hundred kilograms. One thousand *li* correspond to five hundred kilometers.

[9]The basis of this transition from "Cooperative" to "Heshuo county" is a phonetic slide: from "Hezuo" to "Heshuo." Of course, if considered historically it appears that the nation-building motif, that is quite apparent in this story, has actually reversed the direction of the phonetic slide. Clearly, the socialistic drive to establish cooperative farm enterprises is what has generated the narrator's regret—that, for the small difference of a consonant, a famous breed of horses is not being named in honor of socialistic state policy. (Note by Luckert)

The Phoenix and Her City

Place: Ningxia District
Recorder: He Cun (Hui), 1981

According to legend, the city of Yinchuan was at one time called "Phoenix City." Today, if you mention the Phoenix City to old people, they will tell you that the Gaotai Temple east of Yinchuan, by the Yellow River, is the head of the Phoenix; the two wells by the Gaotai Temple are its eyes; the Drum Tower at the center of the city is the heart of the Phoenix; the West Tower and the North Tower are its claws; the trees, flowers, and grass in Zhongshan Park are the tail of the Phoenix—which used to be so long as to extend all the way to the Helan Mountains.

Why is Yinchuan called the "Phoenix City?" It is a long story. Do you by chance know anything about the Phoenix herself? She is the Bird of Happiness. Wherever the Phoenix is, there happiness is.

Seven Phoenix sisters lived on a high mountain peak south of the Chang Jiang (Yangtze) River. They lived there to bring happiness to people. So the place where they lived was very beautiful, with turquoise hills and clear bodies of water. Everywhere was the fragrance of flowers. Rows of trees stood there. The people were good looking and strong. Each year brought them an abundant harvest of the five cereals. People there lived prosperous lives. They had nothing to worry about. They lived together joyfully and pleasantly.

At the same time the Ningxia Plain, to the north, was a land of poor soil, and the people there lived under great hardships. Though the Yellow River flowed past them in the east, the water was so shallow that it could not be channeled into the fields. The Helan Mountains in the west could not keep out the cold air currents which blew in from Siberia. The Liupan Mountains in the south could not keep the sands of the Tengger Desert in check. Nonetheless, the Hui, the Mongol, and the Han people did not lose heart; diligently they continued working on this stretch of land. But though the people's muscles were nearly torn to shreds from hard work, and their blood was nearly desiccated, they could not ease their poverty. Sadly they sang:

Though the river is wide
And the mountains are high
Ningxia—an endless wasteland!

When news of the Bird of Happiness reached Ningxia, all the Hui, Han, and Mongol peoples were looking forward to her arrival in Ningxia, every day and every month. They looked forward to her arrival with so much devotion that their eyes turned red from the strain (and they recited this verse):

Though the river is wide
and the mountains are high,
Ningxia—its people hungry and nothing to wear!

The wild goose learned about this and was deeply moved by the sincere desire of the Ningxia people. She volunteered to fly southward to visit the Phoenix sisters and to communicate the genuine wish of the Ningxia people in detail. There, in the woods, the seven Phoenix sisters deliberated. The youngest insisted that she would go to Ningxia to have a look. The remaining six sisters agreed. They knew her habit—that, once she had decided on a course of action, no one could make her change her mind anymore. But they told her to return home as early as possible.

And so the youngest Phoenix began her journey, immediately. All the birds in the woods came to send her off. Some were playing on flutes and others were singing, while still others frolicked in dance. It was a very thrilling sight. The people from around there also came to see her off. They brought with them many presents, some for the young Phoenix and some for the people of Ningxia.

The six Phoenix sisters, and the lark, sent their little sister across the Chang Jiang river. After bidding farewell to her sisters and her friends, the young Phoenix flew to Ningxia trailing the wild goose who led the way. Riding a red cloud in the blue sky, she arrived in the Liupan Mountain area in almost no time at all. There she was received by Hui people who welcomed her with warm greetings. To them it seemed rather auspicious to have a red cloud in the sky. The Phoenix alighted happily by the Yellow River, between the Helan and the Liupan mountains.

Many tents, huts, and yurta were set up along both banks of the Yellow River. Hui, Han, and Mongol peoples lined the river banks to welcome the Phoenix. Birds arrived from the Liupan and Helan mountains. Cattle, sheep, camels, and horses came from the grass-lands to welcome her. They all chanted songs of welcome to the limits of their voices. Their songs resounded through the skies. Even the water of the Yellow River echoed as they sang.

After the Phoenix arrived in Ningxia she flew here and there without resting. When she saw the Yinchuan Plain she thought to herself, "What a vast expanse of dry land they have here!" She turned toward the Yellow River and, all around, she drew many lines. These lines became irrigation canals which, at their mouths, accepted water from the Yellow River.

The next morning the Phoenix rose very early and began flying about. She was so busy that she hardly took time to wipe away her sweat. The Phoenix scattered her presents all over the Liupan and Helan mountains, and all over the Yinchuan Plain. Flowers, trees, and crops sprang up instantly everywhere across the Yinchuan Plain. Herds of cattle appeared on the grassland. The Liupan Mountains cast off their worried frown and put on a green dress. The Helan Mountains discarded their white hair and covered themselves instead with green trees.

Ningxia altered its appearance completely. People were grateful to the Phoenix, for the happiness as well as for the lush southern scenery which she had brought. Since that time Ningxia has been known as the "Land of Prosperity beyond the Great Wall."

Well watered by irrigation canals the crops grew well. People harvested rich bounties every year, and they sang with joy:

At both ends Ningxia Plain is pointed.
Yellow River east and Helan Mountains west,
The Liupan Mountain range stands south.
Land well irrigated, rich harvests, year after year.

Ningxia had become a place as beautiful as the southlands. "The people around here are kind and hard working. It is now as beautiful around here as is my native place." This the Phoenix thought. "I will remain here!"

And so she regarded Ningxia as her home. Together with the people of Ningxia she worked hard to cultivate the land and to raise cows, horses, camels, and sheep.

At that time there lived, far to the west of Ningxia, a tribe of people of a different race. And one year the chief of this tribe, together with his men, pushed into Ningxia like a cruel beast of prey. They burnt crops and killed people. The Phoenix became very angry. She changed herself into a city to contain all the people inside her, with four city gates tightly sealed. No matter how hard the enemies tried, they could not break her open. The battle raged for three months. In the end the enemy ran out of food and was forced to withdraw. Ever thereafter, whenever an enemy came, the people would withdraw into the city for protection. As soon as the enemy withdrew they would re-emerge to resume farming and herding animals.

Now that the Phoenix had changed herself into a city she asked the wild goose to carry a message to her sisters in the south, telling them that she would not return home anymore. On that account it has become the task of the wild goose to carry a message to the southland once every year. Each autumn, when the crops are ripe, the wild goose flies south. And with the arrival of spring, the next year, the wild goose will fly back again with best regards to the Phoenix, from her six sisters.

Many years passed. A tribal chief appeared. Later came the emperor, the warlords, the bureaucrats, and finally the landlords. The face of Ningxia changed. The masses of people were exploited and oppressed by a small number of people. The mountains became barren and the fields were left uncultivated. The Ningxia Plain became a stretch of dry land again. Cattle, sheep, and camels were dying from hunger. Even the Liupan and Helan mountains were covered with ominous dark clouds.

One year the emperor sent an official with a pockmarked face to Ningxia. Upon his arrival he had a palace built at a place southeast of the Phoenix City. He conscripted young men for military service and robbed the people of their belongings. The Hui, Han, and Mongol peoples suffered a lot under this greedy official. When he learned that there was a gold pony sunk in Heiquan Lake, he decided to steal it.

One night he sat in the government office and thought to himself, "I can steal the gold pony without all the people here knowing it. But how can I hide the truth from the Phoenix?"

He continued thinking, "Ever since the Phoenix has come to Ningxia, the people are increasingly becoming more educated and capable. I have done many evil deeds, so that, if I might run out of luck some day the gold pony will fall into the hands of others."

As he thought in this fashion, he suddenly gnashed his teeth and said to himself, "I must take preventive measures. I must kill the Phoenix first."

He searched out the Phoenix before the night was over. When he found her he cut open her throat with his sword. But, even though the Phoenix died, her heart remained alive. She was still thinking about the people of Ningxia. There appeared a canal which carried the flow of her blood. Her blood flowed from one village to another into the thirsty fields.

The next morning many people were surprised to find a newly dug canal winding its way in front of their houses. When news of the canal spread, the inhabitants came running to see for themselves. They were all puzzled: "Why! Can it be possible that the Milky Way in heaven has fallen to the ground?"

As they admired the water flow, they discovered some red threads in it. Some old men recognized it as blood, and they began shouting, "Ah, there is blood in the water!"

Just then an old ahong came running, as if he had gone mad. He elbowed his way through the crowd. Then, with his eyes fixed on the water he cried with deep sorrow, beating his breast and stamping his feet: "Oh my Allah! It is true!" The people surrounded him and asked what was the matter.

After a pause the old ahong began to murmur, "I dreamt I saw the Phoenix last night. She told me that she was being killed by someone. She could not tear herself from us. Therefore she made a canal with her blood for us to irrigate the land."

Upon hearing what the old ahong told them, the people were overcome with grief. Some shed tears of sadness and others wept in sorrow. Still others broke out into loud crying. They cried and cried for nine days and nine nights until the sky was cloudy, the trees were yellow, and the mountains were bald. The people lamented and chanted:

The melon clings to the vine.
A baby clings to its mother.
How can the Ningxia people live
Without the Phoenix to protect them?

On the tenth day the Phoenix once more appeared to the old ahong in a dream. She informed him that her heart was still alive, that after another ninety-nine years she would rise again. Many capable people would appear then. Ningxia would become a paradise on earth.

She told the ahong, "Wait patiently for me. The Phoenix will return when a red cloud appears over the Liupan Mountain range."[10]

The people were no longer sorrowful, and all things on earth resumed their former state. In memory of the Phoenix, people called the city of Yinchuan the "Phoenix City." The canal that was made by the blood of the Phoenix they called the "Red Flower Canal."

The Golden Pheasant

Place: Ningxia
Recorder: Shu Yuanfu (Hui), 1983

Long, long ago, in a Muslim village, there lived a brave and diligent boy named Yusufu. His father died, and he lived with his mother and his little sister. One day Yusufu went to gather firewood on the mountain. Before sunset he began his journey home. He had walked about halfway down the mountain when, suddenly, a colorful flash of light broke forth, and out of it flew a beautiful golden cock. The bird sang clearly and melodiously and paused right in front of Yusufu. The boy was shocked, but then threw himself upon it. But in just the twinkle of an eye the colorful light dispersed and the beautiful cock disappeared. Instead, before his eyes, a small golden pheasant came into view. Yusufu held it in his arms, lovingly, and hurried back to his home with his firewood. He was singing *huaer*.[11]

---

[10]This is an obvious allusion to the Red Army's arrival, after its Long March in 1935, and its historic climb to safety across Liushan Mountain. The plot of this story has obviously been placed in the service of recent socialistic nation building.

[11]*Huaer* refers to an antiphonal folk tune, sung by Hui people and other northwestern ethnic groups.

As soon as he entered the house he called his mother and his sister to come and have a look. His sister loved that pheasant dearly, but his kindhearted mother asked suspiciously, "My Boy, where did you get it?"

Yusufu knew well the principles of his mother. He was afraid that she might be angry, and therefore he told her exactly what had happened.

The mother looked at the golden pheasant and stroked it repeatedly, but then she said, "Even though the golden pheasant is a miracle-working treasure, the Muslim people cannot escape their troubles and afflictions unless an evil spirit is first gotten rid of. Only after this feat can we hope to live more pleasant lives."

These words caused the hearts of Yusufu and of his little sister to sink.

In recent years some evil spirit, whom nobody knew, had been creating troubles in the village. During spring, when the grass was green and when it was a good time for pasturing livestock, a storm would suddenly blast, and within a minute herds of cattle and sheep would disappear. In late autumn, when people were ready to harvest, thunder and lightning would arise. Hail stones would fall as large as eggs and all crops would be stripped bare. The people could not even harvest as much as a single kernel. In addition, halfway up the mountain clouds of black smoke would break forth that dispersed in the wind. Whoever was infected by that smoke would become ill. The local Muslims prayed to Allah, hoping to escape this affliction and to get rid of the disease. But the disaster worsened, year after year. Thinking about this, the three—the mother with her son and daughter—felt heavy-hearted and lost interest in talking further about the golden pheasant. They went to rest in their own rooms.

At midnight the old mother suddenly saw the golden pheasant radiate, and soon thereafter it began to speak to her, "Old Lady, I am not a golden pheasant but the cock who heralds the breaking of a new day. These years the people here are in great trouble because of a frog who lives in the haystack of Squire Mu, in Mu Clan Village. It has turned into a spirit. Almost no-one who is infected with the poisonous vapors of this frog spirit survives. Squire Mu's only daughter is in danger as well. It is only your son, Yusufu, who can dispose of it."

Hearing this, the mother said without hesitation, "I will let him go anywhere, even up to the mountain of swords or down to the sea of flames, if only he can get rid of that evil spirit."

That night, in his dream, Yusufu heard the golden pheasant speak to him, "Tomorrow, please take me with you to Squire Mu, and tell him you can cure his daughter's disease. Then dig out the old elm tree in his yard. Under the elm tree is a spring. When you see a water lily appear in the spring water, simply pull it up, dry it, and boil it in water taken from this spring. It can cure Miss Mu and other sick people in the village. When Miss Mu has recovered, Squire Mu will believe you and give you his sword, his family heirloom. With it you can kill the evil spirit."

Early the next morning, Yusufu told his mother about his dream. His mother said, "My Dear One! None of us can live in peace until the evil spirit has been killed. For the villagers' sake, please try, even at the risk of losing your life." The old woman looked at her son carefully, gave him the golden pheasant, and saw him off at the gate.

The news that Yusufu would go and kill the evil spirit, at Mu's place, spread throughout the village. Boys and girls came to say goodbye to him. Some old men were breathless with anxiety for him and prayed to God to bless and to protect him—all except a lazy man, Ma Erliu, who was only concerned about his own interests. After he heard that Yusufu had gotten the precious golden pheasant, how could he not try to obtain this wealth? So, the moment Yusufu left home he followed him.

Yusufu climbed hills, descended into valleys, and journeyed through a forest a whole day. He was very tired when he arrived at the entrance of the village. The sun was setting. There was a well outside that village, but there was nothing with which to draw water.

Yusufu was so thirsty that he took forth the golden pheasant from his bosom. He rewrapped it in cloth and slung the bundle sideways on his back. Then he began to slide down the side of the well. Suddenly a hand reached down from the top. It snatched away his cloth bundle and gave him a hard push at his shoulder. Yusufu fell to the bottom with a flop. It was fortunate that the water was not deep. He struggled to climb up. But by the time he made it out, the bad man who had snatched away his bundle had run out of sight. Yusufu shouted angrily, "Allah! Please damn that heartless and poisonous snake."

Yusufu's golden pheasant was gone. Meanwhile, over at Squire Mu's place, a swaggering new housekeeper applicant arrived—Ma Erliu. After snatching away the golden pheasant, Ma Erliu hastily offered it to Squire Mu. Because his daughter was seriously ill, and cures were hopeless, Squire Mu was not in the mood to manage the affairs of his house and he had been unhappy all day long. When he saw someone come to offer him a treasure he asked him to manage his affairs. This made Ma Erliu very happy.

While he was enjoying himself Ma Erliu heard the servant girl tell Squire Mu, "A young man is outside and asks to see you, Master. He said he would get rid of Miss Mu's disease."

As soon as he heard this, Squire Mu asked the servant-girl to invite him in. She led Yusufu into the reception hall. Ma Erliu was flabbergasted about his coming. He wondered, "Why! Is he still alive?" He hastily told Squire Mu, "Sir, how can such a young man be a doctor? He comes just in the dark of evening. I suppose he is either a bandit or a crook. You should chase him away."

But Squire Mu was very anxious about his daughter's health. He motioned to him to arrange board and lodging for the young man. That evening Yusufu stayed at the home of Mu.

Ma Erliu, who had a guilty conscience, was afraid that Yusufu would find out that it was he who snatched away his golden pheasant and would expose him. So, for the second time, he hatched a vicious plot to do away with the person who had survived his first plot. Around midnight Ma Erliu slipped to the door of Yusufu's room, with an axe in his hand. Listening at the door he heard Yusufu's regular breathing. He looked around and pushed the door open when, suddenly, the lamp inside was being lit. He had to slip away. It happened that when Yusufu was in deep sleep he felt a pain in his ears. He got up and lit the lamp and found some red ants on the pillow. After that he could not fall asleep anymore. He got up and put on his clothes.

Early the next morning Yusufu was shown to the reception hall. Squire Mu asked, "Where did you come from? Do you have good medicine for my daughter?"

"There will still be time to tell you where I have come from after I have cured the patient. But first you have to promise to dig out the old elm tree in your yard if you want to cure that illness."

Thinking for a while, Squire Mu said, "It is obvious that I, by myself, cannot dig out that one-hundred-year-old elm. But in order to cure the illness, I will have it dug out." Thereupon Squire Mu asked his servants to begin digging out the tree. As soon as the tree was out, a spring could be seen bubbling forth. Yusufu looked at the water without a twinkle. Soon a jade-green water lily grew forth. Yusufu grabbed it quickly and carefully, and he dried it in the air. He boiled it in the spring water to obtain a medicinal liquid. He asked the servant girl to bring some to Miss Mu and sent some to the other patients in the village as well. Within one day Miss Mu and the other patients in the village all recovered.

Squire Mu was very pleased and took his daughter to say thanks to Yusufu. So did the other villagers. The honest and kind young man looked at the villagers and said excitedly, "You are welcome. We should say thanks to the golden pheasant. It was the golden pheasant who cured your illness."

Yusufu continued to explain where the golden pheasant came from, his purpose of coming here, and how he had been robbed on his way here.

All the people began to curse that nameless scoundrel, except Squire Mu. He hurried back to his room and momentarily brought a golden pheasant to Yusufu, in his hands.

He asked: "Is this the golden pheasant you lost?" Yusufu took it into his hands and recognized it as the same golden pheasant.

Some young men in the crowd could not help shouting, "Squire Mu, how did this golden pheasant get to your house?"

Without answering Squire Mu turned and sent a servant for his housekeeper.[12] Ma Erliu came out and stood before the crowd.

"What an evil thing you have done! You must confess your crime!"

Ma Erliu knew that he could not deny it when he saw the golden pheasant in Yusufu's hands. He had no choice but to admit that he had pushed Yusufu down into the well. Squire Mu became pale with anger and ordered his servant to whip Ma Erliu. But Yusufu stepped forth and stopped him, "Sir, do not whip him. He has lost the Muslim's way. Let him off."

---

[12]This story is one of the rare instances where a good squire appears. Of course, the issue at hand is an illness which afflicts all people; the issue is not land, wealth, or power.

Squire Mu desisted and drove him out of the village. Later, because he was gluttonous and lazy, Ma Erliu was reduced to begging. And finally he died on a desolate stretch along the river.

After he had found again his golden pheasant, Yusufu was even more eager to rid the people of the evil spirit. He asked Squire Mu to lend him his sword. Squire Mu agreed without hesitation. The villagers were excited that Yusufu might kill the evil one. Many strong young men asked to accompany him. But he did not agree, because they did not have good swords. He was afraid that the evil one might hurt them.

Yusufu urged them to go back home, and then he tucked the golden pheasant into his bosom, carefully. He went to the stack of hay halfway up the hill, beyond the back yard. Because it had been sitting there many years, the hay gave forth an offensive smell. He made a torch and set fire to the stack of hay all around.

In a short time the haystack was burning, with flames and dense smoke rising up toward the sky. And suddenly there came a violent storm. Sand and stones were flying about. Heavy clouds rolled in the sky. There was thunder and lightning.

From the storm came forth a monstrous demon. His eyes were like green lamps. His mouth was as big as a dust pan. His arms and legs were as sturdy as hammers of stone. His body, with knots all over, was squirting forth a terrible stench. He threw himself against Yusufu with bare fangs and open claws.

Yusufu dodged nimbly, and the demon failed to do him harm. Before he could turn back, Yusufu, sharp-eyed and quick, stabbed the demon with his sword. Slash! One of the demon's hind legs was cut off. The demon was in pain and very annoyed. He roared and leaped wildly at Yusufu, yearning to swallow him. At the same time Yusufu craved to kill this evil monster. He and the demon were locked in a deadly struggle.

Gradually Yusufu was weakened and could hardly support himself anymore; he was scratched blue and bloody. But then, at a very critical moment, in that smoke, a bright flash shot straight toward the demon's eyes—and with that shiny flash flew forth a golden pheasant. With claws as sharp as knives it scratched out the demon's eyes. The monster was hurt so badly that he screamed at the top of his voice. Yusufu used this opportunity: he raised his sword and gave a death stab into the demon's heart. A fountain of black blood spurted out. The evil frog demon, who had been harming the villagers, was finally defeated. Yusufu swooned and fainted on the hilltop because he had lost too much blood.

The sky cleared again and the sun appeared. The villagers came over. They carried Yusufu back to the village, and after forty-nine days of rest, and after eating nourishing food, he recovered at last.

From that time on the people in Mu Clan Village, and in the surrounding area, told the story of the golden pheasant. They told of Yusufu who got rid of an evil for the sake of the people—they told the story of Yusufu who killed the frog demon.

Xueda and Yinlin

Place: Miquan county, Xinjiang
Narrator: Wang Juenqing (Hui)
Recorder: Liu Yan, Xiaoping, 1984

Once upon a time, in a remote place, sat a mountain named Gancialin. Near its foot was a bend in the river and a very beautiful place. Fertile soil was there, and many flowers grew and bloomed.

On the land lived thirty poor families. All had come and settled after having fled from calamities elsewhere. These thirty families shared everything, comforts and hardships, and they worked with one heart and mind to support themselves by hunting and planting.

Among the villagers was a lad named Xueda, who had come to the River Bend area with his parents when he was still a child. A few years later his parents died and he became an orphan.

After that misfortune the villagers treated him as their own kith and kin. Among the villagers lived a widow who had an only daughter whose name was Yinlin. The widow and her daughter were especially kind to Xueda. Xueda regarded the villagers as his relatives; he viewed the widow as his mother and Yinlin as his little sister.

While he was still very young, Xueda was diligent and brave. By the time he reached eighteen he had become far more handsome and strong; he was very skilled in the martial arts. Shooting with bow and arrows was his favorite sport—a hundred shots for him meant a hundred bull's-eyes. When he came upon wild animals he never missed.

One day Xueda went hunting in the mountains. He met an old and white-haired man who gave him a bow and three golden arrows. After that, no matter who the wild animals were—tigers, lions, even demons and spirits—none of them could avoid his golden arrows.

When Yinlin reached the age of about fifteen she became very beautiful and intelligent. The birds and flowers which she embroidered appeared like real and living ones. Cotton cloth which she wove sold well. Aside from that she was good at singing and the people enjoyed her songs very much.

One day, when she was gathering firewood in the mountains, a very kind grandmother approached her and gave her a wonderful flute. No matter how tired one was, whoever heard the music that she played on her flute would forget his or her weariness entirely.

Xueda and Yinlin often enthusiastically helped the villagers. They often gave away to them the bundle of firewood which they had collected. They would offer a helping hand to whoever was in need. And so Xueda and Yinlin were living with the villagers pleasantly and peacefully.

One year some people in the village became infected with a disease that gradually enlarged the patients' bellies. It spread across the village and there was an increasing number of sick people. They suffered severely from that lingering illness and groaned with pain.

Xueda and Yinlin were deeply grieved by the people's suffering and decided to bring relief. In the village lived an educated man by the name of Ma, he had studied some medicine. And so Xueda and Yinlin came to ask him what kind of illness it was and how it could be cured.

Mister Ma said, "It is potbelly disease which is not easily treated. But I have been told that there is an effective remedy. It is a pity that we do not have the primary herb that is needed. It is the small iris. The other medicine is leopard gallbladder. If you cannot find these two medicines within three months, the patients will die."

Then Xueda and Yinlin asked where the two medicines could be found, so that they each could go and look for them. Mister Ma said, half remembering and half lost in thought, "It has been said by old people that in the fairy cave, at Rock Cliff, there lives a leopard who comes forth only once a year, and only during hot days. Nobody dares to go there because an evil spirit returns to the cave soon after that happens. The place where the small irises grow is called Flower Mountain. To get there you must pass through Birds Cave. But no one can approach that cave without endangering his life."

What Mister Ma said did not frighten Xueda or Yinlin. Instead, it strengthened their resolve firmly to find the medicines, even to the point of risking their lives.

Xueda and Yinlin set out on their journeys, separately, leading four boys and four girls, respectively.

Days and nights Xueda and his four fellows walked straight toward Rock Cliff. In order to get there they had to go over six high mountains and cross six deep streams. Faced by the steep mountains and the deep rivers the four fellows were frightened and would go no further. Only Xueda was left to continue his journey. After countless hardships, and after crossing mountains and streams, he reached Rock Cliff.

In the gully by Rock Cliff grew many types of flowers and trees which he had never seen anywhere else. Birds and small animals of all kinds were playing happily and freely. Yet, Xueda had no time to enjoy this beautiful scenery. Immediately he hid himself in a cave opposite the rocky cliff to wait for the leopard. When he was thirsty and hungry he simply drank spring water and ate some wild fruits. In this manner he waited and watched. There was nothing to be seen of the leopard.

One day, while looking out with his sharp eyes, right and left, he noticed startled birds flying from trees and small animals on the ground escaping. After that the entire Rock Cliff became silent again.

Relying on his hunter's sensitivity, Xueda knew that a wild beast was approaching. He lost no time getting his golden bow and arrows and his hunting knife ready, all the while watching carefully. After a while he noticed a beam of red light streaming from the cave in Rock Cliff; it shone brilliantly over the entire valley. From that brilliant light emerged a very wild leopard spirit.

In excitement Xueda raised his bow and successfully shot two arrows at the two eyes of the leopard spirit. Being in great pain, and blinded, the leopard spirit roared terribly and leaped up and down while trying to flee for its life. Xueda seized the chance and rushed at it with his dagger and killed it. He skinned the leopard and took out its gallbladder. And having been successful he began his return journey.

After parting company with Xueda, Yinlin led the four girls and journeyed in the direction of the small irises. After a long trip they arrived at the Birds Cave at last.

The four girls looked inside and found it to be dark, and deep; and a variety of weird sounds came from it that made their blood curl and their hair stand on end. By the cave some ferocious and gigantic birds stood guard, looking at them fiercely. The four girls were absolutely terrified and retreated from this threat; they went back home. Yinlin also was terrified. But, thinking of the death which threatened the villagers she encouraged herself to approach Bird Cave.

She took out her bamboo flute and began playing on it. When these weird birds heard the beautiful sounds they gradually fell asleep. Yinlin seized the opportunity and passed through the cave and thereby entered another valley.

She felt hungry and intended to find something to eat when, suddenly, she caught sight of a small thatched hut ahead, on a nearby hill. By the cottage sat a kindly looking old man. Yinlin walked up to greet him and begged him for something to eat while, at the same time, she asked the way to Flowers Mountain.

The old man said nothing but went into the hut and soon returned with a bowl of soup and a large cake. When she had finished eating the old man pointed Yinlin the right way and disappeared, together with his hut.

Yinlin walked three full days along the road shown by the old man before she finally arrived at Flowers Mountain. She looked ahead and found it to be a truly beautiful mountain, covered with many different flowers and plants which she had never seen before. Yet, Yinlin was not in any mood to enjoy them but began to search intensively after small irises. After having searched a while she saw some that grew halfway up the mountain.

With great delight Yinlin climbed up the mountain. When she got there she discovered that the small irises were in a basket carried by a girl wearing a red skirt. Two pink flowers adorned her head. The girl looked at her with a smile and asked her about the purpose of her coming. Yinlin explained her purpose. Then the girl, seeing the bamboo flute, asked Yinlin to play. This she did.

Unexpectedly her flute playing attracted dozens of young girls in red, and boys in blue. They surrounded her and requested that she play once more. This time Yinlin played a sorrowful piece, expressing thereby the miserable sufferings of the villagers. This caused the girls and the boys to shed sympathetic tears. Quickly they gathered all small irises into one large basket and brought them to her.

Afterward a girl led Yinlin to the edge of a cliff. Yinlin looked in the direction into which the girl pointed and saw that there were even more patients in the village. Most of them were already at the verge of death, and moaning voices could be heard throughout the entire village. Seeing this situation, Yinlin felt even more grieved and worried. How she wished she could fly back quickly to the village, with her herbs!

The girl had already read Yinlin's mind. She asked her to close her eyes and then blew a puff of air towards her. Within a minute Yinlin had flown back to her village.

And so the diligent and brave young people, Xueda and Yinlin, overcame many difficulties and finally obtained leopard gallbladder and small irises within the required three months. They returned the critically ill villagers to life and thereby saved the whole village.

Later, everybody in the village agreed to hold a grand wedding ceremony for Xueda and Yinlin. They got married, and the villagers lived happy lives ever after.

Duoer Tea

Place: Yinchuan rural area, Ningxia
Narrator: Ahong Zhang Fuxiang
Recorder: Xie Rong (Hui), 1980[13]

A servant of Allah was named Duoer Tea. He was a tea boy in heaven. Because Duoer Tea had not conformed to some heavenly rule, he was made to atone for his offense and to perform good

---

[13]For information concerning this recorder see page 73, note 1.

deeds. Allah sentenced him to do some good deeds, to wash away his sins.

One day, when Allah was reciting Quranic scripture, he blew a tea leaf into the endless sea of clouds. The tea leaf was seen gliding down to the Shapo end of Majia village, where Hui people lived together in their ghetto. The tea leaf became a tall, thick, and strong heavenly tea tree with broad and long leaves.

One year the Muslims in the village caught a contagious disease. Everybody, men and women, old and young, were sneezing and coughing and had headaches with fever. Some of the weak people continued coughing up and began to die after a hundred days. The disease was called "Kh—Kh—" sickness.

Yusufu lived in the first house of the village, and he had become seriously ill. He dragged himself to go and ask the ahong to come to his house, to recite. After he had gotten as far as the tea tree he could not move another step. He wobbled and fell under the tree. There he fell asleep and had a dream.

In his dream a giant, with a green turban on his head, came walking out of the vast desert. The giant wore a yellow garment and had pockmarks all over his face. His eyes were shining brightly. He had a golden axe stuck in his belt.

With his gigantic hands he stroked Yusufu's head and said, "Yusufu, I am the heavenly tea tree in your village. The village is infected with something like a virus. I was told by Allah to come and to save you. Take this golden axe of mine, swing it, and my leaves will fall. Gather the fallen tea leaves and give them to the sick. Tell them to boil the tea leaves, and to drink the tea. In that manner they will be cured. To save more people from becoming infected you can plant cuttings of the tree in spring. With an entire tea garden you will be able to cure many more sick people." After having spoken these words the giant disappeared.

Yusufu suddenly awoke from his dream. He was feeling very well. His head stopped aching and he was exploding with energy. He was still thinking about his dream when he saw a large stone slowly emerge from the ground, right in front of him. It shone brightly in the sun. With a hissing noise it gradually was transformed into a golden axe. There, before Yusufu, the axe bounced three times and he picked it up with great joy. He swung it exactly as the magic tea tree had told him in his dream. Tea leaves fell like snowflakes. He sent them to all the sick people in the village and told them to boil the leaves and to drink the tea. All the sick people got well within a day.

The following day, when Yusufu told the villagers that there should be a tea garden, they all volunteered to help him plant tea trees. When autumn came the trees in the garden were covered with tea leaves. Yusufu distributed them among the sick. Those who drank the tea got well immediately. The good news spread far and wide. From everywhere people came to get the wonderworking tea leaves, to cure their sickness.

In Majia village lived a landlord named Ma Seli who coveted Yusufu's tea garden. He wanted Yusufu to sell the garden to him so that he could make a fortune from it. Yusufu would not sell it. Ma Seli sent his men to secretly cut down the trees. But even though the men inflicted blows to the degree that their hands got worn to the point of bleeding, they could not harm the trees.

When Ma Seli heard that Yusufu had a golden axe with which the trees could be cut down, he decided to rob him of this axe. One dark night Ma Seli broke into Yusufu's hut, together with his hatchet men, while Yusufu was sound asleep. They tied him up and took away the golden axe.

Overwhelmed with joy, Ma Seli viewed and admired the axe proudly. All of a sudden the axe flew out from his hands toward the sky. With the sound of "ka—tza" the landlord Ma Seli was burned to death. His hatchet men were so scared that they fled as quickly as their legs would carry them. The gold axe returned again into Yusufu's hands.

From then on Yusufu took great care of the tea garden. He never refused to give tea to the sick who came to ask for it. Everybody praised the tea garden, because it had saved many people. Duoer Tea continued doing good deeds for the people, which showed that he had repented and turned over a new leaf. Allah therefore permitted him to return to heaven.

Before leaving, Duoer Tea once more appeared in Yusufu's dream and told him, "I am leaving with the golden axe. The tea leaves in your garden will henceforth fall by themselves. But you are required to cut off all the dead branches next spring. New leaves will grow. It will be good for one's health to drink tea every day. You must take good care of these tea trees, and with them you can help cure the poor sick people."

Yusufu woke up, suddenly. He touched his belt, but the golden axe was no longer there. At once he went to the tea garden and found that all the tea trees drooped. He took greater care of his tea garden, in accordance with how Duoer Tea had instructed him in his dream. And sure enough, the next year brought more new tea leaves onto the trees.

Rhinoceros Cave

Place: Yunnan
Recorder: Ma Jianyun (Hui), Zhang Baoshou, 1981

In ancient times there was a divine being named Midan who guarded the fruit orchard in the Western Heaven. Because he disobeyed heavenly rules he was ordered to descend to the world as a rhinoceros, to guard the shiny elixir of life, the *"ganoterma,"* in the White Dragon Cave.

One day two brothers from Sichuan came to Yunnan to do business. Carrying silk made in Sichuan upon their shoulders, the two merchants journeyed through a dense forest. It was hot that day. They were so thirsty that they sat down in the shade for a rest. They took out some food to eat. Not a single drop of water was left in their gourd bottle.

The older brother told the younger one, "Go and find some water to drink. I am quite thirsty."

"Where shall I find water in the midst of this forest?" asked the younger brother.

The older brother was unhappy. "If you will not go, then keep an eye on the silk. I will go myself."

With these words the older brother walked into the deep forest with the gourd bottle. He walked over hills and valleys without finding any water. By sunset he was very hungry and thirsty. He had to return to the place where his brother was waiting.

That night the two brothers slept under a big tree in the open air. While fast asleep they were awakened by a noise and, faintly, they saw a gigantic animal running past them.

Early the next morning, the two brothers got up and were about to go on their way when they noticed several huge footprints. Remembering the gigantic being which they had seen during the night, the younger brother said, "It must be a wild ox."

But the older brother did not think so. He said, "It is not a wild ox. Perhaps it is a rhinoceros. I was told by the local people that a rhinoceros lives in this area. If only we could catch it!"

They decided to look for the rhinoceros. By following the footprints they came to a spring which was gushing forth from a rocky cave. The footprints led into the cave. "Go and call some people to catch it," said the older brother. "I will remain here to guard the cave."

After the younger brother left, the older brother waited at the entrance of the cave with his sword and with a carrying pole.

The younger brother went to Shaba Village, at the foot of Dragonhead Mountain, and he told the villagers about the rhinoceros.

The next day the younger brother came up the mountain, accompanied by villagers. They hid behind bushes near the cave. By midnight it was pitch dark. With two shafts of golden rays the rhinoceros emerged from the cave. The people jumped on him from behind the bushes. The older brother was out front. He was thrown up into the air by the rhinoceros, by its horn, and he fell dead.

When he saw the golden rays the younger brother realized that it was a divine animal. And so he stepped aside to make way for its escape. Then he buried his older brother and returned to Sichuan by himself.

In Shaba Village lived a girl named Banzhu whose father had died when she was only three. Banzhu and her mother depended on each other for survival. The mother was old and weak with illness, and so the girl never left her alone.

Banzhu was very diligent and able to do all kinds of work, indoors as well as out-of-doors. In addition, she had to go and look for good doctors, and medicines, to cure her sick mother.

On her way back from gathering medicinal herbs, one day, she saw a thin white-haired old man in rags lying at the bank of the stream, groaning. Banzhu put aside her hoe and her herbs. She took a gourd bottle from her shoulder and gave to the old man some water. After a few mouthfuls the old man's eyelids began to move slightly. Banzhu asked, "How did you come to be lying in such a desolate place, Grandfather?"

The old man answered slowly, "I come from a place far away. I had little to eat all along the way, therefore I fell ill. Now I am no longer able to walk. That is why I am lying here."

Banzhu took pity on the old man. She helped him along the mountain path to her home and looked after him with care. Within a week the old man recovered, and he said to Banzhu, "Thank you for your kindheartedness. May Allah bless you. I wish you and your mother happiness. As for me, I am afraid I will have to go now." Then he left Banzhu's house and walked away with his cane.

The old man was none other than Midan, the rhinoceros. After Midan left Shaba Village he walked along the road which led to Sichuan. Along his way he found a young merchant who was on his way home to Sichuan. The latter had been tied to a tree by robbers and was almost dead. Midan laid him down and put an elixir of life into his mouth. Momentarily the man regained consciousness, and Midan asked, "Why were you tied to a tree, young man?"

The man answered, "Dear Elder, I encountered two robbers on my way home. They took all my belongings and then tied me to the tree. Fortunately you came to my rescue."

Midan laughed. "You are kindhearted as a golden deer. You saved others when they were in danger. Happiness will certainly come to you. Would you mind becoming my foster son? You will be called Yadan from now on."

Yadan greeted his foster father. He shouldered the old man's clothes and food. And the two of them walked on.

After the old man left, Banzhu's mother progressed from bad to worse. So Banzhu asked an experienced doctor to look at her. After the doctor carefully felt her pulse he told Banzhu, "Your mother is seriously ill. I will prescribe some medicinal herbs. You must find the elixir of life to completely fill the prescription. After taking that medicine she will be well again."

"Where can I find the elixir of life?" asked Banzhu.

The wise and experienced doctor answered, "Go to the White Dragon Cave. You will find it there."

The following morning Banzhu, with some food and water, and with a sword, started out to look for the White Dragon Cave. She traveled across mountains and rivers and, at last, she came to a mountain. She saw a young man riding on a cow. The young man was playing the bamboo flute. It sounded beautiful. Banzhu went up to the young man and, after greeting him, she asked, "Could you show me the way to the White Dragon Cave?"

The young man was none other than Yadan, the foster son of Midan. "What do you go there for?" he asked.

Banzhu answered, "My father died long ago. My mother has been seriously ill. She has been to many doctors, but none could cure her. A few days ago an old experienced doctor gave a prescription that calls for an elixir ingredient. The doctor told me that this elixir of life can be found only in the White Dragon Cave. But I do not know how to get there."

Yadan said: "You are a kindhearted girl. Allah will bless you. You will surely find the elixir of life to cure your dear mother."

Yadan tied his cow to a tree and told Banzhu, "My parents died when I was a little boy, leaving me an orphan. I was brought up by my older brother. Unfortunately my brother also died. Then I came across an old man who took me as his son. I am no longer lonely now. I would like to ask my foster father to help you into the cave. Your mother will be well again with that elixir of life."

"May Allah bless you!" said Banzhu gratefully. "I hope you kind people can save my mother."

Yadan said, "Sister, we are melons of the same vine. We share the same fate. Let us promise ourselves to be brother and sister and then go to see my father."

Banzhu nodded her agreement. So they bowed to each other and thereby became sister and brother.

The two of them walked towards the home. On the way they met their father who led a pair of golden deer.

When he saw the old man, Yadan walked over to him and bowed. "Father, this is the girl I met at the mountain."

The old man smiled kindly. "It is Allah who has sent me a daughter."

Banzhu at once knelt down and kowtowed. After that Yadan began to speak: "My dear Father. Here, Sister Banzhu's mother has been bedridden for months. A doctor gave a prescription which must be filled with an elixir of life from the White Dragon Cave."

Scrutinizing Banzhu from head to foot, the old man said, smiling, "Do you remember me? I am the old man who was recuperating at your home. Banzhu, you are a good girl. You need an elixir of life? That is easy. Just look!" The old man pointed with his hand.

Banzhu turned and saw the golden deer standing there with elixir of life in its mouth. Midan the old man took it out and handed it to Banzhu.

Banzhu was filled with gratitude. She invited Midan and Yadan to her home in Shaba Village. Her mother ate the elixir of life and her health was soon restored.

Banzhu's mother was so moved that she told Midan, "I am very grateful to you for bringing me back to life. I can think of no way to repay you. Please let me betroth my daughter to Yadan."

On hearing this, Yadan was very pleased. He married Banzhu then and there.

Yadan and Banzhu lived as husband and wife, and they loved each other. Yadan plowed the field while Banzhu weaved cotton cloth. They lived happily. A year later Banzhu gave birth to a baby son. The arrival of their child made the entire family happier than ever.

One day the old man was playing with his grandson when he heard someone calling his name. Looking up he saw two angels, sent by Allah, riding on a cloud above him. The angels delivered Allah's order to recall Midan to Heaven.

Midan dared not to linger. He immediately gave the baby to Banzhu and followed the angels into Heaven.

When Midan arrived in Heaven, Allah sent one of the angels to tell him, "I have sent you to the world to guard the elixir of life in the White Dragon Cave. And you have given it to people on earth without my permission. I was thinking about punishing you. But since you did it out of mercy and have saved two lives, and because you have arranged a good match, I will forgive you. But I will now take you back to Heaven."

Midan expressed thanks to Allah for not punishing him, and he continued to say [to the angel], "I have a foster son in the world. I left in such a hurry that I did not have time to say goodbye. Please permit me to go back to the earth once more."

"Go quickly and return as soon as possible," the angel agreed.

Midan descended to the world, said goodbye to Yadan and Banzhu, and went back up to Heaven again. His body on earth changed into a big stone, shaped like a rhinoceros. It was left behind at the entrance of the White Dragon Cave, in Shaba Village.

People in later generations changed the name of the White Dragon Cave to Rhinoceros Cave.

Naxigaer

Place: Zhenbeipu, Ningxia
Narrator: Jin Laohan (Hui)
Recorder: Xu Fujiang, 1983

Long, long ago, at the foot of Helan Mountain lived a diligent and kind young Hui man whose name was Naxigaer. His parents died, and he was so poor that he could not afford to marry a girl. He just barely made a living by gathering wood.

One day Naxigaer went up the mountain with his bush knife and a carrying pole. Later that morning he was hungry and rested from work in order to eat his lunch—two black cakes—when suddenly a voice spoke to him from behind: "Please have pity on me, an old and lonely woman. Please share with me something to eat."

He looked back and saw that it was a pale old woman, clad in rags; her two hands were as thin as dry wood. Naxigaer gave her the two cakes. The old woman devoured them and turned away without saying thanks.

The next day Naxigaer took four cakes with him. At noon when he was about to have the cakes the old woman appeared again. Naxigaer gave her two of the four. The old woman finished them quickly and asked him for more. Naxigaer gave her the other two cakes and endured his hunger. After eating, the old woman left as she had the day before.

When Naxigaer came back home he thought of the old woman who had no one who cared for her. He made ten big cakes with the half bag of flour that he had left. On the third day the old woman came again. Naxigaer gave her all of the cakes before she even asked for them. This time the old woman, instead of eating, spat on the cakes and then threw them into a deep valley.

Naxigaer was surprised and puzzled about this behavior. Just at this moment, boomm! A loud sound reverberated up from the valley and a flash of light followed in its wake. A while later a small golden turtle fell on the old woman's hand. She said with a smile, "Kind Boy! There will soon be a great disaster occurring here. You are very kind and therefore I am going to save you."

Then she gave him the small golden turtle. "Take it with you. When the turtle's eyes turn red there will be a disaster. The earth will shake and houses will collapse. You will have to leave at once for Malian Gully in the northwest. There is a pool of water in which some lotus flowers are blooming. You will be safe there. But you must remember not to tell anyone, or else you will turn into a huge rock." Quickly the old woman transformed herself into a light wisp of smoke and disappeared.

Naxigaer continued to go to the mountain for wood every day. Nothing happened for a long time. A festival was near. But then, one day, Naxigaer happened to see the golden turtle's eyes turn red. He knew that the disaster was imminent and so he hurriedly packed up his things and left for the northwest. Along his way the words of his mother suddenly came to his mind: "It is one's duty to do good at all times."

"What should I do? If I tell others I will change into a cold rock."

After thinking it over he finally decided to tell people about the disaster. He turned back toward the village. At first people did not believe him and thought he was out of his mind. Naxigaer was worried about that, and he tried his best to persuade them by telling the story from the beginning. He showed them the golden tortoise, and then the people believed him. They followed him to the Lotus Pool.

As soon as they arrived there, boomm! With an explosion resounding from it, the turtle in Naxigaer's hand turned into a golden ray and rushed into the sky. By and by it seemed as though the sky was falling and the ground was sinking. In the course of a single minute the prosperous town was reduced to rubble. When the frightened people came to themselves they began looking for Naxigaer everywhere. But they could not find him. By the Lotus Pool they found instead a big rock that stood as tall as a man.

Afterwards people planted some pine trees around that pool, in memory of Naxigaer. Nowadays by the Lotus Pool, in the Malian Gully, still stands that big menhir as tall as a human being. It is said that this is Naxigaer.

The Wonderful Doctor Ma Ahong

Place: Guilin, Guangxi
Recorder: Bai Keyu (Hui), 1984

Once upon a time, in Guilin, there lived an ahong named Ma.[14] He was known far and wide as a miracle-working doctor. But he had actually never studied medicine, and the idea of being a professional doctor had never occurred to him. One day he happened to see an injured swallow that had been bitten by a rat fluttering about on the ground. Ma Ahong took pity on the bird, bandaged its wound, and then recited sacred scripture on its behalf. The swallow recovered and was deeply grateful. She flew around Ma Ahong's head three times and then left, reluctantly.

The next spring the swallow flew back from fairy island and brought with her for Ma Ahong a fairies' magic book. After he read

---

[14]The Hui people use the word "Ma" as a proper name, and also to refer to Muhammad, the Prophet of Allah. Many other Muslims in Asia and Turkey alter the original name of the Prophet as a gesture of respect (Mahmoud Abu Saud).

this book, Ma Ahong was able to cure all diseases and to save many patients. No matter how complicated the cases were, he could bring about miraculous cures and bring the dying back to life. From that time on his fame as a miracle-working doctor had spread far and wide.

In Guilin lived a businessman whom people called Master Bai, who had an only daughter named Zhuzhu (Pear); she was eighteen years old. She was a talented and good-looking girl. One day Master Bai told his family, unexpectedly, that in three days his daughter would marry the richest man in the city, Master Hai. In return he would receive very generous betrothal gifts from Master Hai.

Everyone was shocked by his words, because people inside and outside the city knew that Master Hai was an old fellow with a pockmarked face and a crooked mouth, hunchbacked and lame in one leg. Besides, he had already gotten two wives. Everyone knew that this marriage did not match at all, but they dared not say so because of Master Hai's wealth and power.

Nevertheless, a servant girl secretly went to tell Zhuzhu and, upon hearing the news, Zhuzhu began crying loudly. Suddenly she laughed through her tears. Then she talked nonsense while dancing for joy. She was mad.

All the family members, seeing that Zhuzhu was out of her mind, became frightened. Even Master Bai, who shortly before had been grinning from ear to ear, showed some sadness on his face. He hurriedly sent a boy to the miracle-working doctor, Ma Ahong.

This time even Ma Ahong had difficulty trying to figure out Zhuzhu's illness. For quite some time he could not even determine the condition of her pulse.

At last Ma Ahong was able to write a prescription with some tonic, such as Chinese *angelica* and a preparation of root of *Rehmannia glutinosa*. Master Bai read the prescription and considered it ineffective. Nevertheless, it seemed better to take some medicine rather than none. He therefore sent someone to the apothecary shop with the prescription.

Using an opportunity of her father's absence, Zhuzhu quickly handed a note to Ma Ahong. The note read: "I am not ill, much less insane. I pretend to be mad so that I do not have to marry Master Hai. Last year, during Mawlid an-Nabi, I went to the women's mosque to pray, and there I made a private engagement with an ahong apprentice named Huangqing.[15] You are the kindest Ahong. Please try to help me marry Huangqing."

Not until Ma Ahong finished reading did he understand it all. He sympathized with her misfortune and promised to help her have her wish come true. When he left Master Bai, Ma Ahong shook his head without saying anything about the patient. He just pretended to be perturbed.

The next day a young doctor came to the door of Master Bai. He said, "It is being spoken all over town that not even Ma Ahong could heal your daughter's illness. Nevertheless, truthfully, I can."

Master Bai looked this young and handsome doctor over, up and down, and concluded that he had doctoral manners. He was simply worrying about his daughter's sickness, and so he did not inquire any more. As the saying goes, in an emergency any doctor may be asked. So, quickly he showed the young doctor to the inner room to see Zhuzhu.

Knowing that another doctor was coming, Zhuzhu was about to pretend mad. Yet, while looking at the young doctor she noticed to her great delight that it was Huangqing of whom she was thinking day and night. How happy she was! She stretched out her hand to the young doctor to have him feel her pulse, and she did not pretend to be mad anymore.

Huangqing gave Zhuzhu some dried chrysanthemum and said, "Miss Bai, only if you take a decoction of medicinal ingredients named "Taopao," and then take a small box of "Chenqin" pills, will you recover completely and soon."[16]

The young doctor, turning to Master Bai, said, "Your daughter's illness has been aroused by nervous stress. She needs some rest and quiet to recover her health. It seems that your house is bustling with too much activity and noise, and with turbid air. This will lead to complete madness, I am afraid. So I suggest that you let her rest in

---

[15]"Mawlid an-Nabi" means "Birthday of the Prophet" (Mahmoud Abu Saud). The "women's mosque" is on Xichen Road, in the city of Guilin. It is exclusively for women.

[16]This is a play on homonyms. "Taopao" is the name of a medicinal herb and also means "escape." "Chenqin" identifies another medicine and also means "to get married."

the women's mosque for a few days." Then he accepted the money which had been wrapped for him in red paper, and left.

Master Bai felt that what the young doctor said was reasonable; besides, he was afraid that he would lose that generous betrothal gift if his daughter's illness got much worse. So he sent his daughter to the women's mosque, right away. In order to prevent anything undesirable happening to her he sent along a young boy to keep an eye on Zhuzhu. Master Bai also sent someone to Ma Ahong for a prescription of herbal medicine that would keep one awake all night; this medicine he gave to the young boy to keep him from falling asleep. Ma Ahong, who had already guessed this trick, wrote his prescription quickly.

Huangqing, seeing that Zhuzhu was being taken out of her house, secretly got a sedan chair ready in accordance with Ma Ahong's suggestion. At night the young boy took his medicine, and moments later he fell into a deep sleep. Huangqing took Zhuzhu away from the women's mosque, and they both went off to a lonely place. Ma Ahong hurriedly recited Quran verses for them, and he prayed: "May Allah bless your life and let it become happier day by day!"

Later, when Master Bai noticed that his daughter had disappeared without a trace, he at once sent his men to look for her everywhere. When he found out that his daughter had eloped with Huangqing, Master Bai was too angry to eat anything for three days.

"She has been kidnapped!" he shouted all the time. But in his mind he quietly suspected that it was a scheme of Ma Ahong.

He was ready to get even with Ma Ahong. But then arrived the news that Ma Ahong was going to reason with him—concerning the fact that his daughter pretended to be mad and was about to destroy his fine reputation. All this was rumored at the time when it was also being said that Master Bai was going to take the matter to court to sue Ma Ahong.

He thought the matter over, and he became afraid that Ma Ahong would make unfounded counter charges that would shift the guilt on him. So he had to eat his bitter fruit.

This is how Ma Ahong helped these people get married.

4

Glimpses of
Paradise and Wealth

The Straw Rope Valley

Place: Yinchuan, Ningxia
Narrator: Ma Wencang (Hui)
Recorder: Wang Zhiping (Hui), 1983

In the mountains to the southeast of the Jingyuan region used to be a valley called Straw Rope Valley. A considerable distance from this valley lived a family of three—an old couple and their son Sheba. The old man and his wife were too old to do anything, so Sheba had to work both inside and outside the house.

One day the old man said to his wife, "Sheba has now grown up. We should not be a drag on him any longer." They talked the matter over and decided to send Sheba away to learn some skills.

The next morning, at the break of dawn, they sent Sheba off. As a boy he had been told that a white-bearded divine person lived at the Western Mountain. He made up his mind to learn from him.

For days Sheba walked and walked. At last he came to the foot of the Western Mountain. He was about to sit down to rest when an old man in rags appeared from the valley, holding a cane in his hand. The old man approached Sheba, held out his hands and begged: "Please give me something to eat!"

Sheba reached into his bag to take out some steamed bread and gave it to the old man. After the old man had eaten it, he asked for more. Sheba had to give to him all the steamed bread that was left in his bag. It was getting dark by then. The old man told Sheba, "My home is not far from here. You can stay there for the night."

Sheba followed the old man into the valley. They walked along the mountain path for a long while, and then they stopped at the entrance of a cave. "Here we are," said the old man. Then he told Sheba to hold on to the other end of his cane, and so he led him into the cave. For some time it was so dark that Sheba could not see anything. He followed in the darkness behind the old man. But suddenly it was light again. Before his eyes lay a village with a mountain and a river. In the fields some farmers were busy working. Everyone they met was friendly and warmhearted.

In that village Sheba settled. He began to work as a blacksmith during the day, and at night the old man taught him how to read and to write.

Time passed quickly. A year was gone before Sheba even noticed. One day he said to the old man, "My mother was in poor health when I left home. I do not know how she is now. I am thinking about going home."

The old man agreed and told him, "When you get home, never tell anyone anything about your life here, or you will regret it." The old man put some clothes, some food, and silver into a bag which he slung over Sheba's shoulder. Then he sent him forth from the cavern.

Sheba looked around and found everything in the same condition as before—the path, the trees, and the grass. Cheerfully he went on his way. He pulled up grasses and twisted them into ropes. As he walked he left the straw ropes to lay along the path as markers, in case he would want to come back some day.

News of Sheba's return spread quickly throughout the village. Soon their small house was crowded with people. Sheba greeted them politely. He even gave some of his silver to them. He had been away for only one year, and yet, he brought back many things and much silver. This attracted attention, and the people asked how he had obtained all this. At first Sheba kept it a secret, no matter who asked. But when his mother asked he had to tell the truth.

Walls had ears. He had hardly finished speaking when the landlord Maliu already knew the secret. Early the next morning Maliu, with several of his men, came to Sheba's house. Putting on a false smile he said, "I was told you have been to a good place and made a fortune. Can you show us the way?" It was too late for Sheba to have regrets, and he reasoned that it would be better to go in the company of all the villagers. Perhaps they all could live a happy life there.

The next morning Sheba walked ahead of the crowd of people, along the path which he had formerly taken. They walked on and on and finally came to the valley. But the straw ropes and the cavern were nowhere to be found. Sheba began to search carefully for the straw ropes he had twisted. Momentarily he saw a bundle of straw swaying in the breeze. He ran to it and saw straw ropes spread all over hill and dale. Sheba picked up some. They were the very straw ropes he had once made. He was puzzled.

Who caused them to multiply? Though Sheba had traversed the length and the breadth of the valley, he could not find the entrance to the cave. Anyway, that valley came to be called "Straw Rope Valley" after that.

In Search of the Golden Sparrow

First published in *Min jian wen xue (Folk Literature)*, Beijing, 1962.
Place: Yunnan
Narrator: Yang Shufang (Hui)
Recorder: Wang Dong (Hui)

Long, long ago there lived to the south of Kunming a Hui family of four people—a mother and her three sons. The name of the oldest son was Sha Yixian, the second Sha Yizhen, and the youngest Sha Yide. All three were shoemakers. Although they worked hard, they neither had enough food to eat nor enough clothes to wear.

One year it kept raining for longer than a month. Not a single customer came to the three brothers to have shoes made to order. The whole family went hungry for a day, and that night they all had the same dream.

Early next morning Sha Yixian said, "I had a strange dream last night. I saw in my dream a golden sparrow fly over us here. Its body gave off dazzling golden rays. Whatever was touched by its rays became brand new. When its golden rays shone upon our house, it changed instantly. The golden rays touched Mother and she appeared young again. As soon as the golden rays entered our room, all tables, chairs, and all our worn-out clothes became new again. Even the loquat tree in the courtyard began to bear yellow loquat fruits. A lot of people in new clothes were greeting us, smiling, as they passed our house. The three of us were very busy making shoes. No matter how hard we worked, we could not provide all our customers with enough shoes. We were all smiling from ear to ear. That is where my dream ended."

Their mother listened with her eyes wide open. Just then Sha Yizhen cut in, "Ha, ha! I had a dream exactly like yours." Sha Yide continued, "Mother, how strange it is! I remember very well that I have seen the golden sparrow, too. It even flapped its wings while flying over the roof of our house."

The mother blinked with her eyes and said, "O my Allah! I also had such a dream. We were all wearing new clothes. The rice vat was full. In the kitchen was a stack of firewood and plenty of cooking oil and salt. All the bowls were fine porcelain, and when I went to fetch water, the spring water flowed into my bucket by itself. All three of you had virtuous wives."

"Aha, inasmuch as all of us have dreamt of the golden sparrow, it will surely come," said Sha Yizhen.

Their mother continued, "The dream is a good omen. The golden sparrow will surely come. Its golden rays will make everything new."

"Mother, we should not wait for the golden sparrow to fly here. Why not go out and look for it?" suggested the youngest son. But Sha Yizhen did not agree. He said, "Who knows how far we would have to walk before we could find the golden sparrow. Even if we were to wear out all our shoes, we cannot tell for certain that we would find it. Because the golden sparrow has been here once, I am sure it will come again. Let us wait for its arrival."

Sha Yixian insisted on going. He said, "Oh how happy we will be if the golden sparrow can be found!"

Finally the mother said, "It is better for you to go and to look for the golden sparrow than to starve to death. If the oldest fails to find the golden sparrow the second brother will go; and then the youngest. Inasmuch as it exists you will eventually find it."

Her oldest son Yixian volunteered, "Since there is no work to do, let me go."

His mother was very glad. She borrowed some rice and flour from her nextdoor neighbor and made some porridge for her oldest son to eat. Then she baked a few cakes for him to eat along the way. Sha Yixian took with him a knife and a hammer and said goodbye to his mother. He then started walking in the direction of the golden sparrow.

Sha Yixian walked and walked. By the end of the seventh week he came to a three-road junction and found an old woman lying there. He went up to her and asked, "Old Grandma, will you tell me which road to take if I want to find the golden sparrow?"

The old woman opened her left eye and answered, "The road on the right leads to the mountain of treasures. The road on the left leads to the palace granary. Take the road in the middle if you want to find the little golden sparrow."

Sha Yixian thanked the old woman. He was about to go when he noticed that she was wearing a pair of old shoes, the threads of which had all come loose. She stretched and sat up. Sha Yixian sat by her and said, "Grandma, let me mend these shoes for you before I go."

The old woman nodded and handed her shoes to Sha Yixian. After he had finished mending he rose up to go. Just then the old woman opened both her eyes, looked at him and shook her head, "You better not go. There are mountains after mountains along that middle road. All over these mountains you will see boas twining around trees, and hear tigers and wolves snarling everywhere."

Sha Yixian shook his head and said with a smile, "I will do as my mother has told me. I am determined to cross rivers and to climb the mountains if I encounter any."

"But you must remember to leave the tigers and boas alone if you meet them. Do not answer if you hear someone call your name. Never turn around if the mountains shake and the earth rumbles."

Sha Yixian thanked the old woman again, and he went along the road in the middle.

After another seven weeks he came to the foot of a huge mountain. The mountain was so high and the forest so thick that he could not see to the top. Sha Yixian began to climb the mountain. A week passed. He was only halfway up the mountain when, suddenly, he heard the voice of a woman calling from behind, "Sha Yixian! Sha Yixian!"

Not having forgotten the old woman's warnings, Sha Yixian kept silent. The woman's voice faded away. Sha Yixian continued climbing. The mountain was covered with a thick forest. There were thorns growing everywhere. He climbed up a hundred steps, a thousand steps, and more. His clothes got caught on the briars and his feet were pricked. He continued to climb despite the sharp pain. Sha Yixian's heart began to beat faster when he saw venomous serpents sticking forth their heads from the trees, and when he heard tigers growl ahead of him. A large boa appeared before him with eyes like a pair of lanterns. Its body was as thick as a bucket. The boa swooped down on him with its mouth wide open. Sha Yixian's legs felt like jelly. Just at that moment he heard a bang from behind, which made the mountain shake. Sha Yixian was so frightened that he forgot the old woman's bidding and turned around to have a look. The moment he did so he felt dizzy, fell unconscious, and was transformed into a rock.

Ever since Sha Yixian had left home, his mother had been looking forward to his return, day and night. One week, two weeks, twenty weeks had passed, but he still did not come back. His mother borrowed some rice and flour from another neighbor and made some porridge for her second son, Sha Yizhen, to eat; then she prepared several cakes for him to eat along the way. She told him, "Go, find the golden sparrow, together with your older brother!" Carrying all the cakes and shoes with him, Sha Yizhen said goodbye to his mother and set out in the direction of the golden sparrow.

"May Allah bless you! Let us wait and hear the good news!" said his mother at the door.

Sha Yizhen, too, walked for seven weeks before he reached the junction of the three roads. Seeing an old woman sleeping there, he thought to himself, "This old woman really knows how to enjoy herself. She has gone to sleep in the open air."

Sha Yizhen went up to her to ask, "Old Grandma, which road is the shortest to find the golden sparrow?"

Opening her left eye, the old woman answered in a whisper. "I have gone without food for twenty weeks, and my voice is hoarse." Sha Yizhen took out a cake from his bag and gave half of it to her, "Please have a little cake, Grandma!"

The old woman stretched and ate up the cake, and she told him, "The road on the right leads to the mountain of treasures. The one on the left leads to the palace granary. Take the one in the middle if you want to find the little golden sparrow." Then she opened her right eye and looked at Sha Yizhen, saying, "Well, you better not go. Along the middle road there are mountains after mountains. You will find boas twining around the trees and hear tigers and wolves roar everywhere."

Sha Yizhen replied with a frown, "I have no alternative but to obey my mother's words. I must go and look for the golden sparrow and my older brother."

"All right! Do remember not to provoke the tigers and the boas when you come across them. Do not answer if you hear someone call your name. Never turn around even if the mountain shakes and the earth rumbles."

After thanking the old woman, Sha Yizhen went on his way. By the end of another seven weeks he arrived at the foot of a huge mountain. The mountain was so high, and the forest so thick, that he could not see to the top. After half a week's climbing he could hardly climb another step. So he slept in a tree for half a week. The next week he continued to climb. Then came the tiger. Sha Yizhen was so scared that he dared not raise his eyes. By noon he arrived under a tall tree and was about to climb up to sleep when he heard a woman's voice calling, "Sha Yizhen! Sha Yizhen!" His curiosity was aroused. He forgot all about the old woman's warnings. "Who is she? Maybe she is also looking for the golden sparrow," Sha Yizhen thought.

As the voice came nearer and nearer, he could not help answering, "I am here!" A beautiful woman appeared before him the moment he answered. Sha Yizhen had never seen such a beautiful woman in all his life. Her dazzling beauty blurred his eyes. The woman said to him with a charming smile, "What good is there about sleeping in a tree? Why not come to my place to have a rest?" With these words she came to him to take his hand.

Sha Yizhen fell into a daze because he did not know whether he should go along or not. He simply followed her, unconsciously. When they came to the second tall tree he actually saw a house, a dazzling new house. By the door there was a leather armchair. "Take a seat! Take a seat, please!" the woman kept on saying. Sha Yizhen sat down in great confusion. As soon as his hips touched the chair he was transformed into rock.

After Sha Yizhen had left home, his mother had waited anxiously for his return. One week, two weeks, twenty weeks had passed and he had not come back.

One day Sha Yide, the youngest brother, told his mother, "It is already twenty weeks since Yizhen left. Please let me go."

"You are too young to go. Besides, I will be left alone if you are gone," his mother disagreed. "Perhaps your brothers will come back at any moment."

The mother kept on talking about her two sons. "Maybe they will come back tomorrow with the golden sparrow. Tomorrow!"

The mother waited for another twenty weeks, and they still did not show up. She had to change her mind, and she said, "Forty weeks have passed, and neither of your older brothers has returned. Now you will have to go, my little son. We cannot live a happy life without the golden sparrow." She borrowed a bowl of flour, from a relative, which was just enough to make three cakes. Sha Yide started off with the three cakes and with his mother's blessing.

Sha Yide went in the direction of the golden sparrow. He reached the three-road junction after seven weeks of walking. Seeing an old woman lying there, he went up to her and greeted her politely. Then he asked, "Old Grandma, I am on my way to look for the golden sparrow. Would you please tell me which road to take?"

The old woman sat up with a yawn. Opening her left eye she told Sha Yide, "The road on the right leads to the mountain of treasures. The one on the left leads to the palace granary. Take the road in the middle if you want to find the little golden sparrow."

The old woman gave another yawn and asked, "How long have I been sleeping? Why do I feel so hungry?" Her stomach began to rumble. Sha Yide quickly took out the only two cakes he had left and gave them to her. "Old Grandma, please have some cakes."

Without any words of courtesy the old woman took the cakes and ate them up, all at once.

"Well, there are mountains after mountains along the middle road. You will see boas twining around trees and hear tigers and wolves howling everywhere. Without a treasure to protect you, it will be impossible for you to return home from a search for the golden sparrow."

Sha Yide replied at once, "Do you not think my mother's blessings are the best thing to protect me from any kind of danger?"

"Then also take my advice with you. Leave the tigers and poisonous serpents alone if you encounter them. Do not answer if you hear someone calling your name. Never turn around even if the mountain shakes and the earth rumbles."

Sha Yide thanked the old woman and set out along the middle road. The first week he saw a bee in the water. He thought to himself, "Bees should make honey." He immediately rescued the bee from drowning. Only when he saw it fly away did he continue his journey. The third day he found a green kingfisher entangled in a net. "A green kingfisher should fly freely." He walked up and set the bird free.

By the seventh week he came to the foot of a huge mountain. The mountain was so high that he could not see to the top. The forest was so thick that even sunlight could not penetrate. Thorns were growing all over the ground. He began to climb the mountain. When he was only ten steps up, his coat was torn by thorns. As he climbed onward, his face, hands, and feet were scratched. He bore in mind his mother's words and continued climbing in spite of the pain. A snake fell from a tree into his collar, making his neck feel ice cold. He threw the snake aside and went his way. A huge boa passed him, with its eyes and mouth wide open. Tigers were roaring and wolves were howling. Sha Yide's heart began beating faster with fear. "I will overcome all kinds of difficulties so long as I remember my mother's blessings and the old woman's advice."

As soon as he had summoned up his courage, the tigers and the boas went away and left him alone.

He continued to climb. Suddenly he heard someone calling from behind, "Sha Yide! Sha Yide!" Sha Yide told himself, "Never forget mother's blessings and the old woman's advice." He did not answer, and the voice gradually faded away. The following week Sha Yide was still climbing when he heard a voice calling him from the roadside, "Sha Yide, Sha Yide! It is me! Sha Yide!" It sounded just like his brother's voice. Sha Yide said to himself, "Was it really my brother who called me?" He looked but saw no one except a big rock by the road. "Sha Yide! It is me!"

"It is really my brother?"

"I must keep in mind my mother's words and the old woman's advice. In any case, I must not answer," decided Sha Yide. He kept on climbing with all his might. That voice also died away.

Sha Yide climbed one mountain after another. And as he climbed onward he heard a deafening noise from behind as if the sky had fallen down. The mountain began to shake and the earth was atremble. Sha Yide really wanted to turn around to see what was happening.

But the warning of the old woman rang in his ears; and so he climbed ahead, no matter what happened.

After a little while the noise died down. The mountains before him began to lower themselves, one by one. The leaves of the trees waved and made way for Sha Yide. The mountains then were nowhere to be seen anymore. Before him was a garden so bright that Sha Yide could hardly open his eyes. He blinked with his eyes and looked. "Ah, the little golden sparrow!" It was shining all over, just as in the dream.

Sha Yide stared at that garden for a few minutes and then began running toward it. Quite unexpectedly he collided with something solid, and he fell down. It was a long while before he could rise to his feet again. Before him rose a crystal wall. How high was it? Even if Sha Yide jumped he could not reach its top. Inside the garden he saw a bird fly about. It had to change direction whenever it flew toward the wall.

There had to be an entrance. Where was it? Sha Yide looked for the entrance along the wall. Several hours passed and he found himself standing again at the same place where he had started. So, it was a circular wall!

Inasmuch as there was no way to get in, what should be done? He walked round and round the wall but could not come up with a solution. He became anxious. The scratches all over his body began to ache again. He felt as if he had pins and needles in his legs. And there, by the crystal wall, Sha Yide collapsed.

"Little Brother, come quickly to save me!" his oldest brother shouted, lying on the ground.

"Little Brother, come and help me!" his second brother cried, his body soaked in blood.

"Without the golden sparrow we cannot live a happy life," his mother appeared with a worried look on her face.

Sha Yide tried to open his eyes and struggled to his feet. Attentively he looked at the golden sparrow and the garden. What a beautiful garden! There were flowers of various colors and shapes, big and small, red and yellow. The little golden sparrow was skipping about in the apple tree that was laden with many golden apples. Sha Yide gave a sigh. He could see everything but reach nothing. To him all these things were only like flowers in a mirror.

Sha Yide walked around the garden, again and again. He touched here and there, without finding an entrance. The wall was transparent. He touched it with his hands. It was ice cold and smooth with neither an opening nor a ridge. Within the wall the golden sparrow was skipping about, leisurely. The flowers looked as fresh as ever. Birds were flying and bees were busy making honey.

Sha Yide observed for two days. On the second day he caught sight of a bee coming out. "Well, how strange it is!" He stopped at the place where the bee had come out and watched silently. After a while he saw the bee fly in. He jumped to his feet and carefully touched the wall with his hand. Ah, a hole! It was as big as a keyhole. How he wished he could become a bee!

Or, if only he could find the key! While he was still thinking, he heard the flapping wings of a bird. A little green kingfisher flew up and sat on his hand, with a key in its beak. He quickly took the key and inserted it into the hole. The crystal wall began to move. It opened with a click when he pushed. A soft scent greeted him. It was so sweet that no-one before him had ever smelled anything like it. After having drawn a deep breath, Sha Yide felt very refreshed. He took another breath and felt happy and relaxed. After his third breath he felt as if he had a new brain. His body became light as a feather. His clothes became new and his wounds healed the moment the golden rays shone upon him. The little green king-fisher flew away with the key.

"Thank you very much, little kingfisher!" And then Sha Yide ran quickly towards the golden sparrow.

The golden sparrow would not hide from a person who was earnest and sincere in looking for it. Sha Yide went over to the golden sparrow and implored: "Golden Sparrow! Golden Sparrow! Please save my mother and my brothers! Save the whole city, please!" The golden sparrow nodded. It flew over his right shoulder out of the garden.

Sha Yide caught up with the golden sparrow and kept pace with it. All the flowers and apples in the garden flew outward and followed the golden sparrow's path of flight. Everything along the way changed when its golden rays shone on them brightly. The high mountains were lowered. The huge boas and the poisonous snakes were turned to earth and ashes. The tigers and wolves changed into rocks, and thorns into grass. When the golden rays touched some rocks, the two older brothers of Sha Yide came alive again. With the golden rays shining on the fields, crops yielded good harvests. Bathed in the golden rays, old people became young again, and young people became wiser.

Sha Yide got home soon after the golden sparrow arrived. His mother persuaded it to stay, and so it stayed with them. Two weeks later his two older brothers also returned.

From that time on Sha Yide's family, and all the other people, lived a happy life.

The Serpent Grandfather's Treasure Chest

Place: Mi Quan county, Xinjiang
Narrator: Yang Falin (Hui)
Recorder: Hai Mingyi (Hui), 1984

In ancient times there lived a poor young woodcutter whose name was Wan Gars. Above him he did not have parents and beneath him neither wife nor children. Life was very difficult for him.

Wan Gars was an honest and kindhearted fellow. He did not have the heart to even kill as much as a single bird. Once, while he was on his way to the mountain to cut wood, he saw a hunter who was about to kill a little snake. He stopped the hunter and bought the little wounded snake and kept it at home.

One day Wan Gars looked out of his house and saw a group of boys playing with a frog. They attached a firecracker to the frog. The boys were about to make it blow up when Wan Gars arrived. He saved the frog by giving the boys something to eat. Just as he was going home with the frog he saw a vicious dog bite a cat. He drove the vicious dog away and saved the cat. Not long after that Wan Gars saved a miserable little dog.

By now Wan Gars had saved four little animals. He fed them and treated their wounds. When they got well again the frog, the cat, and the dog ventured out again to fend for themselves. Only the snake still remained at home.

One day Wan Gars came back after a day's work. The snake greeted him with its neck stretched and its mouth wide open as if it intended to devour him. Wan Gars got very angry. He scolded, "What an ungrateful fellow you are! I have saved you and brought you up, now you are trying to eat me. You are really a heartless thing."

Surprisingly the snake began to speak like a man: "How can I bite you after all you have done for me? I just wanted to speak to you. Now it is time for me to repay your kindness. Please come with me to my grandfather's place. When you see him, do not take any-thing except the small box which hangs at the wall. When you go with me you must close your eyes. Do not open them, no matter what you hear. You cannot open your eyes unless I ask you to."

So Wan Gars and the snake started out together. Along the way he was unaware whether they were flying or floating. He could only hear the wind whistling past his ears. Before long he found himself standing again on solid ground. The snake told him to open his eyes. He opened them only to see a boundless forest surrounding them. In front of them was a very large cave with all kinds of snakes guarding the entrance. As Wan Gars was led by the little snake into the cave, all the snakes dodged swiftly to one side and stood erect as if to welcome them. Wan Gars followed the little snake in great terror. At the mouth of the cave several huge snakes stared at Wan Gars, with their forked tongues sticking out and making terrible hissing sounds. Wan Gars was too frightened to walk on.

The little snake told him: "My grandfather has been living here for about three thousand years. Just wait a moment! I will make them all become humanlike, otherwise you will be too frightened."

Then the little snake went into the cave. Soon the huge snakes were all turned into armor-clad warriors. With swords in their hands they lined up along both sides along the mouth of the cave, mighty and grandiloquent. Then the little snake came out to show Wan Gars in. The interior of the cave was resplendent and magnificent. They went onward to the armchair, at the end of the cave, in which a white-bearded old man was sitting. He was full of vigor and his face glowed with health.

After Wan Gars had greeted the old man he looked around. There was an exquisite small chest hanging above the armchair. Under it stood an armed general with a pair of swords, one in each hand. Apparently his task was to guard this little chest. Wan Gars was looking at the box when the old man spoke. "Kindhearted young man, you have saved my grandson's life, so I want to express my heartfelt thanks to you. We have here everything. You may take whatever you like. Tell me what you would like to have."

Wan Gars nodded to the little snake and then spoke in earnest to the old man: "I will ask for nothing except that small chest hanging on the wall."

His request put the old man in an awkward position. He turned to look at the little snake. The little snake said timidly, "It is I who told him what to ask for. He is the man who saved my life. You said you would give him whatever he wanted. You must live up to your promise."

The old man hesitated for a while, then he told Wan Gars, "All right. Because I have promised, I will have to give it to you. But I must tell you that this chest is the most precious treasure I have. I obtained it by way of practicing Daoism for three thousand years. In the box is a piece of cloth and a little hammer. Spread the cloth and strike the box three times with the hammer. You will get whatever you want. The chest will grant whatever is requested."

Wan Gars thanked the old man and took the box. The little snake showed him out of the cave. At the edge of the forest the small snake said to Wan Gars, "We have to say goodbye to each other now. Please look after yourself and take good care of the chest."

Wan Gars gazed at the little snake with gratitude. He could hardly tear himself from it. "I wish you a long life like your grandfather." Then he went away.

When Wan Gars first got that treasure box he asked for nothing but food and clothes.

He came to a river in the Gobi Desert and saw a city on the opposite bank. He wanted to cross the river to have a look, but there was no boat on the river.

An idea occurred to him, "I ought to have a city, too. I will be the king myself so that I will never have to wander about, from now on."

He opened the little chest, spread out the piece of cloth, and struck with the hammer three times while speaking, "I want a golden city. I want to be its king."

He had no sooner finished speaking than a golden city appeared in the desolate and uninhabited Gobi. It was a grandiose city that shone brightly. People were busy coming and going. There were a lot of shops along both sides of the street. It was in fact a prosperous city. Wan Gars found himself living in the palace, and he had become king of this land.

The king in the city opposite the river was surprised and afraid to witness the sudden appearance of a golden city. What would he do if one day this powerful kingdom were to annex his realm? The king quickly called together all his civil and military officials for deliberation. They decided to establish friendly relations with this state first and try to find out how it had come into being. The king himself, escorted by some of his important ministers, went to pay a visit and to present generous gifts.

Wan Gars received the king personally, one on one. They had a conversation concerning matters on both sides. When the king found Wan Gars to be still single, he said cunningly, "In order to express our friendship, I would like my daughter to be your wife. What do you think of it?" Being a former poor woodcutter, Wan Gars was very glad to take the princess as his wife.

Wan Gars lived with his wife for several years without revealing a single word about his own past. Then, one day, his wife went to visit her parents. Her father, the king, asked her, "You have been living with your husband for several years. Do you know what kind of person he is and how he got that golden city?"

The daughter answered, "He is an ordinary man. But I know nothing about how that golden city came into being."

The king told her, "After you return, try to find out this secret. If the secret is a magic object, bring it here."

Another four years passed. Wan Gars and his wife became more attached to one another. He hid nothing from his wife except his past and the origin of his city.

One night they were having a good time when his wife began to ask him about the secret of the golden city. Wan Gars remained silent. Not having obtained an answer, his wife began to weep and to complain that still, after having been married for such a long time, Wan Gars treated her like an outsider. So, seeing his wife weeping, Wan Gars could no longer hold back his secret. He took the precious chest from under the pillow and told her everything without holding anything back.

His wife was very pleased to know the secret. She pretended to be more gentle toward Wan Gars. Yet, at heart, she was thinking how she could take the miracle-working chest to her father. One day, when Wan Gars was out on business, his wife made use of her chance to steal the box. She took it to her parents, and she told the secret to her father who, immediately, did as she had explained. The prosperous gold city disappeared at once, and Wan Gars became again the poor woodcutter he had been.

When Wan Gars was wandering again in the desolate Gobi, the frog, the dog, and the cat appeared to him, unexpectedly. The three said in one voice, "We know you have met great misfortune. That is why we have come to help you. Please tell us what has happened to you." Wan Gars told them all about the miracle-working chest, everything from the very beginning.

The cat, upon hearing this story, said to Wan Gars, "Do not worry. I will find and return the box to you. Since I cannot swim I will have to ask Brother Dog to help me cross the river."

The dog was pleased to be able to do something for Wan Gars, their master. As they were ready to go they sneered at the frog, "You are good for nothing, just stay where you are." The cat and the dog set out for the city across the river.

After the king had gotten the miracle-working chest he was too pleased to know what to do with it. Eager to show it off, he put the chest on a table in the middle of the hall and asked all his officials, relatives, and friends to come and to feast their eyes on it.

The cat had been scouting for a few days. Yet it had not gotten a chance to lay its paws on the box. When it heard the news about the king's exhibit, the cat said to the dog, "Now is the time to act. Let us rush into the hall. You just pretend to be chasing me. When we get to the table I will upset the candlestick, and then, in the dark, I will grab the little chest with my mouth."

Having made their plans they arrived at the gate, and the dog barked. They ran into the hall as speedily as an arrow. The cat jumped onto the table and upset the candlestick.

While the people had not yet recovered from their shock, the cat took the box into its mouth and escaped on the dog's back. They ran and ran until they came to the river's edge. Since nobody came running after them they stopped for a rest.

Then the dog told the cat, "The box is much bigger than your mouth. I am afraid you will drop it into the river. Let me hold it in my mouth."

The cat answered: "You have to exert yourself to swim. The box may drop when you take a breath."

"That is all right. I can manage," the dog insisted, and the cat had to agree.

When they were halfway across the river the dog could not resist barking from joy. The box dropped into the river. Neither of them could dredge it up. So they had to go back and tell their master. Wan Gars looked at the river with grave concern. He could not do anything either.

Just then the frog began to speak: "Do not worry. Just watch how I can get it up." He dove into the water and after a while reappeared with the precious little box.

Wan Gars regained the chest. His golden city came back and he was king again.

The king opposite the river became afraid after he had lost the box. He was overcome with regret. He came to Wan Gars' palace with his daughter to admit his guilt. Seeing that they were sincere about it, Wan Gars gave no thought to things in the past, and the people of both countries have been in friendly contact with each other ever since.

In order to express his appreciation to the animals, King Wan Gars issued an order that nobody was permitted to inflict harm on animals. If they did, he or she would be punished as murderers.

About Mibo Mountain

First published in *Hui zu min jian wen xue (Hui Folk Stories)*, Xinjiang Peoples Press, 1984.
Place: Tongxin area, Ningxia
Narrator: Wang Yi (Hui)
Recorders: Zhang Jin and Wang Zhengwei (Hui)

Long ago it happened that the lavishly green Mibo Mountain turned into a bald monk's head, overnight. At the time there lived about one hundred households in the village at the foot of this mountain. Exposed to the hot sun and to fierce winds the crops dropped their tender leaves and were reduced to empty stalks.

From morning until evening, incessantly, one could hear Muslims pray and children sadly crying. Seeing the villagers suffer so much, two larks flew circles above the mountain for nine days and nights. They were unwilling to leave that scene.

In the village lived a little girl named Suo Yaner. Her father lay bedridden and her mother was blind. Life was very difficult for them. One day Suo Yaner, with a basket and a bag, set out for Mibo Mountain to gather edible wild herbs, begging along her way. Halfway up the mountain she looked up and saw that its top was too high to reach. When she looked down she saw a mountain stream running below. Suo Yaner felt dizzy. She was so tired and hungry that she could not move another step. So she dozed off on a hot slab of stone.

She had a dream. A white-bearded ahong, wearing a six-petals white cap and a loose black robe, was watering Mibo Mountain with a Tang copper kettle. The old man, holding a bowl of glutinous millet in his right hand, called her to come near. Suo Yaner woke up, suddenly, and when she looked around she saw nobody. Not satisfied with that observation she climbed slopes and valleys and shouted until she was hoarse, but the white-bearded ahong was nowhere to be found. Greatly disappointed Suo Yaner walked home with her bag.

All of a sudden the sight of a waterfall caught her eye. She focused more closely and saw a stream of shining millet pouring swiftly from an opening in the cliff, right above her head. She looked back and found, to her surprise and amazement, that Mibo Mountain had restored its green appearance and had dew drops on its grasses. Overjoyed, as if in paradise, Suo Yaner threw herself upon the millet heap and filled her bag. Then, with her bag of millet she ran back home like a gust of wind.

All the people of the village came to enjoy this peculiar scene. They surrounded Suo Yaner and took time to make detailed inquiries. She told them about her mysterious experience in detail. All of them were happy to the point where they smiled from ear to ear. People in the neighborhood, and even those living dozens of miles away, went to Mibo Mountain with sacks to carry millet.

Strange it seemed. The millet which poured forth was only enough to feed the people for a single day. A mason, seeing that the opening was too narrow and that therefore the millet flowed rather slowly, widened it with a chisel and a hammer. As more and more millet began to come forth from the opening, the lives of the people got easier and better.

However, the good life lasted only a few years. In the village lived a lazy young woman. While carrying home the millet, she would carelessly scatter grains all along the mountain path. Upon reaching home she would cook food and share it with her chickens and dogs. One day her uncle came for a visit. As she was preparing meals for him she boasted, "Thanks to Allah, we still have an endless supply of grain from Mibo Mountain, for generations to come!"

Just then her little son relieved his bowels on the brick bed. Her uncle right away went outside to look for something to clean him with. When he came back, he saw the young woman clean the boy's bottom with a piece of dough. He shouted with fear, O my Allah! How can you clean the boy with dough? This will bring disaster!"

"My good Uncle, do not worry! If you want grain, the only sweat will be carrying it home."

Her uncle was very angry. Without spending the night he undertook his homeward journey.

The next morning the young woman, with some villagers, went again up the mountain to fetch grain. Halfway at their goal they were met with a gust of whirlwind. The mountain began trembling. One could not see what was ahead even within a distance of three steps.

It was a long while before the wind ceased. The sun came out again, burning hot. By the time the people reached their destination, they were sweating all over. All were dumbfounded. Not a single kernel was dropping from the opening! What kept pouring forth from it were, instead, threatening sounds of thunder, as if that cliff opening was intent on devouring the people.

Mibo Mountain has ceased pouring forth grain ever since.

The Water Pearl

An ancient story from the Tang dynasty (684 C.E.). Recorded in the *Tai pin guang ji*, by Niu Su, who lived during the Song dynasty.

The Anguo temple used to be the residence of Emperor Ruizong (Li Dan) when he was the prime minister. When Li Dan ascended to the throne the palace was made into a temple at which Buddhist rites were performed. The emperor donated a miracle-working pearl to be kept in the temple. He told the monks that the pearl was worth approximately one hundred million *liang* of gold. But the monks did not think much of it. They put it away in a cabinet.

In the tenth year of Kaiyuan, the monks of the Anguo temple chanted the name of the Buddha and gave alms to the poor.[1] They opened the cabinet to examine the precious pearl. When they noticed a paper-strip seal with some words on it—"This pearl is worth one hundred million"—the monks began to think about selling it. When they removed the seal they found a red pearl looking just like any other piece of stone. But at night it radiated a light as bright as several candles.

All the monks in the temple said, "This is only a piece of ordinary stone. How can it be worth so much gold? Let us try to sell it."

So they sent one of the monks to have the pearl appraised and to monitor the market. The monk lingered at the market for several months. Occasionally some rich people would come to make inquiries about its price. When they saw the pearl they said, "It is just a piece of stone, just like rubble. Why are you asking such a high price?" They went away with sneers.

Ten days later another man came. When he noticed that this was a fabled luminous pearl he wanted to buy it. The monk asked for several thousand *liang* of gold. But the man thought it was too expensive.

A month later a Hu—a western tribesman—came to the temple. He asked to have a look at the pearl. When it was shown to him the

---

[1] "Kaiyuan" is the title of the Emperor Xuanzong's reign (731–741 C.E.), during the Tang dynasty.

man became very excited. He even put it on his hat as if he were to carry it on his head. The Hu was an aristocrat who sent his interpreter to ask, "What price are you asking?"

"One hundred million *liang* of gold." The Hu fondled the pearl admiringly, for a long while. At last he left reluctantly.

The next day the Hu came again. He asked his interpreter to tell the monk, "The pearl is certainly worth one hundred million. But because we have been away from home for quite a long time, there are only forty million *liang* of gold left. Would you sell the pearl for forty million?" The monk was very satisfied with the price, so he at once showed the Hu to the head monk. The head monk readily agreed to sell. So the Hu came the next day and bought the pearl for forty million *liang* of gold. He said to the monk, "I am sorry to pay you so much less. It is really not expensive."

The monk asked the Hu: "Where are you from? And may I ask what this pearl will be for?"

The Hu answered, "I am from Dashi.[2] During the early years of the reign of Emperor Li Shimin, the pearl was paid as a tribute to the imperial court so that Dashi might have friendly relations with China. Since then the Dashi people missed it very much. It was announced that anyone who came into possession of the pearl would be promoted to the post of prime minister. We have searched for it for more than seventy years. I am very fortunate, indeed, to have found it.

"This is a water pearl. When after a long march the soldiers stop to have a rest, and when then they dig a shallow hole, two feet deep, and bury the pearl in it, water will come bubbling up immediately. It is enough for thousands of men to drink. So our army seldom ran out of water while it was marching. After the pearl was lost, the troops continuously suffered from thirst."

The monk did not believe what the Hu had said. So the latter had a hole dug in which he buried the pearl. Spring water soon gushed forth, clean and cool. After the monk had tasted some of the water he recognized the pearl's wonder-working powers.

The Hu picked up the pearl and went on his way.

---

[2]"Dashi" is a transliteration of the Persian "Tazi," the name of an Arab tribe. Since the Tang dynasty the Arabian empire has been called "Dashi" in China.

Water Treasure

Source: Chen Hong-mou, *Yuwen zhishi.*
Time: The Ming Dynasty

During the years of Hongzhi a Hui man passed through the province of Shanxi on his way to pay tribute to the imperial court.[3] One day he came to the foot of a mountain and saw many local people rushing to draw water from a pond. The Hui paced up and down. Then he told his companion, "I would like to buy this spring. Please go and talk it over with the local people."

The companion went to tell them what the Hui intended to do, and one of the men said, "What a ridiculous idea! What is he buying the water for? And how can he take it with him?"

The Hui said, "That is my business. Only tell me the price you are asking."

The man said, casually, "You have to pay a thousand *liang* of gold for it."

"All right," the Hui agreed and handed a thousand *liang* of gold to the man.

Then the man said, "I am only joking with you. How is it possible to sell the spring to you?"

The Hui got very angry and was going to hit the man. The man was afraid and went to the district court to complain against the Hui. The district magistrate further cheated the Hui by saying, "It is worth three thousand *liang* of gold."

The Hui readily added two thousand *liang*. But then the magistrate changed his mind and asked for five thousand *liang* of gold. The Hui added another two thousand *liang*. This time the district magistrate also became afraid. He reported this case to the provincial judge.

The judge told the Hui, "You did it just for fun."

The Hui was beside himself with anger. Indignantly he said, "How can you say I am buying the spring just for fun? Your district

---

[3]"Hongzhi" is the name of Emperor Xiaozong's reign (1488–1505), during the Ming dynasty.

official has promised to sell it to me. That is why I have stayed here for several days. I even used items of the tribute to make up for the shortage of gold. If you still refuse to sell it to me, I will fight it out." Angrily he drew his sword, and the judge was forced to agree.

The Hui took a hoe and proceeded to dig along the spring. He dug a hole deep into the mountain and found the water source. It was a rock from which the water flowed into the pond.

The Hui had it taken out and was about to leave with it when the judge said, "Since you have bought it, I will not break the agreement. May I ask what this rock is?"

The Hui answered, "Do you know how many kinds of magic treasure there are in the world?"

No one knew it. So the Hui proceeded to tell them: "If you possess pearls and jewels, these are false treasures. There are only two real treasures in the world: water and fire. People cannot live without these two. The fire treasure is comparatively easy to get, whereas the water treasure is much harder to obtain. This rock is a water treasure. When you drain the pond it will become full again. The water treasure can provide water for thousands and thousands of people. The army, the cities, and the capital city will not have to worry about water when they have this treasure. The water source will never dry up."

With these words the Hui happily went on his way.

The Wind-quieting Needle

First published in *Min jian yue kan (Folk Literature Monthly)*, 1932.
Place: Shao Xin county, Zhejiang
Recorders: Ling Rong-fu and Ding Men-kui (Hui)

One day a Hui saw a pestle in a mortar. He asked the owner to sell the pestle to him.

The owner knew that this was the Hui who went about collecting treasure objects. Inasmuch as this pestle had caught the Hui's fancy, this had to be a precious object. So the owner asked for a very high price. In the end the Hui bought it for ten thousand taels of silver.

"What do you want this pestle for?" the seller inquired cautiously.

"It is a very useful thing," the Hui replied. "To sail the sea in stormy weather is a dangerous undertaking. The boat may be capsized by mighty waves. But there will be no danger as long as we have this treasure. The wind will subside and the waves will calm down as soon as we put this piece of treasure on a boat. Its name is Wind-quieting Needle."

The Wind-quieting Pearl

First published in *Min jian yue kan (Folk Literature Monthly)*, 1932.
Place: Shao Xin county, Zhejiang
Recorders: Ling Rong-fu and Ding Men-kui (Hui)

One day a Hui passed by the Dashan Temple. In front of the temple he saw a shop. In the shop sat a pot of green onions. The Hui asked the owner of the shop to sell him the pot of onions for one hundred *liang* of gold. The shop owner was willing to sell. To him it seemed extraordinary to obtain one hundred *liang* of gold for his green onions.

The Hui was not in the habit of carrying money with him when he went about. He therefore told the shop owner, "I will come for it tomorrow." After the Hui left, the shop owner took the pot of green onions into the shop for fear that it might get stolen.

The next day the Hui came with the gold. He asked for the pot of green onions. The owner brought it out. When the Hui saw it he said he would not want it anymore, because the black spider, in the pot, had run away into the black dragon tablet in the shop next door.

The Hui went to the other shop to buy the black dragon tablet. The owner regarded it as a rare commodity. He would not sell it unless the Hui would give him five hundred *liang* of gold. The gold which the Hui had brought with him was far from enough. He had to say, "All right. I will come again tomorrow."

The shop owner, seeing the black dragon board so dirty, washed it clean and waited for the Hui to come.

The Hui came the next day. He took out five hundred *liang* of gold and asked to see the black dragon board. The owner took it out, saying, "We have washed it clean for you."

When the Hui saw it, he again refused to buy. "No, no, I will not need it. Who told you to wash it?" This time the spider had run up the tower of Dashan Temple.

The Hui realized that the treasure pearl inside the spider was not for him to obtain, so he went to tell the head monk in the Dashan Temple: "The spider on the Dashan tower has a pearl in its belly. You just put a bamboo basket under the tower, point at the spider with a mirror, and it will come down. When you catch it, make haste to cut open its belly and take out the pearl."

The head monk of Dashan Temple did as the Hui had said. As expected, he obtained the Wind-quieting Pearl.

The Osmanthus Tree on the Moon

First published in *Min jian yue kan (Folk Literature Monthly)*, 1932.
Place: Shao Xin county, Zhejiang
Recorders: Ling Rong-fu and Ding Men-kui (Hui)

A Hui once saw a piece of brick and an old axe in a man's courtyard. He asked to buy them for one hundred taels of silver.

"What is the use of these two things? I will not sell them until you tell me what they will be for."

"They are two treasures. If you stand on the brick it will carry you aloft to the palace on the moon. When you arrive at the moon, you must run quietly into the garden and with this old axe cut down the osmanthus tree. This tree is a rare thing. It is worth several million taels of silver!"

Upon hearing this the man thought to himself, "I can only get one hundred taels of silver by selling these treasures to the Hui. But if I go to the moon myself, and cut down the osmanthus tree, I will get several hundred times more silver."

"No, I will not sell these to you—not even if you pay me a thousand taels of silver!"

The Hui could not persuade the man, and with his spirits low he left.

"The axe is an old one. How can I cut down the tall osmanthus tree with it?" the man thought. He took a sharp axe and went up to the moon upon the piece of brick. He crept into the garden and began to chop at the osmanthus tree with all his might. The axe was really very sharp. It cut quite easily into the tree.

The man pulled out his axe and was about to cut again when he discovered, to his utter surprise, that the wound in the tree was quickly healing. He made another cut and the wound closed up again. The man continued to cut.

After a while the gardener heard the sound of someone chopping at the tree. He quickly ran in the direction of the osmanthus tree. The poor man was caught unexpectedly by the caretaker and beaten to death under that tree.

5

Islam and Other Religions

Why Has the Phoenix Gone?

Place: Urumqi, Xinjiang
Narrator: Su Xiuying
Recorders: Ma Xin and Yang Ruiping, 1984

Majia village lay at the foot of Lotus Mountain. In the middle of the village was a green lake, and by this lake lived an old man with his daughter Moyan. The peonies which grew by the lake blossomed and withered eighteen times, and Moyan was eighteen years old that year. She was a very beautiful girl. She had rosy cheeks like peach blossoms in March. Her eyes were bright and intelligent, just like two black grapes. In the dress which she had made for herself she was even more beautiful than a lotus. At the moment when she began singing a song all the larks closed their bills. None of the girls in the ninety-nine villages could compare with her. All the young men who lived in the ninety-nine villages wanted to court her.

Ever since Moyan was eighteen, more and more peacocks could be seen by the lake. The mountain became greener and the water in the lake became clearer, day by day. The villagers were convinced that their village had become more beautiful because of Moyan.

In the year when Moyan became eighteen, the threshold of her family's house was worn through three times by matchmaker women. But she liked none of the suitors they came up with. She used to go and do embroidery by the lake, where she would ponder about her future and look at her reflection in the water. Often a certain kindhearted handsome young man would appear in her imagination.

She became so wrapped up in that kind of thinking that sometimes she forgot to do her embroidery.

There was a young man named Musa who lived in a village far away from Majia village. The sheep he looked after could give birth to ten lambs in a litter. He was able to cut a huge pile of firewood in one work period. He was also very skilled at planting crops. All the year round he worked, untiringly, from morning till night. When he felt tired he would lay under a tree to have a rest. He would drink from a mountain spring when he was thirsty. That same year he was twenty, old enough to take a wife. He wanted to marry a diligent girl with a heart sparkling like gold, one as beautiful as a flower. Whenever he closed his eyes, such a girl would appear before his eyes.

One day Allah and the Phoenix looked at the people in the world—while together they were speeding across the sky under heaven. Seeing Moyan and Musa, Allah spoke to the Phoenix: "These two are to be married six months from now."

The Phoenix felt this difficult to believe and said, "Even though you are the almighty Allah, these two live far apart from each other. It is impossible for them to even meet. How can they become husband and wife?"

"What if they do get married?" asked Allah.

Not to be outdone, the Phoenix answered, "If that happens, I will never come out of the mountains again. I will never appear to the people anymore."

"All right. Keep your promise." With these words Allah took off—on a cloud.

After Allah was gone, the Phoenix reasoned out an evil scheme. She smiled a sinister smile and then flew to Moyan's house. To Moyan she said, "Moyan, you are such a beauty that the peacocks lower their heads with bashfulness at the sight of you. Lotus blossoms wither by comparison the moment you appear. I am fond of pretty girls. Please come with me."

With Moyan riding on the back of the Phoenix, they flew in moonlight across snow-covered mountains, over glaciers, over lengthy rivers and grasslands. By the tenth day they arrived at a boundless forest. After another ten days they came to a cave in a mountain. The Phoenix held Moyan hidden in that cavern and kept close watch over her. She thought to herself, "Now it will be impossible for Musa and

Moyan to become husband and wife. Whatever happens, I will leave nothing undone to prevent them from getting married."

Moyan cried day and night when she found out about the crafty plot of the Phoenix. And oh how she wished that a brave young man would come to her rescue! According to her, the beloved should be none other than the sweetheart she had long cherished in her dreams. Who and where was he? Why did he not come to free her? She did not know how to answer these questions.

As for Musa, in those days he felt that the sweet girl he had been missing so much was in great danger. He also was worried far too much to do any farm work.

The last day of the sixth month was at hand. All day long the Phoenix guarded Moyan without blinking an eye. By sunset all the birds were back to their nests, and the Phoenix felt relieved. "Another four hours and it will be tomorrow. It is impossible for the two young people to meet each other now. I must go to Allah and show him what I was able to do."

As the Phoenix thought about this, she could not help laughing. She told Moyan, "It is the last day of your stay here. Stay where you are in the cavern yet tonight. Tomorrow morning I will take you back home."

With these words she flew away proudly, to look for Allah. As soon as the Phoenix had left, Moyan ran to the riverside like a bird that has gotten out of its cage. She sat by the river, thinking about how to get back home.

Meanwhile Musa had gotten up very early that morning. He had set out for the mountain to cut wood before daybreak. Hardly had he gotten to the foot of the mountain when he heard someone crying for help in the river below. He jumped into the river without hesitation and swam towards the drowning person. When he got closer he found an old man struggling in the water. Musa, together with the old man, was about to swim toward the bank when white-crested breakers came crushing down on them. He had to take the old man under one arm and swim, while using his other arm, along with the current. By and by he became exhausted. When he lifted his head to take a breath he saw someone on the bank and he cried out, "Help! Help!"

The person on the bank was none other than Moyan. Hearing someone cry for help she raised her eyes to see two men floating in the river. She immediately jumped into the torrent and rescued them from drowning. Then she led them to the cavern. Musa went to sleep as soon as they got into the cavern. The old man could not go to sleep because he was tingling all over. He asked Moyan, who was preparing food for them, "My girl, what is your name? Why are you here?"

"My name is Moyan. I was cheated and brought here by the Phoenix for half a year now," Moyan answered sadly.

Soon breakfast was ready, and the old man told Moyan, "Go with us after breakfast and we will bring you home."

Just then Musa woke up, saying, "Oh, is this not the girl I have dreamt about so many times?" Gazing at Musa, Moyan also became convinced that this young man was the very person who would set her free.

The old man understood everything, from their looks. He said to them, "I would not be alive if it had not been for Musa, and Musa and I would have drowned had it not been for Moyan. You are both kindhearted. It is a match made in heaven. Let me recite sacred scripture for you to get married."

Musa nodded repeatedly. "Good, very good! That is very kind of you!" Moyan agreed with a shy smile. With great pleasure the old man recited the marriage text for them.

As for the Phoenix, she had flown like an arrow to Allah and asked proudly, "Almighty Allah! Do you still believe that Moyan and Musa can get married? Is it true that I will have to hide from people all my living days? Ha, Ha, Ha!"

Without a word, Allah motioned to the Phoenix to go out and see for herself. To her great surprise, she saw Moyan and Musa standing shoulder by shoulder before an old man who was reciting wedding texts for them.

Allah told the Phoenix, "There is nothing that could keep these two kindhearted young lovers from getting together."

The face of the Phoenix turned red. "I am now fully convinced," she admitted. Then she flew deep into the forest, as fast as she could, never to come back out again.

That is why people never again have caught sight of the Phoenix.

Abudu and the Devil

Place: Lingwu, Ningxia
Narrator: Guo Zishou (Hui)
Recorder: Wang Xueli (Hui), 1982

Long, long ago, a big tree stood at a place where, from underneath, a spring flowed with sweet and clear water. It flowed the entire year. When people drank from that spring, its water could cure sickness. It could cure sores of all kinds as soon as people would bathe in it. All the people agreed that it was holy water.

When the Devil (Yibulisi, Iblis) heard of it he changed himself into an old man and began to claim ownership of the spring. People who came for water he compelled to burn incense sticks as well as, on their knees, to worship the tree. Those who did not worship were not permitted to get water. Aside from that, they would be required to hand over five *jin* (pounds) of cooking oil. Muslims suffered much by this evil person.

This situation became known to a young man, Abudu (Abdul). He was very indignant and said, "The Devil is crafty, indeed. He wants to change the religion of the people. I must get rid of him and cut down the tree so that the people can see that this big tree is not God and that the spring belongs to everyone." He took a treasure sword and went on his way.

Along the way he happened to meet the Devil. Immediately they began to fight each other. After a few rounds Abudu got the Devil down. When he raised his sword, as he was about to cut off the loser's head, the Devil flopped down on his knees and asked for mercy: "Please spare my life, Great Hero! I can reward you every day if you let me go free!"

The young man became a bit soft. The Devil used this opportunity to beg again, "Of course, I deserve to be dead since I offended you—but not that huge tree. Be kind and let me off, and forgive the tree, and I will pay a gift of gratitude by putting a gold coin under your pillow every morning. If one day I stop doing so, you can kill me and cut down the tree. Will that be all right?"

Thinking about the benefits which could acrue for him, Abudu set the Devil free.

The next morning Abudu lifted his pillow and under it he actually found a gold coin. He nodded and took it with satisfaction. Another day passed, and he found another sparkling gold coin. He said to himself, "This Devil actually does what he says, and he dares not to cheat me."

On the morning of the fourth day he woke up. He lifted the pillow as usual, but to his disappointment he found nothing. Then he looked for it on and under the bed. He turned the quilt and the blanket, and looked everywhere. He did not find anything. This made him so angry that he took out his sword to get even with the Devil.

Having walked not very far, he met him. Without saying a single word Abudu stabbed at him indignantly. But strangely, after just a few rounds he was too weak to strike. He stopped and asked, "Why is this so? Last time you were defeated. But why, only three days later, am I unable to defeat you?"

The Devil gave a weird laugh and said, "Actually, you are not my opponent. Last time you defeated me because you fought for the people, with justice on your side. You were filled with courage while I fought only for myself. And, of course, I was defeated. Today we both are fighting for ourselves, and so you are defeated."

Abudu blushed scarlet at these words, and he left, disheartened. It has been said that after this encounter he retreated to a remote mountain to learn some skills. No-one knows when, for the good of the people, he will have learned sufficient skills to kill the Devil.

The Devil Troubles an Oil Store

Place: Urumqi, Xinjiang
Narrator: Zhao Changgen (Hui)
Recorder: Guo Xiumei (Hui), 1984

Once upon a time, in a country town, stood an oil store. The oil that was sold there was sweet smelling and had fresh color. And therefore business was brisk.

But, it did not take long before a ghostly demon suddenly made itself heard in this store. It has been said that it was the Devil (Yibulisi, Iblis), the small-footed Great Immortal, who came to trouble the oil store every night. And no matter how well the owner kept the doors locked, he could never keep him out. Late at night heavy footsteps could be heard on the stairs. As the news spread, fewer and fewer people came to buy oil. Business slackened. The owner of the oil store became worried, and finally he called on a wise man to help catch that Devil.

One day a carpenter came who took up the challenge. He claimed that he was going to challenge that so-called small-footed Great Immortal Being. The oil store owner was extremely delighted, and warmly he welcomed the carpenter. That night the carpenter hid quietly under the stairs, waiting for this devil. In the dead of the night, and without hearing the door open, he heard "thump, thump" resounding suddenly from the stairs. The carpenter got nervous. But then he saw something like a small cat jumping up the stairs, one step after another. Small as it was, it made a big noise. The carpenter said to himself, "No wonder the people call it the small-footed Great Immortal Being."

The next day the carpenter borrowed a large wooden tub, a stick, and a rope, from the owner of the oil store. He tied the rope to the stick and with the stick he propped up the tub. Then he waited quietly, holding the rope in his hand.

At about the same time as on the previous night, the small-footed Great Immortal appeared again. The moment it jumped to a place under the tub, the carpenter quickly pulled at his rope. The stick was yanked out, and the small-footed Great Immortal Being was trapped under that wooden tub.

The carpenter asked the oil store owner and the others to come inside. An oil lamp was lit. Then everyone could see clearly that the small-footed Great Immortal Being was actually a rat. It went upstairs every night to steal some oil. Its tail became sticky with oil, and afterward it gathered up mud. After some time its tail had become a huge lump of oily mud. The noise which people heard was just that big lump of oily crust that knocked against the wooden stairs.

The rat was killed. And ever since that time the oil store has been quiet. Along with the quietude the oil business became prosperous again.

The Dragon Tablet

First published in *Zhong guo min jian gu shi ji (Folk Stories of China)*.
Kunming: Folk Literature and Arts Press, 1958.
Place: Yunnan
Recorder: Wang Dong (Hui)

Once upon a time, in a village in Kunmin, there lived an old couple. The name of the old man was Ma Yingsheng. They were a childless couple even though they had been married for over thirty years. And oh—how they wished that they could have a child of their own!

"Compassionate Allah! Please bestow a child unto us!" they would pray to God every day.

Then one year, quite unexpectedly, the old woman became pregnant, and the two of them were filled with great joy. A year passed and the old woman had not given birth. Two years passed and she was still expecting. And the old man said, "I am afraid you are suffering from big belly illness. Who has ever seen a woman pregnant for such a long time?"

The child was born during the third year. The old couple rejoiced so much that tears rolled down their cheeks. It happened that there was a severe drought that year. And so the old man named his baby son "Drought."

Drought was able to walk when he was only two months old. By the end of three months he could speak. By the time he was six months old he even followed his mother to the mountains to collect firewood and mushrooms.

The severe drought lasted two years and there was not a single drop of rain. The land was too dry for people to sow seeds. The farmers had to eat tree bark and grass roots as their food.

Drought asked his mother one day, "Why is it that people do not plant rice to eat?"

"My child! The Dragon King does not rain on us. Without moisture the farmers cannot plant rice."

"Mother, shall I go and look for the Dragon King?"

"My child! The Dragon King lives in the Dragon Palace. You must be a good swimmer if you want to go in search of the Dragon King."

After that, Drought went to practice swimming in the Black Dragon Pool. He kept practicing, come rain or shine, and he searched for the Dragon Palace every day.

The Dragon Palace was located deep down in the water. One day, then another two days, and then a month passed, and Drought still did not find it. A second month went by and he still failed. He searched all of a hundred days, and still, the Dragon Palace was nowhere to be seen. Then, one day, Drought was so tired that he even fell asleep in the water.

The moment he closed his eyes he saw a crystal palace. A beautiful princess was moving toward him from that palace. Her dress was made of coral and her shoes were made of agate and pearl. Her face shone with a colorful light. Her eyes gave off a light as gentle as the autumn moon.

Drought stared at the princess with amazement while she began to speak: "Drought, before you can find the Dragon Palace you must first look for the Dragon Cave. But you must start looking for it now, while the Dragon King is still asleep."

The voice of the princess sounded very crisp, as if something was beating on glass. Every word from her mouth rolled forth like a brilliant pearl. The princess also told Drought how to find the Dragon King.

She had hardly finished speaking when waves surged in the pool. The princess turned to escape. Drought quickly hurried after her, but he emerged from the water and woke up. He took a deep breath and went down again along the road of which the princess had told.

As expected, he found a cave large enough to permit a man to enter. Drought went into the cave. It was pitch-dark inside, and the water was as cold as ice. Drought clenched his teeth and groped his way to the bottom of the cave. The rocks which he encountered were sharp like knives. At last he reached the end of the cave where he found two doors, tightly locked. There were thorns all over the doors. His hands got torn when he pushed with them, and his feet were pricked when he kicked with them. His entire body was scratched and pierced by these thorns. A whole day long he kept pushing against this door, but he failed to open it. He kept knocking at the door an entire night and still it remained tightly shut. His hands and his feet were worn down to bloody flesh.

"Drought, Drought," whispered the princess into his ear, "if you want the door to open, fetch the dragon tablet!"

Drought had to come out of the cave. On the mountain he gathered some medicinal herbs to apply to his wounds.

When he arrived at home he asked his mother, "Where is the dragon tablet?"

"The dragon tablet has been placed in the mosque."

Immediately Drought went to the mosque. The day was a Friday. All the Muslims had gathered at the mosque, ready to pray for rain. They had discussed the problem of the drought for forty days, and they only lacked a person who would go and take the dragon tablet into the Dragon Cave.

Drought greeted the ahong and then said to him, "I have come to ask about the dragon tablet."

"You are going to take in the dragon tablet? That is very good!" The ahong had misunderstood him and concluded that the person who wants to take in the dragon tablet had finally come. And then he asked, "What is your name? And can you swim well?"

"My name is Drought. I can swim. I can even sleep in water."

"Fellow Muslims, thanks be to Allah! We have found the person who would take in the dragon tablet!" This the ahong shouted with joy. All the people cupped their hands. Drought also cupped his hands.

Having gotten a person to take in the tablet, the ceremonial procession for rain got under way. Wearing nothing on their heads and feet, the people all chanted scripture and walked with incense sticks in their hands. The dragon tablet was carried by an ahong. The boy Drought followed the people and together they arrived at the Black Dragon Pool. He had been scorched by the sun, but by now he already felt a bit cooler.

At last the ahong handed the dragon tablet to Drought. No sooner had he taken it, he jumped into the pool even without first taking off his clothes. He groped his way into the Dragon Cave and with the dragon tablet struck the door. The two thorny doors opened as if by themselves, and Drought entered the bright Dragon Palace which resounded with elegant music. The Dragon King, dressed in a black robe, was sleeping with a blood-red precious pearl in his open mouth. Drought quickly approached and snatched the precious pearl. He swallowed it, not forgetting what the princess had told him.

The Black Dragon King was startled from his sleep, spurting flames from his mouth and nostrils. He loudly shouted, "Who has stolen my precious pearl?"

"It is I who have swallowed it, down into my stomach!" answered Drought.

The Dragon King jumped with rage. He grabbed a sword and threatened, "Make haste to return it to me or I will cut you into eight pieces!"

"You black devil! You have starved so many people to death. This day, next year, will be the anniversary of your death! I will remove your head from your shoulders!"

With these words Drought raised the dragon tablet and with it struck the Dragon King.[1] The dragon was struck down with the first

------

[1] The Hui request for rain, in this case, required taking a dragon tablet into the pool. The tablet which we photographed (photograph 10) is made of copper and bears a Quranic promise for rain: "It is he who sends down rain for them when they have lost all hope, and spreads abroad his mercy. He is the guardian worthy of praise" (Sura 42, 29). Applied in the form of a tablet, during the rain-requesting rite, Allah's words open the door and defeat the ancient Chinese god of rain, the Dragon King. The next Rain Dragon is a Muslim.

blow. His horns were leveled by a second blow. Drought then gave a third blow, and the Dragon King's head was cut off.

So the Dragon King died. The boy Drought himself changed into a dragon. He flew out of the Dragon Cave and soaked the thirsty land with a pouring rain.

The Dragon Dish

First published in *Yun nan min zu min jian gu shi (Yunnan Nationalities Folk Stories)*. Kunming, 1979.
Place: Yuxi, Yunnan
Narrator: Sha Mashi (Hui)
Recorder: Sha Yin (Hui)

The beaded rosary which Muslims finger while praying, why does it consist of only ninety-nine beads? And why can the broken tiles on the roof of the minaret at the mosque in Beicheng, in Yuxi county, not be repaired? An old story is told among Hui folks.

Nine Dragons Pool is located some miles away from Beicheng. It used to be famous for its scenic beauty. The water in the pool was both clear and fresh. The pool was surrounded with pine trees, with cypresses and weeping willows. A small river ran from the pool off into the far distance. Nicely irrigated with the water, fields and fruit gardens on both banks of the river produced bumper crops every year.

Yuxi county was rich in rice, in vegetables and fruits. Yellow peaches and brown peaches were special products of Yuxi. Fruits were plentiful and tasted better. Even the wild fruits that grew on nearby mountains were larger and sweeter than those elsewhere.

In the vicinity of Beicheng were many Hui villages. The people in these villages were hard working and honest. They lived and labored together in peace and contentment.

Then appeared a white dragon; no-one knew from where it came. After a fierce battle it drove away the nine dragons in the pool and commenced to occupy Nine Dragons Pool. Ever since the white dragon came, the pool stopped overflowing and the river has been dry. Fruit trees have died of thirst. Crops have been destroyed by the drought. For many years in a row not a single drop of rain has fallen. People have been forced to leave the village in order to survive.

Along came Ramadan, the month of fasting. All Muslim men gathered in the mosque for the first prayers of the day. When those were over they surrounded Gao Haji, the man who had been on a pilgrimage to Mecca, and talked with him about the drought. A young man suggested that Gao Haji lead them in search of the nine dragons. Everybody agreed with him.

Looking at the Muslims, Gao Haji cupped one hand into his other and said, pleased, "Muslims, so long as we are pious and of one mind, with the blessings of Allah we will overcome any natural or human-caused calamities! We can surely expel that cruel white dragon!"

With Gao Haji in the lead the people started out. Marching over parched land and across dry canals, the procession headed for Nine Dragons Pool. By noon they reached the pool. Gao Haji led the Muslims in prayer for a second time, and he recited with them verses from the Holy Quran.

Then he flung his string of beads into the Dragon Pool.[2] There was a sudden gust of wind. Gao Haji and the other Muslims were standing by the pool. The haji took off his white turban and was about to throw it into the pool as well when he saw myriads of bubbles rise from the water. A school of fish, swimming face upward, held up a white and blue dish of porcelain with their mouths. Into the dish had been laid his beads. Gao Haji reached for it as one of the fishes jumped from the water and caused the dish to land in his hands. The haji caught the dish together with the small fish. He wrapped the fish into his snow-white turban. And then, with the dish in one hand and with the fish in the other, Gao Haji led the Muslims back to their village.

Upon entering the mosque he wrapped the fish in one end of his turban and tied the other end to the beam, in the prayer hall. After that he rethreaded all the loose beads that lay on the dish, and he

---

[2]As in the previous story, a material token representing Muslim prayers, which are Quranic words of God, are submitted to challenge the dragon that has caused the drought.

counted them. Why, one bead was missing! When he threw them into the pool there were still one hundred of them. Now only ninety-nine were left.[3] That is why nowadays there are ninety-nine beads in a Muslim rosary.

Gao Haji asked someone to fetch a pail of water. He himself poured the water from the pail into that dish. It seemed strange that a dish, just the size of an ordinary eating bowl, could contain a pail of water without spilling a drop.

The water in the dish began to stir, with a noise, as if nine dragons were playing in it. The people were overjoyed, and they named it the Dragon Dish. A moment later lightning flashed, with a strong gust of wind. When the wind died down it began to rain as if water was pouring from a tub.

At midnight, when they rose to break the fast, they noticed a small white dragon ascend to the sky. Its tail struck a corner of the roof of the minaret, at the mosque, and broke some tiles. Ever since, not even the best artisan has been able to repair that corner. From that time on the white devil dragon remained driven away. The Nine Dragons Pool was returned to its former condition. Water continued to flow out again from the pool. People near Beicheng resumed their former lifeways in peace and contentment.

The dragon dish was kept at Gao Haji's home and was handed down from one generation to the next. Muslims who visited Yuxi would go and have a look at the dish for themselves. They would fill it with water to see the nine dragons play in it.

Once—and it is not known during which dynasty—it fell to the floor and broke into pieces, because many people were trying to have a look at it ahead of others. The people glued it back together. But unfortunately, the nine dragons could never again be seen in it when the dish was filled with water. The blue patterns gradually faded. What a pity!

---

[3]The missing bead seems to have been a token from the people, albeit loaded for the dragon with exorcistic prayer power from Allah. It was accepted by the white dragon in the pool. Inversely, the small fish—a creature that had been subject to the dragon—was thereafter kept in the mosque as a token from the dragon to the people.

The Story of Winding River

Place: Luoyang, Henan
Narrator: Ma Yong (Hui)
Recorders: Yao Xingze (Hui), Li Shujiang, 1983

East of Luoyang, in Henan, flows a river that has the name "Winding River" (Chanhe). Along its banks live a great number of Hui people. And why is that river called Winding River? And why are so many Hui people living by it? Listen to me, I will tell you the story.

It was said that Genghis Khan (1162–1227), after his campaign to the West, proceeded to mount an attack against the Jin dynasty. He left some of his Yuan troops stationed in Luoyang. These soldiers committed murder, arson, and every other imaginable crime. The ancient city Luoyang was in turmoil. Even fowls and dogs were not left in peace.

Among the troops at the station was a battalion of soldiers from the western regions; they were quite different from the other Yuan soldiers. Not only were they brave in fighting battles, but also highly disciplined. In the battalion was a young squad leader by the name of Abudu (Abdul). He was an honest and kindhearted young man. He was disquieted about the Yuan (Mongolian) soldiers on account of the savagery which they inflicted on the Han people.

One day Abudu's battle steed got hurt on the way back from maneuvers. He had to return on foot and therefore lagged behind. As he passed a village in the suburbs he heard the cries of a woman in pain, in a house nearby. Sword in hand he rushed in and saw how a Yuan soldier was about to rape a girl. Abudu gave a loud shout and raised his sword. The soldier met Abudu, sword in hand as well. After several rounds Abudu killed the soldier. Just at that moment the girl's father came home with the wood he had cut. Seeing the scene he thanked Abudu for having saved his daughter.

Abudu persuaded the family to immediately flee to another part of the country. Then he himself ran into the thick forest of Mangshan Mountain, near Louyang.

Soon the Yuan troops found the dead soldier. They set fire to the farmer's house and offered a reward for the capture of Abudu.

It so happened that Abudu came again across the old man with his daughter, in the forest of Mangshan Mountain. The old man led Abudu into a cavern and hid him there. He had discovered this cave earlier while gathering medicinal herbs. No one but he himself knew about it. The old man and his daughter Yinyin went to live in a relative's house at the foot of the mountain.

Every other day the old man took food to Abudu. His daughter Yinyin said to him one day, "Father, you are old. The long way along the mountain path will exhaust you. Let me go instead of you."

"It will not do for a young girl like you to go alone."

"I know what to do," said Yinyin. She disguised herself as a young woodcutter. And because Yinyin was so clever, her father agreed. Rain or shine, each day Yinyin brought food to Abudu.

Several months passed. The situation was becoming less dangerous, and gradually Abudu and Yinyin began to like each other. To Abudu, Yinyin seemed like a clever, pretty girl, kind-hearted and hard working. To Yinyin, Abudu was an honest, brave, and handsome young man.

Once, when they met, Yinyin asked Abudu shyly, "This trouble is over, and you cannot forever hide in this cave. Where is your home? What are you going to do in the future?"

"My home is so far from here that it is impossible for me to go back, even if I wanted to. With Allah's blessings I am thinking of settling down here. But I am afraid your customs are different from ours," answered Abudu with a deep sigh.

Yinyin said, "Just settle down here. We will do everything according to your customs."

Abudu and Yinyin got married at the foot of Mangshan Mountain. Abudu worked in the fields. Besides doing housework, Yinyin sometimes helped Abudu do his field work. They lived together with Yinyin's father. A year later Yinyin gave birth to a baby boy, and the four of them lived together happily.

Then one year there was a severe drought. Crops died from the drought. Without water the people and animals were about to succumb as well. Abudu and some villagers set out to look for water, everywhere. They searched three days and three nights without finding any. Then one day Abudu came near the cave in which he used to hide. He looked around and said to the others, "There must be water here. Let us dig a well right here."

Abudu began to dig with a shovel. The others took out the earth which he had dug with a basket. They continued digging day and night, and on the seventh day they found the earth in the basket dripping with water. Soon they would have water!

Suddenly a loud noise came from the bottom of the well. People hurriedly pulled up the basket. But Abudu was not there anymore. Only his turban was hanging from the basket.

Yinyin was beside herself with grief. She wanted to throw herself into the well but was held back by the villagers. She took the turban into her hand and broke into crying. One end of the turban cloth was hanging down the well while the other end dropped to the ground. Yinyin cried and cried. Her tears soaked the turban cloth and then, all of a sudden, it became a stream of spring water rising up from the well. The spring water flowed on and on, endlessly. It ran past the foot of Mangshan Mountain to the city of Luoyang, and from there on and on, far into the distance like a strip of white, winding turban cloth. Abudu had saved the people, their crops, and their cattle, but he himself never came up again.

In memory of Abudu, the people called the river Chanhe —Winding River. Those who lived along the banks of Winding River adopted the customs of the Hui people, in honor of Abudu.

That is the origin of us Hui people, in Luoyang.

Why the Teapots Are Hung Tilted

Place: Southern Mountain area, Ningxia
Narrator and Recorder: Han Delu (Hui), 1984

The Anshi Armed Rebellion broke out under the reign of the Emperor Xuanzong, of the Tang dynasty. An Lushan colluded with troops from the northern tribes, and together they burned, killed, and looted wherever they went.

One autumn some northern troops attacked a village. Many innocent people died from saber cuts. One day a group of northern cavalrymen were chasing a middle-aged woman. The woman was running for her life while carrying a girl of about six or seven years on her back and leading a very small boy at her hand. The cavalrymen caught up with the woman. One of them lifted his saber and was about to kill her when he heard someone shout in a loud voice, "Stop!"

The man who had shouted was a general. He came up to the woman and looked at her carefully. He saw her lying on the ground and trembling from fear. Although she was about to die, she nevertheless shielded the girl from the saber with her hands. The little boy had fallen to the ground; he held on to the woman's foot, wailing loudly.

"What an unreasonable person you are!" said the general. "Normally, it would only be possible for you to escape and to avoid being killed if you were to carry the small boy on your back and take the girl by your hand. Why do you act in the opposite manner?"

The woman answered trembling, "Oh General, have mercy on us! Perhaps you do not know that the boy is my own son, while the girl was picked up along the road just now. To sacrifice even my own child for the sake of others is a Hui woman's duty." She held the girl more tightly in her arms.

Deeply moved, the general told the woman, "You are a kind-hearted woman. So, all right, I will spare your life. You may go home." The woman could hardly believe what he said, and not until the general urged her again did she get up and leave with the two children.

Staring at her as she withdrew, the general thought to himself, "Though I have spared the woman's life, cavalrymen from my command are everywhere. How can she escape being killed if she encounters them?"

He had an idea. "Wait a minute!" he shouted at the woman. Then he bent over, pulled up a turnip and told the woman, "Hang this turnip from your door frame. I will give orders to spare the one who has a turnip at her door." He threw the turnip at the woman's feet and whipped his horse to gallop on. Picking up the turnip, the woman went away with her children.

When the woman arrived at her home she told the secret to her neighbors. The news quickly spread throughout the village. Those families who were unable to flee the village hung a turnip from their door frames. No sooner had they done this than the northern cavalrymen arrived. Having told the secret to all the families, the woman went back to her own house. As she was closing her door she noticed, momentarily, that no turnip was hung at the door of her next-door neighbor. There lived an old couple of nearly seventy years and their sick daughter with several small children. How careless she was to have forgotten to tell them! She immediately ran to tell them to hang a turnip at the door.

Unfortunately, there was no turnip in their house. The woman decided to go to her own field to get one for them. But she heard the northern cavalrymen approaching. It was impossible for her to go to the field. She ran back to her own house in a hurry, took off the turnip and gave it to the girl she had picked up. She told her to take it next door. Now the clatter of horses' hoofs could be heard outside. The woman forced the turnip into the girl's hands and pushed her out. She entered the room, took the little boy in her arms and intended to go and take refuge in her neighbor's house. But it was too late. Knowing herself to be facing grim possibilities, she took a teapot from the table and hung it at her door, in great panic.

After the attack a silence of death settled on the village. One after another the survivors came out. They talked about what had happened. All families with turnips at their door were safe and sound. Only a woman with a teapot at her door was lying in a puddle of blood. Her little son had died in her arms. Her next-door neighbor, the old woman, came with the girl who had brought a turnip to them. The old woman threw herself on the dead woman's body and wailed loudly, "You have saved my family while you yourself died such a tragic death."

All the villagers broke into tears. "Kindhearted woman, it is you who saved all of us."

The woman was given a large funeral, in accordance with Hui custom. Nobody knew where she had come from or what her name was. They only knew what the girl said—that the woman told her to call her "Aunt Sha." As a result, many Han people desired to convert to Islam. Nowadays, nine out of ten Hui people in this area are surnamed Sha.

At first the people would hang a teapot at their doors, on festivals and holidays. Later they put only a picture of a teapot there. The picture image still looks a little tilted. Those who do not know the details concerning this custom think it is done out of carelessness. But actually, it is done deliberately.

In the teahouses, inns, and shops which are run by Hui people, at least two or three teapots can be found. Especially in teahouses, pots which are not in use are polished and placed in rows on a shelf. If you look closely you will find that not a single teapot is placed straight and upright. If you ask the owner why this is so, he will answer you only with a smile.

Lotus Pedestals in the Mosque

First published in *Hei long jiang min jian wen xue (The Folk Literature of Heilongjiang)*, 1981.
Place: Ar-City, Heilongjiang
Narrator: Yang Guangquan (Hui, age 68)
Recorder: Jin Zhenning (Hui)

The first mosque in Ar-City was built in the forty-second year of Qianlong (1777) of the Qing dynasty. But until the early years of Guangxu a gang of bandits kept coming, headed by Fool Ma. They robbed and plundered, and they even torched the mosque. Some time after that (after 1874) the bandits were put out of business. In the fifth year of Guangxu (1879), people began to rebuild the mosque under the direction of Yang, president of the Islamic Association in Ar-City.

On Wula Street, in Jilin City, President Yang solicited a very wise and skilled carpenter whose name was Song Yulin. According to President Yang's idea, Song Yulin first made a small model of sorghum stalks. Yang was satisfied with it on first sight. So he gave Song Yulin the contract for the project. Contracting for a project at that time was done the same way as it is done today. The first party and the second party would draw up a written agreement and sign their names. If the materials supplied were insufficient or not of good quality, the first party would assume the responsibility; if the construction was not as agreed upon, the second party would be responsible.

When the materials lay ready, Song Yulin began to work with his laborers. When the building was halfway done it was time to erect the main hall, a two-storied structure. For that it was necessary to erect four extra-large columns—that is, trees as tall as the two-storied buildings of today. When the measurements were checked it turned out that Song Yulin had made a mistake and cut the four high columns two *chi* (feet) short, and the other smaller columns one *chi* short. That was too bad! The small ones were not too difficult to replace, but the four extra-high columns were very difficult to find. This really worried Song Yulin a lot. He had no choice but to go back to Jilin and invite his master, Wang Yichang, who was over seventy years old, to offer his opinion. When Wang came and had a look he found that Ar-City was not only rich in wood but also in stone. So he advised Song Yulin to carve stone pedestals in the shape of lotuses—that is, to put a lotus base under each column to compensate for their shortness.

Since that time an elegantly carved lotus pedestal is situated under each column of the Ar-City mosque. Thus, every column seems to be growing out of a stone lotus base that was not only flawlessly done, but also gave the people a sense of beauty and stability. This is, in fact, flawless and wonderful workmanship!

A Temple Appeared from Nowhere

Place: Yunnan
Narrator and Recorder: Ma Yusheng (Hui), 1982

On Panlong Mountain there stood the well-known Panlong Temple which used to attract a large number of pilgrims. In the temple lived an old Buddhist monk. The people called him Founder Panlong because he was known as a man of high prestige—he was also known for being infinitely resourceful.

One day, when Founder Panlong was chanting sutras, together with about a dozen monks, a young monk rushed in and reported that a white-bearded old man had been sighted at the bottom of the mountain, coming up toward the temple. "He carries a large bamboo basket in his hand, and he looks like a Hui," he reported.

"A Hui?" said Founder Panlong with surprise. "The Hui people chant different scriptures. What brings him here?"

Founder Panlong got up from the cattail fiber pad and followed the young monk out. Hardly had both of them stepped outside when they saw the old man enter the temple compound, only a few steps ahead.

Greatly surprised, Founder Panlong thought to himself, "This old man is not just an ordinary Hui, or else he could not have walked that fast. I have heard that there lives an old ahong among the Hui people, called Founder Baolao. He must be that man. Let me take this chance to show off my skills."

And so, turning to the young monk, he said, "It is Founder Baolao who has come to our temple. Let us give him a warm welcome."

"I happen to pass by your temple, so I just thought I would drop in for a visit," said the guest with a smile.

They had a chat under the wisteria trellis. There Founder Panlong invited Founder Baolao to have a rest in the side room.

In the side room Founder Baolao wanted to wash some rice to prepare a meal. He was looking for water when two little monks came in, carrying a sieve filled with water. "Founder Panlong told us to bring you water," they said.

Founder Baolao glanced at them, sideways, and said coldly, "That is too much. Half of it will be enough for me." He pulled out his dagger and cut the water into two portions. He took one half and left the other half in the sieve. "Take this back to Founder Panlong," he said to the two little monks. The two looked at each other dumbfounded.

After he had finished washing his rice, Founder Baolao was ready to cook. He asked the monks for wood. Before they could give an answer, Founder Panlong entered and said, "Panlong Mountain is covered with trees. I will go and pull up a large tree for you." With these words he turned to go.

Founder Baolao stopped him, saying, "Wait a minute! Do not bother to go. Just lend me an axe, I will do it myself!"

A sharp axe was brought in. Founder Baolao took it and began to cut into his legs with it. The little monks stared at him, horrified. Within a moment's time, firewood was piled high upon the floor.

Just then, one of the young monks came running into the side room. He went up to Founder Panlong and informed him that something terrible had happened, that all the columns in the rear hall had been cut into pieces!

"Who has done it?" asked Founder Panlong.

"I do not know."

Founder Panlong knew it fairly well, but he was obligated to keep silent.

After the meal Founder Panlong continued chatting with his visitor under the wisteria trellis. He thought, "This Hui indeed has a great hand. People will regard me with ridicule if I am surpassed by him." He then took off his socks and threw them up into the sky. The pair of socks immediately turned into two pigeons who flew round and about, one following the other. Founder Panlong looked at the pigeons, proudly. He cast a sidelong glance at Founder Baolao.

The latter, very casually, took his white turban from his head and also tossed it up toward the sky. Instantly a white dragon flew up toward the pigeons. The two proud pigeons were so scared at the sight of the dragon that they fled as quickly as they could. They dropped in front of Founder Panlong like two dead leaves. He picked up his socks and was at a complete loss about what to do next. The little white dragon returned to earth and became again a turban wound around Founder Baolao's head.

Founder Baolao rose early the next morning. Before leaving he looked at the monks and asked Founder Panlong, "Can you send someone along to see me off?"

Pointing toward the statues of five hundred bodhisattvas, Founder Panlong answered, "You may choose one of these, if you like."

Founder Baolao shook his head on the bodhisattvas. He did not choose any of them. Instead, he walked up to the four warrior attendants of the Buddha and patted the arm of one, "This one looks quite strong. I will have him go with me."

The statue of the warrior attendant began to move. It walked down from its place, lifted Founder Baolao's bamboo basket and followed him out the gate. All the young monks were shocked and flabbergasted.

Founder Baolao and the warrior attendant then approached the river. There, as they were about to cross this river, the warrior attendant began to cry.

"What has made you so sad?"

"The river is very deep. How can a clay figure such as I make it across?"

"All right! You may stay here. Being here is better than being shut up in the Panlong Temple."

Founder Baolao raised his hands to pray. A small temple appeared at the bank of the river while he prayed. It was just large enough to accommodate the warrior attendant. Founder Baolao then took off the sheepskin which was draped over his shoulders. He threw it into the river and leisurely sat upon it. He waved goodbye to the warrior attendant and floated across the river, easily, on his sheepskin.

When the people came to the river bank on the next day they found there, with great astonishment, a temple of unknown origin with a warrior statue standing inside. News of the temple spread far and wide. People gave a name to the small temple: Fei Lai, or, "the temple that flew in from nowhere." The name of the temple, as well as the story concerning Founder Baolao, was handed down from generation to generation.

The North Pagoda

Place: Yinchuan, Ningxia
Narrator: Huang Cunde (Hui, age 83); Zhao Jinggui (Hui, age 65); Ma Xuanxuan (Hui, age 65)
Recorder: Xie Rong, 1980[4]

The North (Haibao) Pagoda is located in the northern suburbs of the old city of Yinchuan, in Ningxia. The people who live there call

---

[4]For information concerning this recorder see page 73, note 1.

it the North Tower. It is one of the major cultural monuments preserved nowadays by the government.

It has been said that long ago the Ningxia Plain used to be a vast expanse of water. One year the Dragon King in the Eastern Sea got a baby son who was black all over. The baby had red eyes, coarse skin and long legs; it looked neither like a dragon nor like a tiger. People called it Black Monster Dragon.

As a young boy the Black Monster Dragon was rather naughty. He would not heed the advice that an elder gave him. The shrimp soldiers and crab generals could do nothing to keep him in line. He was a nuisance even toward his parents, that is, the Dragon King and the Dragon Queen.

Once the Black Monster Dragon sneaked into the treasure house of the Dragon Palace and stole his mother's jadeite hairpin, along with a tiny wave-quieting needle. With these he ran out into the deep sea to play. When the Dragon Queen discovered this behavior she became furious.

The Dragon King ordered his shrimp soldiers and crab generals to fetch the Black Monster Dragon and to bring him in. Wearing the hairpin, the Black Monster Dragon laughingly waved the wave-calming needle at the shrimp soldiers and crab generals and made them faint. When the Dragon King received this news he became very angry. He took out his dragon treasures—the heart-hooking needle, water-proving pearl, life-saving suit, and dragon-binding rope—and he proceeded to ride on a sea beast in order to capture the Black Monster Dragon by himself.

Hearing that the old Dragon King was coming after him, the Black Monster Dragon opened the dragon-beast stable and rode the Yellow Flood Dragon which belonged to his mother. Then he fled to the depth of the sea in a great hurry. The door of the stable was left wide open, and so seventy-two small dragons followed them out.

He covered miles and miles looking for a place to hide, but it was all in vain. He had to run along the Eastern Sea all the way to the west.

The Eastern Sea flowed to the west. The water became shallow. The Yellow Flood Dragon became tired and struggled for breath, while The Black Monster Dragon began to stagger from fatique. Seeing this, the old Dragon King threw out his heart-hooking needle upon the surface of the water. In a moment the Black Monster Dragon was surrounded by a black cloud. His stomach hurt, and he cried out, "Ouch! Ouch!" And meanwhile he poked the tiny wave-quieting needle at his father.

The old Dragon King hastily countered it with a larger needle and tossed the dragon-binding rope. In this manner he tied up the Black Monster Dragon.

The Black Monster Dragon held the tiny needle in his hand and plunged to the bottom of the sea, generating a towering water column while doing so. All of a sudden there was thunder, accompanied by lightning. The Old Dragon scattered his water-stabilizing pearls upon the water surface. Water immediately began to ripple and play with golden rays. The tide receded and land appeared. With a crack of thunder the old Dragon King, riding on his sea beast, returned to the Dragon Palace with the gust of a tornado.

The seventy-two small dragons, who had been following Black Monster Dragon, were terribly frightened and ran away to hide in what is now the Seventy-two Lianhu Lakes area.

After that the water in the Eastern Sea gradually dried up. The Yellow Dragon was afraid that the Black Monster Dragon would emerge from the water. He therefore descended to the bottom of the ocean. He chopped wood and made bricks. Then he surrounded the Black Monster Dragon with wood and brick fortifications. A few years later there appeared a dragon-shaped tower.

When the water receded, a Haibao Pagoda twelve *zhang* high could be seen. People say that the green top of the tower is the Dragon Queen's jadeite hairpin, whereas the nine-storied tower, with eleven steps each floor, still bears the marks left by the dragon-binding rope. The shape and size of the tower is identical with that of the wave-quieting needle.

Another story has it that years later, when the water gradually dissipated, the Black Monster Dragon felt thirsty. He discussed the matter with the Yellow Dragon, concerning a move to a place where there was more water. Riding on a cloud one early morning, before daybreak, they arrived at a lake. A farmer was plowing his field when he heard someone ask, "Where is the lake?"

The farmer turned around and saw a giant standing behind him. His lips trembled with fear and he could not answer a word. Instead, he pointed toward the lake with his whip. But unintentionally he put too much swing into his movement so that the tip of his whip touched the giant. With a loud noise water began splashing in all directions.

The farmer turned to look. He saw the giant who had asked the way fall into the water and transform himself into a tower that stood at the center of the lake. The Yellow Dragon changed himself into a golden horse to hide at the bottom of the lake and to guard the Black Monster Dragon.

Some people have claimed that, while they stood at the top of the tower, they saw a golden pony gallop down there in the lake.

Tomb of an Unknown Ahong
at Twenty-li Place

Place: Xiji county, Ningxia
Narrator: Haji Ma Zhong-xian (Hui, age 75)
Recorder: Li Shujiang, 1990

At Twenty-li Place in southwest Guyuan county, in Ningxia, sits the tomb of a Muslim saint.[5] It is a unique place because those who go to burn incence and to pray at that tomb are not only Muslims of the Hui nationality. Some non-Muslim Han people also go there. An interesting story is told about this tomb.

It is said that Twenty-li Place became a most sacred place some time after the initial tomb was placed there. The common people always passed that place with feelings of respect and reverence. Even high officials would get off their sedan chairs, and army officers would dismount from their horses when they passed.

But once an army officer who had won many military honors was assigned to the Guyuan area. He was advised to get off his horse when he passed the tomb. But he said, "Will anyone twist my neck sideways if I do not get off?"

---

[5]Twenty-li Pu is a place twenty *li* to the southwest of Guyuan. See photographs 61-62.

Who would have expected it! His neck was twisted sideways the moment he passed. He felt such great pain that he could not help but cry out. From that moment on he believed that Twenty-li Place should be considered a sacred place. He contributed a great sum of money for repairing and enlarging this tomb. Since that time even some Han people go to pray and to burn incense there.

Ahong Shanbaba and the Hui Graveyard

Place: The city of Ar, Heilongjiang
Narrator: Yang Guangquan, Islamic Association of Ar-City
Recorder: Dong Zhenyu, 1980

Shanbaba's real name was Shanshihao.[6] He was an ahong who kept traveling from one mosque to another. In the forty-second year of the Emperor Qianlong, of the Qing dynasty, when the mosque in Ar-city was established, Shanbaba was invited to assume the position of First Ahong. In time he was called Ahong Shan.

Ahong Shan not only had a good command of Arabic and of scripture but also was quite good at medicine, at internal medicine and surgery. Yet, he did not readily take a case, unless it was a difficult and complicated one. And then he would speedily cure the problem.

At that time there was a high-ranking official of the royal court, from among the Man people, his name was Shabintu. People called him Sha Yinjun. No one knew the rank of Yinjun, but he was indeed a wealthy man with power. Rich and powerful men often are said to be also unkind.

At one time Sha Yinjun met a young and beautiful girl. He was attracted to her by her beauty. By every means he tried to get her and to make her his concubine. The girl did not agree and wept all day

---

[6]Shanbaba: The ending "baba" is Arabic with a Chinese pronunciation. It ascribes the title of "Father" and serves as a respectful appellation for an ahong.

long. Sha became enraged. He planned to marry the girl by force. But the girl was not easily bullied. Just when Sha kissed her she bit into his tongue and half of the tongue was bitten off.

Having lost half of his tongue, Sha Yinjun not only had difficulty speaking, but he was also ashamed to face others. He was so anxious about this that he posted a notice to the effect that he would give anything to anyone who could mend that severed tongue.

Nowadays it would be possible to have a severed arm or leg rejoined within eight hours of being cut off. But in those days no-one could rejoin a tongue. Yinjun was frequently depressed. He sent his men to inquire among famous doctors everywhere, but they all failed. At last he heard that Ahong Shan, at the mosque, could cure any illness, especially difficult and complicated ones. Sha Yinjun asked an influential person to invite Ahong Shan to mend his tongue. And the ahong actually consented.

Ahong Shan asked him to stretch out his tongue, and he measured it. Then he asked one of his men to get him a small dog. He cut off half of the dog's tongue with scissors. After that he asked Sha Yinjun to stretch out his tongue again; he then put the dog's tongue on his, saying *"douwayi"* (*du'a'* = prayer). Instantly the dog tongue was joined to the tongue of Sha, and he could speak clearly again. Sha Yinjun was very pleased about that and asked Ahong Shan how much money he wanted. Ahong Shan said he wanted nothing but a plot for a graveyard for the Hui people. Sha Yinjun was even more pleased when he heard that Ahong Shan asked for a piece of land and not for money. He said, "I will give you a horse of land."

What does "a horse of land" mean? It means that a person mounts a horse and gives it a whip. The horse begins to run, and it runs until it stops. The distance that the horse covers in response is "a horse of land." Of course, you can give the horse only one blow, because a witness follows and races after the rider to supervise.

The next day, outside the west gate, Ahong Shan rode on a horse and struck it hard. The horse ran quickly westward. In the west there happened to be an elliptic hill, and west of the hill there happened to be a deep ditch. The horse ran around the hill and then stopped. So Sha Yinjun gave the hill to Ahong Shan as a present. This place became a graveyard to the Hui. It has continually been used for that purpose to this very day.

After Ahong Shan died, people buried him at the highest point at the north side of the graveyard and there they built for him a large tomb. Now there are three special tombs at the north side of this cemetary. The biggest of these is Shanbaba's.

In memory of Ahong Shan the Hui people in Ar-City have called him respectfully Shanbaba. Every year, upon completion of the feast of Fast Breaking, at the end of Ramadan, the ahong says, "Go please. Go to Shanbaba's tomb." The people follow their ahong and journey to Shanbaba's tomb, to honor him.[7]

---

[7]Led by their ahong, Hui Muslims go to the tomb to recite Quranic verses in memory of the dead.

6

Muslims Under the Emperor

The Number One Scholar Fir Trees

First published in *Nan feng (Southwind Magazine)*, 1982.
Place: Guizhou, Guongxi
Narrator: Ma Nai (Hui)
Recorder: Fujun

In the district of Nanlong there formerly was an institution of higher learning—the Nanlong School. In front of that school stood two Number One Scholar Fir Trees.[1] A story about these fir trees was told far and wide by the people of the Nanlong area.

In ancient times there lived, next to the stone lions in front of Nanlong School, a Hui family surnamed Shan.[2] The man and his wife were diligent and hard working. They made a living by selling steamed cakes. Every day they started work early and quit work late. The husband would carry water and turn the millstone while his wife tended the kitchen fire to make the cakes. At the first light of dawn their steamed cakes were ready to be sold. School children and workers who passed by would come over and buy some. Their trade

---

[1] "Number One Scholar" is a title conferred on the one who finishes first in the highest imperial examination.

[2] The surname "Shan," and the word *shan* for fir trees, are homophonic.

was so brisk that the supply often fell short of demand. They earned a happy livelihood by selling cakes.

The moon followed the sun, flowers wilted and bloomed, and in time the wife became pregnant. She gave birth to twins. The entire family rejoiced over the birth of these healthy twin brothers. The husband planted two fir saplings in front of their house to express the hope that his sons would grow up healthy and strong like the trees.

The more the young father and mother worked, the more energy they lavished on their two small sons. Slowly, as the stars kept altering the moon, and while the millstone turned, the twin brothers grew up, gradually. With the millstone turning the two boys began to smile and silently, in their hearts, the parents smiled as well. The more they worked the happier they felt. As the millstone turned, the two brothers not only walked and ran, but with their small sweet mouths they would say "Daddy" and "Mommy." The hearts of their father and mother felt as sweet as if they were drinking honey.

As the millstone turned, the two boys reached the age of seven, and the fir saplings in front of their house grew as thick as an earthen bowl. It was high time for the two boys to attend school. But, being poor they were unable to pay the cost. And so, while watching these boys, who were as fresh and as lovely as bamboo, their parents for the first time became worried. They found no way to solve this problem.

Why did they have to be born into such a poor family! They had to abandon the idea. With tears in their eyes they bit their teeth. The boys carried on their father's trade. In a basket they took some cakes to the school, to sell them early in the morning, each day.

It was indeed appetizing to see two chubby and fair-cheeked boys with a basket of white cakes. The cakes would soon be sold, and then the twin brothers would observe the school children through the window. At first they did so just out of curiosity. They wondered what children were doing at school. Was it more interesting than selling cakes? Little by little their attention turned to what the teacher was saying. They began to learn secretly, and back home they would practice writing. Since they had neither pen nor paper they would write on the floor with a piece of charcoal. Their parents were glad to see the boys so eager to learn, but, at the same time they also felt sorry for being unable to give the boys an education.

Anyhow, the twin brothers grew taller and taller, like the fir trees. The fir trees by now were tall enough to provide shade. The two boys were fifteen. And though they had no one to teach them, because they were intelligent and diligent they came to know many classical works. They also were able to use sophisticated figures of speech to express themselves.

But as the saying goes: A storm may arise from a clear sky. Inasmuch as the twin brothers had grown bigger, they could no longer avoid being noticed as they had when they were still small. One day, as they were listening in on the teacher again, they were caught by the cruel school inspector, who slapped their ears and scolded them, "You miserable Hui—wanting to ride to heaven on a dragon! Just piss! Use the puddle for a mirror! And look at yourself!"

Deeply insulted, the two brothers went home. They refused to eat anything. They both fell ill, lay in bed, and died soon after that. Their parents were so grieved that they wept their hearts out. Their neighbors also shed tears of sorrow. After their sons died, the lonely old couple lived a miserable life. Whenever they thought of their sons they would gaze at the two fir trees, and the sight of the fir trees made them think of their sons all the more.

In those times an imperial examination was held, once every three years, at the emperor's court. When the time came for the examination that year, *xiucai* and *juren* from all parts of the country went to the capitol to participate.[3] All the candidates racked their brains during the examination.

Nanlong was an old town which had produced quite a few gifted scholars, but this time the results of the examination were beyond all people's expectations. Two candidates surnamed Shan, from Nanlong, did equally well. It was simply impossible for the emperor to tell which was better. Greatly delighted, the emperor made an exception that year by granting two Number One Scholar titles. And both of the recipients came from the same Nanlong.

The good news soon spread. The families whose sons or husbands had taken part in the examination prepared a feast; they even collected some monetary rewards in advance of the imperial messengers' arrival. Their houses were decorated with lanterns and with

---

[3]A *xiucai*, during the Ming and Qing dynasties, was one who passed the imperial examination at the district level. A *juren* was a successful candidate in the imperial examinations at the provincial level.

colored streamers. To their disappointment, the messengers passed by without stopping. The people were greatly surprised. No one was able to guess whose son had finished first. They surrounded the messengers and their eyes were staring at the red bulletin, asking, "Could you tell us whose son has been chosen as the Number One Scholar?"

"We would not have gone the long way around town if we knew whose son he is," answered the two messengers, each wiping his forehead and gasping for breath. The people were much surprised, and they asked to be permitted to have a look at the bulletin. The bulletin was passed from one hand to the next. Still, nobody could make it out.

Finally an old man of high prestige stood out from the rest and said, "Please be quiet, I will read it to you!" The people stopped arguing. The old man began to read, "Big Shan and Little Shan from the Hui family, by the stone lions, in front of the Nanlong School."

The people shouted in surprise, "The Hui family, living by the stone lions! Is that not the one who sells cakes? But there are only two of them in the family, the old man and his wife. How is it possible that any one from that family should have become Number One Scholar?"

The old man waved the bulletin and spoke again, "Keep quiet, please! Something is written below. Let me read it! It says—We are the twin brothers who used to live by the stone lions in front of Nanlong School. We died two years ago, leaving our old parents alone. Today we return home after having won high honors."

The people were amazed, and they said, "These must be the twin brothers who have resurrected in order to take part in the examination." They showed the way for the messengers to go straight toward the Shan home.

This day happened to be the seventeenth birthday of Big Shan and Little Shan. Their parents had held a memorial ceremony for them, offering some food and drink. They were weeping under the fir trees when they heard a deafening noise of gongs and drums in the street. Not knowing what was happening they ran out to look. At the front gate they were met by the two messengers, followed by a large crowd. The messengers, kneeling, announced the good news and held the red bulletin over their heads, passing it to the old couple. The couple was unaware of what had happened. They were at a loss about what to think.

Not until people explained to them did they realize the actual state of affairs. The old woman, who had been missing her sons day and night, held the bulletin tightly in her arms and called out, "My sons, how miserable you must feel!" She fell unconscious to the ground. By this the people were thrown into utter confusion. Someone pressed her philtrum.[4] Others poured ginger soup down her throat. It was some time before the old woman regained consciousness.

The two messengers needed a receipt for the reward money. If the Number One Scholars could not be found, how were they to account for it? The neighbors gave to the old parents some reward money. But what could be done about the receipt for the message? More people offered more advice. They suggested that the bulletin be put up on the fir trees, and that a report be made to the emperor concerning the real state of affairs. The two messengers agreed because there was no better way.

The news that the two Shan boys revived after having died, and that they were chosen as Number One Scholars, spread far and wide. People even gave a vivid description of them:

On the day when the two Shan boys entered the examination hall, they were seen riding on purplish-red horses, wearing black suits and turbans. They looked very impressive. Others said that throughout the examination two red lanterns shone brightly above the twin brothers. When they put down their pens to hand in their papers, two golden sparks flew out of the lantern—which made the examination hall come ablaze with golden light.

Hearing the news, and the account of his messengers, the emperor was very pleased. He said right away, "Call the two fir trees, in front of Nanlong School, the Number One Scholar Fir Trees!"

As a result of this imperial edict, Nanlong became a busy town. Hundreds and hundreds of people went there to see the Number One Scholar Fir Trees. At times the house of the Shans was so densely surrounded with people, that no drop of water could have trickled through.

---

[4]The philtrum (*renzhong*) spot is located directly under the middle of the nose. It is pressed to bring people back to consciousness.

Many years passed. Each year the old couple would receive an official salary, sent from afar. With its help they spent their remaining years in relative ease. Then one night they suddenly had a dream. In that dream they saw their two sons come to visit them. They wore black gauze caps and python robes with jade belts.[5] They said to their parents, "We are officials in a distant place. Every year we will send our official salaries to support you. Please present the two fir trees, in front of our house, to the Nanlong School to be used as roof beams, when the school needs an extension."

The old couple woke up quite amazed. They presented the fir trees to the school, as their sons had told them.[6]

It was said that later, when the people extended the school, the two tall fir trees were cut down and set in place as beams of the lecture hall, in Nanlong School. From that time on people of talent kept coming forth from the Nanlong district in large numbers. Nanlong has provided the country with a large number of "pillars of the state."

Personal Visit at Niujie Street

First published in *Min jian wen xue (Folk Literature)*, Beijing, 1984.
Place: Beijing
Narrator: Wang Mengyu (Hui)
Recorder: Ma Jie (Hui)

An imperial edict, and a small jingle bell from Emperor Kangxi (1662–1722) used to be on display in the Niujie Mosque, in Beijing. There is a story about this jingle bell.

---

[5]The black gauze cap, python robe, and jade belt were worn by government officials as a sign of high rank.

[6]Perhaps this story should be appreciated as a graduation speech presented by a teacher at Nanlong School—an object lesson concerning the two roof beams which everyone present could see.

The story begins with a supervisory official. During the Qing dynasty a supervisory official was appointed to go around the capitol and make inquiries. His task was to gather intelligence for the emperor.

One day the supervisory official was in the mood for sightseeing. Accompanied by his wife and concubines, by daughters in sedan chairs and by sons on horses, he left the capitol city for the suburbs. Looking rather majestic, these people toured through the alleys and streets. It happened to be a Friday, the day for the Muslims to go to the mosque to pray. As the official passed through Niujie Street he saw people hasten in the direction of the mosque.

This official was, in fact, foolish and self-indulgent. Although he knew how to bully the common people, he knew practically nothing about their religious customs. That is why he became so suspicious when he saw so many Muslims crowd into the mosque. At first he wanted to get out of his sedan chair to find out what was going on. But it was not very convenient, because he was followed by his family. What is more, sightseeing was more important to him. So he dropped the idea for the time being.

Several days later the Muslim month of Ramadan began. During this month of daytime fasting, after eating their nightly meal, the Muslims would go to the mosque dressed in neat clothes and wearing white caps. This went on for a whole month.

But one day, during Ramadan, this supervisory official came to Niujie Street. He again saw Hui people enter the mosque. This time he became even more suspicious. What were they up to? And why were so many people going to this mosque? In his experience, when common people gathered to meet in great numbers it meant trouble, or even the plotting of a rebellion.

Altogether this appeared not to be a good thing. He had heard of people conspiring against the imperial court in some other places, outside the capitol. So he thought, "Perhaps these Hui people, too, are hatching a sinister plot. The capitol is the place where the emperor lives. If unrest breaks out here, then I, as supervisory official, would be punished severely. I cannot treat this matter lightly."

Meanwhile he also thought that if he could obtain evidence of a Hui rebellion, and report it to the emperor, he certainly would be given a handsome reward. His promotion would be assured. Thinking about this, he was very pleased with himself.

The supervisory official walked around the mosque and, just before entering, he turned and saw a young peddler selling candy.

He asked the peddler, "Little Brother, everyday a lot of people get together here. What on earth are they doing?"

The peddler glanced at him and said, "These Hui people believe in Allah. They gather here every night and dismiss before daybreak each day. They are a close-knit group, prepared to fight back against all those who bully them. You better stay away from them!"

The peddler was a rash fellow, who had come here recently and knew nothing about Islamic customs. The day before, after having sold candy, he bought himself a piece of pork and went into a small Muslim restaurant to have noodles added. Some old Muslim men criticized him. The young man got so angry that he mumbled a few abusive words. Many Muslims nearby came up, and all of them reproached the young peddler for his scandalous behavior. So the young fellow was forced to apologize and to leave. His anger had barely subsided when the supervisory official came to ask. And he took this opportunity to air his grievance.

The words "they revere Allah" astonished the supervisory official in a dreadful way. He thought to himself that in this world, of the great Qing dynasty, these people went so far as to revere Allah instead of the Emperor. How terrible! What else could this be if it was not a conspiracy against the Emperor! There could be no doubt about it. He stalked off, immensely proud of himself for having gathered some real intelligence.

Back home he immediately wrote a memorandum to the throne, on paper folded in accordion-like fashion: "The Muslims in Niujie Street gather secretly for meetings the entire night, daily. They plot to overthrow the great Qing dynasty and to have Allah as their emperor."

The memorandum was sent to Kangxi, the Emperor. After having read it the emperor was surprised. "People along Niujie Street are all Muslims. In recent years the country has prospered and the people have become wealthy. The Muslims are well off. Why would they want to instigate a rebellion? Here, in the capitol city, these Muslims are so bold as to plot against me? How would they dare!"

Kangxi immediately called all the civil and military officials to find a way to deal with this situation. Hearing the news, some of the officials were trembling with fear, and some were shocked and stood with their eyes wide open.

"Make haste! Surround the mosque first!" was the advice which the general of the imperial bodyguards offered.

"Quite right!" continued the military counsellor. "Capture first the man in charge of the mosque and force him to tell who is the head of the rebels."

The voice of an imperial kinsman quivered, "The capitol city is a very important place. It is wise to put down the rebellion as quickly as possible. We must not be neglectful and careless."

But Kangxi still hesitated about making a decision on the strength of their advice. He reasoned to himself, "It has been only a short time since this great Qing dynasty was founded. Yet, it is known far and wide for its military might." He did not believe that someone dared to beard this lion in its own den. But now that a memorandum had been sent by his supervisory official, he had to be watchful. Important as the capitol city was, the case should be resolved with care.

Then he said to all his officials, "Your ideas sound reasonable, but at present the country is at peace. It would be better not to use force. Before reaching a conclusion, I will go and examine what actually is happening."

That night Kangxi went to visit Niujie Street, secretly. In the past, when the emperor had left the imperial palace it had been quite a pompous affair—with banners fluttering, with palace guards clearing the way in front, and with many attendants crowding around. But that night Kangxi went out for a personal visit. He wore the common people's clothes instead of an imperial robe. With a white cap on his head he quietly followed the Muslims into the lighted mosque at Niujie Street.

This was the first time that Kangxi had gone into a mosque. At the center of the place he noticed a large hall, five rooms wide and some thirty meters deep. The hall appeared not grandiose, only a little above the ordinary. Outside the hall stood an octagonal minaret from which the times for Muslim prayer were called. At both sides of the hall sat two pavilions with stone tablets, from previous dynasties. By the large gate stood a two-storied tower, and along its horizontal board were inscribed the words, "Moon Watch Tower." These words could be read if there was sufficient light. Before the hall stood eighteen old cypresses, and a passageway extended between them.

Seeing the Muslims enter that hall, Kangxi followed them. They took off their shoes, and he did the same. They knelt on the carpet, and so did he.

During the days that followed everything happened in the same manner. However, the last day was different from the preceding ones. Just when Kangxi knelt down, he saw some people in long gowns come into the hall, with white turbans on their heads. He surmised that they might be ahongs. One of them began to chant. His voice was loud and clear as if he were reciting. After that recitation the Muslims kowtowed, facing west, and the prayer service was over. They all left the hall and went home.

That particular ahong recited from the Holy Quran, but Kangxi understood nothing. He hastened to join the crowd and asked an old Muslim, "Uncle, I am hard of hearing. I did not catch what he was saying." Glancing at him, the old Muslim said, "What Ahong Wang recited is the forty-seventh sura of the Holy Quran—the teachings of the kind Muhammad."[7]

After returning to the imperial palace, Kangxi requested that the copy of the Quran which had been paid as a tribute be brought to him. And he read from it that very night. He could read the words but was unable to understand their meaning. He thought, "It does not matter, if only I can find the word 'rebellion' in it, that will be sufficient." He looked for it word by word, and section by section, but he could not find a single word or section that referred to rebellion.

Then Kangxi thought, "No wonder I cannot find any trace of rebellion. All these are the religious doctrines of Islam."

As for the assembly of civil and military officials, they grew impatient. Knowing that the emperor was holding court today, they came one after another to stand outside the palace, to welcome His Majesty. In court Kangxi told them, "I have known the truth all along. The Muslims at Niujie Street gather in the mosque at night to do their Ramadan prayers! How could that be a rebellion? The supervisory official has submitted a presumptuous report, which nearly made things bad."

---

[7]Generally the ninety-seventh sura is dedicated to the twenty-seventh night of Ramadan. Sura 44 is also relevant to that occasion.

Upon hearing what actually had transpired, the officials shook their heads and talked about the matter. The general of the imperial bodyguard instantly changed his opinion and said with a loud voice, "The supervisory official, being an important member of the imperial court, could not distinguish between true and false and has submitted a false report about a military situation. He should be punished!"

The military counsellor cut in, "Right! In recent years some people have sought honors by submitting false information, which has endangered our great Qing dynasty. They deserve to be severely punished."

At once Kangxi ordered that the supervisory official be summoned to the court.

After he had submitted his memorandum, the supervisory official was so pleased with himself that he thought some major criminals would be caught and would be decapitated and that he, himself, would be promoted to a higher rank. Thus, upon receiving the imperial order he hurried to the Jinyo Palace to report to the emperor.

Kangxi asked him, "How did you come to know about the rebellion of the Hui people, in Niujie Street?"

"I saw it with my own eyes—that they assembled in the mosque at night and left at daybreak. I felt certain they gathered to plot a rebellion."

"Hui people go to the mosque to pray. That has nothing to do with rebellion. What testimony do you have?"

"The peddler told me that the Hui believe in Allah, and not in Your Majesty."

"Submit the peddler's affidavit."

Being nervous, the supervisory official said, stammeringly, "Noo written statement. He...he told me in the street."

Kangxi went into a rage, "Being a supervisor for the imperial court, you are so ignorant that you do not know anything about Hui people's habits and customs. The presumptuous report you have submitted nearly made me take the wrong action. Come! Banish him from the court. Take off his official cap, and demote him to the level of a commoner."

The supervisor, having in fact come for a promotion, had unexpectedly lost his rank and position. He protested repeatedly that he was being treated wrongly.

Kangxi instructed all his officials and generals to punish severely all those who would submit a false report. To prevent the same thing from happening again, Kangxi gave another imperial edict:

"The Hui Muslims have been going to the mosque since ancient times. Anyone, no matter whether he is an official or an ordinary person, who the next time around makes a false report about Muslims being in rebellion, will be executed first and reported to the emperor later...."

Putting down the pen, Kangxi left the writing table to pace up and down the hall, with his hands behind his back. He thought it over, repeatedly: "I have been to Niujie Street several times and have seen the Muslims united as one. They are not Manchu people, and the fact that they do not now rise up in rebellion against the Qing dynasty does not mean that they may never rebel sometime in the future. Let me present to the Hui Muslims a small bell, to show my kindness toward them, and thereby win them over."

The next day an imperial edict and a small jingle bell were sent to the mosque at Niujie Street.

Today the small jingle bell is no longer there. People say it used to be on display in the large hall of the mosque. But it was destroyed during the early years of the Republic, when the Qing dynasty fell. As to the imperial edict of Kangxi, it is still on display in the Niujie Mosque today.

Muslims, Peace and Happiness Forever!

Place: Gansu
Recorder: Zhao Zhibin (Hui), 1985

It was said that Kangxi, emperor of the Qing dynasty, worked very seriously. He not only listened to the reports of his ministers, but he undertook to examine some matters himself. Once he received a report that in some town the Muslims were about to rebel. In order to ascertain this for himself, the emperor took with him a minister. They disguised themselves as merchants and walked into that town. As they entered the town they saw many Muslims wearing white caps, and they also saw a mosque. As they walked along a street they found a Muslim restaurant and went in. While they ate their meal they talked freely with Muslim people and could see no sign of rebellion at all.

For a whole day they walked around and got very tired; so after supper they found a small guest house and settled down. Before Kangxi fell into deep sleep, his minister hurried in, out of breath, and reported in a low voice, "It is terrible. All the Muslims in this town have gathered in the mosque. It appears that they are going to rebel."

He asked the emperor to leave town and return to the capital immediately, to dispatch troops to put down that rebellion.

Kangxi got up and dressed. But as he was about to leave he thought, momentarily, "I treat my people like my children. Why should they rebel?"

It was better to see something once than to hear it said a hundred times. He therefore decided to go to the mosque to see for himself. He asked his minister to get his clothes ready, and he dressed up as a Muslim.

Calmly he went into the mosque, by himself. He saw a crowd of people kneeling on the floor. There was no noise, no knife or spear, but only a white-bearded ahong reciting Quranic verses. Kangxi listened for quite some time among the crowd and he could not hear a word about rebellion. He was a learned man and knew a little about Islamic rules and doctrine. He left the hall and returned to the guest house.

There he said to his minister, "You are wrong. This evening is the Muslim's Lailat al-Qadr.[8] If I had believed you readily and dispatched troops to put them down, I would have harmed my people

---

[8]Song ye jie or Laylat al-Qadr: the twenty-seventh night during the month of Ramadan, commemorating the "Night of Power," a night in the year 610 C.E. when the Quran descended into the soul of the Prophet Muhammad. Historically the date of this holiday may have been adapted to a Manichaean holiday.

and my country." After he returned to the capital, Kangxi wrote, "Muslims, Peace and Happiness Forever."

He had these words engraved in a golden board and had it sent to that mosque. From then on all his ministers and officials dared not, carelessly, to make secret reports in order to hurt people.

Bai Shuyu and His Mutton Fries

Place: Xuanwu District, Beijing
Narrator: Hei Zendian (Hui, age 68)
Recorder: Ma Jie (Hui), 1984

This happened in the years of Qianlong, during the Qing dynasty. At Niujie Street, in Beijing, lived a Hui Muslim named Bai Shuyu who supported himself by selling mutton fries. Each day, at noon, he came to the T-shaped junction by the Xinhua Gate with his handcart. And from there he returned home in the evening.

Bai Shuyu's mutton fries were well known. The meat was done in just the right length of time, fresh and tender, with seasonings of all kinds. Additionally, the pan, the bowls, chopsticks and plates were shiny clean. The moment he set up his stand the street was filled with a good smell. Whoever saw his food wanted to try some. Unlike some other entrepreneurs who welcomed the rich and disliked the poor, Bai Shuyu treated both rich and poor alike. The rich as well as the poor could buy on credit. Thus, more and more people stopped by for the mutton, and business was quite brisk.

One day a Daoist priest came, dressed in a long robe. His manners were above the ordinary. He sat down at a table and ate two servings of mutton in one meal. "Delicious! Very delicious meat!" He said again and again, then paid the money and left.

Several days in succession he came just when the sun had reached the west. Once, after he had finished eating, the Daoist priest stood up with embarrassment and said, "I am very sorry. I forgot to bring money with me."

The very instant when Bai Shuyu heard this, he smiled and said, "It does not matter. You may give it to me whenever you have some. If you are short of money now, you may pay me later." From then on the Daoist priest often forgot to bring money with him, and Bai did not mind at all.

Once, after eating, the Daoist priest said to Bai, remorsefully, "I have noticed that your business is not a big one. I myself owe you quite a bit of money. I really feel apologetic."

Bai said, "I am not selling it just for money. Courtesy is the road to business success. Though the income is small, I can still afford to have my customers pay me later."

After a while the Daoist priest spoke again: "All these days I have found you to be an honest person. Let us become friends. Shall we?"

"That would be really wonderful," Bai said happily.

"What do you usually do in your spare time?" the Daoist priest asked.

"Being a small business man, how can I find spare time? When I am free, well, I like to play a game of chess," Bai answered.

"That is fine. I also am fond of chess. Please come to my place when you have time. Let us play a game." With these words he wrote down his address on a slip of paper and told Bai to look for him at this address. Bai was half illiterate. Next to the address, on the paper, he also saw a red seal; but he was not familiar with the words which were written on it. So he casually put it aside.

One day Bai Shuyu found the Daoist priest's place in accordance with the address on the paper. He looked up and thought, "Is this not the back gate of the imperial palace?" He said to himself, "So, the Daoist priest is an errandman here in the palace. He is indeed an extraordinary priest!"

The guard at the door examined the paper and at once led him to the inner palace. After a few minutes he saw a man with attendants crowding around him, coming in. It was none other than the Daoist priest who used to eat mutton at his stand. Seeing the man in the imperial robe he realized at once that he was not a Daoist priest, but the Emperor Qianlong. With a quick flop Bai Shuyu knelt on the ground and said repeatedly, "I am very ignorant in that I offended your Majesty. Please forgive me."

Qianlong pulled him up and smiled: "You have come to play chess with me, have you not? I have nothing to do at the moment. Come on. Let us play chess." And Bai played with Qianlong.

Qianlong felt bored living in the imperial palace. He went out in ordinary clothes and strolled through streets and alleys. After having tasted the stir-fried mutton, cooked by Bai, he thought it was far more delicious than any of the dainties he tasted in the palace. If he passed a day without eating Bai's mutton, Qianlong would feel uneasy. So he let Bai come to the palace to cook the mutton for him and to play chess with him.

The story, that Bai Shuyu played chess with Qianlong, made the rounds quickly. Almost all the people in Beijing heard it.

The Dragon-Boat Festival was approaching. Qianlong got bored watching dragon boats in rivers and asked for a small dragon boat made of pure gold for his enjoyment in the palace. The imperial order was given to the jeweler shop outside the Zhengyang Gate. The craftsmen kept very busy with designing models and with smelting gold. In only a few days the craftsmen had made a small dragon boat of pure gold and had delivered it to the imperial palace. Against their expectation, the golden boat was secretly taken by a greedy eunuch who waited on the emperor. This fellow often took advantage of the emperor while serving him. He deceived his majesty by taking bribes. He kept the boat of pure gold as his own. Instead, a gilded dragon boat was made overnight and presented to the emperor.

Qianlong was in the habit of appreciating pearls and jewelry. At first sight he thought the boat to be lovely and rare. But when he took it into his hand—"Well, why is it so light?" he asked.

He shouted, "Come on!"

"Yes, Your Majesty." The eunuch kneeled down before Qianlong. "What can I do for you?"

Qianlong asked, "The golden boat seems so light. Is it real gold?"

The eunuch said, cunningly and hurriedly, "Is it possible that those craftsmen deliberately cheated Your Majesty? They should be punished severely."

Qianlong gave an order to break it, right away, and the boat was broken in two parts. What they saw was a silver boat covered with a thin layer of gold. Qianlong flew into a rage. He immediately condemned the craftsmen to death. As for the chief culprit, his family and nine branches of relatives should be killed as well, and their property confiscated.

Disaster fell from heaven. All the craftsmen were frightened. It was indeed unfair. How could a real gold dragon boat become a fake one? For a moment they could not understand it. But anyhow, someone had to go to the imperial palace to request mercy before the death sentence was carried out. Who would be the right person to go?

They thought of Bai Shuyu, knowing that he was a friend of the emperor who often cooked mutton for him, and played chess with him. If he was willing to go, the emperor might relent. So the craftsmen invited some prominent persons and hurried to Niujie Street.

Bai Shuyu, seeing the people neatly dressed, thought that they had come for mutton. So he invited them into the room and, while making tea, asked, "Do you want mutton?"

They spoke, looking extremely worried: "How could we be in a mood for mutton?" They poured out to him what had happened and concluded with these words: "Today we have come, specifically, to request your help."

For a while Bai Shuyu felt it to be a tough nut to crack. How could a solid golden boat have become a fake one? If it was true that the boat they handed over was indeed a fake, that would have been a crime of deceiving the emperor. In that case he could not obtain favors but would himself become involved. So he began to question the craftsmen carefully. They all answered firmly, "Believe us, the golden boat which we sent was real. How could we be so impudent as to deceive the Emperor?"

Bai Shuyu thought to himself, "The boat might have been changed secretly by someone waiting on the emperor. If so, it will be impossible to find the real boat. And instet of finding it much more trouble could arise. It is better to keep the craftmen's grievances quiet and find a way to save their lives first. But how?" Bai Shuyu thought hard. At last an excellent plan occurred to him. He slapped his leg and said, "Ah, I have an idea! I have an idea!"

The craftsmen kneeled down and said, full of tears, "Thank you! We entrust our lives to you."

Bai Shuyu helped them up and said, "I shall go to the palace and you may go back home, to wait for me."

That afternoon Bai Shuyu entered Xihua Gate to meet the emperor and to play chess, as usual. After a while Bai Shuyu gave a sigh with his head bent low. Qianlong became curious and asked, "Usually you are very happy to play chess with me, but today you heave deep sighs. Is there anything that troubles you?"

Bai Shuyu shook his head, intentionally, and said, "It is difficult to talk about."

"It does not matter. I will not count it against you."

"I heard that the gold dragon boat which Your Majesty has received is a fake one. Is that not so?"

"Those craftsmen are really despicable. They dared to cheat me! I shall have their heads chopped off! But why, why do you mention it?"

Seizing the opportunity Bai Shuyu said, "Your Majesty, I have heard that they did not cheat Your Majesty."

Qianlong stopped playing and asked, "How could that be? I had it broken on the spot. It was a fake, really."

"It was a model for Your Majesty to look at. If Your Majesty is satisfied, a real gold dragon boat will be made according to the model, otherwise they will design a new one."

After seeing Qianlong nodding, Bai Shuyu continued, "In my humble opinion, this is not cheating but showing respect for Your Majesty."

Hearing this, Qianlong smiled and looked over the broken sample again, carefully. Yes, indeed, it was delicately made in an unusual style. He turned to Bai Shuyu and said, "All right, I will consider your words. Let the craftsmen make a solid gold dragon boat. I will spare them the death penalty."

And so the craftsmen were spared. And even though they had to hand over two dragon boats made of pure gold, they were lucky enough to have the calamity of being killed averted. On top of that, their families and relatives were spared as well.

In order to thank Bai Shuyu, the craftsmen sent him a lot of silver, gold, and jewels. But Bai Shuyu declined these. He said, "Muhammad once told us to be honest and to find pleasure in helping others. My help is not worth mentioning." He continued to sell mutton as he had done before.

The craftsmen felt deeply grateful toward their Muslim friend. When he died they raised a large sum of money, built a memorial gate spanning the street between Langfang Number Two and Three in memory of Bai Shuyu. Inside the tower they offered a sacrifice to him with mutton. In accordance with Hui customs there was no portrait or statue. To this very day there is talk about Bai Shuyu within the jewelers' guild. Everyone knows about him and has a feeling of appreciation toward him.

It was said that during the years of Gengzi the Dashanlan business district caught fire. The fire destroyed the entire street, but the memorial gate remained standing. Nowadays a board still remains from this gate.

The Golden Foot Mosque

Place: Gansu
Recorder: Zhao Zhibin (Hui), 1985

When Islam came to China it spread first along the seacoast, and then gradually inland. Along with that dispersion a number of mosques were built. No one could tell when Islam came to the city of Nanjing, or when the number of Muslims began to increase. But before long a mosque was built at Nanjing City.

It has been said that one day Zhu Yuanzhang, the Ming emperor, brought with him several of his Hui generals to the region where Hui people lived. He was accompanied by the two ministers Chang Yuchun and Hu Dahai. Before the gate of the mosque the emperor got off his sedan chair and entered the yard, walking straight toward the great hall. One of his feet had stepped into the hall before Chang Yuchun was able to stop him and say, "Your Majesty, according to the rules of Islam, everyone should take off his shoes before entering."

Zhu Yuanzhang looked as if awakening from a dream, and he said, "Ayah—I do not know the custom." Then he drew back his foot and ordered, "Come! Dig out the footprint I have just made on the floor!" After he went back to his palace he sent his men to have the footprint inlaid with gold. Therefore this mosque became known as "Golden Foot Mosque."

7

Origins of the Hui Nationality

Wan Gars

Place: Xiji, Haiyuan, and Guyuan, in Ningxia
Narrators: Bei Wenhai and Ma Yuanqin (Hui)
Recorder: He Jide, 1979

One night the emperor of the Tang dynasty dreamt that the roof beam of his golden palace was collapsing. The roof beam nearly smashed his head, but it was intercepted and pushed back by the right hand of a man. The man wore a green robe, and a white turban was wound around his head. He had a towel draped over his shoulder and a water kettle in his left hand. He had deep eye sockets, a high nose bridge, and a brown face.

The next day when the officials came to pay respect to the emperor, at his court, the emperor told his dream and asked for explanations.

Xu Mao stepped forward and said, "The man is not a Han like we. He is a Hui from the western regions. The green robe and white turban are worn only for prayer when one goes to the mosque. The towel and the water kettle are used to wash one's body.[1] The great Tang empire needs the Hui people for its defence."

---

[1]This water kettle is used by Hui people for the ceremonial washing of face and hands, before prayer. See photograph 64. Concerning the Wan Gars tradition see also photograph 1.

The emperor said, "Then let us invite some Hui people to come here."

Xu Mao said, "We may not be able to persuade some to come by invitation, but perhaps by trading."

The emperor said, "What shall we give in exchange?"

"Exchange people for people."

"All right, it shall be done!"

Xu Mao chose sixty young men and exchanged them for sixty Hui men who were led by Gens, Gais, and Wan Gars. Because they could not get accustomed to the climate, most of these men died along the way. Gens died in Xinjiang. Gais died in Jiuquan. Wan Gars led the twenty Huis who were left and arrived in Chang'an, on the day of Qurban.

Upon their arrival the Tang emperor himself went to welcome them outside the palace gate; he addressed Wan Gars as Brother. Meanwhile, the emperor decreed that Wan Gars should be permitted to go in and out of the imperial palace freely. No one had the right to stop him. Wan Gars could sit at the same table with the emperor, as an equal. And no one could oppose this decree. Moreover, the emperor ordered his high general, Jingde, to build a mosque where Wan Gars could pray.

After having lived at the palace for quite a long time, Wan Gars became homesick—and so did the teacher who was with them and the men. All day long Wan Gars had a worried look. The Tang emperor then ordered a golden water kettle made for Wan Gars to wash his face and his body. Since that time the Hui people have kept a water kettle in their house, made of copper. It is actually called Tang kettle. Copper has approximately the same color as gold; it is clean and durable. With the Tang kettle in his possession, Wan Gars never again asked to return to the western regions.

Some time later the Tang emperor thought about the fact that the Hui men who had come with Wan Gars were all single, without family. If in the future they died, there would be no Huis to guard the Tang empire, and that would be a big problem. So he held a grand ceremony and permitted the Hui to choose their mates. Since that time the Hui people have been settled in China. Even nowadays there is this saying among the Hui, "Hui father, Han mother!"

Hui Beginnings

This narrative is from *The Origin of the Hui People*, an old anthology of stories concerning Islam in China, by Liu Sanjie, who wrote some time during the Qing dynasty.

On March 18th, in the second year of Zhenguan of the Tang dynasty, the emperor Li Shimin had a dream, at midnight.[2] During that dream he saw in the palace a turban scarf pursuing a monster. When he awoke from the dream the emperor felt surprised and bewildered. He did not know whether it was a good omen or a bad one. The next morning he consulted all his officials.

The official in charge of dream interpretation said, "Turban scarf indicates Hui people in the western regions. There is a country called Tianfang, to the west of Jiayuguan. The king of this country is of noble character and high reputation. His country is prosperous and has a well-trained and powerful army. Inasmuch as Your Majesty has seen a monster enter the palace, there must be some evil spirit. It cannot be defeated without the help of the Hui people."

The military counselor, Xushi, said, "The Hui people are very honest. They never deceive. If we treat them kindly they will remain loyal to Your Majesty and never betray you. Please send an envoy to the Muslim ruler in the western regions. Request the assistance of some able person to defeat this evil spirit."

The emperor listened to their advice and sent an emissary named Shi Mingtang to travel to the western regions to meet with the Muslim ruler. The official carried with him the imperial edict which the Muslim ruler was delighted to receive. He chose three eminent Muslims and sent them to China. They were named Gens, Gers, and Wan Gars. Gens and Gers died along the way because they were unaccustomed to the climate of the new place. Only Wan Gars survived. He traveled across mountains and rivers. After many hardships, at last, Wan Gars arrived in China. He was shown very special hospitality by the Tang emperor.

---

[2]Zhenguan is the name of the reign of Emperor Li Shimin (627–649 C.E.).

The emperor asked him about the difference between their respective scriptures. Wan Gars explained to the emperor that their scripture is the Quran, which was sent by God. It is held in high esteem just as the Five Classics are among the Han people. He also expounded in detail how the Confucian code of ethics differed from that of the western lands. The emperor was very pleased with him. He selected three thousand Tang soldiers and sent them to the western regions in exchange for three thousand Hui soldiers.

The Hui soldiers came to keep Wan Gars company. They settled in China and increased in number. They are said to be the ancestors of the present-day Chinese Hui Muslims.

The Hui People of Lingzhou

Place: Wuzhong, Ningxia
Narrator: Wu Jinlong (Hui)
Recorder: Na Jianggao (Hui), 1979

It has been said that during the reign of the emperor Tang Xuanzong, the general An Lushan rose up in rebellion. The emperor had to seek refuge in Lingzhou.[3] At that time Guo Ziyi was the commander in chief who led the Tang army against the rebel forces. Because Guo Ziyi's army was not large enough, he had to go and borrow some soldiers from the Huihe people. The requirements put forth by the Huihe people was that Guo give ten Han people in exchange for one Huihe soldier. Guo Ziyi complied with their demands because he was in dire need. And so, three thousand Han people were given in exchange for three hundred Huihe soldiers.

The battle lasted a long time. An Lushan was finally defeated and Chang'an (present-day Xian) was recaptured. The Huihe soldiers suffered heavy casualties during that battle. Only Wan Gars and the

---

[3]Lingzhou was an administrative division in the Tang empire, situated in the Lingwu region of present-day Ningxia.

two others were left. The Tang emperor was very appreciative toward them. He asked them to remain in Chang'an and rewarded them with high positions and handsome salaries.

None of the three had brought wives or children with them. As time passed they became homesick, and they all wanted to leave Chang'an. The Tang emperor was worried when he became aware of this, and he discussed the matter with his ministers.

One of the ministers said the Huihe soldiers would settle down only if they married some Han girls. But other ministers said that not a single Han father would agree to give his daughter in marriage to a Huihe soldier. There was only one way for them, and that was to take their brides by force. The Tang emperor thought this over and decided to let the Huihe soldiers take brides by force, during the Lantern Festival (on January 15th).

The time of the Lantern Festival soon came. The emperor had the streets of Chang'an decorated with all kinds of lanterns. The festival was celebrated in a variety of ways. People from within the city and the surrounding area came to watch the lanterns. Chang'an Street was a sea of people.

The emperor told the three Huihe men, "Tonight the streets will be very much alive. Surely, there will be many pretty girls in the crowd. You may go and take them by force. Those taken by you will be your wives."

The three men were happy to hear the emperor's words. They took to the street and there took by force whomever seemed beautiful to them. That night each of them carried away nine girls.[4] Inasmuch as they had taken away that many girls—in accordance with his own permission—the emperor had to accept the outcome as an accomplished fact. Each of the three Huihe soldiers was permitted to have nine beautiful girls as wives so long as he agreed to settle down in Chang'an.

---

[4]Islam permits up to four wives only with stringent conditions. After the death of his first wife, Khadijah, the Prophet Muhammad had nine more. It is significant that Muhammad's emissaries to China are considered his equals regarding this privilege of having nine wives. Such dreams of polygamy, nevertheless, apply in China nowadays only in the realm of legends. Chinese Muslims are committed to monogamy perhaps more devoutly than are some of their brothers in the faith elsewhere.

You may wonder why the Huihe soldiers had moved to Lingzhou. It happened like this. After Tang Xuanzong died, a new emperor came to the throne. He paid less and less attention to the three Huihe soldiers, and he forgot all about the great service they had rendered to the Tang empire. There was no reason for them to stay in Chang'an any longer. So they moved with their families to Lingzhou and Wuzhongbao.[5] There they settled and gradually they increased in number. As time passed they were no longer called the Huihe. People simply called them the "Hui."

The Origin of the Hui People

First published in *Min jian wen xue (Folk Literature)*, Beijing, 1983.
Place: Linxia, Gansu
Narrator: Ma Jin-hai (Hui, age 83)
Recorder: Zhou Mengshi (Hui)

During the period of the Tang dynasty the men Gens, Gers, and Wan Gars were sent by the sage Muhammad to China to propagate the religion of Islam. Gens and Gers died from illness along the way. Only Wan Gars arrived safely in China. The Tang emperor was very pleased about his arrival. He sent his court officials to meet Wan Gars, and he housed him in the guest house for foreigners, in the capital city.

After the day of his arrival in China, Wan Gars retreated to contemplate and to pray in seclusion. One day the emperor had some leisure time when, by and by, he remembered Wan Gars. He had been told that Wan Gars was extremely intelligent, well-learned, and resourceful. So he disguised himself as an ordinary official and went, by himself, to pay a visit to Wan Gars.

He came to the dwelling of Wan Gars, secretly, and observed him from the open door. Wan Gars was seen to be piously reading

---

[5]Wuzhongbao is the present-day city of Wuzhong, in Ningxia.

the Quran, facing west. When he had finished a section, he closed the book and gently placed it on the table. Then he came out to meet the emperor, with a smile. "Your Majesty," he said, "please come in and have a seat! Excuse me for not meeting you earlier."

The emperor was surprised and asked, "How did you know that I am the emperor?" Wan Gars only smiled. The two men sat there talking, each clasping his own hands. To test his knowledge, the emperor put forth on purpose a few tough questions, which Wan Gars answered wisely and without hesitation. The emperor was pleased with his answers. He asked Wan Gars to remain in Chang'an and he permitted him to persuade people to join Islam.[6]

Several years passed. Wan Gars became homesick; he wanted to return home. The Tang emperor urged him to stay for another few months. Some time later Wan Gars again asked for permission to return home. The emperor felt very sad about this. He said to himself, "This Wan Gars keeps asking for permission to return home. I must think of something that will make him stay."

He then told one of his ministers, "Go, and tell that 'Hui' to stay for another month. I will let him go as soon as the weather turns nice."

From that time onward, the name of the "Hui" people became wellknown.[7]

---

[6]Chang'an is the old name for Xian (Xi'an), capitol city of the Tang dynasty.

[7]"Hui" in Chinese also means "to return." On account of his wanting to return to Arabia, the emperor is said to have called Wan Gars "that Hui" (that Returner).

Why Do the Hui People
"Chase Horse" at Weddings?

First published in *Gan su min jian wen xue cong shu (Gansu Collection of Folk Literature)*, 1982.
Place: Linxia, Gansu
Narrator: Ma Quanfu (Hui, age 83)
Recorder: Zhou Mengshi (Hui)

After his minister had left his company, the Tang emperor thought very hard, and he had a good idea. He instructed his officials to do this and that. The next day the emperor invited Wan Gars to visit the imperial garden. In the garden of the imperial palace hundreds of girls, dressed like fairy maidens, strolled about merrily. The emperor showed Wan Gars the garden.

After a while he left Wan Gars alone because he had some official duties to attend to. Before he left he told Wan Gars, "You may choose one from among the girls and take her with you, if you like." With these words the emperor left him and went to his residence.

Wan Gars took a leisurely walk in the garden, by himself. He was about to leave when he caught sight of a very nice girl who had been following him and watching him all the time. Wan Gars felt very strange. He called the girl to come near. She looked like a lotus that had just emerged from the water, or like a peony that had just come into blossom. Wan Gars was very pleased with her. He asked whether she would go with him. The girl readily agreed.

Because the emperor had permitted it, and because the girl liked him, he helped her to get on his horse. Then together they left the garden.

But when they left the garden they were seen by the gate-keeper. He wondered why this foreigner carried away a girl. So he broke a twig off a willow tree and ran after the horse, shouting loudly. But he did not dare to arrest Wan Gars, for fear that he might break the Tang emperor's regulations. Wan Gars was alarmed when he saw someone running after them. He spurred on his horse and got to his place without stopping.

To avoid getting accused of neglect the man in charge of the garden reported the incident to the emperor. Hearing his account the emperor burst into laughter. He wrote an imperial edict to the effect that the keeper of the garden should not be punished. Instead, the gatekeeper was praised for having done a good deed.

Then the Tang emperor issued another edict to the effect that a banquet be given to celebrate Wan Gars' wedding. This happened to be not only the emperor's but also Allah's decree. The result was that Wan Gars settled in China.

Nowadays the Hui people in Linxia county, in Gansu, still have the custom of "chasing horse" at weddings. Relatives of the bride will shout loudly while chasing the bridegroom's horse. It is said that this custom has been handed down from the days of the Tang dynasty.

Hui and Han Are Relatives

Place: Xinjiang
Narrator: Wu Wangliang (Hui)
Recorder: Dong Yi, 1983

After the emperor Li Shimin of the Tang dynasty ascended to the throne, the people lived happily and peacefully and enjoyed favorable weather. But no one could tell when an evil spirit would appear. Now and then the city was covered with clouds, and neither the moon nor the sun could be seen. Along the border there were occasional skirmishes, and among the inhabitants in the land something strange and unusual happened. During daytime the ducks would lay eggs and at midnight hens would cackle. People were in a constant state of anxiety. The ministers of the emperor were disturbed but did not show it. The common people talked about it everywhere. They all thought this to be a bad omen. There may be either great disorder under heaven, or Li's throne was about to shake. The emperor, too, became worried.

One day in the Golden Hall the emperor had a dream. In that dream he saw a big strong man, in a green gown and with a turban wound around his head. He was carrying a water kettle in one hand and in the other he held Li's golden hall. The emperor was so startled that he let out a cry. He woke up in cold sweat.

The sovereign thought about this dream but was unable to decode its meaning—whether it meant good fortune or disaster. So he summoned his ministers and officials to interpret his dream.

Among the officials was a wonderful man, Xu Maogong, who had foresight and often gave wise counsel. He acted as though he calculated and reckoned, and then he said, "Your Majesty, the man you saw in your dream is a wise and able man in the west. If you could invite him to come to our land, I assure you that this land would be safe." Thereupon the emperor of Tang issued an order to the effect that a capable man carrying gold, silver, and other treasures would be sent after that able man in the west whom he met in his dream.

The imperial envoy, together with his entourage, left Chang'an to travel along the Silk Road through the western regions until they finally arrived in Mecca. The imperial envoy met with Hailishuai of Mecca and told him of their intent.[8] Hailishuai saw that the envoys which had been sent by the Tang emperor were very sincere. He decided to send three of his disciples, and each of these brought with him thirty younger disciples to accompany them to the East, to assist the great Tang. The gold and silver, with the other treasures and the silk, would all be distributed among the poor and the working people.

Meanwhile, after the envoys requested it repeatedly, Hailishuai agreed to send the Tang emperor a picture of Muhammad. But it was explicitly instructed that they were permitted only to look at it, not to worship it.

At last the imperial envoy departed, greatly satisfied. The three disciples whom Hailishuai had sent were named Gaisi, Aisi, and Wan Gars. There were about three hundred people accompanying them all the way eastward. Along the way the oldest father, Gaisi, and the second father, Aisi, became ill and died.[9]

---

[8] "Hailishuai" is a Chinese title signifying the rank of a king in a land of Muslims.

[9] The meaning of "father" (baba), in this instance comes closer to "uncle."

When they approached Chang'an, imperial envoys welcomed all these people to the central plains of China. These three hundred people had grown beards and therefore looked older than they were. Actually they were quite young. Upon hearing the welcome they knew that Chang'an was nearby. It was better to stay and accept the invitation than to refuse and travel on.

The approximately three hundred people arrived together at Chang'an city. Within the City a meal had already been prepared for the virtuous guests from the west.

After Wan Gars and his entourage had arrived in Chang'an, the world for them seemed to have changed. Li Shimin, the Tang emperor, was greatly pleased to see the portrait of Muhammad, who was the very man he had seen in his dream. He said, "This is the very person I saw in my dream, and this is the capable man who can protect my reign and the state. He is worthy of worship." Just then, as he had prostrated himself before that portrait, the image of Muhammad disappeared. Only white paper was left.

The emperor issued another order, to the effect that Chi Jingde, one of his ministers, should go to Nine-li Hill to build the Great Shaanxi Mosque. At that place Wan Gars and his people could worship and recite scripture.

From then on the great Tang dynasty had good crops, nice animals, and fine weather. It also had strong soldiers and sturdy horses who together defeated the king of Pan as well as rebellious armies. And so the great Tang had its mighty armies and the land was renewed.

But these three hundred virtuous guests could not understand the local language. They also had different customs and wore different clothing. Although they received double rations of grain and a salary each month, they were not accustomed to the life here. They began to miss their home town, and some among them asked for permission to go back to Mecca. The ruler of Tang was not willing to let them leave, so he pretended not to know about their requests. After a long time even common people knew that the guests from the West wanted "to *hui*" (to return). Day after day, and year after year, they wanted to *hui*. But their imperial host insisted that they stay. So from their wanting to *hui hui hui* was derived the name of the *Hui* people.

Li Shimin summoned his officials to think of a way to have the Hui people stay in the central plains. The advisor Xu Maogong had already gotten an idea, and he told the emperor, "We must get them married. If they have wives and children they cannot go back."

The king welcomed this suggestion. But who would act as go-between to arrange their marriages? Whose daughters would be willing to marry someone who did not know their language? Xu Maogong thought of another idea, and the emperor was pleased with this idea and accepted it.

It was the Lantern Festival. There was a colorful lantern party in the park. The king gave a secret order that the Hui men could go in and out without being stopped or checked. He also instructed his interior minister to tell the Hui men that they could choose their brides from among those present at the party, but that those girls who wore their hair in a knot, at their back, could not be chosen because they were married women. All those with long hair in a tail were unmarried girls. They could choose any one they liked. Those who were chosen the imperial officials would register and report to the court.

At the lantern party were all kinds of diversions—lions, dragon lanterns, boats on land, stilts, fireworks, firecrackers, and more. And there was a crowd of people as large as the sea. Some came for amusement, and others just came to see the excitement. Some girls who ordinarily were not permitted to go out-of-doors had never seen Hui people. So, at the party some of them followed the Hui secretly just to see what they looked like.

The next day, in different counties, all the families of officials and commoners, of rich and poor, whose daughters had been chosen by the Hui, received the imperial notice to go to the Department of Finance to receive gold and silver and, in the meantime to have their daughters sent to the Hui courtyard in bridal sedan chairs. The Hui men could claim the one to which they had taken a fancy. The wedding ceremony, held by government officials, with the imperial court as chief witnesses, was lively and exciting. Young couples entered their bridal chambers.

On the third day after getting married, by custom, newly wedded couples had to go back to visit the parents of the bride. The government could not be sure about their safety, and therefore, for the protection of each couple, they sent along two officials, secretly. All the parents were happy to receive the new couples. Aunts, sisters, and other relatives asked the girls in a low voice, "How do you like your husband?" The answers of the girls were almost all the same:

"He is kind and the food is good, but his language is difficult to understand."

The emperor of Tang continued to give to the parents of these girls some grain and money, every month. And so the Hui men stayed in China. But these Hui men had no family names, and their children were therefore named after their wives. Because the Hui people had different customs, and had a different religion, a new nationality eventually came into being. Generation after generation, to this day, many more Hui and Han intermarried. And therefore, Hui and Han are relatives.

Do Not Listen to the Hui

Place: Gansu
Recorder: Zhao Zhibin (Hui), 1983

It was said that during the height of the Tang dynasty, the Tang emperors sent diplomatic envoys to western regions, and vice versa. They got along peacefully.

One year some Hui people were sent from the western regions to Chang'an to do missionary work. The Tang emperor permitted them to settle and to marry Han girls, in Chang'an.

After they had gotten married, the Hui and Han lived together happily, loving and respecting one another. When the girls returned to the home of their parents to visit, they were asked, "How do you like the Hui people?"

The girls answered, "The Hui people are kind, and their food is good, but their language is difficult to understand."

Their parents said: "As long as your husband is kind, and as long as the two of you can get along well, as far as the language is concerned you do not need to listen to him."

So for a thousand years Hui and Han, in the north and west, have addressed each other as Aunt and Uncle. There is also a saying that spread: "Eat Hui food; there is no need to listen to Hui words."

8

Hui Leaders with
and Against the Empire

Young Sanbao Helps Capture
a Corrupt Official

First published in *Yun nan shao shu ming zu wen xue zi liao (Literary Materials about Minorities in Yunnan)*, 1981.
Place: Yunnan
Recorder: Ma Ruilin and Wang Bao (Hui)

It has been said that the family name of Eunuch Sanbao was not Zheng, but Ma; his given name was He. When he was still young, little Ma He enjoyed listening to his father, Ma Ha, when he told stories. Ma Ha had traveled far away across the sea and visited many countries. The stories which he told to his son were all about the local conditions and customs of people in these foreign lands. These stories impressed little Ma He so much that he often thought about traveling across the sea, like his father, to visit many countries. He knew that he had to be an excellent swimmer if he ever was to fulfil his dream.

It happened that his family was living by the Kungying Lake. He went to the lake and bathed there every day. As a result he became a good swimmer.

One day little Ma He was herding sheep in the mountains when, suddenly, he noticed a man running toward the lake, almost out of breath. Having always been a shrewd lad, little Ma He kept an eye on this man who circled a small hill and proceeded toward the lake.

The man lunged into a dinghy and hurriedly rowed toward the middle of the lake. Ma He was absorbed in watching this man when, suddenly, the noise of hoofbeats could be heard behind him. He turned his head and saw a group of men, on horses, galloping toward him and looking about as if they were searching. The little Ma He drove his sheep down the mountain and an officer, leading his horse, stepped toward him from the troop.

The officer asked him, "Young boy! Have you seen a man passing by, wearing a hat with a tip?"

Little Ma He understood immediately what was meant, but he still asked in reply, "Who are you? And who are you looking for?" Being only a child, his question was substantial. So the officer told little Ma He, "We are the soldiers of the great Ming emperor, and we are searching for a corrupt official of the previous dynasty. Formerly he had been harming the people and has committed every possible crime. If we fail to capture him, the people will never be relieved of their hatred toward him."

Most of all, little Ma He hated such corrupt officials who have harmed the people. Judging by the tolerance and the dignified appearance of these men—compared with the deviousness of the man who had untied the mooring rope without permission and who had fled away like a mouse—little Ma He then said, "Yes, I saw him row away in a dinghy." The officer and his men quickly galloped to the lake and saw the boat far away. No other boat was available at that moment, and nobody knew what to do.

Revealing his shrewdness with a twinkle in his eye, little Ma He said, "Do not worry. I can get that dinghy back." With his action faster than his speech, he shed his coat, dove into the water, and disappeared. At the shore the officer and his men began worrying about him.

There was no sign of the boy for some time. But they noticed the boat suddenly being tossed about, at the middle of the lake, and coming several times close to capsizing. The men stood anxious but were unable to do anything about it. The boat kept turning for a while in a circle and, unexpectedly, it slowly came moving back toward the shore, nearer and nearer. Gradually the nose and the eyes of the man in the boat could be recognized.

Then the officer in charge issued an order, and his men rushed into the lake together. They dragged the corrupt official ashore. And it was little Ma He who had been propelling that dinghy through the water. The corrupt official was so frightened that he abandoned the oars and held on to the side boards in fear of drowning. By doing so, little Ma He brought the boat to within a small distance from the shore.

In this manner the little Ma He helped the Ming soldiers catch a heinous criminal. This brought him great merit. He was brought to the capitol to be presented to the emperor. Could an emperor not like such a clever and shrewd boy? He granted little Ma He a Han family name—Zheng—and kept him at the palace.

Later this boy became the famous court eunuch, Zheng He.[1]

Eunuch Sanbao at the Welcoming Pavilion

First published in *Yun nan shao shu ming zu wen xue zi liao (Literary Materials About Minorities in Yunnan)*, 1981.
Place: Quanzhou and Huian, Fujian
Recorders: Qiujun and Yanyan (Hui)

Along the lower reaches of Luoyang River, outside Huian City in Fujian, by the river bank, there is a mountain named Lion Ball Mountain. The mountain displays picturesque scenery. It is surrounded by the sea on three sides and linked with land on one side. It is Baiqi, a place where Hui people live. At the small harbor of Baiqi sits an ancient pavilion, and from that pavilion one has a panoramic view of Quanzhou Bay. This is the famous welcoming pavilion told about in legends.

---

[1] Zheng He was an outstanding navigator during the Ming dynasty. He was a Hui who had come from the Kunming area, in Yunnan. His original name was He Ma. His small name (i.e. nickname) was Sanbao. From 1405 to 1466 he supervised maritime affairs. He visited more than thirty countries in Asia and Africa. He advanced international traffic and commercial as well as cultural exchange. See the statue of Zheng He, at Kun Yang in Yunnan, in photograph 5.

In his days the king of Yan, named Zhudi, won a quick victory in the battle of Jinnan. The eunuch Sanbao performed great deeds of valor during that battle. So, when the king of Yan became emperor, and when he gave the name Yuan to his reign, the eunuch Sanbao was awarded the family name Zheng. Later, by the emperor's command, Zheng He headed a fleet that sailed westward seven times. During his fifth excursion Zheng He commandeered and sailed a large fleet, with over twenty-seven thousand soldiers, seamen, officials and army officers, assembled in sixty-three large vessels altogether.

It was a hot summer, and many soldiers and seamen fell ill from the hot weather. So Zheng He had to order the fleet to dock at Quanzhou Harbor for a short stop and reorganization. While he lay at anchor, Zheng He went on a pilgrimage, up to Ling Mountain to pay homage at the holy tomb. He also prayed in Qing Jing at the mosque.

After the prayer service he had a heart-to-heart talk with Ahong Xuda, and with other old Muslim men. Among these was an old man named Guo Zhongyuan, from Baiqi. He was more than seventy years old and had white hair, but he still had a ruddy complexion. And he still spoke as loud as a big clock. Knowing that the old man had extraordinary skills in playing chess, Zheng He asked to have a table set for playing a match. He, too, was very good at chess. Guo Zhongyuan did not decline.

Of three games Zheng He lost all. He felt excited to finally have found his match. Zheng He insisted on playing more, and he lost again. After playing they sat down and drank tea together. Zheng He was filled with admiration, but Guo from time to time shook his head with a sigh, as if to express something. Zheng He felt puzzled and asked what was the matter.

Guo Zhongyuan explained his worry: "Your Highness! Since the founding of the great Ming dynasty, the Hui people in Quanzhou have been bullied by the Han, time and again. They have tasted full bitterness—have had to struggle for access to land and sea.

"If the Hui people choose to argue assertively, even on just grounds, they must fear the outcome. If they exercise patience and show weakness, it is very difficult for Hui people to remain living here. We are caught in a dilemma. I earnestly hope your Highness can look into this matter."

Having heard this, Zheng He was deeply concerned. With a tea cup in his hands he nodded his head. He thought to himself, "These complicated disputes which are carried on between two nationalities have been freezing relationships for quite some time. A depth of three feet of ice cannot have come about during a single day of freezing. As an imperial envoy I must not step into this dispute hastily. Instead, I must think of a simpler and better way to settle this."

Then he said, "Well, in three days I will go on an inspection tour to the Quangzhou Bay area. On my way I can drop anchor in the Bai-qi Harbor and meet the people, both Hui and Han."

Guo Zhongyuan was pleasantly surprised at these words and said, "That is very good. Thanks be to Allah!"

That very evening, Guo Zhongyuan hurried back to Baiqi. The Muslims were very much excited about this news. Headed by Guo Zhongyuan they went to the harbor area and began building a stone pavilion in which Eunuch Sanbao could rest and drink tea. Within three days, in a single swoop of nonstop work, they built the pavilion with the best of stones and carvings.

The news also spread among the Han, to the provincial governor, who, in order to wait for Eunuch Sanbao's arrival came to Baiqi Port a day early with an entourage of soldiers and officials.

The third day was a very fine day, and a breeze blew in gently from the sea. Already early that morning a crowd of people began to mingle at Baiqi Harbor, but in the afternoon the weather became quite hot. The people were dripping with sweat. And then they saw three ships approaching with full sails.

Gradually the eunuch Sanbao could be seen, sitting in the middle with the yellow umbrella held over his head. He was surrounded by guards who carried golden swords. From the harbor the cheers of jubilant crowds immediately resounded, accompanied by crescendos of music and bangs of fireworks. Sounds like thunder, of drums and gongs, and of blunderbuss fired toward the sky, could be heard coming from the ships. The provincial governor and Guo Zhongyuan walked together to meet Zheng He, and they accompanied him to the welcoming pavilion—for his enjoyment of cool air, in the shade, and to drink tea. The common people paid homage to him with bent knees, lined up at both sides along the road. A speaker announced the eunuch's order permitting the people to rise and to move into sha-dows under the trees.

Zheng He exchanged greetings with the local governor and then requested that Guo Zhongyuan present to him the younger generation.

When the young people made a low bow, a greeting after the manner of Muslims, he returned a salute and smiled, saying, "Salam!"

Observing these proceedings the people were very surprised. Rather common people, like Guo Zhongyuan, sat at the same table with the imperial envoy as if they were equals. The news spread quickly through the neighborhood that a Muslim sat together with the emperor's men. He had become a very important man. On that account the disputes between the two peoples diminished quickly. The Hui people in Baiqi began living and working in peace, and they prospered.

Three years passed. The eunuch Sanbao began his sixth expedition to the West, and along their route his ships again harbored in Quanzhou Bay. Zheng He again asked to play a game of chess with Gou Zhongyuan.

The first game was won by Guo Zhongyuan by a narrow margin, and the second ended in a draw. Guo Zhongyuan was a little hesitant during the third game. He missed a good opportunity and lost the game during the final few rounds. Guo Zhongyuan stood up and said, submissively, "Your Highness, you have a clear mind and are in the prime of life. Your skills in playing chess have greatly improved, whereas I am old and frail and cannot withstand a single blow anymore."

Zheng He won the game, but he was not satisfied because none of the skills which he had learned during the past three years had been applied thus far. Winning the game easily was not to his liking. He suspected that there might be some trouble. So he said: "No, no, you exaggerate. Are you perhaps still dismayed over the old disputes?"

Guo Zhongyuan shook his head. Then he looked up and saw the concerned expression on Zheng He's face. A long sigh escaped him, and he told about the matter which was troubling him.

It so happened that Guo Zhongyuan's youngest son, Guo Shizhao, served in the military. He was well versed in the art of polite letters and also thoroughly trained in the martial arts. His commander, General Zheng, thought very highly of him. He kept him at his side and put him in charge of confidential work. With this relationship Guo Shizhao could enter the general's house with no interference.

General Zheng had a daughter, who was not only beautiful but also very good at writing poems and essays. The general and his wife loved their daughter very much and considered her to be a pearl in their palm. Guo Shizhao often went to the inner chamber to report to his commander—while the girl did not try very hard to avoid him. The two met often without ever talking to one another. But they spoke to each other with their eyes, more or less.

One day, when she was reading documents on her father's behalf, she inserted a colored note before returning the document to the filing office. The note was a two-line poem:

Hence comes that chivalrous man—
to deprive me of peace of mind?

Guo Shizhao read the poem and completed it in an instant with two more lines:

The spring wind has started to blow—
far and gently over the greens.

Then he sent the poem back to the girl by way of her personal servant girl. From that time on the girl and the young man wrote love letters to each other. Gradually they fell in love and were engaged, secretly. They made a solemn pledge of love, and they planned to elope.

But General Zheng noticed their love and resolved to destroy it. He considered it impossible for his daughter, the daughter of a Han in high position, to marry an ordinary Hui man. He quickly issued an order for the arrest of the young man. The young man was to be punished as an army deserter in accordance with military law. Then, just at the time of this danger, the young lady came forth boldly. She begged her parents to do her a favor and to pardon the young man—or else she would die as a result of her love. This made General Zheng hesitate. If he rashly killed the young man his daughter would commit suicide; and, if he set the young man free they would both insist on marrying. He would lose the respect of the army, as well as his dignity about town. Therefore he firmly insisted on keeping the young man in prison.

After having heard this case, Zheng He comforted the old man and said, "Since General Zheng has not put him to death, I believe I can, in three days time, head off the danger and save the life of your devoted son."

While General Zheng was facing a dilemma with his daughter, and while the girl in her room was crying her heart out, Guo Shizhao was kept in prison and could neither be killed nor freed.

Suddenly a servant entered and reported that a fast-riding envoy from Eunuch Zheng He had arrived. At once the general opened the letter and read it. Because of their identical family name, Zheng He in this letter addressed the general politely as elder brother. He then explained that Guo Shizhao's father was one of his old family friends. And for his part, he would like to act as go-between for the marriage between the Hui and the Han. The letter was written in an earnest tone to convey compassionate feelings. It adequately released the general from his awkward predicament and satisfied both sides.

General Zheng ordered that Guo Shizhao be set free, then and there. And he sent him back home to Baiqi, courteously, as his prospective son-in-law. Of course, the girl then smiled through her tears. Madam Zheng, with her servants, got busy to prepare a dowry.

Another three days later, Zheng He and Guo Zhongyuan drank tea together on the welcoming pavilion while playing again a game of chess. Unexpectedly a large ship appeared in the bay. As it approached they saw that General Zheng himself was bringing his daughter to Baiqi. He kneeled before Zheng He, the go-between, to thank him for his great mediation. After that he exchanged greetings with his son-in-law's father. The girl was meanwhile served by Guo's family members. Then General Zheng sat by the table and watched them play chess.

Later on both families, Guo and Zheng, picked a good day and celebrated the wedding for the young couple. On that day the houses were filled with visitors. The ceremony was accompanied by a display of fireworks and a sea of lanterns, with twelve big ships anchored outside the bay. The marriage caused quite a stir throughout the province.

A couple days later, Zheng He continued to sail toward the West. But the stories about him, that he cared for common people and helped others to obtain what they hoped for, are being told to this very day.

Du Wenxiu's Rebellion

First published in *Min jian wen xue (Folk Literature)*, Beijing, 1961.
Place: Yunnan
Recorder: Yang Liangcai (Bai)

Du Wenxiu rose up in rebellion. It lasted eighteen years. This story came down to us from the Qing dynasty:

In the fifth year of the emperor Xian Feng there was a crop failure in Yunchang, Zhaozhou, Menghua, Dali, and Lijiang in Yunnan province. The people starved and were forced to satisfy their hunger with bark and grass.

At the same time, the taxes and grain assessments which the government wanted to collect were not only not reduced, but were increased instead. Not to mention anything else, the grain assessments alone made it unbearable for the people. First they were required to deliver unhusked rice, then husked rice, and then silver. And all the while the people themselves had nothing to eat. Whence could they obtain rice or silver to pay taxes?

Because the people could not hand over the tax grain that was required of them, they chose Du Wenxiu to go to the court on their behalf.

Du Wenxiu lived in Golden Cock village, in Yunchang county. Though he was a scholar he was still very poor. He defended others against injustice, and whenever he came across anything unfair he would protest against it. On that account he did not get along well with men who were rich and powerful. He enjoyed associating with peasants. He understood their hardships and was willing to help those who were in trouble. Every word he spoke was reasonable, and everything he did was fair. All the farmers showed great respect for him. No one addressed him by his name, or as a scholar, but as Elder Brother Du.

Before he left for the court in Dali, on behalf of his fellow villagers, Du Wenxiu said to them, "Fellow villagers, do not worry! If they ignore us in Dali I will go to the higher provincial court. If the same thing happens there, I will go to the supreme court, in the capital city."

The villagers said, "Elder Brother Du, take good care of yourself."

Taking with him solid food, straw sandals, and the people's petition, Du Wenxiu hurried along. Every day he covered a distance which ordinarily would require three days. Each day he walked from sunrise until sunset, and again from sunset until sunrise. Whether it was raining or shining, he never stopped. When he felt hungry he ate some solid food, and when he was thirsty he drank some cold water. It took him all of twenty-one days to make it as far as Dali.

Du Wenxiu went to see the county magistrate of Dali and presented to him his petition.

The magistrate asked, "Scholar Du, what have you come here for? Speak quickly!"

"Your Highness! There is a terrible famine in our Yunchang. The peasants are unable to deliver the tax grain. Please be kind to them and exempt them from having to pay tax grain this year."

"Since ancient times businessmen have had to pay taxes and farmers have had to deliver grain. You have studied the Four Books and the Five Classics, and you do not know such a basic principle?"

"Your Highness! You do not know our situation. With no rain from the sky there is no grain from the fields. How can the peasants deliver tax grain when there is no crop in the fields?"

"Nonsense!"

Then, before Du Wenxiu could continue to explain any more, the magistrate walked out of the court.

Du Wenxiu thought to himself, "There must still be another heaven above this heaven, and higher officials above this official. Though the local magistrate gave our case a deaf ear, some honest and upright officials will be found."

Momentarily he set out toward the provincial court, carrying with him some solid food, his straw sandals, and their petition. He continued covering a three-days' journey in one day, every day for an entire month. At last he reached the provincial capital, Kunming. Du Wenxiu went to see the governor and presented to him their petition.

The governor asked, "Scholar Du, what have you come here for? Speak quickly!"

"Your Highness!" Du Wenxiu said, "there is a severe famine in our Yunchang. The peasants are unable to deliver tax grain. Please bestow favors and exempt them from paying their tax grain this year."

"Since ancient times businessmen have had to pay taxes and farmers have had to deliver tax grain. You have studied the Four Books and the Five Classics, and still you do not understand such a basic principle?"

"Your Highness! You do not know our situation. With no rain from the sky there is no grain from the fields. How can the poor peasants deliver tax grain when there is no crop in the fields?"

"Nonsense!"

And before Du Wenxiu could explain any more, the provincial governor had already left the court.

Du Wenxiu thought to himself, "There must be still another heaven above this heaven and higher officials above this official. Though the provincial governor gave our case a deaf ear, some honest and upright officials will be found."

And so, carrying with him some solid food, straw sandals, and their petition, he momentarily set out in the direction of the imperial capital. He covered a three-days' journey in one day repeatedly, and so after three months he arrived there at last.

Du Wenxiu went to see the emperor and presented to him their petition.

The emperor asked, "Scholar Du, what have you come here for? Speak quickly!"

Du Wenxiu answered, "Your Majesty, there is a severe famine in our Yunchang. The peasants are unable to deliver tax grain. Please show favors and exempt them from the grain requirement this year."

"Since ancient times businessmen have had to pay taxes and farmers have had to deliver tax grain. You have studied the Four Books and the Five Classics, and still you do not understand such a basic principle?"

"Your Majesty! You do not know our situation. With no rain from the sky there is no grain from the fields. How can the poor peasants deliver tax grain when there is no crop in the fields?"

"Nonsense!"

And just as Du Wenxiu wanted to explain more, the emperor left the court.

Du Wenxiu failed in his mission, and he had to return to Yunchang with nothing but his pent-up anxiety.

Soon thereafter the emperor issued an edict, to force farmers to deliver tax grain within a stated time. It decreed that "those who refuse to deliver tax grain must be executed first and reported to the emperor later."

When the local officials received the imperial edict they set out to press the farmers for grain. As a result, countless peasants were put into prison and had their heads chopped off. In those days the officials simply did not consider peasants to be human beings. They would kill a farmer just as easily as they would step on an ant.

Du Wenxiu could not endure all of this. Assembling several of his sworn brothers he discussed with them the possibility of an uprising: "All crows are black everywhere under the sun! [i.e. evil officials are bad, everywhere!]. The officials leave us no livelihood. What must we do?"

"We were refused when we petitioned peacefully; now let us rise up with force!" said everybody.

"Right! This situation amounts to 'officials forcing the people into rebellion.' From now on we all shall be of one heart, and we shall fight side by side!"

"Quite right, Elder Brother Du! Point east and we follow east! Elder Brother Du, point west and we follow west!"

A few days later Du Wenxiu, together with Yang Zhirong, Ma Rulun, and Lan Dashun, went to Menghua and began to prepare for the uprising.

In Menghua they set up a tea shop. At daytime they did business and during the night they called together the poor. In only a few days they had assembled hundreds of people. The poor people, holding spears and broadswords, fought their way into the city of Menghua and killed the corrupt officials, including the military commander and the magistrate. Because the army of rebels carried flags made of white cloth, people called them the White Flag Army.

The news that the White Flag Army had killed the civil and military leaders and had taken over Menghua City, cheered up the peasants all around. Group after group came to join their army. Very quickly the White Flag Army assembled great strength and gained momentum. It numbered some forty to fifty thousand soldiers. Here today, and there tomorrow, they would defeat Qing army troops and would kill corrupt officials. Half of the world was in uproar.

When the news spread to the provincial city, the governor was scared to the point of where he committed suicide. And when the news reached the imperial capital, the emperor was so frightened that he lost control over his bowels.

A ballad was chanted about Du Wenxiu's rebellion:

First kill the military commander,
Then kill the local magistrate,
Force the governor to commit suicide,
And scare to death the emperor.

Rhymed Couplets

First published in *Ming jian wen xue (Folk Literature)*, Beijing, 1961.
Place: Yunnan
Recorder: Guo Sijiu and Fu Guangyu

In the sixth year of Xian Feng, during June and July, Dali suffered natural disasters. The people were living in poverty. Still, the local government continued to demand shares of provisions and moneys to support its troops. Notices were posted, requiring each person to hand in one liter of grain and three copper coins.

As soon as these posters had been put up the people became very angry; they were shouting and complaining everywhere. It seemed as though something disturbing could happen at any moment. Just then appeared, posted along a main street, a peculiar set of counterpoint couplets.

These counterpoint rhymes were unusual not only with regard to their content, but also with regard to the places where they had been posted. The first couplet streamer was put up at the foreigners' church gate, the second one at the court gate of the local government. The first streamer of couplets, at the Catholic mission, read:

What good is being a Catholic?
They pose as representatives of Heaven.
The justice of bullies, the ethics of diffusion,
Make daytime dusk.
Just wait until Heaven will strike!
Heaven will open their eyes!

The second streamer of couplets read:

> Those local officials are all ruffians!
> They extort fortunes,
> They fleece sums of money,
> They turn nice scenery into hell.
> Alongside of extracting the land tax,
> They scrape from the earth even its skin.

The news about these counterpoint couplets spread from one place to another. They caused a sensation throughout the city. All the people came to see them.

"Yes, indeed! These statements criticize to the point! We feel vindicated as we read them." So they spoke with excitement.

These counterpoint couplets made foreigners terribly angry, and they frightened the county governor.[2] Soldiers were sent to tear them off and to drive away the people, threatening to severely punish the man who put them up, if ever they found him.

However, the couplets had sharpened the people's vision and increased their hatred for foreigners and local officials. In less than one month Du Wenxiu captured Dali and drove away foreigners and local officials, and he quickly set up his command headquarters. Only then did people find out that it was Du Wenxiu who had sent men to post these counterpoint rhymes before attacking Dali.

---

[2]A question may rightly be raised concerning the number of foreigners who actually lived in Yunnan during the 1850s, to deserve this special mentioning. We may here be looking at a benchmark sentiment from later years when the story was recorded. Similar critical questions about later modulations can be asked about every tale in the Du Wenxiu cycle. Regarding present-day attitudes toward Christians in the Dali area, see photograph 9.

Du Wenxiu Becomes Commander

First published in *Min jian wen xue (Folk Literature)*, Beijing, 1961.
Place: Dali, Yunnan
Recorders: Yang Liangcai and Duan Shoutao

After having risen up in rebellion, and after having captured the city of Dali, Du Wenxiu's sworn brothers said, "Brother Du, Dali is our lifeblood, and we must keep it."

Du Wenxiu answered, "Right! There are strategic passes in the north and in the south, there is the lake in the east, and the mountains in the west. Dali cannot be conquered unless the two generals sell out the passes."[3]

Dali was really like a city clad with iron. Several times the Qing dynasty sent troops to attack Dali, but these were utterly defeated by Du Wenxiu's White Flag Army. One time Li Jingxi, general governor of Yunnan-Guizhou, led more than ten thousand Qing soldiers on an assault against Dali. But before they reached Dali all the soldiers had been killed. Li Jingxi himself nearly lost his life. Since that time the emperor has not dared anymore to recklessly attack Dali.

In the Dali area, Du Wenxiu opened the storehouses and distributed grain to the poor. The common people were very pleased with what he did. Those who had been persecuted and who had fled into the mountains to hide returned home one after another. Farmers went to the fields to plant, merchants bought and sold, students went to school, and craftsmen pursued their trades. Everyone lived and worked in peace and contentment. The land looked peaceful everywhere.

There was a market in Dali every fifteen days. Every time when the market began Du Wenxiu would appear. He walked from one shop to another to investigate. While meeting the poor he would give them some money he had saved. Some people received three hundred,

---

[3]The two generals who defended the passes were Dong Zhenlun and Ma Tenlun. They were Du Wenxiu's trusted followers. Du spoke so because he believed in them. Later these two generals betrayed him and surrendered the passes to the Qing general, Yang Yuke, and thereby made Dali easy prey.

and some were given a string of coins. The poorer the people were the more money they would receive. One time, in a herbal medicine store, Du Wenxiu was told that an official in Midu, after he arrived at his post, ignored the military and officer's code of conduct, that he extorted large sums of money from the people and killed innocent persons. That same night Du Wenxiu sent three summons, one after another, to recall that official back to Dali. By way of confrontation and confirmation this official was sentenced to death the next morning.

After executing this official, Du Wenxiu said in public, with tears in his eyes, "My Brothers! We have revolted for the common people. How can we extort money from them? And how can we harm them?"

His words moved the people and his sworn brothers to tears. They all said, "Brother Du! You are our defender."

One day his sworn brothers said to him, "Brother Du! Inasmuch as we have already tens of counties, and prefectures, and several hundred thousands of soldiers and horses, we should choose a commander."

Du Wenxiu asked, "Whom are you going to choose?"

"Of course, it will be Brother Du."

"No! No!" Du Wenxiu did not agree, no matter how much they tried to persuade him. At that point one of his sworn brothers stood up and said: "Brother Du, I have a good idea."

"What is it?" Du Wenxiu asked.

"Since ancient times commanders were chosen by Heaven. Let us ask Heaven."

"How do we do it?"

"On the exercise field, at the south end, we can build a large platform. Upon that platform we must raise a large white flag, and under that flag we bury an iron brick. Then, on a favorable day we choose our commander."

"An excellent idea!" all said with one voice.

The next day the sworn brothers built a large platform on the southern exercise field. They hitched up some white oxen and horses and erected a tall pole with a big white flag. Under the flag-pole an iron brick was buried. Then everything was ready, except selecting a day for choosing the commander.

On September 25th the entire city was decorated with lanterns and with colorful streamers. The common people wore beautiful clothes, beat drums and gongs, and came to watch the excitement.

"Boom! Boom! Boom!" With the sound of guns, three times, the election of the commander began. Wearing a clean suit, Du Wenxiu held a piece of yellow paper in his hand. He stepped with his sworn brothers up to the platform, smiling broadly.

First they offered a sacrifice to the White Flag, and then they wrote the commander's name on the yellow paper. Having completed this, they burned the yellow paper in an incense burner, and then they dug out the iron brick. It was indeed strange that the iron brick had some characters engraved on it. These characters read: "Announce that Du Wenxiu should be commander and exercise control over the whole army."

When everybody saw these words, they all said to Du Wenxiu, "You must agree, Brother Du."

Du Wenxiu could not dispute any more. So he became the commander.

How could the iron brick be engraved with the characters that were written on the yellow paper and burnt in the incense burner? Actually, it was everybody's wish to choose Du Wenxiu as commander. But Du Wenxiu insisted on refusing. The sworn brothers could not persuade him until they got this idea—to engrave an iron brick and to deposit it secretly on the day before choosing their commander.

After he became commander, Du Wenxiu set up headquarters and formally held up the banner of the uprising army—the White Flag. They put up official notices everywhere, clearly stating the purpose of the White Flag Army for the people, calling on them to unite, to overthrow appointed tribal headsmen, to kill corrupt officials, and to resist the imperial court. The notice also still said to reduce taxes and tax grain, and to have fair trade. All the people were very much delighted.

It has been said that Du Wenxiu stayed in Dali eighteen years, and every year Dali had an abundant harvest of all the food crops, and everyone lived and worked peacefully and contentedly. There is a folk song which goes as follows:

Dali City, a fine incense city, too.[4]
Du Wenxiu becomes its commander.
The old and young love Du.
There are no more worries about clothing and food.

Dali City, our Forbidden City,[5]
Wherein lives his Excellency Du.
Down with the rich! Help the poor!
No more sufferings we will endure.

Crossing the Yang River

First published in *Min jian wen xue (Folk Literature)*, Beijing, 1961.
Place: Wei Mountain, Yunnan
Narrator: Yang Wenguang (Hui)

One year, while Du Wenxiu was commanding the rebel army he set out in the direction of Shunning. He came to the ferry of the Yang River at the foot of Dazi Mountain. At that time the imperial court had sent a general named Su on a punitive expedition against Du. The Qing troops were stationed at Dazi Mountain with thousands of soldiers and horses, blocking the ferry. In addition, there was a sheer cliff overhang east of the ferry. You could not see its top even if you raised your head to a point where your cap would fall off. It was extremely difficult to cross over.

The moment Du Wenxiu's army had gotten to the west bank of the river they began engaging the Qing troops with blunderbuss. For longer than a month Du Wenxiu failed to displace the Qing troops

---

[4]Buddhism was prevalent in Dali at the time. The customary veneration of the Buddha and of bodhisattvas required the burning of incense. An "incense city" meant thus a city which traditionally had been Buddhist.

[5]"Forbidden City" here means the place of Du Wenxiu's headquarters—a counter-establishment to the imperial "forbidden city" or palace.

who held on to their positions at Dazi Mountain, and he failed to cross the Yang River.

Then Du Wenxiu's eyelids moved a little. An idea flashed through his mind. He called his sworn brothers to deliberate this matter: "Brothers, as you know, the waves keep rolling in the river, and the Qing soldiers keep blocking the road ahead of us. We must find some different way to cross this river."

What he said spread at fire's speed among his soldiers. On that same day a soldier, short of stature but strong, came to see Du Wenxiu: "Commander, after hard tactics have failed to defeat the Qing troops perhaps some soft methods should be tried."

"What is your soft method?" Du Wenxiu asked.

"Commander, just let them fall for a trick."

After the soldier had told him his idea, Du Wenxiu ordered immediately to move thousands of oxen and sheep. All the soldiers got busy tying torches to the horns of oxen and sheep; they also hung bright mirrors on the foreheads of these animals. When everybody had finished his work, Du Wenxiu said, "All right, you all go and have a rest."

It was getting dark then. Du Wenxiu checked the color of the sky and then ordered, "Now is the time to cross the river."

With Du Wenxiu's instructions the soldiers lit the sticks on the horns. Smoke-laden dots of fire and flashes could be seen reflected in the mirrors here and there. The oxen and sheep were put in a long line, and then driven into the river to swim to the east bank. All the while, on the west bank, soldiers were beating drums and shouting loudly, "Right on!" Their shouting shook Dazi Mountain.

General Su, of the Qing troops, became frightened and stamped with fury. He cursed and ordered, "Open fire! Be quick!"

But the oxen and sheep continued moving forward in a hail of bullets and arrows. Flashes of light were sparkling off in all directions, like bullets exploding; the mirrors reflected like broadswords. It was not long before a Qing soldier came to report to General Su, "General! Du Wenxiu and his army have crossed over to the east bank!"

"What?"

"Du Wenxiu and his army have crossed over to the east bank!"

"Oohh!" General Su was too frightened to walk anymore; he was shaking all over. He turned around and wanted to run eastward for his life, but his legs felt like jelly. He fell over and rolled down to the foot of the mountain. The Qing soldiers fled in fear.

At daybreak Du Wenxiu led his army safely across the Yang River.

Du Wenxiu Executes a Close Official

First published in *Hui zu wen xue cong kan (Collections of Hui Literature)*, Yinchuan, 1979.
Place: Yunnan
Recorders: Ma Yisheng and Ma Yinsheng (Hui)

One day Du Wenxiu went to the camellia garden to water the flowers. While he was by the ditch, getting water, Ma Zhongshan, his highest official, hurried into the garden and reported to him that a villager was outside asking to see him.

Du Wenxiu stopped and calmly asked, "What does he come for?"

"He said that he could not say unless he saw the supreme commander. He would be in danger of losing his head."

"Where has he come from?"

"Midu."

"Oh!" Du Wenxiu started up. He put down his buckets and frowned a little. He thought it probable that the man had come to report Wang Guoan's offences.

Du Wenxiu's suspicion was not unfounded. Several days earlier a few people from Midu had already come to accuse Guoan of dishonesty in performing of his official duties. He extorted sums of money from people and raised taxes at will. On his birthday he not only recited Quranic scripture and gave a big dinner party, he also expected every family to bring him generous gifts. Anyone who refused to comply with his expectations would be beaten or even thrown into prison. Within a short span of time Midu, a good place, had been changed into something where not even dogs and fowls were left alone to live in peace. Complaints were heard everywhere. Thus, Du Wenxiu had been anxious about this for some time.

Wang Guoan had joined the rebellion with Du Wenxiu from the very beginning. Through the years he killed many red- and yellow-capped Qing officials. He performed deeds of valor in battle. He had been one of Du's bravest generals. Only a few months ago he was sent to guard Midu, but now...

"Commander, will you meet him or not?" asked Ma Zhongshan.

"Show him in."

In came a middle-aged and travel-stained peasant in mourning dress. After he had taken his seat, and after he had been offered tea, Du Wenxiu began to ask him, gently, "Tell me, what is the problem?"

The visitor quickly dropped to his knees and burst out crying: "Supreme Commander. We beg you to judge for us. Please redress an injustice for us, for the people of Midu."

The man's name was Zhang Tianbao, a Han person. Because quite a number of peasants were unable to afford gifts for Wang Guoan's birthday, some were beaten and some were thrown into prison. Tianbao's father could not bear such a situation. He thought that Commander Du Wenxiu had fought his revolution to kill corrupt officials, caring about the needs of the common people. What Wang had done had not only done great harm to the people, but had also damaged the reputation of the rebel army.

And so, the old father persuaded some villagers to come with him to Dali, to Command Headquarters, with the intention of bringing charges. But quite unexpectedly, Wang Guoan got wind of this and laid an ambush at Red Rock Slope. Tianbao's father was murdered.

This time the son, Tianbao, came to Dali—hiding during daytime and walking at night. He took a circuitous route, by climbing over Cock-feet Mountain and floating across Erhai River.

Upon having heard this statement, Du Wenxiu frowned and wrinkled his brow with rage. He quickly rose to his feet, from his seat, and asked the man: "Brother, will you dare to confront Wang Guoan with your accusation?"

Zhang Tianbao wiped the tears off his eyes and answered, "If you, Supreme Commander, will judge between us I will surely dare to accept the consequences."

"All right!" Du Wenxiu then quickly strode toward the door and gave an order: "Summon Wang Guoan back to Dali to discuss official business!"

During past years Wang had fought in many battles, as a follower of Du Wenxiu, and he had contributed much to the revolution. But after he came to Midu he deemed himself beyond anyone's authority. He tyrannized the people there.

So, when Du Wenxiu's first order reached him, he did not pay attention at all. When the second order arrived he simply took a condescending look at it, very reluctantly. When he was about to ignore the third order, one of his closest men warned him, "General Wang! A military order should not be regarded as a trifling matter. Besides, it is well known that Commander Du Wenxiu always enforces the law strictly."

These words made Wang Guoan a bit worried. He dawdled away another half a day and then, unwillingly, began his journey. The moment he stepped into the southern gate of Dali he was arrested and thrown into prison. The news of this incident spread quickly throughout Dali, and many people became curious to learn more about it. Naturally, some persons asked to see Du Wenxiu to intercede on Wang's behalf. But word was given that anyone who came to intercede for Wang would be refused.

One day, when Du Wenxiu had gone again to the garden to water flowers, Ma Zhongshan followed him, cautiously, and with wrinkled brows. Du turned toward him and asked, "You seem to have something to say?"

Ma Zhongshan knelt and pleaded, with tears in his eyes, "Commander! For Allah's sake, please forgive Guoan this one time."

Du Wenxiu helped him up and asked, "Why?"

"We often say that all Muslims are one big family. If you kill him, then we Muslims will be laughed at by other groups of people. Please do not be excessively strict."

Du Wenxiu frowned, swinging his arms and turning his back on him. Ma Zhongshan knew that Du Wenxiu was angry. He dared not to say any more. He stood still, with his hands at his sides.

After a considerable time, Du Wenxiu turned again to Ma. "I did not expect that you would offer such an opinion, having followed me all these many years. Without the support of all ethnic peoples, how could we have won? Now that we are being supported by all these people, we should be models. In battle we should lead. We should handle matters impartially, and be loyal. Punishment should be redoubled on those Hui officers and soldiers who have broken the law, so that we can win the hearts of all people."

He suddenly stopped, turned away, and strode out of the garden. Ma Zhongshan stood there quite a while longer, motionless and speechless.

After the third night watch had been drummed, Du Wenxiu began to open a court session. At the gate of Command Headquarters wafted flags on which the name "Du" was written, in large characters. On opposite sides of White Tiger Hall huge banners were draped, with rhymed couplets written on them:

Hold a three-*chi*-long sword to usher in a new era,
Repose in confidence to rebuild the destiny of Han.

Put on martial attire to suppress rebellion,
Do kind deeds and loyally perform the feats of Zhou.

The people, consisting of Han, Hui and Bai nationalities, were crowding around the headquarters gate. They had been told that Wang Guoan would be tried today. After a short wait, Wang Guoan was brought into the White Tiger Hall. Not a crow or sparrow could be heard, neither inside nor outside the hall.

Du Wenxiu asked sternly, "Do you confess your guilt, Wang Guoan?"

Wang was about to quibble when Du Wenxiu beat the court table. "Bring in the witness from Midu!"

Zhang Tianbao, who had been waiting outside the door, came down into the hall. He gave a salute and then stood to one side. Wang Guoan was shocked when he heard that there was to be a witness from Midu. When he saw that it was Zhang Tianbao he was paralyzed with fright. And so, before being asked anything, Wang Guoan had to confess all his guilt.

Du Wenxiu asked Ma Zhongshan to open the Martial and Administrative Code, and to read from it aloud:

"Civil and military officials of high and low rank, regardless of whether or not they have defended or captured cities, when they oppress the people, and when they have committed crimes and thereby have earned the wrath of the people, shall be beheaded."

After that, Wang Guoan slowly lifted his head and seemed to say something. But he choked at his own words and lowered his head again.

The soldiers who stood next to him were about to escort him to prison when Du Wenxiu ordered, "Wait a moment!"

All the people were startled. They saw him leave the table and slowly make his way toward Wang. With a gentle voice he said, "You can die without worries. Your mother is also my mother."

At these words tears rolled from Wang's eyes. He hugged Du Wenxiu's legs and wept, "My Commander!"

Du Wenxiu looked up and gave a speech to the people who stood around: "Elders, brothers and sisters! I rose in rebellion for the sake of common people. Thanks to the support of the different ethnic groups we have won what we have today. All officials must be kind to their people. And henceforth, anyone who oppresses the people—no matter what his ethnicity or group may be, what position he occupies or what contributions he has made in the past—should take a warning from the fate of Wang Guoan."

After that, the story of Du Wenxiu, beheading his official, spread quickly.

The Peacock Gallbladder

First published in *Hui zu wen xue cong kan (Collection of Hui Literature)*,
   Yinchuan, 1979.
Place: Yunnan
Recorders: Ma Yisheng and Ma Yinsheng (Hui)

It had been more than ten years since Du Wenxiu had revolted and became commander. The people within a thousand *li* were living and working in peace and contentment. They were having abundant harvests of all kinds of food crops. One day Du Wenxiu set up camp outside the city and ordered his soldiers to drill. Some old men of the Dai (Thai) people, carrying a small peacock, came to the camp and asked to see Commander Du. In the opinion of the Dai people the peacock was a very special bird. They presented this peacock to express their love and their esteem. After listening to that, Du Wenxiu hurriedly tidied his uniform, accepted the peacock, and bowed deeply to express his appreciation.

From that time on this peacock was kept in the garden of the Command Headquarters. Very often the bird unfolded its tail and, usually, it was quite tame and it understood humankind. The people at Command Headquarters were unable to stay away from it even for as long as a single day. Du Wenxiu liked it even more. He fed it, watched it, and regarded it as a pearl in his palm.

But how could the emperor in Beijing tolerate the peaceful, prosperous times in Dali? Thus, during the eleventh year of the Qing emperor Tongzhi, the imperial government enlisted troops numbering hundreds of thousands, from many provinces. With guns supplied by foreigners they came like wolves and tigers to attack the rebel army. The fighting was fierce, and dead bodies laid piled to the height of a mountain; blood flowed like the sea.

The two generals at the upper and lower fortified access routes were terribly frightened. They surrendered unexpectedly to the Qing troops, accepted amnesty, and served the emperor. The rebel army and its people had to retreat as they fought and, in the end, the Qing troops surrounded the town of Dali.

Du Wenxiu, leading his soldiers and people, resolved to defend Dali to the end. For half a year the Qing troops were unable to break through their line of defence. Du Wenxiu eagerly expected to be rescued from this siege by troops from Ailao Mountain, led by General Li Wenxue of the Yi (Lolo) people.[6] But contrary to his expectation, the relief troops were held up by Qing forces. So the military situation at Dali became extremely critical—with no provisions inside and no relief troops arriving outside their town.

After inspecting the soldiers and the people who were defending the city from the top of the town wall, Du Wenxiu returned to his command house looking extremely worried. Suddenly he saw the peacock display again his fine tail feathers, and his eyes lit up. Du Wenxiu heaved a sigh and said, "I have let the people down."

---

[6]Li Wenxue, the revolutionary leader of the Yi (Lolo) people, was captured and killed by Qing troops while leading his army to aid Du Wenxiu.

By that time the grain in the city had nearly been used up, and Du Wenxiu offered the peacock a bowl of rice soup which he himself had not eaten that day.

Again the Qing troops gave the town wall a terrible pounding. Du Wenxiu was just about to go out with a sword in hand, when Cai Tingdun[7] rushed in and reported, "Dasihen has surrendered to the Qing, acting in collusion with forces attacking from the outside. A large opening has been blasted into the city wall!"

Du Wenxiu erupted, cursing, while gritting his teeth, "That shameless traitor!"

Momentarily some people arrived who had blood dripping all over, and they reported, "At the gap in the city wall our people are now fighting the enemy hand-to-hand."

Upon hearing this, Du Wenxiu realized that it was impossible to resist the Qing troops much longer. Very quickly they would storm the eastern part of the city.

At this moment, wave upon wave of people, bringing along their old and their young, came fleeing to the Command Headquarters. The sound of guns and the rolling noise of battle were coming nearer and nearer.

Du Wenxiu felt as if a knife was being twisted in his heart when he considered how the Qing troops would massacre the inhabitants. Cai Tingdun urged, "Commander-father, hurry up! Let us try to break through the enemy lines, per chance we can escape with our lives!"

After having thought a moment, Du Wenxiu contrariwise put his sword back into his scabbard and patted Little Yang Wei on his shoulder, saying, "Our original purpose for the rebellion was to seize the chance of staying alive and to save the people from their miserable condition. Now that the people are facing imminent disaster, how can I abandon them and slip away?"

"Commander, please do not think anymore about us. Just leave quickly," the people said repeatedly.

---

[7]Cai Tingdun was the son-in-law of Du Wenxiu. He was the son of Cai Fachong, the governor of Yang Wei. After taking over his father's post, in the army, he was called Little Yang Wei.

"No. What that pot carrier wants is my head.[8] To save the inhabitants of this city I will give him my head!"

After having spoken that, he turned around and went into the house, asking all his family members to bathe and to dress in clean clothing. At the same time he asked an ahong to recite from scripture the "prayer before death."

The peacock seemed to have read his mind and strode toward Du Wenxiu. Gently stroking his feathers, Du Wenxiu spoke to the peacock: "For several years I have kept you company, but now I cannot even protect you. Just fly away!" But the peacock shook his tail.

"Then you just stay behind and be company to Yang Yuke." And again the peacock shook his tail.

When he found him to be such an understanding peacock, Du Wenxiu could not avert shedding some tears. He took out his sword, closed his eyes, and thrust it into the peacock's heart. It fell. Du Wenxiu took out the gallbladder and held it in his hand. Then, turning around, he had a vision of all his family members, old and young, who had ascended to heaven before him. He looked up and shouted toward the sky, "Allah! Save the hundreds and the thousands of people!"

Walking out from his headquarters, in white clothes and with a white cap, Du Wenxiu was met by the people of the city who kneeled along both sides of the street. Some of them burned incense sticks.

A big sedan chair, to be carried by four men, was waiting at the side. Du Wenxiu bent over and made an obeisance toward the people by cupping one hand in the other. Then he said loudly, "My dear people. My dear people! I do not want you to become involved on my account. For eighteen years we have relied and depended on one another, alive or dead. Now, farewell to you all, and may Allah protect you!"

Again he made an obeisance toward the people, and then he got on the sedan. At once the people broke forth into weeping.

The sedan chair was carried to the eastern part of the city. Soldiers at both sides had already stopped fighting and were watching Du Wenxiu being carried in the sedan. The sedan chair was seen

---

[8]Yang Yuke, a leading officer in the Qing government, was a humpback. He was called Baiguo by the people—which means "carries a pot on his back."

to move straight toward Yang Yuke's headquarters at Xia Rui Village, east of the city.

Having heard that Du Wenxiu was coming forth from the city, alone, Yang Yuke hurriedly came out to look. Though with sword in hand, he still looked somewhat flurried.

At the moment when Du Wenxiu had gotten on the sedan chair he swallowed the peacock gallbladder. By the time he arrived at the Qing camp, the toxicity of the gall had begun to take effect. Sweat, like rain, was rolling down from his body all over, and he was suffering great pain. But he clenched his teeth to display a steady and enraged face—which frightened Yang Yuke so much that he backed off a little.

Du Wenxiu walked up to him and said, "I, Du Wenxiu, have come to bring you my head on which you have set a bounty! The people of Dali are kind and innocent. I am the only person who rose up against the Qing dynasty. Now that I have dared to do what I did, I accept full responsibility and also accept the consequences. The people had nothing to do with it."

He felt his throat constricting, and he could speak no more. Yang Yuke, as if awakening from a dream, and taken aback, ordered his men right and left, "Fetch him!"

But Du Wenxiu had already fallen to the ground and lay on his back facing heavenward—he had already returned to Allah.[9]

------

[9]The headless body of Du Wenxiu lies buried a few kilometers from Dali. See photograph 6.

9

Family Affairs

Musa

Place: Changjie, Xinjiang
Narrator: Li Guifang (Hui)
Recorder: Yang Ruiping (Hui), 1984

Once upon a time, in Majia village, lived a family of three people—mother, father, and son. On his deathbed the old man said to his wife, "My dear wife, since we have been living together we have never quarrelled. Now I am leaving before you do. You may sell everything except one room to live in. You and our son will have to live diligently and thriftily. If life becomes difficult you may ask our son, Musa, to go to a place along the Nanshan Road, which will require eighty-one days of travel.[1] There he will find a peony garden, by which sits a house built of turquoise."

Then the old man died, and not long thereafter their living conditions got worse and worse. A famine had struck the village. The old woman worried so much that even her hair turned completely white. One day she suddenly remembered what her husband had said. So she sent Musa to look for the Old Man at Nanshan Mountain.

Musa said farewell to his mother and to the villagers and went on his way, provisioned with dry food and straw sandals.

---

[1] "Musa" is the Chinese equivalent of "Moses." Quite distinct from the biblical Moses, who was a Hebrew, the name here is that of a Chinese person. The Chinese transliteration is therefore retained.

279

It was getting dark, one day, when he walked through a grove along Nanshan Mountain. He smelled a fragrant smell, and he walked toward it in hope of staying there overnight. Passing through the dense grove, just as he expected, he found a gate at the corner of the grove. He knocked, and then went in. It was a clean and tidy courtyard. The turquoise stone slabs before the door were polished as shiny as mirrors. Presently, out from the house came an old and white-bearded man. Musa took some steps forward to him and said, "Grandfather, I am on my way to Nanshan Mountain to see an old man. It is dark now. Could you let me stay overnight in your house?"

"Yes, please." The old man showed him in.

Musa just sat down by a table and drank a cup of tea when, before long, a girl came in carrying a wooden plate with a meal on it. She put the plate on the table for him.

Musa was attracted to this girl as soon as he saw her. The girl was very beautiful, with bright and intelligent eyes, thin and long eyebrows, and black and shiny braids. He thought to himself that she was quick to prepare for him a meal—even before he could finish a cup of tea. How happy his mother would be if he could marry such a girl!

After the meal Musa told the old man of his father's last words and his mother's hardships. The old man could see that Musa was an honest and filial young fellow. He said to him, "The girl you saw is my daughter. She can do all kinds of housework very well, such as cooking and sewing. She is also very filial toward me. Yet, from the day when she was born she has been unable to speak. Please do me a favor and ask the old man at Nanshan Mountain why she cannot speak."

"Grandfather, I promise to you that I will find out about this," he replied.

The next day the old man and his daughter accompanied him, mile after mile, before bidding him farewell. They did not turn back until he disappeared in the distance.

Keeping the old man's words in his mind, Musa continued his journey. He walked and walked before he stopped at a large meadow of grassland. He caught sight of a house, went over and knocked at the door. In a minute, out came an old woman with snow-white hair all over her head.

"Grandmother, I am going to see an old man at Nanshan Mountain. It is getting dark now, could you offer me a place for one night?" Musa asked.

"Yes surely!" the old woman said and led him into the room.

After the meal Musa helped the grandmother to clean the yard, fetch water, and to look after cows. The old woman could see that he was a diligent boy.

She said to him: "My boy, as you have seen in my garden, the grass is green and flowers bloom in red and white colors. Only, this jujube tree has never blossomed and bore fruits, not in ten years—in spite of the fact that I water it very often and apply much manure. Can you ask the old man at Nanshan Mountain for me why this is so?"

Musa promised her and kept her words in his mind. Before the sun rose the next day he went on his way.

Along the way his path happened to be interrupted by a very deep lake, with bright green water. Along its shores grew various trees, grasses, and flowers which he had never seen. The clear water mirrored the clouds in the sky and the trees along the shore. Looking at the lake, Musa said to himself, "What a large lake it is!" and "How can I swim across?"

Just as he was becoming anxious about it, the water began to recede little by little, until at last the bottom could be seen. Musa walked forward into it with great delight. But while he was running forward the water began to rise again, and in the water swam a big fish—a carp.

Musa asked for help: "Carp fish, Carp fish, I am going to see the old man at Nanshan Mountain. Could you help me get across the lake?"

The carp said, "I cannot take you unless you do me a favor."

"What is it?"

"I have stayed in this lake for two thousand years. Oh how I wish to become a flying fish, able to hover in the air! I have tried more than ten thousand times, but have never succeeded. Can you ask the old man for me why that is so?"

"Yes, big fish. I promise you," Musa said.

So the carp fish asked him to sit on his back and to close his eyes. The moment Musa got on he heard the gurgling of water and the sound of waves passing by his ears and fading away. When after a while Musa opened his eyes he saw the deep lake far behind him.

Filled with joy he continued walking. Finally he arrived at Nanshan Mountain and in the distance he saw the peony garden. The flowers were so pink that they reflected a reddish cast over almost half the sky in the west. In front of the garden was a spring by which a copper kettle was sitting.

"Is this the place where the old man lives?" he wondered. Unexpectedly he saw a group of white pigeons. Plum-blossom deer came running over toward him. And meanwhile, from among the flowering peony bushes emerged a distinguished looking old man.

Musa quickened his steps and went forward to offer a greeting, and then he asked his questions, "Grandfather, I came only for your advice. In a deep lake there is a big fish, wishing to become a flying fish. Why did he never succeed after trying ten thousand times? Secondly, a very kind grandmother has had a jujube tree in her yard for ten years which never blooms. Why is this so? My third question concerns an old man's daughter who is intelligent. She is already eighteen years old but cannot speak. What is the reason for that?"

The old man answered, "Young man, the big carp cannot fly to the sky because in its body are many pearls and agate stones which weigh him down. It can turn into a flying fish if all of these are taken out. The jujube tree never blossoms because under the tree was buried half a sack of gold and silver, which keeps the tree from blossoming. As for the girl, she will speak as soon as she meets her bridegroom."

Just before Musa was ready to ask what his mother told him, the old man stopped him and pointed to an inscription, on the turquoise lintel above the door. Musa looked up and saw these words engraved in stone, "Three Questions Only!"

Musa felt rather sad, because he could not ask for advice on what his mother told him. But the old man gave him a smile and with the twinkle of an eye he disappeared, without a trace.

Musa did not know what to do. He thought, "It is not easy to get here. It is lucky that I have seen the old man, but it is a pity that I have not gotten any advice concerning my mother's troubles. What can I do? But even so. I did not make a fruitless trip, because I have gotten advice for the old grandmother, the old grandfather, and the carp fish."

He turned and began his journey home. When on his way home he came again to the lake, the big carp swam over hurriedly to him and asked, "Did you ask the old man about my question?"

"Yes, it is confirmed," Musa replied. "The old man at Nanshan Mountain said that you have too many gems in your body which weigh you down. After removing all of these you can become a flying fish."

"Then come and pull them out. All the gems will belong to you."

When Musa finished pulling out gems from its mouth and body, the carp immediately became two to three feet long. It was so happy that tears ran down its face.

"Thank you, dear Musa. Take these treasures home with you." This the carp said and then flew up toward the sky, surging a huge water column in its wake, ten feet high.

Musa continued along his way and again came to the grassland. Entering the yard he was greeted by the old grandmother: "My Boy, did you ask my question?"

"Yes Grandmother! The old man of Nanshan Mountain said that under the tree lies buried half a sack of gold and silver, which burns the tree. Only if the gold and silver are dug up will it blossom."

Immediately the grandmother asked Musa to dig and, as expected, he really dug out a half a sack of gold and silver. Along with a gentle wind the leaves on the tree began to rustle and within one hour the tree had begun bearing large red dates. The grandmother said, "Thank you, Musa. Just take this gold and silver, and go home quickly to see your mother."

With the treasures, and the gold and silver, Musa went on his way and came to the old grandfather's place. When the daughter of the old man saw him returning, she hurried toward her father, three steps in one, "Father, Father, that boy Musa comes again." So the girl spoke.

The grandfather was astonished. He thought, "Why could she speak all of a sudden after having been mute for eighteen years?"

Just before he had a chance to ask, Musa came in and said, out of breath, "Grandfather, your daughter will speak the moment she sees her bridegroom."

Hearing this, the grandfather shook his white beard and said, "Haha! Yes! Just before you entered my daughter was able to speak!"

Musa and the girl both turned red. The girl hurriedly went back into the kitchen, to prepare a meal.

After the meal the grandfather told Musa that he would like him and his daughter to get married soon, and to live with them. But

Musa did not agree, because he did not want his mother to be alone in Majia village. He suggested that they both come and settle down in his village. At last they accepted his idea.

On a day when Musa's mother was washing vegetables by the stream, she heard magpies twittering. She raised her head and saw her son Musa coming towards her, followed by a very pretty girl and by an old man. Musa ran to her before she could stand up, and said, "Mom, I am sorry I did not get to ask your question because of the words above the door: 'Three Questions Only.' I asked those three questions for people whom I met along the way to Nanshan Mountain."

The mother gently stroked his head and said, "My son. It is quite enough to have clarified these three things. What else did you need to ask? You see. You brought home a wife and riches. Are these not the answers to my questions?"

Musa understood at once. He hurried to support his mother with his strong hands. The whole family went home together, happily.

Yinbolaxi

Place: Qing tong xia, Ningxia
Recorder: Ma Shenbao (Hui), 1979

Long, long ago there lived a very kind old couple in a mountain village. They had an only son twenty-one years of age, Yinbolaxi.[2] They lived by farming a plot of land on a south slope. In years with normal harvests they could make it fairly well. But one year there was a drought in spring and a flood during autumn. They got nothing from their field. Because of constant overworking the old man broke

---

[2]In stictly Islamic stories "Yinbolaxi" refers to the Quranic Ibrahim and the biblical Abraham. Here the Chinese version of that name refers to a Hui Chinese story character.

down and laid in bed. Daily his health deteriorated. The old woman and her son could do nothing to help him, but wept every day.

One day, knowing that his death was near, the old man asked his wife and his son to come close to his bed, and he told them, "After I die, you should not be too sorrowful. If you really have trouble surviving, just send Yinbolaxi to a very far away place to visit an old ahong. He will help you out of your difficult situation."

Then the old man breathed his last breath. The mother and the son were almost weeping their hearts out. At last they buried the dead one. Life became more difficult after the old man died. So Yinbolaxi took leave from his mother and set out, eastward, to find the old ahong.

While he was walking he kept asking about the way. He was completely tired and hungry by nightfall. Unexpectedly he saw some light from a house in the distance and he walked toward it. When he got to the door he knocked lightly. An aunt came out and asked, "What can I do for you?"

He told the aunt about the troubles of his family and his father's deathbed instructions. The aunt began sobbing sadly at his words and then allowed him in. In the room he saw a beautiful girl, about nineteen years old, sitting at the edge of the *kang*, sewing something. This, too, was a very poor family. Still, the aunt asked him to sit down on the *kang* while she made tea and baked corn cakes for him. After he finished eating, the aunt said, "When you see the ahong, please do me a favor to ask him the reason why my daughter suddenly ceased to speak when she came to be fifteen years old."

Yinbolaxi promised that he would do this. That night he stayed at the aunt's house, and the next morning he had his breakfast there as well. Then he thanked the aunt and left.

All along his way he asked travelers whether they knew that old ahong, and he failed to obtain a satisfactory answer. He got tired again and hungry. Then there, by the roadside, he noticed a house before which stood a huge apple tree with many branches and leaves, but with no fruit at all. He went up and knocked at the door. Out came an old man who asked whom he was looking for. Again he told everything. The old man sympathized with him and invited him into the room. Later a meal was ready for him.

After the meal the old man said, "Please ask the ahong for me why my apple tree blossoms but does not bear any fruit—even though it is more than seven years old."

Yinbolaxi agreed. And that night he stayed at the old man's place. The next morning after breakfast he left and continued on his journey.

By midday he came to a large river which blocked his way. There was no ferry. Anxious he stood on the bank while great waves rolled and foamed. Then, from the river emerged a big fish, as big as a door board. It spoke to Yinbolaxi: "I know your bitter experience. Let me take you across the river."

The fish asked him to get on its back, and to hold on to its teeth, and so it swam steadily toward the other bank. With astonishment Yinbolaxi thanked the fish and then asked, with embarrassment, "How can I cross this river when I come back home?"

"I will take you back as well," the fish answered and swam back into the river.

Yinbolaxi went on his way in a cheerful frame of mind. When darkness fell again he wondered where he could stay for the night. At that very moment he caught sight of a mosque, ahead in the distance, and he hurried to get there. Upon entering the great gate of the mosque he saw an old ahong with a long beard, reciting scripture. He went over, made a bow, and then said, "Peace!"

The old imam returned his greeting: "Peace be with you also!" He told Yinbolaxi to have supper and to sleep first, and to postpone what he wanted to talk about until the next day. Then the ahong continued reciting.

A *mullah* came and led him to a room. After breakfast, the next day, Yinbolaxi went to pay a visit to the old ahong and told him why he had come. Upon hearing his story, the old ahong told him, "On your way back you will ride again on the back of the fish. In its mouth there is a valuable jewel, you may take it from its cheeks. With the jewel your mother and you will be able to have a better life."

Yinbolaxi also asked concerning the two strange situations he had encountered along the way. The old ahong gave him a satisfactory answer to these as well. Yinbolaxi therefore thanked the ahong and begun his homeward journey.

Because he was in a happy mood, his steps quickened. By midday he arrived at the river bank where the fish was ready and waiting for him. As before, he straddled its back, and as they moved toward the other bank he held on to its teeth. When they neared the other side, Yinbolaxi reached with his hand into the fish's cheek and, as expected, he found a jewel. He bade farewell to the fish and continued on his way.

By evening he arrived at the house with the apple tree. Invited by the uncle, he entered the house and had supper. After the meal Yinbolaxi said, "The old ahong said that there were silver pieces buried under the apple tree. That is why it does not bear fruit."

So the uncle with his family went out to dig the ground around the tree. Having dug to one meter's depth, they actually found two jars of silver. Everybody was quite happy, praising the old ahong as a great diviner. The next morning after breakfast the old uncle gave Yinbolaxi a horse and some pieces of silver and saw him off.

In the late morning he arrived at the old aunt's house. And it happened that the daughter of the old aunt, fetching water in a well by the gate, saw him returning. The girl hurried into the house, shouting, "Mom, the young fellow who was here a few days ago is coming back."

The old woman was very surprised and asked, "You could not speak for three or four years. Why can you suddenly speak now?"

By that time Yinbolaxi came in and spoke a greeting. The old aunt asked him to explain the reason for her daughter's dumbness. He said, "The old ahong said, 'At the moment she sees her future husband she will be able to speak.'"

The old mother quickly realized what had happened. The girl's face blushed, and shyly she ran to her room. The next day they packed up their things and went to Yinbolaxi's home together. Yinbolaxi told his mother what he had seen and heard. The mother was moved to tears. She went out to welcome her daughter-in-law and her mother. They talked cheerfully and merrily throughout the night. From that time on their lives became easier.

The Stone Monkey

Place: Lingxiazhou, Qinhai
Narrator: Ma Mingyi (Hui, age 67)
Recorder: Sha Cunshan (Hui), 1984

Once upon a time, in a Hui family, there were two brothers whose parents had died years ago. The older brother never treated the younger one as his blood brother. What is more, he and his wife often tormented his younger brother.

One day, shortly after dark, the older brother and his wife found again an excuse to beat up his younger brother. The latter could no longer tolerate their cuffs and kicks. He ran away from home to sit on a stone in the village, crying bitterly.

Momentarily he saw a white-bearded old man coming toward him, with a staff in his hand. The old man asked why he was so sad. With tears in his eyes the young one told the old man how his brother and sister-in-law treated him. The old man took pity on him and told him, "Poor young man! Go toward the mountain behind your house early tomorrow morning. Continue walking until you see a stone monkey squatting in the ravine. Reach into its mouth and you will get some silver. With the silver you can afford to live by yourself."

The younger brother was very grateful. But the old man disappeared before he could say a word of thanks.

The next morning the younger brother started out toward the mountain before daybreak. He walked and walked. Suddenly he found, there in the ravine, a stone monkey, squatting, with its mouth wide open. He ran quickly to it and put his hand into its mouth. True enough, what he took out was silver. He only put a small amount of silver into his pocket for he thought he should not be too greedy. Now that he had silver he bought a house with some furniture. He took a wife and began to live a happy life.

Great changes had taken place in the younger brother's life which made the older brother and his wife envious. By every means they tried to elicit from him the secret of his wealth. One day the older brother came to the younger brother with some crystal sugar and tea. With sweet words he begged his brother to tell him the secret. His brother was so honest that he told him how he had met that white-bearded old man and what the old man had told him to do. The older brother clapped his thigh and said, "Oh I see! I see!" He bounced back home to tell his wife.

The wife sewed a dozen bags that very night. Shortly after dark on the next day the older brother went to sit on the stone to cry. When a white-bearded old man appeared, as he hoped, he was overjoyed but wept even louder.

The old man took his hand and asked him what had happened that made him so sad. The older brother made up a story about being ill-treated by his brother. After the old man heard this he gave a sigh. Then he told the older brother to go and to take silver from the mouth of the stone monkey. But he admonished the older brother to keep one thing in mind—he should stop and leave when he heard the old man's voice. The older brother thanked the old man over and over again. When he finally lifted his eyes, the old man was nowhere to be seen.

The next morning before daybreak the older brother and his wife started out toward the mountain. On the way they saw a stone monkey squatting in the ravine just as they were told. They were wild with joy. They rushed to the stone monkey. The husband asked his wife to hold the bags for him. Then he reached into the white mouth. Ah, silver as white as snow! They were busy filling bags, one after the other. They did not stop even after the sun had risen high in the sky.

After all the bags had been filled they stuffed silver into their coats and trousers. Just at that moment the old man shouted, "It is time to descend from the mountain! It is high time to go!"

They were so taken in by the silver that they heard nothing. The older brother continued working.

All of a sudden the stone monkey closed its jaws with the man's hand still in it. He was frightened. Hastily he tried to pull back his hand, but in vain. It seemed as if his hand had taken root in the stone monkey's mouth. His wife could do nothing but watch him suffer.

When after a while it was proven it was impossible for him to take out his hand, she told him to wait there. She would go home first with the silver and then come to his rescue. But then, to their great disappointment, when she opened the bags to take out some silver, all of it had in the sunshine become pieces of stone—stones of all sizes.

At last they came to realize that it was Allah who brought them disaster. So they asked Allah for forgiveness. But no matter how piteously they prayed, the older brother still was unable to get out his hand. His wife had no alternative but to go home and to prepare food for him.

The older brother remained on the mountain with his hand in the mouth of the stone monkey for quite a long time, during which time his wife had to bring him something to eat every day. As time went by he could bear it no longer.

One day, when his wife came again he said to her with tears, "Do not bring any more food to me from now on. It is Allah who is punishing me. I deserve to be punished. We should not have been so cruel to my brother. But it is too late to regret."

His wife cried bitterly and was reluctant to leave. He pushed her and said, "Go, and apologize to my brother on my behalf. Take good care of him so that I can die with nothing to worry about." His wife said good-bye to him with tears in her eyes. Just as she was about to leave the stone monkey burst out laughing. At the moment when it opened its mouth the older brother took out his hand and dashed down from the mountain with his wife.

When the older brother returned home he went to the younger brother's place to apologize to him. They were on good terms ever after. On account of the lesson, taught to him by the stone monkey, he decided to turn over a new leaf. He told people that brothers should love one another, and help one another—as a boat helps water and water helps the boat—to live happily on the land given them by their ancestors.

The Ugly Mother

Place: Tongxin, Ningxia
Narrator: Wang Yiguo (Hui)
Recorder: Wang Zhengwei (Hui), 1979

Once there was a man called Bump whose father died young. With him in the family lived only an old mother. This mother was ugly looking and she had a pair of large feet. But she was good-natured and diligent. If she saw rice being dropped to the floor by the children, during meals, she picked it up and chatted endlessly, "Do not waste grain, or you will be punished by Allah."

The hens she bred were sure to lay eggs, sheep were sure to get strong, and crops were assured to come to harvest. As time passed the family's standard of living rose to a level of well-being. People in the neighborhood praised Bump as an able man. But actually, it was the ugly mother who had accumulated all this by way of hard work and frugality.

One year, at the end of Ramadan, which happened to be the ten-year anniversary of his father's death, Bump invited an ahong. He slaughtered an ox and more than ten sheep, and also made baskets full of fried food. He also invited many relatives and friends to dinner.

When guests arrived, and before they ate their meal, they asked to see his mother to say "Peace" to her. Upon hearing that, Bump felt uneasy. He despised his mother for her ugly-looking face, which disgraced him.

Outwardly he hemmed and hawed, and then went out. Bump told his two laborers in the backyard, "I am so proud that many guests have come today. But they want to see my mother. My mother is so ugly looking that I shall lose face if they find out. You two go and hurry, and carry her to the Black Valley."

The two laborers looked at each other with surprise, but they dared not to say anything. They had to obey.

After sending his laborers away, Bump went inside the house and told the guests, "I am sorry that my mother has become too ill today to see you. Please give up that idea."

Upon hearing this, everybody began to pick up chopsticks to eat the meal.

Meanwhile the two laborers took the ugly mother on their backs and left quietly through the back door. They brought her to an abandoned cave dwelling in Black Valley. A dog followed the mother all the way and stayed with her.

Above the old cave dwelling were some fields, the owner of which was called Outsider. Every morning at daybreak he plowed these fields, carrying with him dried food.

One day, after having plowed until midday, Outsider was tired. He opened a bag of his steamed bread. There were only two pieces of bread left in the bag. He did not care, and after eating he went on plowing. The next day when the time came for his meal he again found only two in the bag. This went on for several days. Outsider became very annoyed and gave his wife a scolding.

His wife did not know what was supposed to be wrong with her and asked him immediately, "What on earth makes you so angry?"

"I am doing such hard work as plowing, and you only give me two pieces of bread. How can I endure that?" said Outsider angrily.

His wife found it hard to discuss the matter, and she said while crying, "How can you say that? It is unfair. Every day I put four into the bag, not two." Upon hearing this, Outsider was puzzled and was determined to find out tomorrow what the matter was.

The next day Outsider went to the fields with dry food, and he laid his bag on the ground. While plowing he looked back now and then. A little later he saw a small white dog come over to the bag. And from the bag it took two pieces of bread into its mouth and ran off. Outsider ran after it and followed it all the way to the cave dwelling. In the cave he saw the dog lying next to an old woman. The old woman was covered with dust all over her body. No quilt nor bed was on the ground. Even the white cap on her head had become worn and dirty. She looked skinny and exhausted, and pitiful, indeed.

Outsider then asked, "Mom, where is your home? And why are you staying here?"

The old mother looked up, and sighed, "It is heartbreaking to mention it. On the day of fast-breaking many guests came who wanted to greet me, but my son Bump was ashamed of me because of my ugly looks. He was afraid to lose face. Therefore I was left here."

All this she explained with tears running down her face. This reminded Outsider of his parents who had died long ago. He sympathized with her, and made up his mind to take her home and regard her as his mother. So he said, "Aunt, do not be sad. My name is Outsider, and I am poor. My parents died when I was a child. If you agree, I can be your son."

The old woman became happy and said, "That is very kind of you! If you do not care about my ugly appearance, I will go with you and look after your children and do housework."

Outsider led his donkey up to the mother, pleasantly, and helped her get on. Then they went home together.

Ever since the mother lived in Outsider's home, all the family members, young and old, showed her respect. Being the pleasant mother she was, she refused to stay idle. She fed sheep, pressed manure. She did everything quickly and well. Within a few years Outsider had enough grain and herds of sheep, and their lives were becoming increasingly better.

The years passed faster than they knew. It was the festival of fast-breaking again. And it was also the thirty-year anniversary of the death of Outsider's father. Outsider slaughtered sheep, made fried food and invited many friends and guests.

When the guests asked to say "Peace" to his mother, Outsider happily brought out his mother from her room. The guests greeted her one by one, and among the greeters were the two laborers of Bump. To their great surprise they found that Outsider's mother was their master's only mother. They ran back and reported it to Bump.

Bump had become poorer and poorer since he had abandoned his mother. Sheep died off, grains were eaten up, and bad luck poured in on him continuously. He once tried to look for his mother but could not find her. Now, knowing where she was, he hurried to Outsider's house.

When he got there, Outsider and the mother were entertaining the guests. Bump shouted, "Mother, why are you here?" Outsider looked at the stranger and said, "She is my mother."

"She is my mother! You have stolen my mother! You have stolen my mother!" argued Bump, making a scene in the courtyard. The guests were puzzled.

Then out from the crowd came an old ahong. He said, "Do not argue! Let the mother herself say which of you is her son."

The mother stood up slowly and said, "My son's name is Outsider."

Bump did not give up yet. Outsider therefore said to him, "I do not want to argue with you. All the guests here are witnesses. Let us go and dig a large pit in the road. He who can jump over it shall be the son of the mother. Do you agree?"

Bump thought in his mind that, naturally, the woman was his mother. So he agreed and replied, "All right, all right."

Outsider sent two of his men to dig a pit. Afterward he and Bump went to the spot, while many people followed them to watch.

Bump said, "You jump first."

"You first," answered Outsider.

"All right!" Bump made a leap, but then fell into the pit. Before anybody knew what happened the pit closed and left only his head exposed. Soon the head turned into an earthen bump on the road.

In the smooth road that bump of earth kept sticking out. And therefore, whenever people passed there they would mutter an insult: "What a bad Bump!"

The Origin of Jiaozi Alley

Place: Xuanwu District, Beijing
Narrator: Wang Mengyu (Hui, age 80)
Recorder: Ma Jie (Hui), 1984

Along Niujie Street, in Beijing, there is an alley called Jiaozi Alley. Old people say that the name of this alley used to be Sedan-chair Alley.[3] A sad story is told about this change of name.

Opposite Sedan-chair Alley used to be Pot Alley. A Hui family lived there, many years ago. There were only two people in this family, a woman and her son. The father had died when the boy was

---

[3]*Jiaozi*, in Chinese, means to teach, to rear, or to bring up a child. It is pronounced like the word for sedan chair.

only three years old. The mother had to make a living by washing clothes for others. She would spend all her hard-earned money on buying good food and new clothes for her son. Moreover, she hated to spend a single penny on herself.

The mother pampered her son to the effect that he became a spoiled child. When he was only four or five years old he would demand whatever he wanted. If it was not exactly to his liking he would make a tearful scene. If the food was not good to eat he would throw his bowl and chopsticks on the ground. If the clothes did not fit him well, he would throw them on the floor and trample on them. His mother always did as he wished, even when he was obviously in the wrong. She would pick up the things he had thrown away and plead with him, repeatedly, to eat the food and to put on the clothes.

Several times her next-door neighbor, an old grandmother, told her, "Do not pamper the child like that."

She agreed in words but thought to herself, "You do not care much about your children because you have many. I have but one child. How can I help spoiling him?"

At the age of ten the boy neither went to school nor worked as an apprentice. Every day he roamed from street to street with other children to make trouble. Repeatedly an old grandfather in the neighborhood said to the mother, "You should be more strict with your son."

The mother would nod her agreement, while thinking, "I know how to love my own child. A tree will become upright when it grows up into a tall one. There is no doubt about this."

Now the boy was grown up. He had become a greedy and lazy young man, good for nothing. He was no better than an illiterate who could recognize only a few Chinese characters. The money his mother earned was not enough for him to squander. He learned to gamble and to steal. He would spend all his money on good food and clothes. Sometimes he would be absent from home for days.

One day his mother lay ill in bed. A group of court officers suddenly burst into the room to tell her, "Old woman, you have a good son indeed! He robbed a pedestrian and committed murder yesterday. He has been arrested and put into prison."

Upon hearing this the mother fainted. The neighbors immediately brought her some water and medicine. It was some time before she came to herself again.

It had happened like this. Her son, with a gang of others, had gone to Guang An Men early in the morning. They had robbed a pedestrian. The man had grabbed the son's jacket and would not let go. The others had run away from fear of getting caught. The woman's son had become desperate. He had drawn his dagger and stabbed the man in the chest. The man had died on the spot.

On the day when the son was to be executed, he was sent under guard to the execution place. Thousands upon thousands of people came to watch. Among them was also his mother.

Before the moment of execution arrived the executioner asked the son, "Have you anything to say?"

"I only want to have a word with my mother," was his answer. People moved aside to make way for the mother.

When the mother came up, the son gazed at her and asked her to move closer. Then he spoke into her ears, with resentment, "Mother! Mother! Oh how I regret having done this! Though you have ears, you refused to listen to earnest advice. The reason why I have come to such an ignoble end is because I was brought up without being taught proper behavior."

Then suddenly he bit off his mother's ear and turned to go up to the execution platform. Seeing her son about to be executed, the mother felt regretful for what she had done. She smashed her head against a big rock by the road. By the time people came to pull her up, she was already dead.

All the people were deeply grieved at the death of the woman and her son. To keep this lesson firmly in mind, they changed the name of Pot Alley into Guan'er Alley.[4] For the purpose of warning later generations, the people who lived in Sedan-chair Alley changed its name to Jiaozi Alley—to Teach a Child.

---

[4]*Guan'er* means "pot" or "jar" and is pronounced the same as "to spoil a child."

An Evil Woman

Place: Tongxin, Ningxia
Recorder: Wang Zhengwei (Hui), 1979

Long ago lived a cruel-hearted and sharp-tongued young woman. She was very cruel toward the old people. She made her sixty-year-old mother-in-law do housework all day long. The mother-in-law cooked meals, did the laundry, heated the *kang* (brick bed), etc. People therefore referred to the young woman as an "evil woman."

That year the old mother-in-law suffered a serious illness. Later she became farsighted and a bit deaf, and she lost some teeth. She could not do housework anymore. The evil woman had to do the housework herself. For this she often made the old woman suffer by leveling oblique accusations against her while she was working.

One year, when the new crop was still in the blade and the old harvest had been consumed, no grain was left at home for cooking. The husband went out to borrow some grain. Before he left he told his wife, "There is only some millet left. Just cook a little each day. Let mother eat millet while you drink the millet water."

After he left she smiled coldly. She put two handfuls of millet into a pot. As the water in the pot was ready and viscous she skimmed it from the millet, then she poured some more water into the pot. When it was again ready and viscous she skimmed the water and drank it again. She did not take the millet to her mother-in-law until, in the end, she had drunk all the millet essence off the top.

Several days later the husband returned without any grain. He found his mother pale and emaciated. So he asked his wife, "Did you let Mom eat millet while you drank millet water?"

The evil woman, pulling a long face, replied unhappily, "If you do not believe me, go and ask your mother."

The husband thought, perhaps the millet water was more nourishing. He told his wife, well-meaningly, "Tomorrow I will go out again. This time you eat millet and let mother drink millet water. Mother is old and she is in bad health."

The evil woman answered sweetly, with cunning, "I do not care what I eat, as long as Mother will become healthy."

Later she put some millet into the pot. When it barely came to boiling she hurriedly poured the water out from the pot and took it to her mother-in-law. And she herself ate the thick millet.

When the husband came back with grain he saw that his mother was even more weak while his wife was in ruddy health. The husband thought that perhaps his mother was old and needed some meat to build up her health. He told his wife: "Go and cook the leg of lamb which I have brought home. It must be thoroughly steamed."

The evil woman smiled from ear to ear when she heard this. After a while she brought a plate of cooked mutton to the table. The husband ripped the soft mutton into pieces and asked his wife to take the soft mutton to his mother. Seeing this, the evil woman thought that he had shown too much bias toward his mother. And rolling her mouse-like eyes, she walked into the kitchen. She hid the meat and cut a piece of sheep skin, cooked it a while over the fire, and then took it to her mother-in-law.

"This is the mutton your son has brought for you—have it!" she said.

The old woman was so happy that when she heard it was meat she snatched it into her toothless mouth. The meat was too tough to chew. She had to throw it back up.

A moment later the son came in and asked: "Mom, do you like the meat you had? Was it delicious?"

"It was tasteless and just like a piece of leather. I could not chew it and gave it to a cat."

The son thought: "Mom could not even chew such soft meat. I will make some noodles for her."

Before supper, sitting at the edge of the *kang*, the son told his wife, "Go and cook some noodles for Mother, and make them soft."

The evil woman rolled up her sleeves and in a short time she finished cooking. The husband ladled out a bowl of noodles and poured some vinegar on it. In succession he asked his wife to carry two bowls of noodles to his mother.

The son thought his mother must have eaten her fill. But contrary to his expectations, his wife had eaten up the noodles in the yard, secretly.

After supper the son went to see his mother and asked, "Mom, did you like the noodles today?"

"My Son, I have eaten nothing today." The mother did not know whether to laugh or to cry.

The son became angry, "What? You become more and more confused. With my own eyes I saw your own daughter-in-law bring you two bowls of noodles. Why do you say you did not have any?"

The son stepped out of the room, and the old woman was compelled to suffer in silence. She prayed, tears in eyes, "Allah! Why do you not provide justice? Let me die as quickly as possible. Do not let me suffer any longer."

Day after day the old woman became skinnier. With sunken eyes she laid on the *kang*, weak, and without any strength left to turn over. The son was worried about her but did not know what to do. One day he found an excuse and scolded the evil woman: "A few days ago I asked you to take noodles to Mother. But she said she did not get any. Where did you take them to?"

But far from admitting her bad behavior, she responded shamelessly and accused her critic, "By Allah—this is unjust! You saw me with your own eyes take the noodles to your mother that day. If I have taken your mother's meal to others, let me become a pig and die." She cried and shouted for quite some time, swearing all the while.

The husband believed that what she said was true. He softened and became reconciled. "Mother is too old to think clearly anymore. So never mind. Treat Mother filially and you will go to heaven after you die."

The next day, when the husband saw his wife's face brighten up, he told her again, "Today you better make some soft steamed bread, and take more to Mother so that she can eat whenever she wants."

She nodded and said obediently, "I will do so at once."

As soon as the husband had gone out she picked up a kitchen knife and went over to the old woman, and said, "From now on, if you dare make trouble for me with your son, I will kill you." And with deliberation she rubbed the knife at the edge of the *kang*.

The old woman did not dare to say a word. After a short time the evil woman fried some board beans for the old woman and said, "This is your food for these two days."

The old woman, with her hands shaking, took one into her mouth because she could not see clearly what it was. How could she chew it? It was as hard as a rock. But she felt very hungry. So she chewed it in her mouth over and over. At this moment the son came in. When he saw his mother's mouth moving he thought she was still eating steamed bread. He felt relieved. Such things continued for two days. The husband thought he really had wronged the evil woman.

On another day the son went over to see his mother and said: "Mom, these days you have eaten well. Have you not? Later I will ask my wife to bring you more steamed bread and water."

The mother replied, "My Son, I raised you in vain. I am on my last breath. I am waiting for my end."

The son became annoyed. "Mom, why do you speak against your conscience? I saw you chewing from morning till night with my own eyes. You mean you want ginseng?"

The old mother became increasingly more heartbroken. Her nose twitched, and she opened her mouth and cried out. A board bean dropped from her mouth.

The son wondered at this sight: "Why! Mom has few teeth. Why did she eat beans?" He held the old mother in his arms and asked, "Mom, why do you eat beans instead of bread?"

The old mother kept crying, shaking her head constantly. Seeing his mother so heartbroken, the son asked for the exact reason.

The old woman choked with sobs. "You saw me eating without stopping. But what do I eat? Your wife brought me some board beans. I cannot chew them, but I kept them in my mouth. For two days I have not had anything." Saying this she began to weep again.

When he heard this, the son fell into a rage. "This evil woman! She must pay for it!"

He ran out into the yard and looked for the evil woman. Yet, there was no-one in sight—except a pig grunting. He was greatly surprised. How could this be?

Suddenly black clouds were rolling in on the sky, with thunder and lightning. The son hurried into his mother's room. "Crack!" A series of thunderbolts smashed the evil woman out of sight.

From then on the old mother was served carefully by her son. And she lived happily the remainder of her life.

Colorful Stones

Place: Ningxia
Narrator: Ma Wencheng (Hui)
Recorders: Long Fengyun and Ma Xueli (Hui), 1980

Long, long ago, in Wuja Village, lived an old man named Wu, who carried loads of goods on a shoulder pole. He was selling them from village to village. His wife managed the affairs at home. His two sons and their wives farmed ten *mu* of rice fields. Together they lived a fairly prosperous life.

One day the old Wu came home, walked to the edge of the *kang*, and with a sudden slump he lay on it stiff-like. Cold sweat broke forth from his forehead. He was breathing hard and praying with a murmur, all the while, "Allah—I am dying!"

For several days the old man did not seem to recover, although he had taken many doses of herbal medicine. One day, after visiting their father, the two sons went back again to their homes. The moment the younger son entered his house, his wife pulled him to the inner room and said, with an angry face, "What a fool you are! Your older brother has already taken away many pieces of family property. He has locked them up in a big chest, while you are still boxed up in a drum."

"What can I do about it?"

"If we are to depend on you, we would have nothing but north-west wind to drink." While speaking so, she opened her wardrobe chest, pointing to the wrapped and bulging things inside—which she had already taken. She said, "We must hide and transfer these things to another place in darkness, tonight. And do not let anyone know."

But the mother found out about this matter, and she was quite indignant. All day long, with tears in her eyes, she was thinking about what she would live on after her husband passed away. If she were to live with the oldest son—his wife was a shrew and nobody dared to deal with her, including the old woman. And if she were to live with the younger son—his wife was full of unnecessary suspicions. Thinking thus to and fro, she came up with no idea. She looked at her husband who remained unconscious, and tears rolled down her face.

"Mother of our children!"—the old man awoke, and called out to his wife—"Under the gate I have kept two silver ingots for you. After my death, you better live separately so as not to be bullied by the daughters-in-law."

"My Allah!" The old woman could not help but cry out loudly. The crying shocked the sons and daughters-in-law. They came one after another gathering round their father who was not yet dead. The oldest son said, "Dad, how shall we brothers do it if you go to Allah?" The younger brother, fearing that his older brother would take advantage, added before his father opened his mouth, "Dad, if you go to Allah, our family property will..."

The old man suddenly raised himself on his hands, scolding, "You wretches! I raised you with great difficulty, and here you do not think about supporting your mom in the future. You think about family property."

The old man gasped for breath, fell back on the *kang*, and then died.

The next day already, after the dead one was buried, the two sons fought each other for the property. Their near neighbors came and stopped them. After dividing the family property the oldest brother put up a new house outside the courtyard. Following the man's instructions, the widow lived alone. Everyday she got up early and went to bed late, doing her prayers. Once a week she prayed for her husband.[5]

One midday she thought about her days and what her life in the future might be like. She could not hold back her tears and broke forth into crying. This happened to be heard by her oldest son and his wife when they were passing by. So they came in. Putting down his spade, the oldest son said, "Mom, the winter is coming. It is getting colder and colder. If you stay here alone we shall be blamed."

"Mom, just come and live with us," chipped in the wife, adding to her husband's words. "Although we have no good meal, we can serve you with our warm hearts. The younger brother and his wife care nothing about you, even though you live here."

---

[5]Seven days after a person dies prayers should be given for the deceased. These prayers are repeated seven times in the course of forty-nine days.

The widow stopped crying. "Just let me be..." she said, wiping her tears.

"Mom!" the oldest son's wife said, smilingly and meekly, "you need not give us anything if you will live with us. If we make you unhappy we would be no better than animals."

"It is enough for me that you have such a filial sense of duty"—the widow's heart was convinced by their words. She gave a long sigh and said, "All right. Tomorrow I will move to your house."

After that they served the mother with meals and tea and made the bed warm for her in the evening, to sleep. Day by day the grief in the widow's heart gradually was reduced and she became satisfied with her life.

But one day, after coming from work in the fields, the daughter-in-law pulled a long face and began beating her child, and chided him, "You little dog, only eat and eat.... We have little grain left."

"Why do you beat him? He is too young to know anything," said the oldest son as he came in and sat on a chair, sighing.

The widow came over and asked her son, "My Son, what is the matter?"

"Hai...." After heaving a long sigh, the oldest son replied, "After my father's death I held a funeral ceremony for him and then set up a house. The three *dan* [three hundred pounds] of grain are almost used up."

"Why did you not let me know earlier?"

"I did not want to disturb you."

"Do not speak so. Being a mother, no matter how old I am, I cannot avoid worrying about my children. I can contribute."

That night the widow dug out the silver ingots. She kept one in her wardrobe and gave the other to the oldest son. The oldest son swore, "If I do not provide for you all my life, I deserve to be punished by Allah."

The widow lived in the oldest son's house, and very soon spring came. One day, after breakfast, the oldest son and his wife went to town. The widow was just feeling numb when the younger son's wife pushed the door open and came in, calling "Mom" and throwing her-self into her arms, crying.

The mother touched her head and asked, "My Child, what troubles you?"

"Mom." She stopped crying, wiped the tears from her face and said, "Look at your broken nails and thin face. One night I was missing you so much that I could not fall asleep. I got up and came to see you. But I was greeted by a nice smell of meat. Looking inside from the window I saw the older brother and his wife having meat while you were sleeping in the dark." She began crying again. "Allah! What heartless people they are...!"

These words dumbfounded the widow. For a long time she remained silent.

"Mom, come home with me!" said the younger son's wife after having cried enough. "It is enough to see their cold faces here." Then she started to pack up the old woman's clothes.

"Wait, just wait until your older brother-in-law comes back."

"What is the use of waiting for him?" The younger son's wife said. "He stands by his wife to bully you. Let us go!" And so she dragged the old woman away.

From then on the mother came again back to her own house. The younger daughter-in-law took good care of her and did not let her do any housework. She not only cooked meals for the mother, but also made new clothes for her. When the mother felt bored she would have a walk in the village. As time went by, her lean face was glowing with health. This situation lasted until summer came. Then the mother offered the younger son that other silver ingot.

It was autumn now. Early one morning, before the widow finished her prayers, noises of wrangling between her younger son and his wife were suddenly heard in the courtyard. The wife threw chopsticks and bowls on the ground, making oblique comments: "How rich are you? Is the old woman only your mother? Where is her older son? Why should I serve her?"

The younger son did not speak. He held his head in his arms and squatted on the ground. The more she listened the more unbearable she felt. She went into her own room to sob.

When the oldest son heard these scoldings he came into the courtyard to reason with them. With the authoritative manner of an older one, he kicked the door open and shouted at his brother, "It was you who took mother here, secretly. It is also you who wants to kick her out. You are heartless!"

"Are you or we the heartless ones?" With these words the younger son's wife lashed out while her husband still kept silent. "You are the oldest son; you took much more property. Now you want us to support the old woman. How can you have the heart to do so?"

Hearing this, the wife of the oldest son joined in. Pulling a long face she assaulted them with sharp words: "Parents in the world always make a favorite of the younger. You got most of the property—you received some publicly while quietly you stole some. And now you sound off."

The widow did not want to see them quarrel so fiercely. Shedding tears she begged, "Stop quarrelling. None of you has to support me. Just pay back my silver."

The oldest son's wife said with a red face, "Do not talk nonsense. You lived at my house for several months. I provided you with good meals. Your silver is not enough for the meals, let alone my service."

The younger son's wife broke in, "You cheated her out of her silver and now you want to kick the mother out. We have taken neither more property nor the silver. Mother must be supported by you."

The two sons could not bear any more of this quarrelling. Each of them jumped toward his own wife, and each fought with his. The people who came to watch finally took them apart and persuaded them to stop. Now only the widow was left there, together with some old women who spoke some words of comfort. The widow was crying sadly.

The more she thought about it the more she felt that this was no way to continue living. At night when the moon was rising over the trees she finished praying and went to the river, alone. On the bank she again had a good cry. When she was just about to leap into the river, all of a sudden her clothes were grabbed from behind by someone. Momentarily she turned around and saw an old man standing in the moonlight, wearing white clothes and a cap. Across his shoulders he carried a long rectangular bag.[6]

"Who are you?" she gave him an angry stare.

"I am an ahong, passing by."

"Oh Ahong," she said with grief, "my sons do not support me anymore. I cannot go on living." And so she told him the whole story. The old man said, "I really cannot believe that such a thing has happened. But thanks be to Allah, who let me meet you!" Then he took out some colorful stones from his bag and handed them to her.

---

[6]A bag sewn up at both ends, with an opening in the middle.

After that he whispered something into her ears. By the river he got on a black donkey, and quickly he disappeared.

The next morning a white-bearded man on a donkey came to the village. Along his way he kept calling out, "Collect jewels, treasures, and colorful stones."

When the white-bearded man was passing by the widow's door, the widow came out with a silk bundle in her hands, and said, "Please wait, I have colorful stones."

At that moment the younger son's wife was having lunch. Hearing the mother's words she at once put down her bowl and chopsticks and ran out. Watching by the door she noticed that the white-bearded man got off his donkey and walked over. He took the silk bundle from the widow's hand, untied it, and then looked very surprised. "How much do you want for each one?" he asked.

"One thousand taels of silver," she said.

"How about nine hundred?"

"No."

"Nine hundred fifty!"

"No. I do not want to sell them. Actually, I just wanted to have their value appraised." And she asked, "Where do you live?"

"I live on Ox Mountain." Then he left on his donkey.

The younger daughter-in-law witnessed all this. She returned to her room and was in no mood to eat her meal anymore.

During the afternoon, the news that the white-bearded man wanted to buy colorful stones spread all over the village. Everybody was talking about it. Some said that the widow had fifty colorful stones. Some said that she had more than that. And others said that the widow would not sell even when the white-bearded man offered her nine hundred and ninety-nine taels of silver for each. It was evening when the news reached the oldest son's ears. He told his wife about this curious happening as soon as he entered the house.

"Really?" His wife asked unbelievingly.

"Yes, indeed."

"Then go and bring mother back!"

And on that account they took the mother back into their house.

From that time on the sons and daughters-in-law took great care of their mother. One family presented the mother with chicken and mutton, the other with eggs and fish. One made new clothes, the other sewed a new padded coat. The widow's life was becoming more and more bearable.

Eight years flew by unnoticed before the widow died.

After their mother was buried, the oldest brother said to his younger brother, "Brother, the white-bearded man has not been seen coming around. I think we should go to him and sell the colorful stones. We can divide the money half and half. Shall we?"

"All right. That is the same idea my wife has."

So the next day the two brothers got up at dawn and set out in the direction of Ox Mountain. When they got to the foot of the mountain they looked up at its steep peaks, one appearing higher than the other—and hawks were circling around them. Goats could hardly climb up, let alone human beings. The two brothers sighed in despair while sitting on a rock.

At this moment a strong man came down the slope carrying an old woman on his back. The two brothers walked up to meet him, and they asked, "Big Brother, is there a white-bearded man living on this mountain?"

The man looked at them and asked, "You come to see him for something concerning your parents?"

"Yes, yes."

"Follow me, then."

The strong man walked ahead and the two brothers followed him closely, climbing on a very narrow and winding trail, up the mountain. The farther they walked the narrower the path became. Halfway up the mountain there was only one stone ledge for a single person to pass. Below that ledge was a dark abyss, too deep for its bottom to be seen. The two brothers became so afraid that they were dripping with cold sweat all over, and their legs could hardly support them.

The strong man, carrying the old woman, walked steadily, with no shivering in his legs and no swaying of his body. In short, he left the two very far behind. The older one shouted, "Big Brother, wait for us please!"

The strong man turned around and called back loudly, "This is called Heart-judging Cliff. As the saying goes: 'For the sake of one's mother the narrow winding trail becomes wider; for the sake of money even a broad road becomes narrow.' So you need not be afraid. Come on up. I will wait for you ahead."

Their faces suddenly turned pale at these words. They stared at each other and knew not what to do. At this moment they caught sight of a white-bearded old man, on a donkey, coming up from below along the stone ledge. He narrowed his eyes into a line. The two brothers knelt down hurriedly and cried, "Help! Help!"

"Why do you not continue walking? Why do you shout for help while blocking my way?" the old man asked.

"We are terribly afraid!"

The old man threw them his reins and said to them, "One of you take my reins, and the other hold his hand!"

Accepting the old man's advice, they climbed upward—their hearts in their mouths.

Ahead of them was a large open space; it seemed as if they had come to another kind of land. The strong man, supporting the old woman, walked toward the white-bearded man and said, "Grandfather, this is my mother, she became blind and mute all of a sudden. It is said that you can cure such illnesses. Please help my mother."

The white-bearded man took out a paper wrapper from the bag across his shoulder, and gave it to him and said, "Though this medicine is of the longevity kind, it is effective on eyes and ears as well. It can stimulate the circulation of the blood and cause the muscles and joints to relax. Its local name is Rejuvenation Medicine. Boil it and then let her have it. She will recover very soon." The strong man thanked the old man, took his mother on his back, and went away happily.

Then the white-bearded man turned and asked the two brothers, "You are the sons of the widow. Are you not?"

"Yes we are," they answered. "And you are the old man collecting jewels and precious stones?"

"Yes I am," said the old man. "Have you brought the colorful stones with you?"

"Yes." The oldest brother took out the colorful stones.

"All right," the old man said. "I will ask you two questions. If you can answer, I shall pay ten thousand taels of silver for each one."

Then he asked, "What is the sweetest? And what is the most bitter?"

The oldest brother thought for a while and answered, "The sweetest is honey..." and the younger brother interrupted, "The most bitter is a very young melon."

"You are wrong," said the old man. "The sweetest is young married couples and the most bitter is to be widows and widowers."

When they heard this, the two brothers stared foolishly. The old man said again, "Now follow me to examine your colorful stones."

By the time the sun went down they had arrived at the edge of a river. Colorful stones lay everywhere. The white-bearded old man grasped a handful of stones and mixed them with the five they had, and then he said, "Look! They are ordinary stones!"

The two brothers took a look at the stones and stood there motionless, like rocks.

Four Sons of Aisima

Place: Lingxia, Gansu
Recorder: Han Chang (Hui), 1980

Once there was an old couple, the Aisimas, who raised their four sons while working very hard. By living frugally they had married them all off. But after they had married, the four sons had wives and forgot their parents.

Ever since that time none of the sons or their wives served the old couple a hot meal or sewed them clothes. The old couple lived a very difficult life. Now and then they had something to eat for one meal, but nothing left for another meal.

The old couple thought about this, repeatedly, and an idea finally came to their minds.

One day, after praying in the morning, Aisima went out as usual to the river bank, carrying a basket on his back. There he gathered some sticks and branches which had been washed up on the bank. And he picked up some stones the size of eggs, and then came back slowly. In the evening he cleaned every stone shiny and bright with a cloth, and made marks on each one. He wrapped them in paper and placed them into a chest at a corner of the *kang*.

This odd behavior was observed by a child of his neighbor. There is no child who is not curious and, accordingly, one child told another. When darkness had fallen and lamps were lit in every home, a group of children quietly looked into the old man's room through the window crack. As expected, they saw the old couple wrapping some things in red paper and then putting them into a chest.

The news spread very soon and also reached the ears of the four sons. When night fell, the big son sent his child to find out what on earth his grandfather was doing. The boy returned later and said, "Grandpa was really busy, wrapping something like a lump! Yet, he did not let me come close enough to see."

Meanwhile the other sons also sent their children to investigate the matter. They all got the same answers.

The next day the four sons, each striving to be the first and fearing to lag behind, began to invite the old couple to live with them. In each family the sons would heat up the brick bed for them. In the morning the old couple would be served milk in tea, with soft and crisp breakfast cakes; fried eggs or steamed bread with soup, for lunch; and noodles with mutton, or dumplings with a mutton filling, for supper—which were the old couple's favorites. Clothes were made for them for different seasons, as well as shirts, padded coats, socks, shoes, and new quilts. Even by doing all this the four sons felt that they were not filial enough. Every morning they would come to say "Peace" to the old couple, bowing down before them.

The old couple lived no more than a month with the oldest son's family when the second son came to invite them to his house, pretending to complain. "Brother! Mom and Dad have lived in your home for quite a long time. It is their turn now to live with me." And even though the oldest son did not give his consent, the second son took the old couple away that very moment.

After the old couple had just lived half a month in the second son's home, the third son came, pouring out his dissatisfaction. "Brother! Dad and Mom have stayed here for quite a long time. It is my turn now."

After having been only about a week in the third son's home, the fourth son came to blame his brother. "How can you keep Mom and Dad here so long? It is my turn now. I will have them stay with me a year or two." So the old couple had to move into the fourth son's house.

Yet, only a couple of days passed and the oldest son came again for the old couple. The four sons all felt that the old couple did not stay long enough at each of their houses. They all wanted them to stay as long as possible.

Three years passed like this. The old mother suddenly caught asthma; later she died by choking on excessive phlegm. Unfortunately, within the next seven days the old man died also, from heart disease and general poor health.

The four sons, in order to show their filial hearts, spent a lot of money on the old couple's funerals. Four days later, according to local custom, they invited all their neighbors and relatives to dinner. When the dinner was over, the oldest son took out a key and, in front of everyone, opened the chest which sat at the corner of the *kang*. He placed all the red-wrapped packages on the *kang*, in a row.

Each of the four brothers picked up one and unwrapped it. Each contained nothing but white stone. They all stood there, astonished. They complained, and then they wept.

Nuha and Suoli

Place: Ningxia
Narrator: Huang Cunde (Hui, age 83)
Recorder: Xie Rong, 1979[7]

At Taolinyan, in Lajiahu, lived two brothers. The older brother, Nuha, was kind and honest and was nicknamed "Old Sheep." The younger brother, Suoli, was sinister and crafty, and was called "Scorpion."

Scorpion was gluttonous and lazy. He lost all his family inheritance by gambling, and he owed Heersa, a merchant, five taels of silver on top of that. How could he pay this debt? He knotted his brows and a plot flashed into his mind. One day he secretly lured away Lihu, Nuha's five-year-old son, and he took him to Heersa. He lied that the boy was his own son, and he offered him as payment for his debts. The merchant only had a daughter. He had come to pity himself for not having a son of his own. When he saw that Lihu was

---

[7]For more information concerning this scholar see page 73, note 1.

handsome and clever he became so excited that he gave Suoli another five taels of silver.

Having lost their son, the Nuhas became worried and broken-hearted. They looked for him everywhere, their tears nearly drying and legs swollen. But Nuha was not discouraged and he was determined to go look for his son and to do some business along the way. Before leaving he urged Suoli repeatedly to take good care of his wife.

Eight years had passed since Nuha left home. He was never heard from. When Suoli saw that his brother was gone forever, he rolled his eyes and another scheme occurred to him. He told everyone whom he met that his brother died of a sudden disease along his way. Hearing the news, Nuha's wife wept and wailed. Suoli took advantage of this situation to force his sister-in-law to remarry. But the sister-in-law cried and cried and said that she would rather die than remarry. For seven days in a row she took neither water nor rice.

When his first ruse failed, Suoli plotted and tried another. He secretly sold her as a slave to a rich man for twenty taels of silver. They agreed to clinch the deal that night. The rich man was told to take away the woman who could be identified by wearing on her head a white mourning veil.

As for Nuha—Old Sheep—he had not found his son on his journey; he had suffered business losses instead. As a result of his anxiety he had fallen seriously ill. It had been several months before he could struggle to rise up, but he had spent his last penny on his room and medicine. Being penniless he had to go begging along the streets. Nuha thought about how he not only failed to find his son but that he himself had become a beggar. He felt ashamed to face his wife, and he concluded that he better accept this fate. Perhaps, with Allah's help, he would have better opportunities and luck some day.

One day it was snowing and blowing hard. Nuha did not get a single mouthful of food. He was feeling cold and hungry. With a stick in his hand he dragged himself to a forked intersection in a village. He slipped and fell, and at that moment he saw a small white bag near his feet. He quickly untied it, and in it were two hundred taels of silver, wrapped in four packages.

He was pleasantly surprised. But meanwhile he thought, "The owner must have gone through hardships to earn this money, and now he must be feeling very anxious. I could not spend the money even if I starved or froze to death."

So he waited for the owner, in the snow, enduring hunger and cold till deep into the night. But no one came. And so he made his way to an old cave nearby to find shelter for the night.

At the break of dawn, the next day, he took the small bag with him and hurried back to the fork in the road. There he found a man who looked like a merchant sitting by the roadside, sighing, cheeks in his hands and his brows frowned. Nuha walked up to him and asked, "Friend, what troubles you?"

"Oh, do not speak of it! I cannot go on living!"

"We are both wanderers. Tell me your trouble. Maybe I can help you."

"What lousy luck! I lost two hundred taels of silver which I earned with much difficulty. How can I support my family of four without these?"

"What was your silver packed in?"

"A small white bag, which was sewed by my wife."

On hearing this, Nuha took him by his hand and said, "My friend, do not worry. I have picked up your silver." Then he handed the white bag to the merchant.

The merchant was stupefied. Looking at the man in rags, thin and emaciated, and then the bright silver in his hand, he could not prevent tears from rolling down his face. He opened his arms and held Nuha's shoulders and said, "My Good Brother. You are such a kind man as can rarely be found. I am Heersa, living in Dengkoubao. If you do not mind, please come and stay at my house for some time. I now regard you as my brother."

They both started on their way to Dengkoubao. The Heersa family made fried cakes, mutton, and other things to show hospitality to him. The family's reunion and prosperity reminded Nuha of his lost son and his wife of eight years ago. Tears filled his eyes.

Heersa asked him for the reason and then comforted him, "My brother. Do not worry. Your son can be found. I will try my best to have your family reunited. Just describe to me your son's appearance and let me help you."

"My son is very handsome, with a white face, a pointed chin and long eyebrows. His infant name is Lihu. And beyond that, there are three black moles on his left knee."

Heersa was shocked when he heard this. He opened his eyes wide and was speechless. Momentarily he turned and rushed out. A while later he brought in a good-looking boy. As soon as he entered he said to the boy, "Lihu, say 'Peace' to your father." While he so spoke he rolled up the boys trousers on his left leg.

Seeing the three black moles on his knee, Nuha was pleasantly surprised. He was choked with sobs, and finally burst into tears: "Lihu, my dear son. Your mother and I have been missing you so much."

Heersa told him in detail the story of Suoli selling Lihu to him. Not until now did Nuha realize that his own brother was as ruthless as a wolf. He thanked Heersa time and again. Heersa said with pleasure, "Well, well. A chance encounter, indeed. It will be a pleasant thing to let my daughter marry your son; they are well matched in age and character. I suggest we simply become relatives."

Nuha readily and pleasantly agreed and decided to take Lihu home to his own mother first. Then they would fix a date for marriage. Before starting, Heersa gave Nuha twenty taels of silver to pay for his traveling expenses. The father and his son hurried happily along their way. They wished they could fly to their home!

Our story returns here to Suoli, the Scorpion. That night Suoli had agreed with the rich man to carry away his sister-in-law, secretly. He took a piece of white silk from his wardrobe chest and went to visit his sister-in-law:

"Sister-in-law, it has already been told that my older brother has died, but you do not believe. Now you see, somebody brought a message and told me that my brother, before he died, asked him to send this piece of white silk as a remembrance. Please put it on your head to show your feelings in memory of my poor brother." And as he spoke he pretended to squeeze out a tear.

Nuha's wife believed him. She kept weeping and wailing, holding the white silk in her hand. She thought that she had lost her dear son and now also her husband for sure. What should she live for? It would be better for her to die. So she stopped weeping, closed the door, and put the white silk on her head. She found a rope and hanged herself at the roof beam. But the rope was not strong enough and broke, and she fell to the floor, unconscious.

Meanwhile, having noticed that Suoli gave his sister-in-law a piece of white silk, Suoli's wife felt angry and envious. Secretly she went to ask her sister-in-law for the white silk. She broke in through the window because she could not get the door open. She paid no attention to her sister-in-law as she was lying on the floor. She snatched the silk off her head and put it on her own: "A beggar's wife! Do you deserve to wear such a thing?"

She was just about to step out when a band of masked men broke into the room. The moment they saw her head, wrapped in white silk, they dragged her away without saying a word. Suoli, who hid behind the trees, saw them carrying away a woman and then went back home, delighted with the twenty taels of silver in his hands. Entering his own house he found his wife gone. Instead, in her house, he found his sister-in-law sobbing on the floor.

Only at this moment did he realize that he had lifted a rock only to drop it on his own feet—that he has sold his own wife for twenty taels of silver. He turned around and ran to the river bank in a great rush. But where could he find a trace of his wife? While he was regretting his foolishness, beating his breast and stamping his feet, a boat came into view in the distance. Up front in the boat stood a man, looking over toward the bank. Suoli thought that he looked familiar. And while he was wondering about this, a voice shouted, "Lihu, come out. We are almost home."

Upon hearing this Suoli was shocked and turned pale. It was his brother who returned with his son. Thinking about what he had done, how could he face them? He threw the silver into the river and ran back into the dark woods and hanged himself on an old tree.

Nuha returned home with his son, and the family was reunited—the wife and her husband, the son and his mother. After years of peaceful life they fixed a good date and went to Heersa's place for their son's engagement. Somewhat later Lihu got married.

Lihu and his family lived a happy life.

A Small Wooden Bowl

Place: Ningxia
Narrator: Ma Chengui (Hui)
Recorder: Xie Rong (Hui), 1980[8]

Long ago, in Nanliu village, there lived a family, the husband and wife of which were not respectful and filial toward their old father. The father was weak and ill, but every day he had to gather firewood, carry water, herd sheep, and clean the house. After some years the father had become too old to lift water, and eventually he walked only with much trouble. The husband and wife regarded the old father as a burden. They thought of a convenient way to mistreat him, so that he might die more quickly. A large eating bowl was replaced with a smaller one, and the smaller one was replaced with a small child-size wooden bowl. Each day the old father failed to fill his stomach.

One day their five-year-old son, Mugao, took the usual leftovers in the small wooden bowl to his grandfather. The innocent child asked the old father, "Grandpa, Dad and Mom have said that you would be full by having one bowl of food for a meal. Why are several bowls of food not enough for me?"

The old father, pointing to the small wooden bowl, replied with tears in his eyes. "This bowl is a precious one. The food in it shows the kindness of your parents. So, I can eat my fill."

The grandson told his parents about these words. The unfilial couple said, "Son! Your grandpa is right. This bowl is really a precious bowl. One can eat his fill with little food."

Hearing these words, Mugao secretly hid the bowl. At another meal time he took food to his grandpa in a big bowl. As soon as his parents found that there was less rice in the pan, they at once ran after the child and snatched the big bowl and shouted in anger, "The wooden bowl, where is it?"

---

[8]For more information concerning this recorder see page 73, note 1.

Mugao answered, crying, "Grandpa and both of you said that it is a precious bowl, with which one can eat his fill. I have hidden the small wooden bowl. I will save it and use it for you, someday in the future."

The husband and wife stared at each other, silent and speechless. From that time on they no longer treated their old father badly.

A Clever Wife

Place: Haiyuan, Ningxia
Narrator: Laoyang (Hui)
Recorder: Yang Shencai (Hui), 1980

Long, long ago, lived an old couple who had many fields and horses. And though they were rich, they were still unhappy. Why? Who was there to inherit the family estate? Their only son was stupid and dimwitted, and he could neither conduct any business nor oversee the house.

The old man tried hard to make him clever. First he tried every possible means to educate him, and then he had him marry a very bright and kindhearted girl. And after that he taught him how to do business.

One day the old man said to his son Yesaier, "You may choose one of the best horses and take it to sell in the market. Then slowly you will learn how to do business."

Hearing what his father said, Yesaier walked to the horse barn, chose the best horse, and then took it to his wife and asked her how much it would cost. The wife looked at the horse and said, "Two hundred taels of silver."

As soon as Yesaier reached the market, a rich merchant wanted to buy his horse. The rich merchant said, "Hello Guy! What is the price of this horse?"

Yesaier answered, "Two hundred taels."

The merchant bartered, "Will you take anything off?"

"No, my wife told me two hundred taels."

Seeing that the young man looked foolish, the rich merchant said, half-jokingly, "Will you sell it for more money?"

"I only want two hundred taels, not a bargain."

The rich merchant thought that the horse was very fine and that the price was quite reasonable, but that the young man was simple-minded. He decided to play a trick on him.

The merchant looked around and then whispered, "As the common saying goes 'it is not proper for a millionaire to carry cash.' And so, today, I have no cash with me. Will you come and get the money when the horse's hooves have gotten round?"

The selling being done so quickly, and smoothly, Yesaier became very excited, and so he readily replied, "All right."

"I live in the north of West Street. There is a horn tree and a rice-eating bug in front of my house," said the rich merchant.

Yesaier cheerfully arrived back home.

Seeing him back the father asked, "How much did you get?"

"Two hundred taels."

The father was glad to see his son's progress. He then asked with a smile, "Where is the money?"

"I will go and get it when the horse's hooves are round."

"The horse's hooves are round already. You gave it away for nothing. You fool!" The father poured forth a stream of curses.

The son's wife could not sit inside any longer. She came out and comforted the father: "Do not be too angry. Anger is not good for your health. The money will come back soon."

The old man turned back and walked inside, giving a snort.

In the evening the wife told the husband, "You may go and ask for the money when the moon, like horses' hooves, is round. That is on August fifteenth of the lunar year. The 'horn tree' in reality is a honey locust tree, and 'the rice-eating bug' is not a bug but a stone mortar with a crooked pestle."[9]

------

[9]A horseman's way of referring to the moon was by way of associating it with "round horse hooves" which to him were more familiar. "Horn tree" and "rice-eating bug" are descriptive labels. The first description is based on the shape of this particular honey locust tree; the second is descriptive of the action of the pestle in a mortar—when the bent pestle is worked it appears as though it is eating the rice in the mortar bowl.

The fifteenth day arrived. Yesaier went to the north of West Street and at last found a house with a honey locust tree and a stone mortar in front of it. He entered the yard and caught sight of the horse eating grass at the manger and the rich merchant chatting with some people. Yesaier went over and said loudly, "Hello, I come to get paid for the horse."

The rich man looked at him and then pulled a long face. "Why do you come today? Did I not tell you to come when the horse's hooves are round?"

"The horse's hooves are round—and the moon is round too. Please have a look if you do not believe," Yesaier replied with perfect assurance.

These words made the rich man lose face in front of others. Abusively he shouted, "You fool! Why did you break the handle of my conversation [Why did you interrupt?] while I was talking to others? Be off! Go away!"

Yesaier returned with his pent-up grievance. He told his wife everything that had happened. After the wife heard this she told him, "Tomorrow morning you go to the back of his kitchen with a pick-axe, and dig at his chimney. If he asks you why you dig it, you may tell him that you are looking for the smoke root. If he says 'smoke has no root,' you may tell him that indeed smoke has no root, and neither is there a handle on conversation. Why not give me my money!"

The next day Yesaier started to dig at the rich man's chimney as his wife had told him. When the rich man saw what he was doing he became anxious and said: "You fool. What are you digging for?"

Yesaier answered, "I am looking for the smoke root."

"Who told you that smoke has a root?"

"Indeed, smoke has no root, and neither is there a handle on conversation. Why not give me my money?" This Yesaier said in a deep and gruffy voice.

The rich one no longer thought, as before, that the young man was foolish. Moreover, he was afraid that this fellow might do some more rough things. So he had no choice but to give him the money.

10

Love and Courtship

Not To Die Until One Sees Huang He

First published in *Ning xia wen yi, Ningxia Literature and Art,* 1962.
Place: Guyuan Mountain area, Ningxia
Narrators: Ma Xinshui and Ma Fengying (Hui)
Recorder: Zhao Yuru

There is an old saying which goes: "...not to die until one sees Yellow River (Huang He)." Actually, this proverb is mistaken. Originally it was "...not to die until one sees Yellow Lotus (Huang He)." It is a sad story to tell.[1]

Once upon a time, in the Liupan Mountains, lived a Hui family surnamed Huang. They had fields and oxen. In that family the old father was the boss. But what did not conform to his wishes was the fact that he had no son—and only one daughter. To his joy, however, the daughter was very beautiful. Her face had a touch of rosy red. While smiling she looked as beautiful as a lotus flower in water. Old Huang loved his daughter so much that he took great pains in caring for her. He named her Huang He (Yellow Lotus).

When Huang He had grown up and reached the age of eighteen, it was time for marriage. Her father kept her in the house, an earthmade building, to sew clothes and flower shoes, to embroider a

---

[1] "To reach the Yellow River" ordinarily implies tenacity and endurance even to the end of one's road. The Chinese names of "Yellow River" and "Yellow Lotus," are homonyms—"Huang He."

321

small colorful bag (an engagement gift), and to wait for a match-maker. But the girl refused all suitors. This caused Old Huang many worries.

The building in which she lived overlooked a canyon from its back window. Below the cliff was a winding path that led off into the distance. One morning Huang He was embroidering the small bag when she heard a bamboo flute being played. She pushed the window open and saw a young shepherd playing on a bamboo flute and coming across with a flock of sheep. The young shepherd often passed below this window and the girl always listened inside. With the passage of time, the girl became acquainted with the young shepherd, and they began to talk to each other. The shepherd learned that the girl's name was Huang He, and the girl in turn found out that the young man worked for a landlord in the village and that his name was Xiyu—also that he was a Hui Muslim.

Early in the morning when Xiyu was playing his bamboo flute while passing by on his way to herd sheep, Huang He would always lower to him on a rope some solid food, a large toasted cake. In the evening when Xiyu came back, playing the flute, Huang He would lower a package of roasted potatoes for his supper.

One day Huang He herself slid down the rope and went with Xiyu to herd sheep in the mountains. By a clear spring, with the bamboo flute acting as matchmaker, and with folk tunes as their witnesses, they were engaged. Xiyu picked up the flower of a morn-ing star lily and inserted it in Huang He's hair as a betrothal gift. Huang He tied her small bag with tassels to Xiyu's bamboo flute, showing her consent. They looked at each other in the clear spring water, laughing and talking.

Xiyu said, "Your father has no son, I would like to join your family." Huang He said, "There will be no one to wait on your mother. I would like to accept her into my family, and let us make two families into one."

It often rains in one mountain valley but shines in another, and the road to happiness is always marred with setbacks. When the secret engagement became known to Old Huang, he flew into a rage. He took Huang He and locked her up in her room; he blocked up the back window; he covered the wall with heaps of wild thorns. Then he went to see Xiyu, scolding him with such anger that his goatee stood upward:

"A man can marry a girl from a lower level; but a girl must marry a man of high position. You are not a gentleman, so do not get the idea of marrying my Golden-Bough Jade-Leaves Fresh-Flower. You are good at nothing but blowing a bamboo flute."

The more he cursed the more furious he became. He picked up a stick nearby and with it he hit Xiyu severely.

Because he could no longer see Huang He, Xiyu became increasingly more depressed. His health declined. And seeing that he could no longer do heavy work, his landlord dismissed him.

Xiyu returned to his home town, one hundred *li* away. He refused to speak or to eat food. He missed Huang He from morning till night, and his condition worsened. His old mother looked after him, day and night. She wept so many tears that she became blind.

It was no use crying. Before his death, Xiyu took his mother's hand and told her his innermost thoughts and feelings: "Mother, I am dying of love sickness for Huang He. I am very sorry I cannot support you anymore. When my dead body is being washed, my heart will jump out from my mouth. Please fetch a bowl of water from the spring by which I engaged myself to Huang He. Then put my heart into the water, and, along with the bamboo flute, place the small engagement bag on the bowl. My heart will start beating and the flute will play melodiously. The music will come from my heart, and my heart will continue to beat for Huang He. The flute will never stop playing until the heart stops beating. Take it with you wherever you go, and people will give you alms."

Then he closed his eyes, and died.

The mother cried herself almost to death. When her son's dead body was washed, a red heart actually leaped forth from his mouth. She had great difficulty feeling her way toward the spring, but in the end she did as her son had asked her. The heart all of a sudden started beating and the flute began playing mournful tunes. It was heart-rending. The blind mother took the heart with her and went begging from door to door. In this manner she lived year after year.

One day, when she passed by the spring again, she met, head-on, people who carried a bridal sedan chair. It was an exiting occasion. The blind mother still had good hearing, and therefore she hastily withdrew to one side. But the sedan chair stopped in front of her. It was Huang He in the sedan chair. While she was sobbing in the chair, strong and sudden tunes from a bamboo flute had reached her ears. She had ordered the sedan chair to be stopped at once.

Huang He got off the carriage and caught sight of an old blind woman with a bowl in her hands. In the bowl a brilliant red heart was floating, and the bamboo flute lay across the bowl. The heart continued beating, and the music broke her heart. The small bag with the tassels was precisely the one which she had knitted. She immediately understood it all.

The old mother begged in her misery, "Please take pity on me, and give me some alms!"

Huang He cried out, "Mom!" and she threw herself at the old blind mother's feet. Then the old mother knew that it was Huang He kneeling down before her. And so she told Huang He how Xiyu had died. After that they wept in each other's arms so grievously that the mountains shook and the sky was darkened.

Old Huang pressed Huang He to get back into the sedan chair. But she did not move. She held the bowl in her hands and watched the beating of the heart, and she listened to the playing of the flute. Her tears dropped into the bowl. The heart then stopped beating. It was exactly as Xiyu had promised: "It will not die until it sees Huang He."

Having now seen Huang He, the heart died. And the bamboo flute stopped playing.

Old Huang again tried to get Huang He to move on. Yet, instead, she took off all her jewelry, gave it to the old blind mother in exchange for the bowl and told her to leave at once. Holding the bowl in both hands, with Xiyu's heart in it, she suddenly ran up against a boulder by the spring. Crash! Her blood splashed over the spring water and dyed the water red. Meanwhile, a shadow flew swiftly upward into the clouds. The people did not clearly see his face, but judging by his posture and by the way he held his bamboo flute, they knew that it was Xiyu.

Where did Huang He go? The water in the big spring turned to become a clear lake. The spilled blood of Huang He was transformed into many lotus flowers. Among thousands of brilliant flowers was a large golden lotus flower which never blossomed. It would bloom only late, during a quiet night, when Xiyu appeared in the clouds, playing the bamboo flute, and when rains were drizzling on all the flowers in the lake including the big golden one. Huang He would then come out from the pistil and begin to dance on the petals of the lotus flower, along with music from the flute.

The Black Moss Girl

Place: Southern mountain area, Ningxia
Recorder: Li Dexiu (Hui), 1979

Once upon a time there lived in the village of Hongshigang, at the foot of Mibo Mountain in the southern mountains of Ningxia, a poor farmer named Haadan. Haadan and his wife were both over fifty. They had a daughter by the name of Fatumai (Fatima). Fatumai was a kindhearted girl. She was beautiful, virtuous, kind, and well liked. From the cruel landlord, Yang the Black Wolf, the Haadans were renting five *mu* of land, on a slope.[2] But the grain they harvested yearly was not enough to pay the high rent for the land. The Haadan family survived with great difficulties.

One snowy night, Yang the Black Wolf and his men pushed into Haadan's house to collect payment for rent. Haadan could not pay the rent, and so Yang the Black Wolf carried away Fatumai instead.

Haadan went to court against Yang the Black Wolf. But instead of winning his lawsuit he was beaten and thrown out of the court. When the old man arrived home he took some poison and killed himself. His wife cried herself blind and was driven out of the village by Yang the Black Wolf.

At Yang's house, Fatumai would rather die than yield, so she was made to toil the year round. Yang the Black Wolf had a farmhand whose name was Yusuf. Seeing the girl suffer so much, Yusuf took pity on her and took care of her secretly. As time passed they fell in love. Unfortunately, Yang the Black Wolf sensed it, and he decided to let Fatumai be the concubine of his cousin, Pockmarks Yang. How could Fatumai know about this scheme?

One day Pockmarks Yang arrived on horseback, dressed as a bridegroom and escorted by his men with drums and gongs to take her away. Fatumai was unaware of it until the bridal sedan chair stopped in front of the gate. She thought to herself, "I would rather die than be insulted. I must run away."

---

[2]A *mu* is a unit of land, 0.0667 hectar; five *mu* are a third of a hectar.

While she combed her hair, Fatumai cut off her long braids and asked an old woman to give them to Yusuf to keep—to remember her by.

After having been dressed, Fatumai was carried and lifted on to the wedding horse.[3] When they came to the edge of Lake Sanbra, Fatumai suddenly leaped down from the horse into the lake, and she drowned herself. Momentarily there was lightning accompanied by rumblings of thunder. Rain fell as if it was being poured from buckets. Torrents of water rushed down the mountain. The earth was shaking with rage. All the villagers ran up the mountain to take refuge—all except the miser Yang the Black Wolf. He stayed behind to take care of his courtyard. The village of Hongshigang was inundated by the mighty flood waters, and Yang the Black Wolf was washed away. People never even caught as much as a glimpse of him again.

Yusuf missed Fatumai very much after she died. He thought he should make her live in her native place forever. He cut her braided hair into short pieces and scattered them over the fields.

A sudden gale was blowing. The entire Mibo Mountain was covered with the hair of Fatumai. From that time on black moss grew here and there along the hillside. In commemoration the people henceforth called Fatumai the "Black Moss Girl."

Every year when spring and autumn come around, groups of young women and girls, with baskets in hand and iron rakes on their shoulders, go to the mountain to gather black moss, talking and laughing. It is said they are combing the hair of the Black Moss Girl.

---

[3]The narrator's slip from sedan chair to wedding horse suggests the presence of a variety of wedding customs.

Mansuer

Place: Ningxia
Narrator: Yang Ke (Hui)
Recorder: Wang Zhengwei (Hui), 1978

Once upon a time a boy named Mansuer, whose parents had died, was reduced to living a difficult life. He had to herd sheep and gather wood for the landlord Dulaxi. In return, this landlord gave him bran cakes or leftovers to eat. He was indeed a pitiful sight to behold. When he did not gather enough wood, or when he did not herd sheep exactly as expected, he would be beaten.

One day Mansuer, as he was herding sheep on the hill, saw a black snake bite into the head of a white snake. With his whip he pushed the black snake down into a ditch. He sprinkled some cotton ash on the head of the white snake and placed it into a cave.

He was tired and fell asleep on the hill. He dreamt, and in his dream he saw an ahong with a white beard who stood before him and said, "Today, if a man in black on a black horse comes to give you a ride, do not go; but if a man in white on a white horse comes to carry you, you may go with him."

Mansuer woke up and saw that nothing had actually happened. "Oh, it was just a dream."

He turned and suddenly caught sight of a man in black, on a black horse, standing in front of him. He said, "My dad has asked me to take you home to play."

"I am herding for Dulaxi. I would be beaten if some sheep were missed," Mansuer said. The man tried to persuade him, but failed. So he went away.

After a while another man came, dressed in white and on a white horse. The man said, "My father asked that you come to our home, and he will thank you."

Mansuer answered, "Why should he want to thank me? And what can I do if I lose a sheep?"

"I have an idea," said the man in white, taking the whip from Mansuer. He drew a big circle on the ground which, at once, turned into a sheep corral, and the sheep were enclosed.

The man in white said, "Now sit on the horse and close your eyes." As he sat on the horse's back, Mansuer heard the wind whistle past. The man in white told him, "When you reach my home you should not accept anything my father offers you, only, you might ask that he give you the third flower hanging in the front room."

"Yes," said Mansuer.

After they traveled a long distance, Mansuer heard water flowing. He opened his eyes and stole a glance. To his surprise he found that the man in white, riding into the sea and pushing the waters aside, was actually a beautiful girl. After only a while they reached the Dragon King's palace. The girl in white asked him to open his eyes. When he opened his eyes he found himself in a different world. It was all filled with treasures. The Dragon King personally served him sea cucumber. The son of the Dragon King brought him two plates of gold.

Then the Dragon King said, "You killed the spirit and saved my daughter. I have nothing else to repay you with. Please accept the gold."

The words of the girl in white came to his mind. So he said, "No, I do not need gold. If you really want to thank me, would you please give me the third flower which hangs in the front room?"

The Dragon King was shocked and hesitated for a while. At last he agreed. He took out the flower and accompanied Mansuer with the flower, out through the sea.

Keeping the flower hidden in his bosom, Mansuer quickly hurried back to his sheepfold. It was nearly dark when he arrived there. In haste he cut some firewood and drove the sheep back home. On his way he thought of the flower, and so he took it out. It was so fresh and brilliant that the whole mountain was reflected in splendid red when he turned to look back. What a mysterious flower that was!

Back home he stuck the flower into a crack in the wall and went to eat his lunch. When he returned he found his *kang* (brick bed) in such a condition that not even a piece of a straw pad could be seen anymore. The bed was covered with a five-inch-thick felt blanket and a cotton-padded mattress. Upon it lay two quilts of red satin. Looking up at the flower he found it to be brilliant and wonderful. It was red in one moment and white in the next, and presently it turned into a beautiful girl. Jumping before him, she said, "I am your wife."

Mansuer was surprised and dumbfounded; he thought that he was dreaming. The girl came over to him and took him by the hand, and from the very first moment on she spoke forth to him her innermost thoughts. The more he listened the happier he got.

"Thanks be to Allah! What good luck I have!" he said to himself.

The next day, even after the sun had risen high, Mansuer had not yet gone to herd sheep. The landlord sent his son Hasai after him. When Hasai came, Mansuer and his wife were talking and laughing on the kang. Seeing this, Hasai ran back and told his father, "Mansuer has a beautiful wife in his house, and they are just talking."

Dulaxi did not believe it and said, "Nonsense! How can a golden phoenix stay in a chicken coop?"

Hasai replied, "It is true. Go and have a look yourself."

Dulaxi went to see for himself, and he found that she was a beautiful lady, indeed. She had big eyes with double folds on her eyelids, and she had a round and white face, just like a fairy.

At the very moment when he saw Mansuer's wife he hatched a malicious scheme: "We must kill Mansuer and let her marry Hasai."

That same day Dulaxi said to Mansuer, "Before tomorrow morning you must gather firewood, as much as a hill, or I will kill you."

Mansuer became worried. His wife asked, "Why are you so sad?" Mansuer told her what Dulaxi had said.

"Do not worry. Very early the next morning you just open our door and shout three times 'Firewood, as much as a hill, come before daybreak, please,' then come back to sleep."

Mansuer did so early in the morning. The next day, to his great surprise, Dulaxi found a pile of firewood as large as a hill. He said to Mansuer, "Today you must go and carry back for me the chopping board, which is in the wolves' den."

"The wolf has devoured so many people that the road there is impossible to travel; almost no one goes there anymore. Do you want me to lose my life?" said Mansuer.

Dulaxi gave him a stern look, with triangular eyes, and said ferociously, "Go, or I will kill you!"

Mansuer told the matter to his wife. And she said, "Do not be afraid. Just take four eggs and four pieces of red thread with you. If the wolf pursues you closely, you just put down an egg and keep on running. If he comes near again, put down a piece of red thread."

The wolf was asleep when Mansuer entered the den. He quietly picked up the chopping board and started running homeward. The wolf woke up, found the chopping board gone and began to run after him. But before the beast could catch up with him, Mansuer put down an egg. The egg instantly grew into a high and steep mountain which stopped the wolf.

The wolf crossed over the mountain and again caught up with him and chased him closely. He laid down a red thread. Immediately the red thread turned into a deep and wide ravine. By the time the four eggs and the four pieces of red thread had been left behind, Mansuer arrived at his home.

Dulaxi, seeing Mansuer alive, said to him again, "Today you must dig a fire pit as large as the sea, make a pan to place over it, fill the pan with water, and heat the water to a boil with no more than three sticks of wood."

Mansuer said to his wife, "It is impossible to do what Dulaxi has asked. He just wants me to die."

But his wife comforted him. "Go and dig three spadefuls. Go to the sea and shout three times, 'Old Dragon King! Please lend me the iron scoop with which your daughter often used to play when she was a child.' With the iron scoop I will then accompany you and heat up the water."

Mansuer got the iron scoop and set it over the pit he had dug. In a short time the scoop had turned into a pan full of water, as large as the sea. His wife took three sticks of flax, lit them, and gave a puff. The water began boiling at once.

Having observed this situation, Dulaxi was overcome by fear. He thought, "Mansuer must be gotten rid of, or else he will bring disaster on me." So he ordered Mansuer to go down into the boiling water, to reemerge later. Mansuer hesitated. He could neither afford to offend Dulaxi, nor did he want to leave his dear wife. With tears in her eyes his wife put a couple of golden bracelets on his wrists and said, "Go and be back quickly. I will be waiting for you back in the house."

Mansuer closed his eyes and jumped into the boiling water, with a splash. Dulaxi was extremely delighted that, no doubt, Mansuer would surely die this time, and then his wife would belong to Hasai.

Three days passed, but Mansuer had not yet come back. Dulaxi succeeded in forcing Mansuer's wife to marry his son Hasai. But at night the wife put a stick beside her, then clapped her hands. Each time the stick became a wall which kept Hasai on the other side of the bed. In this situation the wife spent more than forty days.

One day Mansuer came back with two large lumps of gold on his back. Dulaxi was scared stiff—he had remained alive after such a long time! "What is on your back?" he asked hastily.

"Gold."

"Is there a lot of gold in the sea?" Dulaxi asked again.

"Yes, quite a lot. You can get as much as you want," answered Mansuer.

Dulaxi became jealous and ran to the pan to heat the water. But it did not give forth any steam, much less was it boiling, even though that big pile of firewood had been used up.

He sighed and asked Mansuer for help. "How did you heat the water? Tell me, please!" he begged.

Before Mansuer could give an answer, his wife went over there and gave a puff. The water began to boil right away. Dulaxi laughed and offered Hasai a couple of bracelets to put on his wrists. "You get down first. If there are many pieces of gold down there, just wave your hand and I will join you!" he instructed his son.

"All right!" Hasai closed his eyes and jumped into the water. The moment he descended his hands waved confusedly, because of the scalding water. Dulaxi caught sight of the waving hands and also jumped in, because he believed that there was a lot of gold down there. As a result both father and son died in the boiling pot.

Mansuer and his wife, in spite of it all, lived a happy life after that.

The Zither Master Hasang

Place: Ningxia and Shaanxi
Narrator: Yang Zhouwen (Hui)
Recorder: Yang Bing (Hui), 1982

Long, long ago, in a poor village, lived an old couple. They worked diligently year after year. And although their seven sons had grown up, their living conditions remained poor.

One day the old father asked his sons to come to him, and he told them, "My sons, you see, your mother and I are getting too old. Today we are still alive, but we cannot tell whether or not we will still live tomorrow. You all should go out, learn a trade, and come back to support your parents for the years that remain. Otherwise we will all die of poverty."

His sons all said with tearful eyes, "Dad, we will do as you have told us, and we will surely come back to take care of you." A little later they kowtowed to their parents and left with some dry food provisions.

The seven brothers came to a road which divided into seven branches. At each fork happened to stand an old and very tall pine tree. The brothers stopped by these trees for a while and each chose one of these pine trees to represent his fate. As long as a tree was alive it meant that the respective brother was living happily and also was good at his skill. If the tree died it meant that the brother had also died. Then they departed.

Three years later the seven pine trees had grown to a mass of branches and needles. And seven brothers came back, one after the other, with the trade they had learned. The father was so happy that he asked his sons to demonstrate their skills.

The oldest son, the second son, the third through the sixth, all pleased their father very much. Now it was the turn of the seventh son, Hasang. He took out his nice zither and played for his father.

But the father did not praise him. On the contrary, he scolded him angrily: "You have learned nothing. Can you live on playing zither? You are not my son. Out! Get out!"

Hasang tried to explain, "Dad, do not be angry. Playing zither can earn money to support you, besides...."

But being in no mood to listen to him, his father interrupted him and drove him out.

"What shall I do?" Hasang wondered, and each new day he was full of anxiety as he sat by the seaside playing his zither. During these days the zither appeared to be his closest friend. He could be relieved from his depression only by playing on it.

The wonderful music he played attracted birds who flew over and listened from the woods; the wind seemed to stop; the trees and even the sea seemed to quiet down and listen to him, attentively.

One day, suddenly, upon the sea, there appeared an old and kind man who straightway walked toward Hasang. He said in an earnest tone, "Dear Hasang, how splendidly you are playing! Would you be so kind as to teach my daughter to play the zither?"

"Of course I would, but I have an old mother and an old father. Who will support them if I leave?"

The old and kind man said, "You need not worry about them. Your brothers will look after them. Besides, I will help them too!"

Hasang asked again: "If you can help them, that is fine. But who are you, and where do you live?"

Pointing to the sea, the old man said, "I am the Dragon King of the sea. I live at the Dragon Palace at the bottom of the sea."

Hasang thought, "He surely can help my family if he is the Dragon King." And so he accepted the invitation. He closed his eyes and, as he was instructed, sat on the back of the Dragon King. Feeling only a moment of cooling, they reached the Dragon Palace, which was a place inlaid with gold, silver, and pearls. It was an extravagant place indeed.

He settled down in the palace, and each day he gave careful lessons to the daughter of the Dragon King. The girl was beautiful, intelligent, and adept. In a short time she had mastered all the skills of playing. Eventually she could play as well as her teacher.

After that Hasang thought he could go home. But when he told the Dragon King of his intention, the latter shook his head and declined. He was not willing to let Hasang go. But Hasang insisted so firmly that the Dragon King had to agree at last—though, he stated a condition. He would give Hasang a pair of copper shoes and promised to let him go if he succeeded in wearing holes into the tips of these shoes. In the meantime, of course, he would be given a generous gift. How long would it take for him to wear holes into the tips of these shoes? This really troubled Hasang. He went to bed unhappily that night.

After falling into deep sleep he dreamt a curious dream. In the dream he met an old man with a white and long beard. That man told him to wear the copper shoes upside down and to kick the threshold twice when going in and out. Then the shoe tips would break. The old man also told him, "After breaking the shoes you will surely be repaid by the Dragon King. Then you should ask neither silver nor gold, but a peony flower from his palace. With the flower you will live happily in the future." And, waving his hand in the air, the old man disappeared momentarily.

At daybreak, the next day, Hasang got up to see the Dragon King and told him he would like to do as he required, but the king should not break his words. With a smile the Dragon King promised him. Hasang put on the copper shoes, and he kicked them in the manner the old man told him. Just as expected, the shoe tips were broken. With the broken shoes he went to see the Dragon King: "Your Majesty, the copper shoes are not very durable. It was easy to break them."

The dragon was surprised and speechless. He regretted the situation, but he could not go back on his word. Before Hasang was to leave, the Dragon King said to him, "Hasang, initially I wanted you to remain in the Dragon Palace, but you insisted on leaving. I have to give in. But how can I reward you? Please tell me what you want. I shall give you whatever you ask for."

Hasang remained silent.

"You want silver? That is easy." The Dragon King sent for ten plates of silver to give to Hasang. Hasang shook his head.

"You want gold? That is easy too." And so ten plates of gold were brought to him. Hasang shook his head again.

"Your Majesty," Hasang said, "if you really want to reward me, I would like to take this peony flower above anything else."

After a long time of silence the Dragon King said, "All right, Hasang. You may take it, but be sure to take good care of it!" And unexpectedly tears rolled down his face. Hasang felt puzzled about what this might mean. He took the peony flower in his hand, with great care, and closed his eyes. Within the time it takes to blink an eye the Dragon King had sent him back to the seashore.

Hasang came back to his home town. His parents were much older but happy to see him. Nevertheless, they suggested that he should not play zither. They found him a small house to live in, at another place, so that their prayers would not be disturbed by his zither playing. Being very tired, Hasang lay down and soon he fell asleep.

When he woke up the next morning the sun was already high in the sky. He saw a beautiful girl cleaning the room, and the peony flower was gone. He hurriedly put on his clothes and went quietly towards the girl. The girl turned, and then Hasang understood immediately. It was none other than the daughter of the Dragon King.

No matchmaker, no betrothal gifts—they got married then and there. The young couple was in mutual love. They gave presents to their old parents and lived a happy life.

But good times did not last long. The news that Hasang had married a beautiful girl got around. When the emperor, a lecher, found out, he wanted her to be brought to him. So he sent for Hasang to come to his imperial palace. There he promised to make Hasang a high official if he gave up the girl to the emperor.

Hasang got very angry, and feeling greatly insulted he turned back and left immediately. The emperor, of course, did not let the matter rest at this point. He sent an official to Hasang who informed him that the emperor, who brought with him an army, was challenging him to a contest. Nearby were two large mountains of the same size. He who first covered one of them with white cloth would have the girl.

Being afraid of losing his wife, Hasang told her about the situation with a worried look on his face. But the dragon girl smiled and did not worry at all. She told Hasang to tell the official that he would accept the challenge, on condition that the emperor keep his word. He determined that the contest should begin at daybreak the next day.

As soon as the official had left, the dragon girl told Hasang the way to win the match. He became delighted like a happy bird, running toward the seashore, calling loudly, "Sea Brother! Sea Brother! Sea Brother!" He called three times in succession. As expected, a red and shiny wooden box appeared on the sea. He picked it up, easily, and ran back home.

The contest began on the next day when the sun had just risen a little in the east. The emperor's soldiers were lined up in huge formations, bales of white cloth in their hands. But in Hasang's hands was only a wooden box. The moment the emperor gave his order to start, Hasang unlocked and uncovered the box. White streamers of cloth flew out from the box to cover the mountain, as if they fell from the sky. Within a few minutes the mountain was tightly covered. As for the emperor's soldiers, they had not even run to the top of their mountain yet. And so the emperor lost the competition.

However, the emperor did not keep his word and challenged Hasang to another competition. "This time," he said, "let us dig a canal and see whose is longer." Having no choice, Hasang had to agree. He went back to ask the dragon girl's advice. And in accordance with her instructions he went to the seashore and shouted, "Sea Brother!..." three times. And from the sea came forth a golden shovel.

The next day, at the same hour, the competition started. At the emperor's side stood a long row of soldiers, each holding a polished shovel in his hands. They exerted all their strength to dig the canal, with dust flying everywhere.

What Hasang needed to do was only to dig a shovel full at each end of his canal—and to run along the stretch where the canal was to be dug. The earth behind him turned over, and soon the canal was dug. By then the soldiers had just dug a small hole in the ground. The emperor lost again. He was so angry that it took him a long time before he could speak.

Later the emperor thought to himself, "Could Hasang be afraid of anything in the world?...All right! I will ask him to show me something called 'Horror.'"

"If you can show me such a thing as Horror, we will stop the competition. But if not, it means that you fail."

Hasang was unable to make head and tail of it, and he wondered whether there was anything called "Horror." He thought of the dragon girl. She must be able to help him, and so he nodded his consent.

Upon hearing this, the dragon girl was struck dumb for a moment, and very soon smiled: "Naturally, there is nothing in the world called 'Horror.' But since the emperor wants it, we shall show it to him."

Once more she sent Hasang to the seashore, and he called, "Sea Brother!..." What he got this time was a very heavy copper box. The dragon girl said, "Go and tell the emperor to wait at the foot of the mountain for Horror, early in the morning."

The next morning the emperor and his soldiers had already come when Hasang came to the mountain with his heavy box. He unlocked the box. Just at the moment he shouted, "Horror!," out toward the emperor and his soldiers ran a monster.

"Allah! How horrible!" the emperor shouted, running away for his life.

Still, the monster kept running after him all the way, shouting, "I am Horror. Are you horrified?"

Earlier the emperor had made a plan to get something horrible to subdue Hasang. But then against his expectation he himself was horribly threatened. He tried to flee quickly. But the monster did not let him go. The emperor then fell to the ground face down. And there, on the ground, he was horrified to death.

Afterward, Hasang, with his family, began to live a peaceful and happy life. His six brothers, too, lived happily with his assistance. In order not to disturb the prayers of his parents, Hasang and the dragon girl moved their home to a place not very far from his parents. There they played zither, and their beautiful music resounded all over the place. Their lives became still happier because of that.

Asking Permission

First published in *Ming jian wen xue (Folk Literature)*, Beijing, 1963.
Place: Kaifen, Henan
Narrator: Zhen Xinsun (Hui)
Recorder: Yuan Ding

Once upon a time there lived an honest young farmer whose name was Haersan. His parents had died when he was still a boy. He had to work as a farmhand, for a landlord. Haersan was very strong and he could do the work of several men. But the landlord never gave him enough to eat and often beat him. Haersan could not stand it any longer. And so one day he ran away from the landlord's house to find a way to live elsewhere.

It was very hot that day. Haersan walked in the burning sun. Soon he was sweating all over. He felt rather thirsty. Just then he saw some green trees ahead of him. He quickened his steps and found an orchard. Fruits were hanging heavy on the trees, and some ripe ones had already fallen to the ground. He picked up one to eat. After he had finished eating he washed his face with clear water from the ditch and sat under a tree to rest.

When he arose to go, it suddenly occurred to him that he had eaten fruit without permission. He decided to go to the owner of the orchard and ask for his permission retroactively. Walking along the ditch he saw an old man trimming dead branches off a tree. Haersan went up to him and asked, "Excuse me! Are you the owner of this orchard?"

The old man turned around to look at Haersan, then he answered, "Yes, I am. What can I do for you?"

Haersan told him, "I am a passerby. I was so thirsty after a long walk in the hot sun that I ate a fallen fruit from your orchard. I should not have eaten it without your permission. I have come here to ask your permission."

Hearing Haersan's words the old man stopped working to assure himself with his own eyes. He knew at first glance that the young man who stood there before him was an honest fellow. He said, "You want to ask permission. That is easy. You have to do only one thing first."

"Just speak out. I will do whatever you ask me to do," answered Haersan readily.

The old man continued, "I have an only daughter. She is blind and dumb. She has no hair nor feet. You will have my permission if you agree to take her as your wife."

What the old man said put Haersan into an awkward situation. He was unwilling to take a maimed and ugly girl as his wife. But if he would not, the old man would not give his permission. He thought for a long time. At last he decided to marry the old man's daughter in order to obtain permission.

The wedding was to be held right away. All the old man's relatives and neighbors were invited to attend the wedding. The guests were very glad to find Haersan to be such a nice young man. They congratulated the old man. But Haersan was not happy. He was afraid to see his ugly wife.

The sun had set and the guests were gone. Haersan was led to the bridal chamber. He went there slowly and saw his bride wearing a beautiful skirt which reached to the ground. She had a pink gauze veil over her head. Haersan hesitated quite a while. Finally he went up to her and said, "I will be your husband for the rest of my life."

He did not expect an answer from her because she was a dumb person. To his surprise, however, the bride answered right back, "I will be your wife all my life." Her voice was so sweet that Haersan could hardly believe his ears.

He quickly took off the veil. It turned out that his bride was a beauty—as beautiful as a flower. She had a pair of bright beautiful eyes. Her hair was black and shiny. And Haersan wondered why she was not as the old man had described her. So he asked the girl, "Are you really the old man's daughter?"

"Yes, I am his only daughter," the girl answered shyly.

"Then why did your father tell me that you are a blind and dumb girl with no hair or feet?"

"My father was not telling a lie. He just said it in a clever way to see whether you would act in good faith."

Haersan asked, "What did he mean by these words?"

The bride explained, "To him I am blind because I have never seen evil things; I am dumb because I never gossip; I have no feet because I have never been to improper places; I have no hair because I have never shown my face in public."

Haersan was very pleased with the words of his bride. But he was still puzzled. "Since you are so beautiful and innocent, how has he ever decided to make you my wife?"

"It is like this," said the girl, "my father came to own this orchard by hard work and thrift. He wants to hand it over to the most diligent and kindest person. You are the very man he has chosen."

Haersan married the girl. He worked hard in the orchard, with his wife. And they lived happily ever after.

The Fifth Daughter

Place: Tongxin, Ningxia
Narrator: Ma Guangyuan (Hui)
Recorder: Ding Yi (Hui), 1980

Long ago an old man named Hasang owned nothing but a copper axe with a silvery handle, which was handed down from his forefathers. He would rather starve than sell it. He called it "silver handle golden axe."

The Hasangs had five daughters of whom the fourth and fifth were twins. It was a pity that the mother had died when the twins were less than a month old. From that time on Hasang acted both as their father and their mother. He had to provide his five daughters with food and clothing.

Eighteen years passed. The five daughters grew up. Each was more beautiful than the other, even surpassing peonies. One day on his way home, after cutting firewood, Hasang passed Shelengge's garden. Above the edge of the sunken garden he was eager to pick five of the most beautiful flowers for his daughters. His axe happened to drop down into the garden below that was surrounded by cliffs at three sides. At the remaining side was a locked gate, and so, Hasang could not get in.

He was obliged to beg the gardener: "Shelengge, Shelengge, my silver handle golden axe has dropped down into your garden."

Shelengge was a young man. His parents died when he was a child. He was simple, honest and frank, but still single. While he was cooking he heard someone calling "silver handle golden axe." He thought it must be a rich man. So he replied with deliberate slowness, "I am putting on my trousers."

"Shelengge, Shelengge, my silver handle golden axe has dropped down into your garden."

"I am putting on my shoes."

"Shelengge, Shelengge, my silver handle golden axe has dropped down into your garden."

"I am washing my face."

"Shelengge, Shelengge, my silver handle golden axe has dropped down into your garden."

"Wait, I am coming." He dawdled for a while longer before he came forth from his cave dwelling. When he saw that it was a poor man, carrying firewood on his back, he quickened his steps toward him and made an apology.

When Shelengge found out that he was after flowers, and that he had five daughters, he picked one of the most beautiful flowers from his garden and wrapped it carefully in a piece of cloth. Then he picked up the axe and said, "Uncle, I am not married yet. Please be so kind and permit me to marry one of your daughters. If you agree, please accept this flower as a gift of engagement."

Hasang could see that Shelengge was good-natured, honest, and frank. And so he promised.

Then Shelengge said "Peace" to him. Happily he handed the golden axe and the flower to the old man.

As soon as Hasang got home he told the story to his daughters. Hearing that story, the oldest daughter pouted her lips; the second pulled a long face; the third frowned; and the fourth displayed an unpleasant grimace on her face.

Hasang knew that these four daughters were all greedy and lazy. They would dislike and avoid Shelengge's poverty. But he had promised this young man, and he had accepted his "Peace." What should he do?

When the fifth daughter came back from finishing the laundry, outside, she noticed her Dad's unhappiness. She instantly put down the clothes and asked him what the matter was. Hasang told her the whole story exactly as it had happened.

Before Hasang asked for her advice she said to him a little shyly, "Dad, my sisters are not willing to marry him—but I will do so if only he is a kind man."

"Are you not worried about his poverty?" asked Hasang.

"For generations our family has been planting, and gathering wood. And none was too poor to live."

"Are you not afraid of hard work?"

"Dad, you are probably getting old and you are forgetting your daughter's behavior. Do you not know how your daughter works?"

Several days later Hasang chose the Friday on which Shelengge and the fifth sister were to be married. Because they were both diligent and hard working, their life together after marriage improved steadily.

All the sisters got married, except the fourth, who was picky and never accepted anyone to be married to. When she saw her fifth sister living a very sweet and happy life, without having to worry about food or clothing, she regretted that she had not married Shelengge.

One day, when Shelengge was in the field, the fourth took the opportunity and went for a visit to the fifth sister's home. When the latter saw her sister coming she became really flustered. She did not know how to be a hostess to her. The fourth sister said, "Fifth Sister, I was told you have to do housework all day long. So, I came to help you do laundry during my free time."

Seeing her sincerity, the fifth sister pleasantly went with her to the river bank.

After having washed for a time, the fourth said, "My Sister, we have not seen each other for ages. Let us look in the water to see whether we are still alike or not." The fifth sister agreed.

While they were looking into the water, the fourth sister spoke again, "Fifth Sister, why do I look older than you?"

"That is because I wear bright-colored clothes while you wear plain-colored ones," the fifth sister replied, smiling.

"I do not believe that. Let us change our clothes and see whether you are right or not." The fifth agreed.

After having changed their clothes, while the fifth sister was looking at herself in the water, the fourth suddenly pushed her into the river.

Then the fourth sister went back to Shelengge's house, hastily, with the laundry basket in her hands. When Shelengge came back from the field he did not even notice a change in his wife.

It was not long before Shelengge went to the river to carry water. He found a lotus growing forth at the side of the river. It became more lovely day after day. He told his wife about it. The fourth sister went to the river and only saw a drooping lotus. She returned and accused him for it.

The next day when Shelengge was carrying water he saw how the lotus had become larger and more lovely. Again he told the fourth sister about it. She trotted away to the river and caught sight of a lotus drooping even more. She pulled it up with anger and threw it into the fire back home. The next morning when Shelengge was emptying the ashes, the pit of a honey peach dropped from the ashes down into the courtyard. It was not long before a large peach tree grew there. Shelengge and the fourth sister were puzzled. What was even harder to understand was the fact that at night, when they went to bed, peaches as large as a fist came straight into Shelengge's mouth, one after another—never into the fourth sister's mouth.

When she could not eat any peaches she decided to switch places with Shelengge, while sleeping. But still, the peaches flew into Shelengge's mouth while into her own flew some bitter and astringent peach pits. For several days they regularly kept changing their sleeping positions, but never did the fourth sister eat a single peach.

One day, when Shelengge was gone, the fourth sister chopped down the peach tree. When he returned and saw the peach tree he embraced the stump and burst into tears, and his tears moistened the root. Three days later, from the root of the peach tree grew forth a big lotus flower. It was getting bigger and more lovely. Shelengge was so happy that he went nearly out of his mind. He guarded it and never left it alone. The fourth sister became frightened.

When the lotus flower blossomed toward ripeness there appeared, inside, a little girl, which grew larger and larger and at last became a beautiful girl. Shelengge looked at it, transfixed, and to his great surprise it was his own wife, Fifth Sister. He turned back to look for the fourth sister and saw her hurrying out the door.

At this moment Fifth Sister leaped forth from the flower. She knew that Shelengge had been deceived—kept ignorant, boxed up in a drum. So she told him the truth about what had happened. Shelengge suddenly realized what had transpired. After the fifth sister's return, their life together became better and better.

As to the fourth sister—she hurried away and never came back again. Shelengge and Fifth Sister looked for her everywhere but could not find her. As time passed she was forgotten.

Yaya and the Golden Sparrow

Place: Ningxia
Narrator: Yang Zhuhua (Hui)
Recorder: Xie Rong (Hui), 1980[4]

Long, long ago, at the foot of Jing Mountain (Golden Mountain) lived a girl named Yaya. One day, while digging bitterroot at the slope, she saw a mountain bird flapping its wings, unable to fly. Yaya picked it up and found that it was, in fact, a downy male golden sparrow. It glistened like gold. Its left wing was hurt. As it gazed at Yaya the eyes of the golden sparrow were filled with tears. Yaya understood what it meant. She looked at it full of pity and wrapped its wound with thread. Then she carried it home in her basket.

Back home she made a birdcage and placed a forked twig and dish inside. She hung the cage from the middle roof beam. Gradually the sparrow's wing was getting restored. The bird looked again healthy and acted lively. It even began to sing a song:

No sparrow lives who does not want to fly!
Wings are too heavy
To lift the deep emotions in the cage.
Preening my golden feathers I sing a song
To my appreciated friend.

Every time when Yaya came back from the field the golden sparrow would sing to her that same sweet and wonderful song. Each time when she fed it, it would alight on her palm.

One clear day, with a gentle wind caressing her face, Yaya was looking up to the sky outside the gate. And then, in the twinkling of an eye, there stood before her a smart young fellow, with solid features and a round face. The moment she caught sight of him Yaya's heart was somehow touched. The young fellow, too, was looking at Yaya with a smile. Neither of them spoke.

---

[4]For more information concerning this recorder see page 73, note 1.

Yaya being a girl, after all, turned back and shyly ran into the house. In the room she looked up and saw the golden sparrow sitting with a blank gaze, on the forked twig in the cage. Then she suddenly thought of the young fellow again. She hurried back to the gate to have a secret look through the door, but the young fellow had already gone.

Not long after that a horse race was held in her village. Riders, businessmen, and spectators from all directions gathered on the grassland at the foot of the slope. Outside the racing ground many tents were pitched, many banners were flying, and there was a sea of people. It was indeed a scene of bustle and excitement. All the horses on the racing field were decorated with colorful silk garlands; they were dashing to and fro swiftly, clip-clap, accompanied by shouts that shook the sky.

Yaya was in high spirits and ready to enjoy the race when, suddenly, she saw a tall white horse at the horizon galloping straight toward her. Upon the horse sat a smart young fellow. He wore a red sleeveless jacket and leather boots. In one hand he was waving a snake-leather thonged whip and in the other he held a bouquet of red peony flowers. When he stood before Yaya he gave her the fresh flowers, and then he wielded his whip to prod his horse to move on. Just like a wisp of smoke he disappeared into rosy clouds.

Yaya stood there, dumbfounded, holding the red peony flowers in her hands. As she thought it over she came to realize that the young fellow was the same fellow she had met at the gate of her home. While she thought about this her face turned red. So she hurried homeward. The moment she entered the room the bird began to sing a song:

Peony flowers are fresh and fragrant,
Petals unfold at daybreak,
Flower buds grow on Ninth Heaven cliff.
Do not guess or think, Girl!
While the young plant is still under morning dew
Clip-clap will resound, on both sides of the path.

This wonderful song robbed Yaya of her peace of mind. Thinking about the young fellow's smart and good looks, and about the sweet-smelling peonies, Yaya was dreamingly lost in thought.

Then a woman appeared and said, "Yaya, you must be thinking of that young fellow. If you really love him, just burn the sparrow in the cage at once—because the sparrow is an embodiment of that young fellow. Only after you burn the sparrow can you have the young man!"

And having spoken so, the woman disappeared.

Upon hearing this, Yaya thought back and forth. Is it true? She remembered the songs and the joyful and lively activity of the golden sparrow, and also the sight of the golden sparrow staring blankly when she was meeting the young fellow. Why! What was the matter? These may be instructions given by Allah. Finally, because she was eager to see the young fellow, she believed the woman's words. She lit up a big fire and threw the cage with the golden sparrow into the flames. At once the sparrow began to sing a song of sorrow:

> Love's fire unexpectedly comes as roaring heat.
> Hate, Hate, Hate.
> I hate infatuation that confuses true and false.
> I call on Allah with a sigh: Wrong, Wrong, Wrong!
> Give the Muslim golden eyes to discern people from demons!

This miserable song surprised Yaya greatly. Who was that woman? Why did she plot this scheme? How could she know these mysteries? Oh, evil spirit! Immediately Yaya hurried to rescue the golden sparrow from the fire. Standing on her palm and flapping its wings, the sparrow stared at Yaya with tears rolling from its eyes. Yaya felt deeply sorry; she blew and patted gently the burned feathers all over its body.

Just at this moment Yaya did not know why her eyes were slightly sore. Even though she tried hard, she could not open her eyes and thereby she floated off into a dream.

Then she saw the young fellow speak to her sadly: "Yaya, you were easily cheated to burn me because you wanted to see me soon. But you did not know that at one time I was Alifu, a boy servant in heaven. I was punished to descend to this world for a whole year, because I broke a heavenly rule. The evil woman who schemed to burn me to death is a fox spirit who deliberately steals and robs others of their achievements, and who saps their life to nourish itself. Last time it bit my wing and almost stole the celestial root of my immortal nature. Thanks to your rescue, that time, it failed. This time it wanted to get rid of me by means of your hands. The evil fox spirit should be punished for its evildoing.

"Because of all this I cannot yet assume my real appearance. If you really love me, please go up to the top of Jing Mountain three times a day to pray. Each time you must pray three hundred and sixty-five times. You should keep praying three hundred and sixty-five days without missing a single day. Only in this manner can I return to you."

Yaya opened her eyes and knew that, actually, it had been a dream. The bird on her palm had disappeared.

But since that time, each day three times, Yaya climbed to the top of the mountain to pray. She stopped neither for rain nor wind, neither for the heat of summer nor the cold of winter.

On the last day of the three hundred and sixty-five, when the sun was setting in the west and the sky was overcast with evening clouds, as expected, the Golden Sparrow came again onto this world. After she was done praying, Yaya was about to go home when, suddenly, she saw a person run toward her and take her hands. A strong whirlwind carried both of them up into the sky and caused them to float over many mountains and rivers. In a very short time they landed in a quiet and beautiful garden, between two mountain peaks. They got married there and began living a happy life.

But several days later, the evil fox spirit transformed itself into a soldier, with a broadsword in hand, and groped its way into the room through a window. It wanted to kill Yaya. But at this moment Alifu, the celestial boy servant, was startled and woke up. He jumped up at once and came to blows with the fox spirit. The fighting continued from the house into the yard, outside, and still neither of the two was defeated. Just then dark clouds appeared in the sky. With a sudden clap of thunder exploding, the fox spirit was burned to a skeleton.

From that time on Alifu and Yaya lived a peaceful and pleasant life. From the garden between the mountain peaks their happy song echoed forth:

From the flowing waters of the mountain stream
    I know it is her voice.
The beauty of the peony does not compare

with the beauty of my sister.[5]
My sister's heart has been stitched
    into my padded red vest.
I declare to say that the dearest to me
    is my sister.

From the call of a wild goose in the sky I know
    that my brother is calling me.
Jingle-bells ringing from the mountain path I know
    that my brother is returning.
As long as spring water is flowing
    our love will last forever.
I feel unhappy if only for a single day
    I fail to see my brother.

----

[5]"Sister" in this stanza, and "brother" in the next, are poetic terms of endearment which mean "wife" and "husband."

11

Poor and Rich—Good and Bad

Alifu and Erbudu

Place: Southern mountain area, Ningxia
Recorder: Li Zhongwu (Hui), 1980
Translation adjusted, approximately, to the original uneven rustic rhyme
by Karl W. Luckert and Zongqi Yu.

This story happened long, long ago:

> There was a high, high mountain, named Hongyuanlin;
> Its peak reached Heaven, amidst clouds floating.
> Where was the end of that mountains' tip?
> There is no-one who knows this answer glib.
> Half up the mountain there was a plateau,
> Neither squared nor rounded, nor just so.
> From its top a bird would see the valley below,
> Half down, in plum blossom glow, the Plum Plateau.

At the center of Plum Plateau a village was located, and on account of its location it was named Flower Village.

> Though that village was small in size and name,
> Its poor and its rich were not the same.

349

The wealthiest was Erbudu,
The poorest man was Alifu.

Erbudu had herds of sheep;
Cattle and camels were his to keep.
If a meal for him no meat contained,
The master's face would frown, disdained.
His summer shirt was silk and smoothy,
His winter coat of fur was cozy,
Going forth on mule he sat quite lazy,
Home in his soft chair he lounged eas'ly.

Erbudu's wife was a vicious woman who often laughed at poor people's misfortune. She claimed that their wealth had been given to them by Allah. And to this she would add:

"My family can never go poor or unfed,
Not before Quan Canal dries up or the stones turn red.
The Alifus' poverty is a pity and a wail,
Days on end their pan hangs empty on the nail."

The Alifus had an old mother, age seventy-eight. They had seven children each taller than the other. The husband and wife worked day and night, but still, they never had enough to eat or to wear. Alifu's wife was very kind. She respected her mother-in-law, loved her children, and was a good helper to her husband.

One winter brought cold and sheer bitterness,
Even stones were split by the icy stress.
No birds could be seen to fly in the air,
But in Erbudu's house roared a cozy fire.
Inside the air was mildly abake,
They had just eaten mutton and cake.
And then they drank the tea,
While Erbudu's wife belched A'heeeh.

And twisting her narrow mouth she declared:

"No fierceness no wealth,
No freezing no winter...

They say I am a woman with scorpion heart,
Such-hearted I savor cold weather.
Just look at Alifu's wife!
Poor looks! Poor fate! Poor bones!
In summer black and shiny shining,
In winter pale and shivery shivering.
I wonder why Allah does not dispose of her!"

Thereupon Erbudu his goatee did stroke,
He spat into dirt, and his throat cleared he spoke:

"Even a stone feels chilled in December,
How can Alifu's family survive this winter!
A fence door shuts the cave where entrance is gained.
His children in gunny shreds are contained,
And Alifu himself his ankle has sprained.
With Alifu's wife having naught in the pan to give,
How can his children continue to live?
Those miserable wretches should die of poverty!

"They say that I am fierce-hearted,
This is so because they are jealous of me.
They must look on in despair.
And the more they look and envy me,
The happier, eventually, they will be."

Alifu left his home one day, his foot a-sore,
Alifu's wife remained behind as mistress of the floor.
His mother suffered and lay ill,
His children cried from hunger,
Making sounds no longer.
Alifu's wife survived as best she could:
She had to go to Erbudu's, to borrow food.
With tears in her eyes and basket in hand,
She hoped to obtain millet, another two *sheng*.
She shivered walking through their gate,
And entering their room she hid her face.

And entering she did hear the sound of a cold sneer:

"You come to borrow more? Ai-eh you!
You ought to learn from me how to make a living.
Have never you heard how it is said, that
'Borrowing flour and borrowing grain
Makes two households never to greet again?'

"No more lending this time!

"But then, because you are such a pity,
I offer you to earn a bitty.
Lice abound among the hairs on my head,
You are quite welcome to squeeze them dead!
If before dark you can fetch them clean,
Millet shall be given to you, a full two *sheng*.
But if as much as the shadow of a louse does remain.
You will not even get to borrow that grain...
And then do not complain!"

Alifu's wife embarrassed stood,
Insulted, degraded, and up-shook.
Mother-in-law needed hot millet soup jellies,
Nothing was left in her children's bellies,
So she closed her eyes and nodded assent.
Standing by the *kang* she worked her hands.

Then her hands became numb,
Then her eyes became drab,
Then darkness descended,
And Erbidu's wife awoke from her nap.
She rose from the *kang* and swayed her posterior,
And took a long stare into her mirror.
To the left she did a look-look.
And to the right she did a look-look.

From her body broke forth cold sweat,
Completely clear now was her head.
As though to someone—so it seemed—
She had to give two *sheng* of millet.

Then suddenly a ploy occured to her. She decided that she would continue to check that hair of hers, more carefully, after she returned from the toilet.

> She left the room and her waistband she groped,
> She at last found her louse, just as she had hoped.
> She finally found happiness—and without being duped,
> She held up her mirror, pretending, she probed.

> Shouts erupted from her voice:
> "You have not gotten all the lice!
> Immediately get out of here!
> You make me angry, standing there!"

> Alifu's wife thought here and there:
> Empty-handed how could she bear...

> To enter her own gate?
> Two smooth pebbles into her bosom she laid.
> The old one saw her in-law enter the gate.
> Her eyes on the woman's bosom she laid.
> And seeing their mother had entered the gate,
> Children cried, hands reached to her bosom and stayed.

> She took her children and led them aside,
> Put the pebble stones into the pan.
> She lit a fire in the stove,
> She tended flames, teardrops rolling down her cheeks.
> She pondered how to cope with this impossibility.

> The fire burned to ashes,
> The water boiled dry to naught,
> Her worries turned to gruesome fate,
> Her children could endure no longer.

> It is better to be dead!
> The mother thought—by far!
> She took a knife to sharpen its edge,
> At the rim of a water jar.

But before it was used, the knife began to speak to her:

"Lift the lid off the pan!
Lift the lid off the pan!"
Befuddled in mind the troubled woman approached her pan,
And as the lid was lifted, silent she became.

And look at that pan...!
It was filled with bowls...
One, two...all the way to eight
bowls, and a plate.

In these bowls and on that plate were various kinds of meat, vegetables, and cakes which ordinarily could only be seen at Erbudu's
banquets—a formal dinner of eight bowls and a plate.

The mother became happy,
The children became joyful,
The mother-in-law smiled.

They began to eat their meal together when, suddenly, that strange
voice resounded again:

"Lift the lid off the pan!
Lift the lid off the pan!
Lift it up and look!"

They saw the two round stones shining, just like the treasure cache
calabashes of Erbudu.

From then on Alifu became well-to-do.
The old mother would no longer suffer,
The children would no longer go hungry,
The wife no longer went to Erbudu's to be tormented.

It was really strange how Alifu became richer and how Erbudu
became poorer. Alifu's family could bear poverty, but Erbudu's
family was too spoiled to endure.

The Erbudu's prayed some here,
They confessed some there,
They tried everything and went still farther,
But life for them became harder and harder.

It occured to Erbudu's wife that she had not yet asked the Alifus concerning the means by which they had become wealthy. And so she went to ask. Alifu's wife was very honest and told her the entire secret.

Erbudu's wife, the secret now disclosed,
Her beams of joy were readily exposed.
She told her husband with smile and glee:
"Tomorrow here a banquet will be!
After tomorrow to market we take, treasure calabashes.

"We hire astute men to herd our sheep and cattle.
We hire permanent caretakers for our camels.
For me we will make silk dresses.
For me we will hire a young maid."

Her husband's mind had baffled she,
His wife he could not understand.
Yet sayeth she: "Just wait and see,
Until the lid is lifted off the pan."

Next day she pretended to borrow some millet grain.
She cleaned someone's hair till evening came.
And she failed to borrow, as she hoped, with shame.

Likewise—she went home and cried along the way. She picked up two black and smooth pebble stones. Back home she bellowed the fire, and told her squire: "Just wait aside, here, until we lift the lid."

They waited and waited while nothing did happen.
While the one focused his eyes to see,
The other perked her ears to listen.

Suddenly! With a noise of cracking and reeling,
The lid flew up against the ceiling.

They rubbed their eyes and hastily they looked.
Two stones, transformed to iron eggs, had cooked.
One egg toward Erbudu jumpeth,
The other upon his wifey bumpeth.

They ran too slow. The stones flew faster.

After a while they could run no more.
Iron eggs had smashed them, on their floor.

Saierdong's Stick

Place: Tongxin, Ningxia
Narrator: Yang Dehu (Hui)
Recorder: Wang Zhengwei (Hui), 1978

At one time there lived a rich man who was so greedy and cruel that people called him "Black Scorpion." The more money he got the more merciless he became.

In the village also lived a boy named Saierdong, whose father and mother were too old to do any labor. And so the mother and the father both depended on their only son. But Saierdong could not find employment. In the end he had to be a full-time servant of Black Scorpion.

He worked day and night sweeping the floor of the yard, and gathering firewood. If what he did was not liked, Black Scorpion would slap him across the face. The pitiful boy had to swallow such insults, and he could only lament for Allah's blessings in his dreams.

One day when Saierdong went out to cut firewood on a mountain, he saw a white crane lying in the fields. He went over and discovered that one of its legs had been broken when it was shot by a hunter. The bird was bleeding and lay motionless. Saierdong tore a piece of cloth from his shirt and bound up the wound, and then he took the crane home.

After a month the crane's wound had healed and the bird wanted to fly to the Qing River. So, one morning the white crane flapped its wings. It raised up its head and suddenly said to Saierdong, "My kind host, you have done a lot for me, and I must repay you. If you have difficulties, please come and visit me at the bank of the Qing River." Then the bird flew towards the river.

Saierdong did not quite believe what the crane had said, but upon contemplating his poor life he was eager to try his luck. The next day he went to the river. Soon a green blanket came floating toward him. He reached for it with his hand and felt that it was very soft and thick. "Ho! I have never had such a good blanket in all my life," he thought. He took it home and spread it on the floor.

At noon the next day he came back from work and, to his surprise and delight, he found four bowls, filled with noodles and mutton, sitting on the corners of the green blanket. Saierdong felt as if he were in heaven. After eating he rolled and rolled on the blanket as if he were a child. It would have been next to impossible to describe his happiness.

For some reason, Black Scorpion suddenly noticed that Saierdong did not have his meals anymore in his home. One morning, when Saierdong was out plowing, he took time to go to Saierdong's house. When he pushed the door open he saw, to his surprise, a green blanket on which sat four bowls of food. Black Scorpion was envious. This was a magic treasure, indeed. This blanket is wasted being spread out in this poor guy's room, he thought.

He hurried back home and brought a similar blanket to Saierdong's house and exchanged the green one with his own.

When Saierdong came back for lunch his heart began to sink. There was no meal for him, as before. He examined his blanket carefully and found that it had been exchanged by someone. After thinking for a while he reasoned that it must have been done by Black Scorpion.

He kept his anger in his heart and, without eating anything, he went to the river and poured out his unjust sufferings to the crane.

The crane said to him, "Do not be sad, I will give you a hen. With the hen your life will become better soon."

The crane flapped its wings and then a yellow hen flew up to Saierdong. He carried it home in his arm and set up a roost for it. He, however, continued to work for Black Scorpion, as before.

Every day when he returned home he would find a golden egg laid by the yellow hen. This continued for three or four days and Saierdong felt excited.

One day, while Saierdong went out to fetch water, Black Scorpion passed by his house. He heard the cluck-cluck of a hen. He went to the roost and saw a golden egg glittering. Black Scorpion thought he would be rich all his life if he could have such a hen. Again he played the same trick of exchanging the yellow hen with one of his own.

When Saierdong came home he found that the egg was not a golden one, and then he discovered that the yellow hen had been exchanged. His face turned now pale and then red, and he was gnashing his teeth in anger. Allah, why do you not punish this greedy man? Where is there an end to my sufferings?

The more he thought about it the more angry he became. Saierdong went to Black Scorpion to reason with him. But Black Scorpion stamped his feet with fury and refused to admit what he had done. With tears in his eyes Saierdong went again to see the white crane. After listening to his misfortune the crane could not help but also shed some tears. "Let me try again to help you. Here is a club. With it you can protect yourself against thieves," said the crane.

Saierdong thanked the crane and went home with the club. He put the club behind his door and went to work again for Black Scorpion.

Black Scorpion felt very strange on account of the fact that Saierdong so frequently obtained magic treasures. Entering the room he looked here and there and discovered a club behind the door. What a nice club it was! He reached for it with his hand when, suddenly and unexpectedly, the club jumped up and pounced right and left, pouring a shower of blows on him. He was beaten black and blue. Seeing no place to hide he knelt down, begging for mercy.

Momentarily his shouts for help alarmed his wife and his children. They ran over and saw the club beating on Black Scorpion who, in vain, tried to dodge the blows. His wife was too worried to cry.

At that moment Saierdong returned, and seeing what he saw he burst into laughing.

"For Allah's sake, I beg you, Saierdong, catch this club!" pleaded the wife. Yet Saierdong remained motionless. After a while Black Scorpion fell down and blood was running on the ground, and all the while the club was still bouncing in the air. The old and young of the whole family knelt down with fear and pleaded, "Saierdong, please catch this club, we will give you whatever you want."

Saierdong said, "I want nothing but my blanket and my yellow hen." Quickly they returned to him his treasures. Then Saierdong gave a shout and the club stopped. After that he always took the club with him, and no one dared to bully him anymore.

A Clever Manla

Place: Yanchi, Ningxia
Recorder: Ma Guangjian (Hui), 1979

Long, long ago there existed an owner of a coal mine. He and several other scoundrels captured people who passed by—such as merchants, load carriers, and travelers, and forced them to go down the mine shaft to dig coal. At the entrance of the shaft hung a basket in which insufficient food was sent down and by which much black coal was pulled out.

It happened that Manla lost his way, was caught by these scoundrels, and was subsequently forced to work in this mine.[1] When he reached the bottom of the shaft he found, in the dim light, an old man bent over and digging. He asked him, "Grandfather, how long have you been here?"

The old man looked up and viewed the young man. "I do not know. I was your age when I came here," said he.

Manla walked along. In the dark mine here and there lay dead men, and there was a deep pit filled with bones of the dead. Manla was so moved by sorrow that he began to cry.

---

[1] The name "Manla" here is derived from *"mullah"* which originally referred to a student who prepares to become an ahong. However, here the name simply designates someone who has knowledge—specifically, the skill of writing.

"Why are you crying, Older Brother?" a young voice was heard asking.

When Manla lifted his head he saw a small boy in front of him, whom he answered, "I am afraid I can never go back home for the rest of my life."

The boy said, "I have been here for more than three years and have been thinking about going home every day. But I cannot."

Manla became hopeless as he had to work with these people in the mine.

One day he saw the boy scratch the wall with coal, inscribing many lines. He asked, "Younger Brother, what do you draw these for?"

"One line means one day," answered the boy. Manla made up his mind right then. From then on he carved his name on each piece of coal. These pieces of coal were carried out and sold far and wide.

It happened one day that Manla's father saw his son's name on a piece of coal. He reasoned that Manla must be digging coal in a mine somewhere. So he reported it to the local authorities. The authorities sent soldiers to the mountain and found the coal mine. They saved Manla and the others in the mine and threw the owner and the scoundrels down the shaft.

To Borrow Sheep

First published in *Heilongjiang min tian wen xie* (*Heilongjiang Folk Literature*)
Place: Heilongjiang
Recorder: Sui Shujing, 1984

Once upon a time, in the Muslim village south of the Sunhua River, lived a family with the surname of "Ma." There were four people in the family. The old parents had two children, one daughter and one son. The daughter was approximately fifteen years old. When she was still a small child she already was very bright and lovely, and her pleasant voice sounded like jade striking upon jade. Therefore she was named Lingling—Jingle Bell.

The son whose name was Laifuzi (Good Fortune) was two years younger than the girl. Old Ma supported his family by tending sheep for a landlord. But the landlord only gave him part of his pay, and every year he would owe him months of back pay. One summer day, when there was an unbroken spell of wet weather, Old Ma could not go out to tend the sheep. The landlord deducted his pay for the entire summer.

The Ma family was so poor that they did not even have pennies to jingle. Laifuzi was so hungry that he had to eat wild herbs. He was reduced to skin and bones.

The mother felt very sorry for her children and she explained their sufferings: "A father of children, and grownups, they can bear hunger, but children are at an age when they must grow. How can they be starved? Just go and beg some money from the landlord."

Old Ma knew that the landlord was cruel and merciless. But to avoid going hungry he forced himself to go. "Master, my whole family has not had any grain for days."

"Why have you not gone to buy some?" said the landlord off-handedly.

Old Ma said to himself, "You owe me my pay. Where can I get money?" but he dared not to speak it aloud. He was afraid of offending him.

He said patiently, "Do me a favor, my Master. Please reckon my pay and pay me some. Help us please, or my children will starve and die."

Hearing Old Ma ask for back pay the landlord became annoyed and a cold expression appeared on his face. "It is neither a festival nor New Year's day. Why do you want me to consider your pay? When you Ma people came here, if I had not taken mercy on you and kept you on to tend sheep, you all would have died of hunger long ago. Wait until next year for that pay."

Old Ma's heart sank. But thinking of his children he kept imploring the landlord and said, "Master, please have pity on me. I have tended your sheep for years, but I have never received full pay. I think I can still ask for some. Lately it has always been raining. I cannot go out to tend the sheep. And still, you deduct my pay. What can I live on?"

The landlord, who often hid a dagger in his bland smile, was crafty. He often amused himself at the expense of the poor. He thought for a while and decided to have some fun.

"Old Ma, I see you are pitiful. Though it is not the end of the year, I cannot look on with folded arms and laugh at you. Well, I will lend you five sheep tomorrow and you may sell them at the market in order to buy some rice so that you can tide over the starvation..."

Old Ma was so thankful to hear his master's promise to lend him five sheep that he said in a hurry, "Great thanks to you, My Master. Thank you very much."

"Wait, I have not finished yet.... But you will have to return to me five sheep tomorrow evening, or else I will not spare you, under any circumstances."

Old Ma was very angry at such bullying. He turned and walked home.

Seeing her father come back empty-handed, Ma Lingling knew that he had made a fruitless trip—also judging by her father's pale and sad face. So she spoke to him, "Dad, do not be grieved. I will go and pick some edible herbs with my brother. Everything will be better. The gourds and beans are ripe."

Old Ma felt sad at these words, and with tears in his eyes he sighed, "How can we live through this?"

Lingling noticed that her father was more grieved than ever. She thought that perhaps he had run into additional difficulties.

"Dad, has the landlord not lent you any money?" she asked.

"Money? That cursed landlord not only refused but also bullied me."

"Dad, what on earth did the landlord do to you?" Lingling asked, wishing to know more precisely.

Then Old Ma told her the entire story. Having gotten very angry herself, Lingling said to her father, "Dad, you always are the one who gets chided. Why don't we teach him a lesson? It will help vent your anger."

Though Old Ma knew that his daughter was clever, he was nevertheless afraid that she might get into trouble. So he said, "My dear Child, do not do that. The landlord is a tricky and slippery fellow. You are too young to take him on."

"Dad, did he promise you he would lend you five sheep?"

"Yes, but he asked me to return five that evening."

"That is easy, Dad. Do not worry. Let me deal with him."

The next morning Lingling and her little brother went to see the landlord. Before that the landlord had only intended to have fun at Old Ma's expense, but now, unexpectedly, they actually came after the sheep. In order not to lose face he decided that he would lend them the five sheep and see how they could return them.

He said to Lingling, "I never break my word. Neither can you. You may take five sheep away but you must return to me five this evening, otherwise I will not let you off."

Lingling answered angrily, "Do not look down on the poor. Though we have no money, we have dignity. Please put your mind at ease. I will pay you back in full this evening."

Lingling and her little brother drove the five sheep away. They neither drove them to town nor to their home, but to a forest. Lingling, with the help of her little brother, tied up the legs of the sheep. She brought out a pair of scissors and said, "The landlord bullied our father, bullied poor people. Today we shall turn his trick against him and make him understand that the poor are not foolish and cannot be harassed without doing anything in return. Come, Brother, let us put down the sheep and cut their wool. Then we go to the market and sell the wool for grain. As for the back pay, I will have it out with him later."

It was not very long, and the wool of the five sheep was sheared off completely. She sold it and bought some rice which was carried home by other people. Then she and her brother drove the sheep back to the landlord.

The landlord, seeing the five sheep back, but bare, got very angry. Lingling said to him with a smile, "Thank you for your help! Here are the five sheep for you! I am sure you will also want to clear the account of my father's back pay. So long, for now!"

The landlord was unable to express his annoyance; he opened his mouth, flabbergasted. He had only asked them to return sheep, not wool!

From then on this story of borrowing sheep spread quickly. And the people praised Lingling for being a clever girl.

The Treasure Pan

Place: Yinchuan, Ningxia
Narrator: Chen Fu (Hui)
Recorder: Ma Yu (Hui), 1980

Once upon a time, in a Hui village, lived a rich landlord called Master Ma the Second. He had a big head and large ears. He was fat like a water bucket and he walked like a duck. He often tried to do harm to the poor, and the poor in the village suffered a lot.

The poor people gathered and discussed how to play a trick on him in return, but they could not think of a good way. So they came to the home of Dawu. After some deliberation they agreed to teach Master Ma the Second a lesson, on the day of Dawu's mother's memorial ceremony.

Soon after that the news spread that Dawu had a treasure pan, one which could give you whatever you wanted. Now he was going to hold a grand memorial ceremony for his mother. The news reached Master Ma's ears, and therefore he sent one of his men, named Mazy, to investigate whether this was true or not.

Mazy slipped into Dawu's house, just like a mouse. Dawu and the others had noticed him but pretended not to have seen him. Suddenly, from inside the house the voice of Dawu's wife resounded: "Get out! Out! Out!" Then followed the voices of several women: "All right, the meal is ready!"

Many fried cakes were brought out and set before everyone. All the fellows cried out happily, "Well, well! It is indeed a magic treasure pan!"

Thus, with shouts of "Get out! Out! Out!" many fried cakes were brought out.

Dawu appeared to be afraid of losing his secret. He lowered his voice: "Hush! Do not let others hear!" And while he so spoke he looked and saw Mazy slip away, in a hurry.

Mazy ran back breathlessly to his master and told him what he had seen. Master Ma the Second became curious and asked, "Is that true? Perhaps I should go to investigate this myself." Before arriving there he had an idea.

"Dawu, I came for debts you owe me!" Ma called out the moment he entered the door. Seeing Master Ma the Second arrive, Dawu walked over to meet him and said peace to him.

"What wind brings you here? Sit down please!" He immediately brushed off the couch (*kang*). Master Ma the Second sat down at the edge and said in a cold tongue, "Dawu, do not pretend to be a fool! Will you repay the money or not?"

Dawu pleaded, "Master the Second, I have spent a lot of money on my mother's funeral. I really have no money on hand."

Master Ma the Second gave him a hard stare and said, "No money on hand? What did you poor folk eat just now?"

Dawu muttered, "Master, the Second, it is..."

Master Ma the Second interrupted, "What? Speak it out!"

Dawu turned a smile, "Master Ma the Second, do not be angry. Let me fix something for you to eat. After eating we shall discuss the debt." Then he asked his wife, in the inner room, to cook a meal. Master Ma the Second just wanted to know the secret of the treasure pan, so he left the debts aside and listened carefully, with his ears perched.

In the inner room Dawu's wife shouted, "Dawu, come! The treasure pan does not work!" Dawu did not seem worried at all. He said, "Keep your mind sincere. Do not be afraid. Master Ma the Second will not take it away. Just speak the incantation sincerely."

Soon a shouting was heard from the inner room: "Get out! Out! Out! Quickly!—All right, there, the meal is ready!" And immediately a nice meal was brought out.

Upon hearing all this, Master Ma the Second felt delirious in his mind. But still, pretending to be generous, he said, "You do have such a pan? It might pay half of your debts."

Dawu looked awkward. The poor who were present came and begged on behalf of Dawu.

Then Ma gave a long sigh and said, "For Allah's sake, and for the sake of the poor, and also for Dawu's sake as a sincere Muslim—I do not blame you for your crime of trying to keep the treasure pan secret for yourself. But I must take the pan, to cancel your debts."

Dawu sighed and said, "Master, since you said 'for the sake of the poor,' why not cancel the debts of all the people? Then you will own the treasure pan." Because Ma the Second was so excited about the treasure pan, he nearly flew into the inner room combining two steps into one. He snatched the pan away.

Having gotten the magic treasure pan, Master Ma the Second decided to hold a banquet to show off the pan to his guests. When all of his guests had arrived he invited them to the table to await dinner. Master Ma the Second whispered at his wife's ear and took time out to teach her the incantation. Then he turned back to the hall and declared to everyone present, "Thanks to Allah, now I have a magic pan. This pan now offers you fried cakes. I hope you will enjoy them." And after having spoken this, he turned toward the kitchen and called out, "Bring out the fried cakes!"

He had already called several times. Yet, his wife was not coming out. Master Ma the Second became annoyed and abusive. "You Deaf Ear!" But before he stopped abusing her, his wife came out with the empty pan, and said, "I have recited the incantation many times, and still it does not work."

Master Ma the Second stared at her and said, "You have no experience. How could it not work! It must be because you have an insincere and unstable mind and you forgot the incantation."

Ma's wife fell into a rage and, waving her hands, she shouted, "Get out! Out! Out! Quickly!" Upon hearing these words the guests thought she was driving them out and they stood up aghast.

When Master Ma the Second saw that his wife's incantation was not working, he also waved his hands and shouted, "Get out! Out! Out! Quickly!" Three times he repeated these words. Now the guests could no longer remain, and they left, cursing.

After the guests had left the treasure pan still refused to work. Thereupon Master Ma the Second and his wife began to quarrel, terribly. And the more they quarrelled the more angry they got. Finally they came to blows. Without giving it any care, the magic treasure pan was smashed to pieces.

Gold Could Not Buy

Place: Ningxia
Recorder: Li Dexiu (Hui), 1982

Long, long ago there was a rich man named Nasima. He had a family property which included over a thousand *mu* of land, ten thousands heads of sheep and cattle, and many pots of gold and silver. Nasima hired dozens of laborers to herd his sheep and cattle. He cared for money as much as for his life, so much so that in his eyes even a copper coin seemed as big as a bottom millstone. He was cruel and evil toward his laborers. He was as fat as a pig, while his laborers were just skin and bones and suffered from hunger.

One year it rained so heavily that a terrible torrent of water rushed from the mountains into town. The flood drowned the streets and lanes of almost the entire town. Carrying with them bran cakes, the laborers fled from that calamity to the western mountains.

Nasima, by way of risking his life but not his money, carried with him silver and gold. Assisted by all members of his family, old and young, he too fled to the western mountains. The next day the flood waters rose, quickly. Half of the town was washed away.

The laborers satisfied their hunger with bran cakes. But on the third day Nasima was too hungry to bear it any longer. He took out some gold and silver to trade for some bran cakes among the laborers. But the laborers said, "Master, you cannot do that. The gold and silver is given to you by Allah. You have your gold, and we have our bran cakes."

On the fifth day the flood receded. Each of the laborers went his own way. However, the Nasimas all died of hunger on the mountain. Their eyes were staring at the gold and the silver.

Zhang Sanwa

Place: Ningxia
Recorder: Yin Weizhong, 1980

Once upon a time there was a poor single man called Zhang Sanwa, who was working all the year round for a landlord called Wang Shanren (Wang the Charitable). But still, he could not afford to get married, even at an age of almost forty.

As for Wang Shanren, people far and wide knew that he was very cunning and crafty, so he was given the nickname Trickster. Laborers who had once worked in his house would never come to work for him again. But Zhang Sanwa was an exception. It was said that Zhang Sanwa's parents had died very early when the boy was still only a child. Wang Shanren, who pretended to be very kind, helped bury the dead parents. From that time on Zhang Sanwa was a long-term hired hand in Wang's house.

One spring Wang also employed four laborers from another region. At first each laborer could have three meals a day, with three steambread pieces for each meal.

A few days later Wang thought to himself, "If I provide for them in this manner, a huge amount of grain will be eaten up in the course of a year." And so he instructed cooks to prepare two meals a day instead of three, but the laborers each could have five pieces of bread with each meal.

Wang became worried again. He discovered that it was more to have ten pieces for two meals than nine pieces for three meals. He changed two meals back into three and gave them porridge instead of bread. The alloted grain made then seven small bowls of porridge per meal for each worker.

When he noticed this, Wang was surprised and went to talk to the laborers in a hurry: "I only have a limited amount of grain. So as not to let you work hungry, I will have to serve you porridge. As the saying goes: 'Not overeating brings well-being.'" This he said while he pretended to feel awkward.

Then Zhang Sanwa said, "Yes, you think nine pieces of bread are too much, and ten are not worthwhile. Though it is porridge now, only twenty-one for each."

Wang felt snubbed, and he slinked off, angrily.

Two days later Wang played another trick. He woke up the laborers before the cock crowed. He made them feed grass to the cows and had them go to the fields at the first cock-crow. For breakfast he gave to each three hard and coarse pieces of bread to eat while walking to the fields. The laborers became very angry, but they had to obey.

Two days passed like this, then Zhang Sanwa said to his fellows, "We should think of a way to deal with him."

"What can we do?" the fellows asked. Zhang Sanwa whispered his idea, and everyone agreed.

On the third day before cock-crowing, Wang knocked at the window and shouted, "Get up! Get up! Feed the cows and go to the kitchen for food!"

The laborers got up and went to the kitchen first, for bread. But they did not feed the cows. Wang thought that the cows had been fed, and so he urged the laborers to go to work in a hurry. They led the cows to the gate and Wang saw that at the mouth of each cow hung a basket with straw in it. He was puzzled and asked, "Why have you put a basket at the mouths of the cows?"

"You urged us to hurry, and we had no time. But it does not matter. The cows can eat their fill as they go to the fields."

Wang became very angry, but he could do nothing but accept the situation.

It was time for weeding. Wang again played a trick. He offered everyone a small cake for breakfast, and then said, "As you know, I am short on grain. Nevertheless, this is a cake of good quality."

The laborers went to work, cursing Wang all the way to the fields. Zhang Sanwa said, "Do not curse anymore. Let us carefully hoe off the weeds on a small plot. Then we will have a nice nap. I have a way to deal with Wang."

So everyone began to work, and after a while they went to sleep under and around a tree. At midday Wang did not see the laborers return for lunch. He thought they must be working. So he asked his men to help him carry a meal to the field. Along the way he wondered how he would flatter his laborers. But contrary to his expectations he saw them sleeping, here and there, and only a small amount of work had been done.

He got into a rage and began abusing them: "Damn you! Are you dead? Get up!"

Everyone woke up and they saw Wang standing before them, looking ferocious. Wang shouted at them, "You heartless people. I treat you well, but you repay me with sleeping at work during such a busy season!"

Zhang Sanwa walked up to him and said, calmly, "Master, how can you say so? All of us know very well how you treat us. This morning we had a small cake. And really, it was of good quality. So, in order to repay you properly we hoed a small patch of weeds as accurately as we could. You may examine it with your own eyes!"

Wang made an uproar: "Very well! Very well!" Then he turned away, angrily.

When winter came, Wang sent the laborers to the mountain for firewood. Everyone must bring back a bundle of firewood each day. When it was a cloudy day, Wang offered two persons just a bowl of mush, to share. If one said that it was not enough he would answer, "A cloudy day has a shorter span of daytime, so you need less food in your stomachs." It seemed as though what he did was right and proper.

Zhang Sanwa said, "I have never heard of that."

Wang smiled and said, "You are too young to know it. That is why you have heard me tell it only now."

After the meal the laborers went up to the mountain to cut firewood as usual. Zhang Sanwa suggested, "Today two of us cut one bundle of wood. You let me answer him when he asks why." Everyone agreed.

In the evening they came back with bundles of firewood, each carried by two men. Wang asked them with dissatisfaction, "Why do you have one bundle of wood being carried by two men?" Zhang Sanwa replied, "On a high mountain, with strong wind, two men can carry only one bundle. Does that seem so strange?"

Wang shouted, "I have never seen that!"

"You have seen it now. Have you not!" they all answered in one voice.

The Masons' Wise Revenge

Published first in *Ning xia wen yi (Literature and Arts of Ningxia)*, 1961.
Place: Pinluo, Ningxia
Narrator: Ding Lianyin (Hui)
Recorder: Ding Yibo (Hui)

Once there was a landlord named Zhang whose nickname was Qiedao (Knife). He was a sinister and fierce-looking fellow, with a hawk nose and with mouse eyes. By hook and by crook he was trying to squeeze the poor, and so the poor people hated him very much.

One year Zhang the Knife wanted to build a large house for his son to get married. He sent a servant to call Wang Yong, a mason who was well known, far and wide. But knowing this landlord to be of an evil disposition, the mason found an excuse to refuse. But then his wife said to him, "We cannot afford to offend him. He is a man of power. You better go!" The mason dawdled a while and went with his tools.

Three other workers were there to help the mason build the house. Zhang the Knife summoned the men to him and said, "I want to have the house built with walls made of lime, the floor of bricks, and the ceiling of good felt. After all is done, each of you will receive ten taels of silver." The mason suspected that he was trying to cheat them as usual. So he thought to himself, "If this landlord refuses to pay the silver, they would surely find a way to punish him."

All the masons got up early in the morning and went to bed late in the evening. Going back in mud and coming forth in water they hauled earth, they carried water, mixed mud, and moved bricks. All the while they were hungry. They did not distinguish between day and night. They worked on building the house for longer than ten days, in a constant state of exhaustion.

Just when the house had been built and the masons were ready to apply their second layer of mud, Zhang Knife paraded up to them, fan in hand, and said, "You are good-for-nothings. Look at the house for yourselves. It is too ugly. It looks just like a pig stall! What a pity! You have wasted my materials!"

Hearing this, Wang Yong became so angry that his lungs were about to explode. And how he wished to hit this fellow with his spade—twice! The other workers were incensed as well.

They knew that Zhang Knife had bad intentions again, that he was looking for a thorn in cotton. So they discussed it among themselves and came up with a harassment for this landlord. They put a straw rope on the eaves and inserted a reed pipe in the middle of the roof, and Zhang Knife knew nothing at all about these things.

On the day when the work was finished, Zhang Knife talked sweetly to the masons: "I keep my word, even though you have wasted my materials and have built such a bad and ugly house. At first I wanted to request compensation for the materials, but you are too poor to pay for it. So I give up. You have had my meals. I also will not ask you to pay for them. Because I pity you, each of you can go home with a *dou* of bran."[2]

The mason held back his rage and said, "Thank you for your kindness, but you may keep the bran for your pigs."

Having heard this, the wife of Zhang Knife said in a hurry, "If they do not want it, we will keep it."

A few days later the wedding ceremony of Zhang Knife's son was held in the newly built home. At night some strange noises were heard from the roof. Snap! Snap! The bride was frightened to death, and the bridegroom shouted in fear, "Father, Father, there is a ghost in the house."

Zang Knife did not know what was happening and asked the wife to start praying, immediately.

Because he knew that Zhang Knife, the landlord, believed in gods and was afraid of ghosts more than anyone, the mason that night climbed on the roof of the new house and in a fearsome voice spoke through the reed pipe: "I am the god of the earth. You told a lie and treated the masons unfairly, and I will come again in a few days..."

Again the terrible snapping noises resounded, on account of tension transmitted to the dry straw. All the family members became terribly frightened.

Zhang Knife stuttered, "Grandfather bless us. We will do as you order."

---

[2]One *dou* is a unit of dry measure for grain, approximately ten liters.

So the next day the wife urged her husband to send silver to the mason and the workers. Yet, Zhang Knife, still reluctant to pay the silver, promised his wife, "...in a few days, depending on the situation."

On the third day it began to rain, so hard that the rain ran down through the reed pipe into the room and transformed the room into a complete mess. Their silk quilt and their clothes were drenched. And the wife shouted at her husband, with a temper, "You Old Evil. You lied again, and therefore trouble has come again! How can you dare to offend the Earth god?"

After the rain stopped, Zhang Knife immediately sent someone after the mason. When the mason came with the other men, Zhang Knife walked to welcome them and said, hypocritically, "It has been raining these days, and it is getting colder. Now, there are ten taels of silver for each of you to get some grain and clothes." This time he actually paid out the silver, well behaved.

That same night the mason climbed up on the new house, quietly, and took away the reed pipe and the straw rope, and patched the hole with mud. From then on there were no more snapping noises and no more rain leaked into the house.

Carrying Mud

Place: Tongxin county, Ningxia
Narrator: Wang Diyi (Hui)
Recorder: Wang Zhengwei (Hui), 1979

Once upon a time a rich man hired more than ten fellows to build a house for him. Among them was a boy named Musa. The rich man was cruel and merciless. He chatted endlessly, cursing them, no matter how quickly the fellows worked or how well they did.

One day the rich man was acting as an overseer and gave orders here and there. Some of the fellows were carrying water, some were building the wall, others were mixing up mud, while Musa was carrying mud with a shovel.

The rich man came over to scold him for being too short and not applying his strength. Musa became filled with pent-up anger. A while later the rich man walked up to him again. "Why do you work so carelessly?" he said, with his triangular eyes wide open. "You must put mud at the places to which I point!"

"Yes Sir!" replied Musa.

When the rich man pointed here, Musa put mud here; when the rich man pointed there, Musa put mud there. After some time, when the rich man was scratching his head, Musa quickly put mud on his head.

The rich man began to curse him with rage, wiping the mud off his eyes: "You poor wretch! Why did you put it on my head?"

Musa answered, unhurriedly, "I only put the mud wherever you pointed, just as you told me to."

While all the fellows could not help laughing, the rich man was too angry to speak.

Little Kalimu

First published in *Qin hai hu (Qinhai Lake)*, 1963.
Place: Qinhai province
Recorder: Shi Jiyuan

Once upon a time there lived some dozens of Hui families on a stretch of fertile land, below the Ji Mountains. They went out to work early in the morning and returned late in the evening. Day by day, and year by year, they labored diligently on the land. They lived a fairly pleasant life.

But things changed. During one particular year, at a place not far from the village, a compound of houses with tiled roofs was being built, with a golden dragon carved on the left door and a colorful phoenix on the right. In the mansion lived a rich but bitterly sarcastic squire. Because of the looks of his face he was called, behind his back, Beardy Pockface. At times he sent his men to the farmers to collect taxes, and grain, by inventing excuses such as a mosque needed to be built, or scriptures were to be recited at the occasion of a religious festival. This evil man caused the farmers to suffer a lot.

In the southern portion of the village lived a family of two people, a grandmother and her grandson. They had two *mu* of land and a dog called Huahua. The grandmother was old; she had white hair, but she was still strong and healthy. Her twelve-year-old grandson, Kalimu, was good looking and clever. He seemed like an obedient lamb when he was quiet, but when he was working he would become lively like a calf. His parents had died when he was a child and he was brought up by his grandmother, enduring all kinds of hardships.

Spring came after winter. One morning after breakfast the grandmother went to the fields with a hoe to dig up weeds. She left Kalimu at home with the dog.

While hoeing, the grandmother suddenly heard the clatter of a horse's hooves. A cloud of dust arose, and out of it ran a mule. It was the squire with his mouselike eyes, his hooknose, and pockmarked, bearded face, who came riding along the road toward the fields.

Beardy Pockface rode up to the field. The moment he saw the flat and green land, his mind was actively hatching an evil plot. Reins in one hand and a whip in the other he asked the grandmother, "Hi there—tell me how many shovelsful of weeds you have hoed up?"

It was quite a long time before the grandmother could answer, "Ahr...ahr...Gentleman. I am too old for counting. Besides, what is the use of counting them?"

Beardy Pockface replied with a cunning smile, "Listen, if you cannot tell me by tomorrow, you will not own this piece of land any longer." Then he bumped the mule and rode off.

The grandmother, being interrogated, felt her body become so weak that she could not go on working any more. She thought for a long time but could not find a way to deal with this trouble.

Kalimu was sweeping the courtyard when his grandmother came back. Being sharp-eyed, he at once noticed the strange expressions on her face. Usually, when coming back from the fields, Grandmother would kiss him and make warm inquiries. She would keep saying,

"My Dearest, my Love," and such like. But why did she look gloomy today and remain speechless?

"Grandmother," Kalimu said, holding her by the hand, "Who made you angry? Just tell me."

The grandmother said coldly, "That is enough. It is none of your business."

Kalimu did not give up that easily. Kneeling before the grandmother, holding her legs in his arms, he said, "Grandma, Grandma, please tell me. I am old enough now to help you. Otherwise I would."

Tears were already running from his eyes. The grandmother could not stand the begging of her dear grandson, and she told him exactly what had happened.

"That is easy!" Kalimu smiled through his tears. "Grandma! Let me answer him tomorrow. You just pay no attention to him."

The next day the grandmother and her grandson went to the field together, followed by their dog. While hoeing they heard the dog barking. Bow-wow! They looked up and saw Beardy Pockface riding toward them, in the distance. When he approached the grandmother he asked, fiercely, "Tell me how many shovelsful of weeds have you hoed up today?"

Kalimu walked up to Beardy Pockface. Pointing at his mule he asked calmly, "Your Highness! Tell me how many steps has your mule taken today?"

Beardy Pockface did not expect to be talked back to by such a small child. And the jab was so powerful that he was surprised, annoyed, and a little frightened.

"You little devil. What nerve you have. Wait and see!" he said. Then he bent down and gave the mule a sudden whipping, and he sped away.

At dusk, when the grandmother was busy in the room, and Kalimu was cutting firewood, the dog suddenly barked. Momentarily some fierce-browed and cold-eyed villians rushed in, who poured forth a stream of abuses. "You old wretches! What a nerve! Our master's precious mule, granted by Allah, was enraged by you, little devil. The only way to avoid the disaster is to hand over your land as a pledge and to make your grandson his little page for three years. Go with us!" they said.

With all the villains lending a hand, they were just about to catch hold of the boy. The grandmother was quite indignant at their overbearing rude manner. She rushed at them with her hands raised up and said, "Damned bandits! Just kill me, but do not bully a small child!"

Seeing the grandmother throwing herself at them, one of the villains kicked her cruelly. She fell to the ground with a fierce yell and fainted.

The moment they saw the grandmother faint the villains disappeared in a tumult—because this was becoming a case involving a human life.

Kalimu kept crying until his grandmother regained consciousness. He helped her lie down on the *kang*.

The grandmother groaned from pain, "My Dear! I feel my end is drawing near. Try to win justice for me, and do not forget our hatred!" After so speaking the old woman laid her head on the pillow and died.

Kalimu was in deep sorrow, crying bitterly and wishing to wake her up again. But the grandmother would never again be with him.

With the help of kind farmers and an ahong, Kalimu buried his grandmother at the foot of the mountain. Now when the time of mourning was over, Kalimu came to the house of Beardy Pockface, seething with hatred.

"The poor one, Kalimu, now reports to see the master. Just assign what I have to do!" said Kalimu to Beardy Pockface, coldly.

"Go and feed my mule!" Beardy Pockface said, sneeringly. And he cursed him silently in his mind: "You brought your own destruction on you before I sent for you. All right, sooner or later I will get rid of you!"

One day he said to Kalimu, "Go get the saddle and the mule ready. We will go to collect taxes very far away. Take along your dog Huahua, and you will be promoted to be *manla* when we come back."[3]

Beardy Pockface sat in the saddle, Kalimu waved a whip, and the reins were in the dog's mouth. They walked on and on and went from door to door. They passed many villages and collected much silver.

---

[3]A *manla*, ordinarily in Hui speech, refers to a *mullah* who has been educated to become a teacher in the ways of Islam. However, in this instance it merely means promotion to the status of a clerk.

One day they came to a river with no village ahead nor an inn behind them. Beardy Pockface cast a sidelong glance at Kalimu and said: "Allah! We have to pass the night by the river today." He dismounted from the mule, took down a luggage roll, and then began to sleep. Kalimu took off the heavy sack full of silver and put it between himself and Beardy Pockface. He laid himself down by the river side.

While Kalimu was dreaming about his grandmother telling him a story, he suddenly was awakened by the dog Huahua. He was shocked but understood at once. Softly and quietly he got up and removed the silver sack to the place where he slept. He lay down in the middle, instead.

It was so dark and quiet, only the water of the river swirled and flowed. Sitting up stealthily, Beardy Pockface looked about and then gave a sudden kick to the black bundle which lay at the river side. With a pit-a-pat sound the sack fell into the river. Delightedly he said while laughing, "Little Kalimu, little Kalimu. Be tricky no more! Your dead body is floating downstream."

Kalimu heard clearly and burst into laughing, "Do not be so cunning, Master. It is your silver that is sinking in the stream." Upon hearing this Beardy Pockface wailed loudly, while stamping his feet and beating his chest.

The next day they journeyed onward and arrived by evening at a small inn. Beardy Pockface rented three cabins. "I will have the eastern cabin so that I can pray during the night. Tie up the mule in the middle one. You and your dog go to sleep in the western cabin."

Kalimu fell asleep, dreaming about his grandmother making for him a paper horse. Again the dog Huahua woke him up, nudging him with his head. He was startled but understood quickly. Kalimu quietly walked out of the cabin, led the mule into his own and tied it up. He and his dog went into the middle cabin to sleep.

Around midnight Kalimu was awakened again, not by his dog but by crackling noises.

"What is that villain doing now?" he wondered. He went out, followed by his dog, and saw the western cabin burning and aflame. All the wood burned, crackled, and sputtered.

Beardy Pockface laughed and said, "Kalimu, little Kalimu, laugh no more. Your white brains are now sizzling in the fire!"

"Do not laugh, Master. Your mule right now is being burned to ashes!" Kalimu said loudly.

Not only had Beardy Pockface failed in murdering Kalimu, but he also had lost his silver and his favorite mule. In addition, he had to pay for the house. Being no longer in a mood for collecting taxes, he just swallowed the bitterness and went back home.

Since that time Beardy Pockface treated Kalimu far more savagely than a wolf would have. He gave Kalimu less to eat and more work to do. But in order to avenge his grandmother, Kalimu just bore the endless sufferings and indignities.

One day Beardy Pockface said, "Kalimu listen! While I am out collecting taxes you must clean the courtyard. Do not let dog or chicken droppings be scattered about, or I will force you to eat them."

After Beardy Pockface left, Kalimu locked all the doors, and opened a window and crawled through it. In the other room he filled a bowl, half with honey and the other half with pan-roasted flour. He mixed them together and kneaded them into small and round balls. After having done that he swept the ground of the courtyard clean and scattered the honeyed, roasted flour chunks on the ground.

In the evening, when Beardy Pockface got back, he found droppings everywhere. He shouted for Kalimu, covering his nose with his long sleeves: "You lazy sluggard! Eat up these droppings! None must be left!" he ordered.

"Yes Sir!" Kalimu picked up the chunks, one by one and threw them into his mouth without delay. He munched sweetly and deliciously. Kalimu really had good meal.

At first Beardy Pockface held his breath and closed his mouth. But the more he watched the more curious he became. He also picked up one. It smelled all right; so he tasted a little and it was lip-smacking sweet. Presently he smiled at Kalimu and asked, "What is it made of, good boy?"

Kalimu answered, "Rub garlic on your head, obtain fresh honey from a beehive, and mix it with half a bowl of pan-roasted flour."

Beardy Pockface seemed mad. He ran into his house and actually embalmed his head with garlic, climbed up the ladder and put his hands into a beehive.

Smelling the garlic, the bees instantly flew and buzzed all about, stinging Beardy Pockface on the head.

"Heh...Be quick! Help!" shouted Beardy Pockface, overtaken by the bees. He was unable to move as much as a single step. His scoundrels came running, one after another, but none dared to help their master. They just stood there, dumb.

"Beat!...Beat! Beat with a hammer," shouted Beardy Pockface. Yet, who dared to beat the master with a hammer?

Now Kalimu asked slowly, "A wooden one or an iron hammer?"

Beardy Pockface was in too much pain to think any more, so he said, "An iron hammer. Please beat, beat hard!"

So Kalimu lifted the iron hammer quickly, and with all his strength he hit him on the head. In an instant Beardy Pockface fell to the ground and died.

Kalimu felt avenged and left the place, with his dog Huahua. He then went to his grandmother's grave, and by it he cried aloud.

In order to thank the little hero who had rid the people of a scourge, the villagers helped Kalimu find a kind and pretty girl, and they held a big wedding ceremony for them.

Kalimu and his young wife lived together happily ever after.

The Fairy Maiden's Descent

Place: Miquan, Xinjiang
Narrator: Qi Zhenhua (Hui)
Recorder: Qi Wenjuan (Hui), 1988

Long, long ago, the Sage decided to send a fairy maiden to determine whether the earth had more good people or more bad people on it. He instructed the fairy maiden that she could test only three people whom she would meet.

When the fairy maiden came to the world of humankind she first disguised herself as a beautiful young lady and was resting at a quiet road side. After a short while, a clear and melodious clatter of a horse's hooves was approaching and a cart came within sight.

The young lady got up and signaled: "Dear Driver. It is indeed Allah's providence that we should meet here. For Allah's sake, please let me ride on your cart."

The driver agreed without any hesitation, for he thought it a pity that she should have to walk on foot.

When the cart drove into the deep desert, the lady squinted and slid closer toward the driver. The driver, when he noticed this, appeared as if he was stung by a wasp, and he quickly moved sideways. But the young lady did not relent. She came closer again and, at last, she simply leaned on the strong man.

The driver jumped off the cart, in a flurry, and said, "Madam, if you feel uncomfortable, please lie on the cart."

The young lady could do nothing but pout her lips. Unhappily she lay down and pretended to be asleep.

By the time they came to an inn it was completely dark. The driver asked the young lady if she would take his cart the next day. She said yes. The driver asked the owner of the inn to help the lady settle in, and he himself, with his quilt, went to the horse shed.

It was quite late the next morning by the time the driver had harnessed his horse. He waited for some time, but the lady failed to come out. A little impatient, he went to knock at the door where the lady stayed. He knocked for some time, but no one answered. He became worried and asked the owner to unlock the door. In the room was nothing except a bed.

The driver thought that, because of the way she had behaved the day before, she might have felt ashamed to face him again. He therefore walked away without much ado and quit worrying about her. He got on his cart and sat down. Just at that moment he felt something hard under his straw cushion. He picked up his cushion and saw, laying there, a shiny shoe-shaped piece of gold.

The fairy maiden went on her way. She walked along the Old Dragon River, toward the entrance of a village. In the field not far ahead a man was clumsily plowing, with a strong ox. She thought this to be the time for sowing and this fellow, here, was just beginning to plow. He had to be a very lazy man. Before long the fairy maiden turned herself into a calf which walked along the road toward the strong man, mooing.

The man squinted at the calf, thinking it was a lost one. A smile appeared on his face. He ran over at once and grasped the short rope that was slung around the calf's neck, and he dragged it onto his field. He detached the plow from his own ox and hitched the calf to it. Then he began to whip it hard and to make it plow his field.

At this moment another farmer came walking alongside the field. When he saw how that man's strong ox ate grass, leisurely along the ridge, while the calf was plowing, he said, "Hey there, my Brother! How will you ever finish plowing by letting the strong ox rest and making a calf do the work?"

That strong man looked immensely proud and said, "My Brother, if you do not know the situation, please inquire before you speak. This is a lost calf, and I found it. Allah has sent it to me. Why should I not use this opportunity? I will use my own ox again when the calf's owner comes for it."

Hearing these words the calf became very angry. It let out a roar in a deep gruffy voice. Momentarily it transformed itself into a small dragonfly and flew away.

Then the fairy maiden went along the Old Dragon River, thinking, "If I meet another evil-hearted man like that one, I must ask the Sage to let disasters befall this region."

Entering the city she changed into a pitiful old woman. Dressed in rags, holding a very thin stick in her hand, she begged along the streets.

An orphaned and helpless beggar came along, with a piece of rice crust in his hand. He was running to a secluded spot.

The old woman staggered to him and begged in a trembling voice, "For Allah's sake, please have pity on me." The young beggar looked at her, as if struck dumb.

"For Allah's sake, please give me some rice crust," repeated the old woman.

The young beggar was hungry, indeed. He glanced at his only rice crust, hesitatingly. But when he looked up at the pale woman, in rags, he concluded that she was poorer than he. He handed over the rice crust to the old woman, with both hands.

The old woman gazed at him with deep emotions and said, "You are the kindest son of our Muslims. You have given me your rice crust. As a result you will have to starve."

"Grandma, you may have it. Hunger means nothing to me. I can bear it for a couple of days," said the young beggar with a smile. The old woman smiled cordially. She accepted the rice crust and looked at it for a while. Then she handed it back to the young man and disappeared in a flash. The young man looked at his hand, and in it he held bright and shiny silver.

So it happened that on her journey to the world of humankind the fairy maiden discovered that there were more kind-hearted people than bad ones. And although she was not completely satisfied, she decided to tell the Sage all of it. She asked him to spare humankind.

12

Social Satire

Three Gold Bricks

Place: Jimosaer county, Xinjiang
Narrator: Lixin (Hui)
Recorder: Zhangyi, 1984

Yes, there is such a story, handed down from long, long ago. There were two farmers. The one who was named Muhama was a fat man; he lived on the upper reaches of the Quan River. The other who was named Yiliya was a thin man, and he lived at the lower end of the Quan River. They were almost the same age, but quite different in nature. Muhama was greedy and crafty while Yiliya was honest and kind.

On a market day these two men pooled some money for dried food and then walked to town together. On their way the thin man carried the provisions on his shoulder and the fat one followed behind, humming *huaer*—a Hui antiphonal folk tune.

After passing through a portion of the Gobi Desert, the fat man sat on the ground and asked for food. The thin man took out all the three cakes and went to a house nearby for water. When he returned with the water he found that only one cake was left. Yiliya complained, "Why do you only think of yourself? You have eaten two of the three cakes..."

The fat man stared at him and denied it. He gestured to the sky and then to his heart: "Allah knows, there were only two. That is certain. How could you accuse an innocent person!"

The thin man thought that, unless the fat man confessed, there was nothing he could do. There were no witnesses. It seemed better to walk on. When he was about to stride forward he suddenly caught sight of something shining, far ahead. He walked over. It was three gold bricks! At this moment the fat man also walked up, with open eyes.

Seeing the gold bricks the fat man again began to scheme for himself: "We both found the three gold bricks at the same moment. How shall we share? I must get more."

But he was embarrassed to say so directly. And so he asked, "Hi there, Respected Brother! Allah gave us these gold bricks. How shall we divide?"

The thin man still wanted him to confess that he had eaten three cakes, so he replied readily, "It is easy. Three cakes and three bricks. One who has eaten one cake will get one brick, one who ate two will get two bricks as well."

The fat man was satisfied. He then had the nerve to say, "Hey, to tell you the truth, it was I who ate the two cakes. I denied it because I was afraid you would be displeased."

The thin man thought, "This fellow has a totally black heart. Being together with this fellow I might yet lose my life at his hands." Then he said unhappily, "I do not want any of them. You may take all." And with these words he turned quickly away.

That was just what the fat man had hoped for. He picked up the gold bricks in his arms. Looking at the thin man in the distance he thought, "A fool, destined to be a beggar indeed."

The fat man walked toward the town, thinking and planning: "Allah has bestowed on me this much gold. With it I will build a large tile-roofed house, I will buy all the land up and down the Quan River. I will run a store in town and marry a pretty girl..."

While thinking about his happiness he found himself nearing a robbers' hill. He held the gold more tightly and looked around nervously. Momentarily he saw the grass below the roadside move, and out ran four bandits to confront him. Before he could even shout, the fat man was cut down by the bandits, with a knife.

The four bandits got the three gold bricks, but they began to quarrel about how to share. Among them an older man, nicknamed Bold Ma, said, "Well, it is important that we first eat something. Then let us divide the gold." Thereupon they sent the youngest to buy some steambread.

While the youngest was absent the other three bandits shared one gold brick each.

But the youngest bandit was even more cruel. He bought a bag of steambread from which he took out and ate his own share. Then he put poison into the other pieces of bread. Upon reaching Bandit Hill he put the steambread on the ground, and before he could say anything he was stabbed by Bold Ma. The three bandits began to eat the steambread with pleasure. After a short while, Bold Ma was the first to feel a stomach ache. A minute later he fell and died. Within a few minutes the other two lost their lives as well, with foam and blood in their mouths. And so the four bandits all died.

After half an hour's rest the thin man continued to walk toward town. When he got to Bandit Hill he found a dead body lying on the ground nearby. He walked up to it—it was the fat man, Muhama. He looked around and saw four dead bodies not far from there; three of them each held a gold brick in his hand. He was astonished to the point of shouting, and he ran to report it to the county official. The county official sent his men for a postmortem investigation. After that they endorsed what the thin man had said, that it was true. They decided that the gold bricks should belong to him.

What Do They Respect?

Place: Wuzhong area, Ningxia
Recorder: Qi Qing (Daur) and Ye Xiuhua (Hui), 1979

There was once a poor but learned ahong. He often gave away to the poor what he received, such as money and clothes. All the while he himself became poorer and poorer.

One day a rich man heard about the poor ahong's learnedness. He invited him to dinner out of admiration.

The poor ahong attended the dinner in shabby clothes. All the wealthy men looked down on him and he was therefore seated as a commoner. All the while another ahong, magnificently dressed and rich, who had neither learning nor skill, was asked to sit at the place of honor.

Later, for some reason, this rich man gave another dinner. He invited the poor ahong again. The ahong declined: "You better invite the rich ahong who sat at the place of honor."

The messenger said, "Be sure to come, but you better come in fine clothes."

This time the rich man asked him to sit at the place of honor and respectfully invited him to eat. Then all the others lifted their bowls. But the poor ahong took off his gown and shoes and put them on the table.

"My gown and shoes, please help yourselves," he said. All the guests were surprised and asked why.

The poor ahong replied, "You do not respect knowledge, but clothing."

A Magistrate Judges a Case

Place: Xinjiang
Narrator: Ma Xinfa (Hui)
Recorder: Chang Qiang, 1984

There were three men who saw a penny lying on the road. They ran to get it at almost the same moment. And so their three right hands were all together on that penny. It happened that a county magistrate came by, with a fan in his hand. When they saw the official, each of the three men said that he had found the penny first. No one was ready to yield. So the case was left to the county magistrate to judge.

The county magistrate was, in fact, himself greedy for money. He would not give away as little as a single penny. Nevertheless, being an esteemed official he did not wish to grab it by force.

His eyes rotated and he hit upon an idea. "Stop shouting. Each of you just compose a poem which describes your family's financial situation. The poorest of you will get the penny." This the county magistrate spoke.

Everybody thought for a moment. Then one of the men, with a ragged felt hat on his head, said:

"Sky shows through the roof,
No wood in the stove,
No cover on the *kang*,
Hens and even mice are gone."

The county magistrate nodded his head slightly and muttered, "Poor, he is poor!"

Then an old man in a ragged felt coat said:

"Sky and earth are my room,
The moon is my candle,
My belly is my blanket,
My back is my mattress."

The country magistrate, perking his ears, listened and said in a hurry, "He is without anything, poorer than the first man."

It was the third man's turn now. He spoke calmly, word after word:

"Thirty years since I was born,
Never seen tea or grain.
Northwest wind is my drink,
Spring water is my meal.
If you do not believe,
Open my belly and see!"

Before the magistrate had finished listening to all of them, he began abusing them in his mind: "The poor wretches! Surprisingly they were all good at making poems, and one did better than the other." He became anxious, and therefore he shouted out his words of judgment in haste:

"Being an official from afar—
Working for nice clothing and for food.

Plucking a penny from the street,
I do not care about appearances."

Before he finished these words, the county magistrate jerked off the hands of the three men and grabbed the penny. He left them as he swaggered away.

The Treasure Mirror

Place: Linxia, Gansu
Recorder: Fen Jun (Hui), 1980

Once upon a time, in the Dongchuan Plain, lived a man of wealth named Master Ma. He owned much land, extending tens of miles. There were three people in his family. Rich as he was, he was extremely brutal and a scrooge. His wife and son were just as miserly as he. Local people called them "Iron Cocks." They said, "The Ma people are after money more than anything else."

One day their son wanted to look around in town, so his mother gave him several strings of copper coins and told him, "My dear son, for these coins bring back some white silk cloth for your father, some satin to make a coat for me, and some velvet to make shoes for you."

The son nodded in reply. Riding on his horse he was counting his money all the way to town—thinking how he could buy all the things requested by his mother.

Hardly noticing it, he arrived at the town's east gate. It happened to be a market day. The streets were crowded with loud and confusing voices. On both sides along the streets many booths were set up, to sell all kinds of goods for daily use—snacks, shoes, needles, cold and steamed noodles—everything was available. Business was flourishing, indeed.

He first rode through the streets on his horse. When he felt hungry and tired he went to a restaurant and asked for a plate of steamed stuffed dumplings, and he devoured them. After the meal he asked for a small bowl of tea with crystal sugar, and he drank, while tasting it with leisure.

Finally, after he had recovered from his weariness, he remembered what his mother had asked him to buy. He hurried into the shop next to the restaurant, looking here and there, but he hated to spend his money even on the things he wanted. Just at this moment he caught sight of a light flashing by the counter near him. Immediately he walked over and saw a pretty young lady buy something shiny, which he had never seen before. In it you could see a very beautiful lady, like a flower and jade, and all the goods in the store.

He stared at it and thought about it, again and again, a little bewildered. Water dripped from his mouth momentarily. He said to himself, "It must be a treasure with all kinds of things in it.... Right! I will get it."

Fortunately it was inexpensive. And so he happily paid the money, tucked it away at his chest, and rode home on his horse. Along the way he touched it now and then, being afraid it would fly away.

His mother had been waiting by the gate since even before he returned. Seeing her son grinning from ear to ear she thought that he might have had a good time in town and that everything went smoothly, so she, too, became overjoyed.

"Mother, I am lucky today that I was able to bring you a treasure. Everything you want is in it. I even have brought you a daughter-in-law." He took out his shiny mirror and handed it to his mother. "Just look at it yourself if you do not believe."

But the mother, taking it in hand, became terribly surprised and pale, because there was not a thing she wanted in there, much less a daughter-in-law. Rather, there was the wrinkled face of an old woman wrapped in a scarf. She lost her temper and pointed abusively at her son's head: "You idiot! Is this the treasure you got for me? An old woman with a wrinkled face? What on earth do you mean? Could she serve me or should I serve her? My Allah! What a pity it is to have lost my money on this!"

The son was startled at her sudden scolding, and he muttered, "Mom, maybe you are dim-sighted!"

The mother shouted angrily, "Just look with your own eyes, if you are not blind!"

The son took it over and, indeed, he saw an old woman in the mirror. "Why..., it...it...." He was too shocked to speak. The mother and the son gazed at each other in despair, speechless, not knowing what to do.

Crash!

The mirror fell to the ground and broke into pieces.

Terrible Worms

Place: Changji, Xinjiang
Narrator: He Yin (Hui)
Recorder: Hai Mingyi (Hui), 1984

Long, long ago, no watermelons were raised here. One year a merchant passed through, driving a camel, carrying some watermelons. He was tired. He lay down under a tree next to the wheat fields and fell asleep. So the camel went down to the wheat fields and ate up a big patch of wheat. When the merchant woke up he worried about what his camel had done. He wanted to apologize, but there was no-one around. Thinking for a while, he chose one of the biggest and brightest watermelons and put it on the spot where the wheat had been eaten. Then he went on his way.

The next day the landlord's supervisor came to inspect the wheat fields. When he saw that a large swath of wheat was gone, and that instead there was at that spot something round, black and green, he thought it to be a terrible worm. He was so frightened that he ran back at once and told the old landlord, "It is terrible. A big and round worm has appeared in the wheat field, west of the village. The wheat over which the worm has crawled is eaten up."

After he heard this, the old landlord took with him a few of his men ("dog legs") to have a look. When they reached the field they saw that big, round, and strange thing lying at the spot where it had eaten up some wheat. They were astonished and turned back in a hurry. When the landlord returned he told the villagers to find a clever and strong man to get rid of that terrible worm.

When a poor man named Yusuf heard of the news, he laughed into his sleeve and volunteered to get rid of that terrible worm. The landlord was glad and welcomed his help. All smiles, he praised Yusuf, and pretended to make many promises. But Yusuf cared little for that. He said to the landlord with a displeased look, "The fact that strange and terrible things appear here shows that somebody is too cruel. For example, you often cause us trouble, you bully us and treat us unfairly. That is why this strange thing has appeared here."

The landlord was frightened at these words and shivered all over.

When Yusuf saw this, he said, "Actually, yes, there is a way to remove it."

"Can you remove it?" he asked as he came closer to Yusuf.

"Yes," said Yusuf, "but you must promise something. First you must give up your rent for the land this year—let us say you give it to the poor people, in charity. Secondly, you should butcher fifty sheep, to offer a sacrifice to Muhammad and recite verses from the Quran. Aside from that you must give to each poor man two fried cakes and two pieces of meat—so that there will not appear any more such terrible worms. If this is not done, it will be difficult to eradicate such strange things completely. If you do as I said, I myself will remove it."

The landlord was both glad and distressed. He was glad that Yusuf could rid him of this terrible worm. But meanwhile he also became distressed because this year he would lose not only all rent for the land, but also fifty sheep, and much food.

But at this point he had no alternative but to make this promise, painfully.

The fact was, Yusuf knew that it was not a terrible worm but a very nice watermelon. The year before, when that merchant had passed through and taken a rest along the village road, he had helped him lift the baskets off his camel. The merchant had thanked him by giving him a watermelon. From then on he was thinking about eating more such melons. He would be lucky to enjoy one again.

That afternoon, when Yusuf saw that the landlord had slaughtered the correct number of sheep, had given each villager some meat and two fried cakes, and also declared publicly to exempt the villagers from paying land rent for that year, Yusuf told his friends the truth and went with them to share the watermelon in the wheat field.

Everybody thought that it was really good to eat. They kept the seeds to plant next year. In this manner the terrible worm was removed.

At the beginning of the next spring, Yusuf turned over the soil of the field where the merchant had put the watermelon; he dug the same ditch as he did for planting calabash. Then he spread some manure on the land and planted the seeds. Formerly that piece of land belonged to the landlord, but from the time when the terrible worm appeared in the field, neither the landlord nor others dared to till this land. So Yusuf was given this opportunity.

Soon it was August. The foreman of the landlord strolled to the field. When he caught sight of so many of the same worms as before he was scared out of his wits. He hurried back and told the landlord, "Oh Allah! In that field have appeared terrible worms over a large stretch, the same as the last ones..."

The landlord turned pale with fright and said, "It is not a good omen. Last year one terrible worm appeared, but this year there is a large stretch."

The more he thought the more scared he became. He was without recourse.

The supervisor said to him, "Last year Yusuf said he could get rid of such a worm, but this year more have come after. He should be punished."

The landlord thought that reasonable. He sent for him immediately.

Yusuf knew that the landlord would send for him sooner or later. So when he was brought to the landlord, just before the latter began to accuse him, Yusuf said calmly, "Last year you killed sheep and offered a sacrifice to Muhammad as I told you. Our Muhammad has therefore turned the worms into a kind of fruit. You may have a taste if you do not believe me."

He went to the field and brought a ripe watermelon for the landlord, and cut it into slices. He took one piece and began to eat, then handed one to the landlord. The landlord accepted it, nervously. Hesitantly he tasted it with his tongue. Alas! It was quite sweet. And so he began to eat greedily.

When he finished his first piece, and when his hand was reaching for another, Yusuf stopped him and said, "Do not be in a hurry. This is watermelon, which has been given by Allah to all the people. In order to let everybody have it, the seeds must be kept and will be used to plant some more next spring. But all the watermelons shall be shared by all, and not only taken by you. Otherwise Allah will have them changed back into worms again."

"All right. All right," the landlord nodded and began to have another piece.

Since that time the people here have had watermelons. And Yusuf became a famous watermelon planter.

13

Tricksters
And Wise Guys

Abudu Goes Fishing

Place: Mountains and plains of Ningxia
Recorder: Jin Wanzhong (Hui), 1980

Although Abudu was poor, he always looked happy and enjoyed laughing and talking. What he liked to do most was to engage in a battle of wits with the rich. All the rich men regarded him therefore as a liar. They referred to him as a fabricator of lies.

One day, while Abudu was on his way home from work, Ayoubu was standing and idly watching. He stopped Abudu and said, "You are said to be fond of lying, but you cannot fool me by your lies."

Abudu said, grinning, "Usually I only tell jokes. How would I dare to tell a lie and to make fun of you? Besides, I have something very important to do. I cannot have fun with you now."

"What is it you must do?" Ayoubu asked excitedly.

Abudu answered in a low voice, "To tell you the truth, the small river east of here dried up suddenly. Large carps flip along the bottom. Some cowherders are busy catching fish. I am hurrying home to get containers for fish." With these words he rushed on.

Ayoubu thought that this was a good opportunity. So he went with two of his men. With large and small baskets they rode on horses to the bank. Upon reaching its bank he found the river still winding its way downward, full with water. Some cowherders were playing in the water.

397

Ayoubu became so angry that smoke poured from the seven holes in his head. He rode back to get even with Abudu.

Abudu Digs for Gold

Place: Shanchuan, Ningxia
Recorder: Jin Wanzhong (Hui), 1980

"You rascal! How did you dare to deceive me?" Ayoubu arrived and complained to Abudu in a huff. But at that moment Abudu was digging a hole behind his house, sweat pouring down all over him.

"Oh revered Ahong!" said Abudu with a friendly smile. "I saw you standing witless by the gate. Do you not feel happy about having sauntered along the river bank on horseback?"

Sitting there, on the back of his horse, Ayoubu knew that he had been fooled. Still puffing with rage, he again put forth a challenge: "Abudu, I now bet you this horse that you cannot deceive me to get off it."

Abudu wiped away the sweat from his head and said, "Just now I made you take a stroll along the river bank. How could I dare to inflict a joke on you again? The horse is your throne, I am afraid to gamble for it."

After speaking this, he immersed himself again vigorously in the business of digging his hole.

Ayoubu felt strange, and then asked, "What are you digging for?"

At first Abudu hesitated to speak, but a little later he said quietly, "Last night I met my departed grandfather. He appeared in my dream and told me that behind the southwest corner of the house lies buried a piece of gold, three feet deep, which was left there by my forefathers. As you see, I am looking for it!"

The moment he heard that a piece of gold was buried in the ground, Ayoubu quickly slid off the horse. He took over the spade and said, "Look, you are tired. Let me help you dig. We can divide half and half if we find it."

Abudu then said, "It is too slow to dig only with one spade. I will go and get another spade from the field."

"Just ride my horse to go, it is quicker," Ayoubu said, hurriedly.

Abudu rode off while Ayoubu continued digging with all his strength. A long time passed and there still was no sight of the gold. The sun had already disappeared in the west, and there was still no sight of Abudu either. Ayoubu became tired, and suddenly it occurred to him that he might have been deceived again.

Finally Abudu returned, walking leisurely and carefree. Ayoubu jumped up angrily and asked, "Where is my horse?"

Abudu replied calmly, and slowly, "Did you not say that the horse belongs to me if I fool you down from it? You must keep your word. Inasmuch as the horse belonged to me, I sold it in the market."

Ayoubu was struck dumb, shocked by these words, and he almost fell over.

Abudu Washes Mud Bricks

Place: Shanchuan, Ningxia
Recorder: Jin Wanzhong (Hui), 1980

The landlord asked Abudu to do work which he estimated would require a full day. But Abudu worked fast and finished it before noon. He wanted to have a good rest in the afternoon. But the landlord did not feel good when he saw his laborer idle. He especially hated Abudu, who often deliberately made things difficult for him. Now he wanted to teach him a good lesson in return. The landlord gave Abudu a piece of mudbrick and said, "I pay you not only money, but also provide your food. It is unreasonable for you to be idle. Since you have nothing to do this afternoon, you will have to wash this mudbrick with water, until there is no dirt left on it."

Abudu took the mudbrick, quietly. And then he said, "It is too bad that a mudbrick is entirely made of dirt. All right, let it soak in water."

With a splash the mudbrick was thrown into water. The landlord shouted, "Mischievous! I asked you to wash it with your hands."

Abudu answered, "After soaking it, washing it clean will be easier. If you do not believe me you may take it out after a while and see." Abudu left and went to sleep in his room. The landlord was too angry to say another word.

Abudu Apologizes

Place: Qinhai
Recorder: Zhu Gang (Hui), 1980

Abudu was not only poor, having ordinarily one meal and not a next, he also was turning a blind eye on pious recitation. Being very busy earning a livelihood he was unable to perform the five prayers, and so the ahong of the mosque disliked him.

Yesterday it was his turn to provide the ahong with meals. But, as before, the three meals he sent were steamed bran bread and weak tea. This angered the ahong even more.

Today, however, Abudu left his work and went to attend Friday prayer in the mosque. Just as he entered the mosque he met the ahong, who had the facial expression of a black wind, and who said, "Abudu, you offended. Do you know that?"

"Yes, I know, reverend Ahong! My conscience enlightened me yesterday, and I have learned a few verses for my atonement. Please listen."

While speaking, Abudu knelt down in the prayer hall and began to pray, publicly and sincerely:

"I enter the mosque,
Kneeling toward the west,
Great Allah, please forgive me two things.

First, I have no skills,
And second, I have bad relations with the ahong."

The Hui men all around could not help but burst out laughing.

Abudu Gives Alms

Place: Ningxia
Recorder: Jin Wanzhong (Hui), 1980

Abudu, a poor man, lived next door to Ayoubu, a rich man. Abudu lived in a thatched cottage while Ayoubu lived in a splendid mansion. Abudu worked day and night in the fields but could not keep his body and soul together. Ayoubu was an ahong in a mosque. He recited Quran and lectured every day and he did not have to worry about his food or clothing. Every Friday when he recited scripture he always urged the people, "You should do good deeds, often, and as many as you can. If someone comes to you begging, whether you are rich or poor, you should give him at least a mouthful or a *dou*."[1]

One day Abudu was having his meal at his door. He saw that Ayoubu had his grain taken to be dried in the sun; the surplus grain had been stored so long that insects crawled out of it. At this very moment a beggar walked up, and Abudu gave him the only half piece of bread which he had.

In contrast, Ayoubu was a miser whose deeds did not match his words. He saw the beggar ask for alms but he pretended not to see him.

Abudu became angry. And he had an idea. Smilingly he took the beggar to Ayoubu and said loudly, "My revered Ahong. You often told us when you recited scripture that, whether poor or rich, one should give to a beggar at least a mouthful of food, or a *dou*. I had

---

[1]One *dou* equals approximately ten liters.

only a half a bread and gave it away. You have so much grain. You should give him a *dou*."

Ayoubu filled a whole bag of grain for the beggar. It made his heart ache. But what else could he do?

Suoli's Story

Place: Shanchuan, Ningxia
Recorder: Niu Geng (Hui), 1979

A landlord who was named "Bigbelly Ma" took quite a fancy to the red horse of Wang Sheba, a poor old man, and he wanted to exchange his own black and thin horse for the red one.

Wang Sheba, even though he was a robed ahong, has never been asked to speak in a mosque—because he was too honest and straightforward. Fortunately Wang was good at acupuncture. He tried to make his living by curing illnesses; and so he rode from village to village on the red horse which was led by his son Suoli.

Wang and his son had bought the horse when it was still a foal. They had taken good care of it. The horse was not only good looking with shiny satin-like hair and a long black mane and tail, but it was also very strong with a broad breast and straight legs. It could run fast and steady.

Each day, in the evening, the red horse returned carrying its master and half a bag of grain. Wang often asked Suoli to feed grass and to give water to the horse, and to let it stroll a while before sleeping—because they loved it dearly.

Once a horse dealer took a fancy to the red horse and wanted to buy it. Wang said jokingly, "Two hundred taels of silver!" Unexpectedly the dealer offered one hundred fifty.

Immediately Wang corrected himself: "My friend. I was joking. I will not sell it, no matter how much you will pay."

Now the landlord Ma wanted to trade his black thin horse for the red horse. But how could Wang agree to let it go? However, Ma was rich and powerful. If Wang refused, his son Suoli would be grabbed to join the military.

Old Wang Sheba had no other choice but to agree. Bigbelly Ma gave him his black horse and pretended to be so nice as to give him ten taels of silver on top of it. Then he took the red horse away.

Aside from looking ugly and skinny, the eyes of the black horse were sunk deep in their sockets. For each feeding they gave it half a pan of grass which it would smell, and smell again, and then begin to eat gingerly. In the end still some grass would be left. The horse swayed as it walked, and it could not support itself enough to get up without being helped by two men.

How could such a weak horse carry Wang on his rounds from village to village? Wang got so angry that he fell ill. Fifteen days later he died.

Suoli was just sixteen years old then. He was very grieved and angry. Young and weak as he was, he made up his mind to avenge his father and to get back the red horse.

One day, at the crack of dawn, Suoli got up, put on his ragged padded coat, tied his mourning sash around his waist and put on his white mourning cap. Then he began to feed grass to the black horse which was tied up in the dilapidated shed—which was a horse shed and a mill shed all in one—where the red horse used to be tied.

In the middle of the shed sat a small stone mill, and at the corner a crib was built of mudbricks. Into the crib Suoli put half a pan of grass and then stood aside waiting for the horse to eat it, slowly. It did not finish until midday, but then its belly was filled round. Suoli took out some silver pieces from his pocket, which had been paid by Bigbelly Ma, and one by one he shoved them up into the horse's behind.

After this was done he walked the black horse to the big street where landlord Ma lived.

Even a half month after the landlord had bought the red horse, and had taken it home, he rarely succeeded in getting on it. It went wild with strangers. And even when he got on the horse it would break away from the reins and run erratically. Besides, while being fed it would snap at him or give him a sudden kick.

Now it happened that the landlord was attempting again to get on the red horse. But when the horse caught sight of its former young master, Suoli, whom it had not seen for days, it began to neigh loudly and kick happily. Ma, who had just gotten on, was forced to slide off. Suoli glanced at the red horse but pretended to pay no attention to it; he proceeded to lead the black horse to walk past slowly.

But the black horse suffered too much to hold back the pieces of silver in its rectum. And just at the moment when they were passing in front of Ma it began to shit. What fell to the ground, as droppings, were pieces of silver.

Suoli turned back at once to pick up the pieces of silver, pretending to keep himself from being seen by others. But actually, Ma had already seen this, and he was surprised. He immediately asked, "What was it that the horse dropped?"

Suoli deliberately answered in a very low voice, "Silver. Hmm—it shit much less today. Why was that?" weighing it in his hand and appearing dissatisfied.

"Silver?" Ma really did not expect that. He stretched his head to make sure that what was in Suoli's hand was really silver. Then he asked, "How often does it shit silver?"

Seeing that Ma was falling for his trick, Suoli boasted, "How often? To tell you the truth, twice a day and about fifteen taels each time." And he continued to tell with pride, "The silver which I got this morning is about ten taels!" And, after weighing the pieces in his hands again, he tucked them into his breast pocket and pretended to leave.

Ma began counting. Twice a day meant twenty. Two [twenty] times three [thirty] is six—then six hundred taels in one month. How regretful he was! He stopped Suoli and grabbed the reins: "I have changed my mind! Take back your red horse and return to me mine, and you can keep my ten taels of silver," he said.

"No, no!" Suoli insisted emphatically. "You proposed to trade, how can you go back on your word?"

Ma did not listen to him but shouted at him, "Be gone!" He led the black horse by force into his yard, quickly, and bolted the door inside.

From then on Ma looked after the black horse, carefully, feeding not grass but beans to it, and making good tea for it. He had been waiting a full three days and three nights to find silver under the horse's rump. He did not even get manure, much less silver. On the morning of the fourth day the black horse died of overeating. Not until that moment did Ma realize that he had been fooled. Right away he sent his men after Suoli, but no one knew where he had gone.

But the landlord never gave up easily. Because he had lost ten taels of silver and the black horse, he hated Suoli very much. He therefore tried with all his means to get back the red horse. Yet, Suoli had already taken precautions and left his red horse with Brother Zhang, forty miles away.

As for himself, Suoli lived by cutting firewood from morning till night. One winter day he was caught by Ma's men in the mountains. Ma asked for the red horse, but Suoli refused. These were cold days and Ma held evil intentions of having him freeze to death. He stripped off Suoli's padded coat and left only a worn-out shirt on him. Then he kept him in his old mill shed which was as large as three rooms. It was winter and bitter cold. That night Suoli nearly froze to death, at first.

In order to keep himself warm he kept stamping his feet. Later he remembered that he used to push a stone mill. He took hold of the roller stone and began to push. Ma's stone mill was made of a huge black boulder, and usually it was pulled by a mule or a horse. After pushing tens of rounds he felt much warmer all over. Suddenly an idea to fool Ma once again came to his mind.

He slowly and steadily pushed throughout the entire night. Before daybreak he quickened his steps and after a while he was dripping sweat all over. He thought that perhaps Ma had gotten up. So he stopped to sit on the stone mill and to fan himself by shaking his shirt.

In fact, Ma, thinking that he must have frozen to death, came to look as soon as he got up. Contrary to his expectations, he saw him still alive, and he asked, surprised, "Do you not feel cold?"

"Cold? Can you not see that I am sweating? Though you are rich, you do not know about the shirt I am wearing."

Ma curiously felt his worn-out shirt and said disdainfully, "What can it be, that shabby thing?"

"Shabby thing? Haah," Suoli said with an air of complacency. "It is a warming shirt. The colder the weather is the warmer you will feel when you wear it. It has been handed down in my family for generations."

Ma became jealous again. He put on a smiling face and said, "Suoli, let us switch. I will give you silk padded clothes, and a leather overcoat in addition. All right?"

Suoli shook his head, pretending: "No! No! My father told me it could only be handed to the sons or grandsons of my own family. How can you have it? I cannot surrender it."

Ma could not resist this temptation. He did not have time to start caring for "sons and grandsons." And he said, "It does not matter. Give it to me." And he began to take off the shirt by force.

Suoli intentionally did not let him take it off easily. Ma finally pulled it off Suoli's body and ran away. After a minute Ma actually brought a silk padded coat and a sheep-leather overcoat back to Suoli, and set him free. There was nothing else Suoli could do. And having no choice in the matter, he went away in a new padded silk coat and a new overcoat.

To test the effect of the heating shirt the landlord chose a snowy and windy day. He put on the shirt and went into the garden to enjoy winter-sweet flowers. But before reaching the garden his hands and feet were numb with cold and he turned around in a hurry. By the door he slipped. His mouth hung open and he was speechless.

Ma was extremely enraged at having been fooled twice. He tried very hard and succeeded in catching Suoli again. This time he lashed him very hard, with a whip, and put him into a large sack. Then he made his men carry the bag to the bank of the Yellow River—with the intention of throwing him into the river. Because the river was frozen, Ma asked his men to dig a hole into the thick ice. He himself went home and told them to let him know when the hole was ready, because he wanted to see the sack thrown into the river with his own eyes.

The men finished digging and could no longer bear the cold. No one was willing to be left behind, so they all went home to tell their master about the hole being finished. At the bank only Suoli was left, in the sack.

It just so happened that Ma's oldest son, who had pinkeye, came riding across the river on a horse. Hearing hoofbeats, Suoli thought that his death was coming near. This must be Ma who was coming to throw him into the river. So he bit into the sack a small hole through which he saw that it was Ma's oldest son. He called out, "Red eyes can be turned into black eyes; black eyes can be turned into red eyes. It is a secret cure handed down by our ancestors. It works every time."

Ma's son was delighted to have found someone who could cure pinkeye. He was already thirty years old and, although he was rich and powerful, no girl would marry him because of his pinkeye troubles. Ma had seen many famous doctors, and still, none of them could cure this disease. Upon hearing that the man in this sack could cure his disease, he got off his horse and immediately released Suoli.

Suoli told him, "My eyes were red before. Just now I went into this bag and covered my eyes with my hands, in darkness, for only a short time. They became black. Can you see my black eyes?"

"Yes, yes!" Ma's son said. "Please help me into the sack. If my eyes become black, I will pay you as much money as you ask for."

Suoli—pretending of course—said a few words of courtesy and let him in. Then he tied the bag. "Just wait. I will be back when your eyes have recovered," this he said and ran away.

Soon thereafter Ma and his men came. Ma shouted proudly, "Throw the sack into the icy hole!"

Two men carried the sack and moved toward the hole. Upon hearing these things said, Ma's son became fearful and shouted loudly, "No! No! It is me!"

Ma sneered and said, "Yes, I know it is you who I am throwing. Off with him!"

With a splash the sack dropped into the icy hole. A few days later Bigbelly Ma discovered that it was indeed his son who had been thrown into the river. He hated Suoli so much that he wanted to eat him up in a single bite. Suoli therefore went very far away on his red horse. No one knows where he went.

Sailimai Asks the Way

Place: Tongxin and Guyuan, Ningxia
Recorder: Wang Zhengwei (Hui), 1979

One day Sailimai's father-in-law had something important to discuss with Ahong Ding who lived rather far away, in Ding village. But he could not go out, because he had hurt his back and also had a pain in his legs. And there was no other man at home at the moment. Seeing that her father-in-law was so worried, Sailimai said, "Let me go, Father."

The father said, "You are a woman, how can you go out?"

"I have an idea," said Sailimai, and quickly she dressed up as a man and started out on her journey.

Having arrived at Ding village, Sailimai found that it was a large place, with hundreds of families—too large for her to find the ahong. While she was still worried there came a man who was known in the village as Sharp-mouthed Mosquito. Sailimai walked toward him and asked, "My friend, can you tell me where Ahong Ding's house is?"

"It is the house with a door in the wall!"

Hearing these words, Sailimai thought that the man was really skillful in speech. "All right, I can find it myself." She paid no longer any attention to him and began looking around.

Sharp-mouthed Mosquito looked "him" over, up and down, and concluded that "he" must be a *xiucai*.[2] He asked, "Whose son are you?"

Sailimai turned her head back and replied, "I am the son of my father."

Sharp-mouthed Mosquito said angrily, "You senseless boy! I just asked what your father's name is. How can you answer like that?"

Sailimai took him by his word and replied, "And I asked you where Ahong Ding's house is. But you told me it is the house with a door in the wall. What house has no door in the wall?"

---

[2]*Xiucai* is a scholar who has passed the imperial examination at the district level, during the Ming and Qing dynasties.

Sharp-mouthed Mosquito was shook up. He was unable to come up with anything to justify himself. So he led Sailimai to find Ahong Ding, right away.

Sailimai Goes to an Examination

Place: Ningxia
Narrator: Wang Yanyi (Hui)
Recorder: Wang Zhengwei (Hui), 1979

On one of his inspection tours, to various places, the emperor one day heard that Ali's daughter-in-law, Sailimai, was a talented and knowledgeable woman. She could answer all kinds of questions with a glib tongue. So the emperor sent a man to summon Ali and said to him, "I was told your daughter-in-law's wisdom is extraordinary. If this is true, I will place her in an important position. Let me examine her."

Ali became scared and said to himself, "Allah! How can a woman take an examination before the emperor?"

After he came home he went down to the kitchen with a worried look and told Sailimai the story. And then he said, "You better stay home. Many *xiucai* scholars have failed this examination. Why would you want to put yourself through that much trouble?"

Thinking for a while, Sailimai said: "Dad, since the emperor has already come our way, we cannot simply avoid meeting him. Just let me try. Perhaps I can answer the questions, more or less."

Ali had to agree.

When she stood before the emperor, Sailimai said, "Peace!" The emperor looked at her who, wearing a round white cap and common clothes, did not look like a talented and learned woman at all. Then he began to ask, "How many words have you learned?"

Sailimai answered unhurriedly and clearly, "Not one word learned."[3]

Upon hearing this, the emperor no longer thought that she was ordinary—because only one word remained which she had not learned.

Because she talked so confidently, the emperor continued to ask, "Who was the first one born in the world?"

Sailimai thought it over. It had been said that Pan Gu was the earliest man, but I would not say so![4] "The earliest man is Pan Bian Gu (Pan, sire of Gu)," she answered.

"Nonsense!" the emperor scolded. "Ever since ancient times it was known that Pan Gu separated heaven and earth. From where comes Pan Bian Gu?"

Sailimai answered wisely, "Your Majesty, if there was no one to generate Pan Gu, where could Pan Gu have come from? He who generated Pan Gu was Pan Bian Gu—Pan, the father of Gu."

These words cheered the emperor, and he said, "A good answer, indeed! I only remembered Pan Gu, but forgot his father Pan, sire of Gu!"

Hearing the emperor speak in this manner, Sailimai grinned over her shoulder.

Once more the emperor asked, "There are so many Chinese words, but only one word you do not know. Then—on earth—how many volumes (of books) have you read?"

Sailimai said, "As clay scrolls up under the sun (*ri shai jiao ni juan*)."[5]

---

[3] *Yi zi bu shi*—"one word not learned"—may mean "have learned not one word" as well as "only one word not learned."

[4] Pan Gu or Panku is the primeval man to emerge between heaven and earth, or between the two halves of a primeval cosmic egg shell. Sailimai's quibbling pokes fun at both the emperor and at Panku mythology. From a Muslim point of view concerning the world's origins, the humor is obvious.

[5] "Volume" (*juan*) and "to scroll" (*juan*) are homonyms.

What did it mean? The emperor was absorbed in deep thought. Correct! Clay after a rainstorm, exposed to the sunshine, scrolls up endlessly. Ah! she had actually read endless volumes of books!

"Extraordinary!" In his mind the emperor praised this Hui woman who had such a wealth of knowledge.

Then the emperor continued to ask, "Now that you have read that many books, how many articles—on earth—are there?"

Sailimai answered, "As pieces of leaves blown by the wind (*feng chui shu ye pian*)."[6]

Upon hearing this the emperor concluded, "She is such a wonderful lady. She has read as many articles as there are leaves. Truly extraordinary! I have quizzed many people, but none of them had learned so many words and read so many books and articles as she has. No wonder she has a reputation of being wise."

At once the emperor proclaimed her as the Female Number One Scholar. Sailimai's name became famous after that.

Sailimai's Four Precious Things

Place: Xiji, Ningxia
Narrator: Wang Yanyi (Hui)
Recorder: Wang Zhengwei (Hui), 1979

Sailimai's father-in-law, Ali, was conscripted to do repair work in the palace for the emperor. One day, when Ali had been working till midday, the hard work made his head swim. This gave him a pain in the back and caused his hands to shake. Quite unexpectedly he knocked over one of the emperor's precious vases. It broke into pieces. When the emperor heard of it he opened his eyes so wide that it seemed as though sparks would fly from them.

---

[6]"Piece" (*pian*) is a homonym of "article" (*pian*).

He drew his sword and was about to kill Ali. Being tired and hungry, and seeing that the emperor was about to kill him, he was too scared to think. Panic-stricken he implored, "Forgive me, your Majesty! I will pay for it. I will pay for it."

The emperor said with scorn, "Ah! Such a poor old Hui even talks big! You will pay for it?"

A minute later he spoke again: "All right, Ali, I will not ask you to pay for my precious vase. I only ask four things of you: The first, something more black than the bottom of a pan; the second, something clearer than a mirror; the third, something which is harder than steel; the fourth, something that is as large as the sea. You must have these four things in ten days, or I will chop off your head."

Even though Ali had avoided death at that moment, he felt sick as he went home. All day long he was depressed and unable to eat or fall asleep. Sailimai saw all this with her eyes, and she asked, "Father, what is the trouble? Do not depress yourself like this."

The deadline set by the emperor was drawing nearer. Ali wanted to speak about it, but he thought it useless to tell her and only gave forth a long sigh. But Sailimai did not give up and persuaded him with all the words she could muster: "Just tell me. Maybe we can find a way."

Ali could not refuse her repeated questions. With tears in his eyes he told her the entire story, exactly as it happened. After hearing the story, Sailimai said, "Father, do not worry! I have all these four things. When the emperor comes tomorrow, I shall present them to him myself."

Ali reckoned that Sailimai was just trying to comfort him, and said, "Do not be a fool, Sailimai. There are no such things anywhere in the world. The emperor made his request of these things deliberately difficult for me!"

Still, Sailimai said, "Father, I really have these four things. You can see tomorrow even if you do not believe me now."

The next day the deadline for having the four things had come. The emperor wondered why Ali did not appear. He went to punish the crime himself, followed by a troop of soldiers. Ali and Sailimai were just waiting at home. When the emperor entered he asked ferociously, "Ali, have you got the four things ready? It is high time now!"

Sailimai stepped forward and said, "Your Majesty, the four things are ready. Please name them, one by one."

The emperor said, "The first thing I want is that which is more black than the bottom of a pan."

Sailimai said, "Yes, I have it. A bottomless heart with avarice is more black than the bottom of a pan."

The emperor was shocked. Hmm! Initially I wanted to put him on the spot, and now I lose! How sharp she is! And so the emperor spoke again: "The second is something clearer than a mirror. Do you have that?"

Sailimai answered quickly, "Yes. Knowledge in one's mind is more clear than a mirror."

The emperor could hardly believe that a rural woman had spoken these words. He cleared his throat and said, "Something that is harder than steel—do you have anything like that?"

Sailimai answered loudly, "Yes I do, it is the unity of the brothers."

The emperor for a long time remained speechless, and dumbfounded. He blushed scarlet with shame. And after that he asked, "Do you have something as large as the sea?"

Sailimai said, "Yes, a virtuous woman's heart is as large as the sea."

The idea had never occurred to the emperor that Sailimai could come up with the four things. And she did it so well. He shouted at his soldiers who stood about, "Get out!" Then he left dejected and surrounded by his men.

Since that time the story about the wise Sailimai spread far and wide.

Yimamu Questions a Stone

Place: Yinchuan, Ningxia
Narrator: Ma Chenshan (Hui)
Recorder: Xie Rong (Hui), 1980[7]

Long, long ago in Sufang county a new governor arrived—his name was Yimamu.[8] He was a tall man about thirty years old, with blond hair, deep eyes, a high-bridged nose and a resounding voice. He was unusually intelligent and judged fairly. Within a couple of days the news spread that he was an old Hui-Hui from Hami.

Even though he was a county governor he never paraded his power and prestige before the poor, and he never accepted any presents or bribes. It was not long before he had listened to the complaints of many people from the town of Aolu about having been treated wrongly. He decided to go there and see for himself what the matter was.

One day he put on common people's clothes and rode on a donkey down to the town, with only one official.

On the street he saw a little girl of about twelve, in shabby clothes, sitting on the ground and weeping grievously. The girl was such a sorrowful sight that Yimamu dismounted and stood next to his donkey to question her. He thought that there must be some reason for this sorrow, and so he asked her kindly, "Dear Child, what is the matter with you? Tell me, will you?"

The girl wiped her eyes and began to share her sorrows. Her mother, a widow named Fatumai (Fatima), had skills for making fried foods of various kinds which had been handed down through generations. Everyday she did this business in her store, and the little girl helped her mother sell the foods on the street, with a basket on her shoulder. As time passed, the widow earned a lot of money and so

---

[7]For more information concerning this recorder see page 73, note 1.

[8]Yimamu literally translates into "Imam." But the subject here is a secular Hui official, and "Yimamu" simply happens to be his Hui name. For parallel traditions to this story cycle compare Han stories about Judge Bao and Judge Di.

the people called her "Rich Widow." Last night a scoundrel broke into the store and choked the widow to death. He took along all the money and did not leave even a few pennies. The girl became an orphan. Upon hearing this, Yimamu resolved that he must get to the bottom of this matter.

Yimamu sent his official to summon the mayor of the town, and also some townsmen, whom he questioned about the matter. He also made a careful examination of the scene of the crime and of the body. He discovered that a pot of sesame oil had been broken on a stone. This stone was covered with oil; even the finger marks on the dead person's neck were oily. He concluded that the murderer must have broken the oil pot. His hands might have gotten oily, and also the money. So he said to himself, "Oil, oil, oil is the clue for solving this crime." He instructed his officer accordingly.

The next day was a market day. Some officials who carried a big stone through the streets and beat bronze gongs, shouted along their way, "People, listen. The murderer has been found out. The governor is going to question the stone in the big yard at the West Gate. Everyone is welcome!"

This event roused the people and left the murderer panic-stricken. Very soon a crowd of people gathered in the big yard, and the murderer was drawn along by the crowd, unthinkingly.

The big yard by the West Gate was a sea of people, and the officials locked the gate. By the door stood a large water jar, at both sides of which were stationed a couple of court runners. In the middle of the yard was set up a makeshift platform for questioning procedures. At its center stood the stone and next to it a stove and a burning iron.

All the people sat on the ground and became very quiet when the governor appeared. In official dress and hat he walked to his place. Yimamu stared at the stone. Then he gave a sudden shout in its direction:

"Stone! Why were you so cruel? You stole money, killed the widow, and made the poor girl an orphan. Confess your crime, right now!"

Stopping for a while he inclined his head toward the stone and listened attentively, saying, as if speaking to himself, "It is not you? Who could it then be?"

The crowd burst into laughing. But Yimamu waved the burning iron at the crowd and said, "Do not laugh! The stone confessed that the murderer is among you."

The people were struck dumb by these words. The murderer was overcome with fear and trembling, and he hung his head. All the while, Yimamu continued to ask the stone, "Who is it? You do not want to tell right now? But what can that girl live on?"

"Ask the people to contribute?"

"Oh yes, yes, yes."

Yimamu talked with the stone in his own voice, now high and then again low. Then he spoke loud to the people: "You cannot hear the stone talking, but I can. It told me, to ask you, to contribute some money for the girl. There is no limit on how much you may give. The money must first be dropped into the water jar. After that is done, let us listen to the stone's testimony."

Two officials brought over the water jar. Yimamu sat on his chair and kept eying the water jar closely. Seeing him act in this manner, the people began talking about the matter secretly: "What on earth is he doing with the jar?" All passed by the jar with puzzled expressions. Copper pennies were thrown into the water like raindrops. A middle-aged man, who was pale and looked sideways, came to the jar from the crowd. He took out some pennies from his pocket and threw them into the jar. As soon as the pennies went into the water, oil droplets appeared at the water surface. The man turned away without looking up, but from that moment on Yimamu kept his sharp eyes on him.

The money was collected. The governor stood up and began to walk around the stone, again and again. Yet, his eyes were kept on the man all the time. He asked the stone, "Now, has the time come for you to tell me who this merciless killer is?" Again he inclined his head and listened carefully. Then he said, "Oh, it is him! I see!"

He strode toward the crowd followed by two officials. Then he pointed at the middle-aged man and said, "You come out!" The officials dragged him out and took him to the questioning platform. They searched him in public and put the copper pennies which were in his pockets into water. Oil floated on the water surface. Upon questioning, the man confessed that he was the murderer of last night.

The people of the town praised Yimamu not only as a righteous judge, but also as a wise governor.

Yimamu Examines a Corpse

Place: Yinchuan, Ningxia
Narrator: Ma Chenshan (Hui)
Recorder: Xie Rong (Hui), 1980[9]

One day Yimamu went down to the troublesome village Shija-keng, in Aolu county, for a private visit. Along his way, when he was passing Camel Hill, he saw a young lady kneeling before a grave. She was about twenty-five years old, dressed in black with a white mourning cloth on her head. She seemed to be thinking about something. The moment she caught sight of the passerby she began to cry, "My Caide Old Brother! You have gone to Allah! Wait for me at the Suiladi Bridge! How can I live without you, my Old Brother?"[10]

Yet, there was no grief in her crying. The more he listened the more curious he became. He patted his court runner on the shoulder and told him something in a whisper. The runner hurried to the grave and asked the young lady something. Soon he came back and said, "Your highness, the lady said she was crying for her husband, Bai Caide, who died last night of a sudden illness. She lives in Shijakeng, Aolu."

Yimamu instructed his man to find a local investigator to examine the circumstances. And the investigator said, "Bai Caide was a Muslim who came from far away and settled down here, years ago. He obeyed the law and behaved himself. He got along well with his neighbors. We were shocked to hear of his death last night, because he has been very strong and healthy. His wife, as everyone in the village knows, has not been a decent person."

Having heard this, and thinking about what he had seen at the grave site, Yimamu became even more suspicious about this matter. He therefore entered the village again and visited the homes of

---

[9]For more information concerning this recorder see page 73, note 1.

[10]Suiladi Bridge, the "bridge of no avail." An eschatological belief apparently related to the Persian-Zoroastrian "Cinvat Bridge."

farmers. One old man said, "Bai Caide was a good fellow. He was as strong as a horse. That very evening I still saw him carry water."

Another investigator said, "Bai Caide's wife is like a tigress. She loves being idle and hates work. She is fond of gossip. She has seduced a scoundrel named Maly, from the village. They have often gotten together. That night, when I was passing by, I saw the shadows of three persons at their window. The morning after that I heard that Bai Caide had died."

Yimamu thought this matter over, carefully, while listening. It seemed that a lot could be read from this evidence. He asked a Grandma, Maihu, to look for suspicious things, and she found a coat which Maly often wore and brought it to Yimamu as evidence.

Even though Yimamu had this evidence, he could not be sure whether these two licentious people actually had killed Bai Caide. He questioned Bai Caide's wife in court. Seeing the governor she turned pale and hedged: "While Bai Caide was lighting an oil lamp, he felt a sudden stomachache. After a while he fell to the floor and rolled over, holding his stomach. Within a very short time he died."

Yimamu asked, "Who washed the dead body?" She began to speak and then hesitated for a moment." —An ahong who was passing by washed his body in the house."

Yimamu gave a cold smile and concluded that, inasmuch as there were no witnesses, the evidence was limited to the dead body. Then he cleared his throat and said, "All right. Inasmuch as there is no witness, I have to examine the dead body."

When the grave was dug open, they saw a bluish-purple body, the lips of which were black and the eyes of which were half closed. On the belly there was a black blue lump, as large as a bowl. Yimamu asked his men to do an autopsy to investigate what kind of a disease he had. Yet, to his surprise he found a poisonous seven-inch snake in his belly. The snake was still alive.

Later, for the second hearing, Bai Caide's wife and Maly were brought into the court under guard. They were forced to kneel in court. Bai Caide's wife was paralyzed with fright and hung her head without speaking. Maly did not confess his crime until Yimamu became angry and presented the clothes and the snake as evidence.

Actually, the two scoundrels put some narcotic into the tea which they made for Bai Caide. After drinking it, Bai Caide gradually lost consciousness. Bai Caide's wife held his head and opened his mouth with force, while Maly put the snake down his throat. Thus, Bai

Caide was killed and buried on the same night, his body covered with a white cloth. The next morning they hypocritically asked an ahong, an outsider, to pray in the house and by the tomb. Bai Caide's wife and Maly intended to get married one hundred days after Caide's death—an interval required by local mourning custom. But unexpectedly, their deed was found out and exposed by Yimamu. They were thrown into prison to be sentenced.

The story made its rounds throughout the county. The people clapped their hands and cheered.

Yimamu Questions a Hen

Place: Yinchuan suburbs, Ningxia
Narrator: Ma Ziling (Hui)
Recorder: Xie Rong (Hui), 1980[11]

One day Yimamu, the county governor of Sufang, followed by two of his court runners, was going about and making inquiries in the city. At the crowded street crossing two men were fighting. One was beaten black and blue, and the other was bleeding at his head. From among the onlookers no-one dared to stop them. Yimamu ordered his men to stop the fighting and to ask for the reason. One, appearing like a farmer, said, "My name is Ding Sheba. My mother is ill, and I came to town to sell grain to get some money—to buy medicines for her. But being afraid that the money would not be enough, I also brought a black hen with me as pay-ment. In order to get the grain sold first, I had the black hen kept in his stall, with his permission. After I sold the grain, when I came back for the hen, he denied the fact that I had left it here."

The owner of the stall, Nasi, shouted then, "What a country bumpkin! Who has ever seen his hen? What a curious thing!" He

---

[11]For more information concerning this recorder see page 73, note 1.

pointed at a shoemaker by the stall, who was mending a shoe, and said, "You may ask him if you do not believe."

The shoemaker broke in at once, "No, I have never seen this farmer."

Yimamu said nothing. Instead he went straight into Nasi's yard, by the house.

While he entered the yard he saw a group of hens, looking for feed here and there. Yimamu asked Ding Sheba, who followed him closely, "Can you recognize your hen?"

He looked among the chickens and saw his black hen standing aside. "Yes, my hen is among them," he said.

Yimamu whispered something into the ear of one of his officials, and returned to the mansion. His two officials caught all the hens and put them in a basket. And one of them requested that the plaintiff, the accused, and the witness come with him to the court. Another court runner began beating a bronze gong in the street, while calling out, "The governor is to question a hen. Come to the court, please." Many people quickly assembled in the court yard.

While some official runners were beating the court drums, some others had already been stationed at their proper places. The governor came out and sat down at his table. He pounded on the table and gave an order: "Call the plaintiff, the accused, and the witness." The three men were brought before him and made to kneel.

Another order was issued: "Carry them out!" A basket of hens was brought in and placed on the ground. An official released the hens from the basket.

Another official scattered some rice on the ground, and immediately all the hens began to peck at the rice, except the black one which stood aside and dared not to take any kernels.

Yimamu spoke to the crowd: "As the local saying goes, 'what you hear may be false, but what you see is true.' It is also well known that 'dogs like to be alone and hens are afraid of strangers.' It is obviously true that the black hen belongs to the farmer. Do you have more to say?"

Facing these facts, Nasi had to admit his wrong. The shoemaker looked embarrassed and hung his head. The entire court yard was rocking with laughter.

Yimamu continued: "Nasi swindled Ding Sheba and lied to the governor. He should be severely punished. But because this was the first time he did such a thing, he will be punished lightly....Moved by Ding Sheba's filial piety toward his mother, I will award to him all the hens of Nasi.... The witness, the shoemaker, dared to give false testimony to the governor; he will be awarded twenty strokes."

The people in the court agreed, almost as if in a single voice: "It is fair. Very fair."

The Donkey Knows Its Way

Place: Yinchuan suburbs, Ningxia
Narrator: Ma Ziling (Hui)
Recorder: Xie Rong (Hui), 1980[12]

In the late afternoon of a hot summer day, Yimamu went to inspect the granary, followed by his runners Zhang Qian and Li Wan. Before the storehouse, in the huge crowd of people, there was a boy of about sixteen years, covering his eyes and crying so loudly that his throat was hoarse. Yimamu stopped to ask him the reason for his behavior.

"My name is Ding Li, and I am from Heshui village. Today I came to visit my relatives in town, and to deliver also tax payments for the farmers while I was here. But there was such a large crowd of people here that I could not push in. Just then, a man over forty came over. He pretended to be kind and said he would hand in the tax payment for me, as he would also be paying his own tax. So he asked me to look after his own donkey and wait for him. But the whole morning has passed and the man is nowhere to be found," he said.

Yimamu asked him about the amount of money that was involved. He opened the donkey's mouth to look at its teeth and said to himself, "This cheater got away with money equal to three donkeys." Immediately he instructed his men to lead the donkey to his court and told them not to feed it in the course of that day.

---

[12]For more information concerning this recorder see page 73, note 1.

The next day Yimamu told three of his men how to carry out their assignment. With the donkey leading the way, the official runners left town. After having covered over seven *li* the donkey turned off into a farmer's yard.

Someone there was talking in a room. A woman's voice could be heard: "Did you sell the donkey? Was it a good bargain?"

A man replied in a laughing voice, "Everyone knows that I am good at business. Would I sell it at a low price?"

Before he finished his words, a boy was shouting, "Dad, our donkey is coming back!"

Upon hearing these words the man's heart sank. He muttered in an angry voice, "Oh, where?"

The three court runners appeared before him. Without a word they tied him up and escorted him to the court.

Before that incident the man had been a notorious gambler. He had lost money and was unable to pay his debts. Therefore he had to sell his donkey in the market, but no one came to take it. The donkey was very old. He wanted to borrow some money from one of his acquaintances who worked in the grain storehouse. Then he happened to see Ding Li carrying a large sum of money in his hand. A ruse came to his mind at once. He talked the boy out of his money and slipped away from the crowd.

Nevertheless, the man at first did not admit what he had done. And so the governor asked, "Do you not know that an old donkey knows its way home? The boy did not know you and could not find you. But the donkey could."

So the man had to confess what he had done.

Pushing the Millstone

Place: Yinchuan, Ningxia
Narrator: Ma Chenshan (Hui)
Recorder: Xie Rong, 1980[13]

Long, long ago lived dozens of Hui households at the foot of Moon Mountain. In the village lived a rich man named Shelizi. He was bald, with shifty eyes and an evil look on his face. He would try to take liberties with young ladies by any means, whenever he saw any. Behind his back the people named him Jackass.

One day, during the twelfth month (December), Fengerde fell on a Friday. All the people, the men and women in the village, went to the mosque to listen intensely to the ahong who was reciting from the Quran. But the rich man, Shelizi, was not in the mood for it. It was as if, upon seeing a young lady's nose and her eyes, the man's soul had left his body; he fixed his weasel eyes secretly upon a young lady, Ma Musa's wife. His mouth drooled unawares.

After that, for a couple days, he was unable to sleep well. One day, after having seen Ma Musa go to the market, in town, he happily went to knock at Musa's door. "Is Musa in?"

A minute later the yard door opened. Ma Musa's wife stuck out her head and answered, shyly, "He is not at home."

Shelizi squeezed in before she finished speaking: "You are the prettiest among the ladies in our village. Please call at my house if you are free. I am willing and ready to help you whenever you need me. Hihihi...."

While he so spoke he moved very close to her. The young lady got angry about his manners and guessed that he might be Shelizi. "Be respectful! Get out!" she shouted. But Shelizi did not lose his temper and still pestered her, shamelessly. At that moment Musa's little brother came back with firewood, from the outside. Shelizi had to leave, disappointedly.

---

[13]For more information concerning this recorder see page 73, note 1.

When Ma Musa came home from the market, that evening, his wife told him exactly what had happened. The young couple was very angry. They thought it over and decided to teach this tailless jackass a good lesson.

As they expected, a few days later while Ma Musa was again at a market, Shelizi came and knocked at the door again. The young lady saw that it was Shelizi and said in a low voice, "Right now I have relatives in the room. You can come tomorrow evening when the moon is up. Ma Musa will take the donkey to the mountain to carry coal." Upon hearing these words he left in a happy mood.

That very evening Ma Musa cleaned his millstone and fitted the carrying pole in the center. When everything was ready he went out to his neighbor's home, for a friendly chat. The young lady filled the lamp with oil and lit it; then she latched the yard door. She sat alone by the mill, getting the tools ready to grind wheat.

The moon rose and Shelizi arrived, stealthily. When he found the door latched he moved some earth bricks from nearby and made a small platform, high enough to climb over the yard wall.

He happened to fall right into the manure pit which was covered with ice. He had such a bad fall that he strained his back. His nose was badly hurt and his hands were bleeding. Yet, he had to endure his sufferings.

Seeing the rich man with mud and blood all over him, who looked neither like a human being nor like a ghost, the young lady could not help but laugh under her sleeves: "You are not young. On top of that you are fat and clumsy. But here, you have to come climbing in over the wall! It is Allah who punishes you."

The rich man Shelizi pulled a piece of cotton from his padded clothes, and on the oil lamp he burned the cotton into ashes. He used it to stop his bleeding. Then he stretched his arm out to touch the young woman when, suddenly, a knocking noise was heard at the door.

The rich man trembled with fear and asked in a broken voice, "Who might it be? What shall I do?"

The young lady, pretending to be afraid as well, said, "It must be my husband. But why does he come back so early? You just go to the mill and push the millstone. Let me deal with the situation."

The rich man calmed himself a little and hastily went into the mill shed. The young lady went to the door. "Who is it?" she asked while walking toward the door.

"It is I, your husband!"

"Why, have you not gone yet?"

"I have not been able to borrow money for the coal."

The door creaked open, and was latched again. And loudly the husband asked, "Have you ground the flour?"

"It is being ground now!"

"Whose donkey did you borrow?"

"The jackass of Laosi."

The young couple entered their room. The young lady pointed toward the mill and smiled secretly.

"Let me go and look how much flour has been ground," the husband said in a loud voice.

"Just sit down and have a cup of tea. Let *me* go and see."

The young lady went to the mill shed and saw the rich man pushing the millstone, with every muscle strained. She said to him, quietly, "Be quick. Do not let the hothead find out. Otherwise he might kill you with a knife."

While she was speaking she cleared away the bran and put on more wheat. Back in their room the young lady smiled to her husband. They began having tea and cakes while keeping an ear tuned to the movement of the mill.

In the mill the rich man was going out of his wits. He knew that Ma Musa was a man of unusual strength. "If by any chance he finds out, he will beat me to death." And while he thought in this manner, cold sweat kept oozing from his body. He had to behave well and push the millstone. Step after step he pushed until he was tired out, and then he rested with his hands on the pole.

Suddenly he heard the voice of Ma Musa, "The jackass has stopped. Let me go and look."

After that the lady shouted, "You need not go. Just give it a shout. It will walk."

And then he shouted, "Go!"

This really worked. The rich one started up again quickly, as his fatigue was frightened away. The noise of the millstone could be heard again.

But then the husband shouted, "This damned jackass. It needs whipping!"

"Why do you have such a bad temper today? Grinding flour is my business. Go to bed and sleep! Perhaps the blinders have come off the jackass's eyes. Let me go and have a look."

When the young lady came in, the rich man hurried to beg in a very low voice, "Please find a way to get me out of here!"

The lady said, "Be patient, there is not too much wheat left. Just hold out a little longer until Ma Musa falls asleep."

The rich man did not know whether to laugh or to cry. With all his strength he finished grinding the flour, at last. And by that time Ma Musa was fast asleep.

The young lady opened the door and the rich man quickly slipped away.

Half a month later the young lady chanced upon the rich man. She said to him quietly, "Why are you not dropping in these days?"

Looking very much embarrassed, he said, "Perhaps you need to grind flour. Do you?"

A Hui Fool

Place: Inner Mongolia
Recorders: Li Keda and Ma Deqing (Hui), 1978

In the town of Tuoyang, where Hui people live, everyone knew him. His name was Hui Kuanzi. He was homeless and without a job, and a bachelor. "Fool" was his nickname.

When people talked about "Fool" they all regarded him as a peculiar man. He was often in a situation of having one meal without a next. But poor as he was, he was always cheerful and happy. With his unusual disposition he never saved money or food for the next day; instead, he shared these things with poor people. Along with that he liked to poke his nose into other people's business. The people said that he was a bit silly; and for that characteristic the Fool became known near and far.

One day, when the Fool passed a shop where rice and flour were sold, he noticed a crowd of people standing there. He pushed himself amongst them and saw that the shopowner Yiu, with force, pushed some excrement into a boy's mouth with one hand, while he twisted one of the boy's ears with the other. The boy was already beaten black and blue in the face.

Seeing this, Fool tried to dissuade Yiu not to do that. But when the shop owner saw that it was Fool, he became even more angry. He shouted abusively, "Be gone! And you, poor fellow! How dare you steal my things? I must make you throw it up."

After inquiring about the matter, Fool learned that the boy was terribly hungry—that he had grabbed a handful of millet from the shop and put the grain into his mouth before the shop owner could stop him.

Fool said, "Master, we are all Muslims. The boy is an orphan. Have pity on him, please. He has already been beaten hard. How can you force him to eat excrement. No! You just cannot!"

"It is none of your business!" the shop owner shouted. "You are both the same stuff. It is obvious that you are poor."

With a smile on his face Fool walked over and took the boy away with him.

The next day the shop owner returned from the mosque, after prayer. He looked immensely proud. All of a sudden the Fool hurried past him with some nice fried cakes in his hands. He dropped one deliberately and walked away in a hurry. The shop owner caught sight of the cake through his glasses. He bent down and picked it up. He then bit off a big mouthful and chewed, savoring. He thought he was lucky today. And oh, how happy he was!

No sooner than the shop owner had swallowed the last mouthful, humming at the height of his enthusiasm, than Fool came running back nearly out of breath. He pretended to be worried and asked the shop owner, "Hello, Master, did you pick up a fried cake?"

"Yes, what is wrong?" asked the shop owner while rotating his eyes.

"It cannot be eaten."

"Why?"

"There is some poison in the cake."

"My Allah! But I have eaten it." The shop owner was frightened out of his wits. He showed the white of his eyes, with his mouth wide open.

"Alas! You are in great trouble. That was to be used to kill yellow weasels," the Fool said with great deliberation.

All the six vital functions of the shop owner suddenly began to fail. He was too frightened to turn around and to wring his hands. Momentarily he put his fingers into his throat in order to throw up the cake. It seemed that in fact he already had a bad stomach-ache, that he was feeling worse and worse.

Fool looked at him and pretended to be worried. "Master, be quick to find a way before the poison takes effect and you lose your life. But perhaps it is already certain that you will die in this manner. Go and ask an ahong to make your funeral arrangements!"

This the Fool said, moaning as well. It seemed as though there was no way to save this shop owner. As you know, rich men are afraid of death.[14]

The shop owner felt much more terrified when he saw the Fool's manner of worrying. He held the Fool's arm: "My good Brother! Help me, help me! I am dying." This he said with a trembling voice. Only the whites of his eyes, behind his eye-glasses, were still moving.

Fool had already decided. Nevertheless, he pretended to be helpless—sometimes thinking with his fingers on his head or wringing his hands. He glanced at the shop owner and saw sweat breaking out all over his face.

"Oh, I remember," muttered the Fool. "Yes, there is a way to get the poison out of you, but...but..."

The shop owner's heart became relieved when he heard that, and he answered even before the Fool had finished his words: "I will do anything, if only I can rid myself of the poison."

Fool cast a glance at him, sideways, and said, "It was said by the old folks that...that...Oh I am afraid you will not accept this."

"Yes, yes. I must. If only you can help me. My Brother please tell me," the shop owner begged, holding his stomach with his hands, moaning. "O what a pain I have in my stomach!"

"Come along." The Fool led the shop owner to a toilet and said, "Wait a moment."

---

[14]"Rich men are afraid of death" may be an old Chinese proverb, but in China it became a popular political platitude during certain periods after 1949.

Fool went inside and brought back a ladle loaded with excrement and handed it to him, "It is the best way to get the poison out."

The shop owner looked at the ladle. The terrible smell went straight to his nose. He shook his head and closed his mouth tightly. The Fool put the ladle on the ground and pretended to leave. "Have it, or not, as you like. When the poison takes effect it will be too late to have it."

The shop owner was afraid of death. He said to himself, "It is too terrible to die." He could hardly think anymore, and he seemed to be facing death. "Oh, it is terrible." He could not help but cry out, covering his face.

"Will you have it? I have got other things to do. I am going to." said Fool slowly.

The shop owner was anxious, and again he held on to the Fool and said, "You cannot go, my good Brother. I will have it. It is to cure me. What should I be afraid of?"

"Yes, it is to save you. You should not be afraid," the Fool said. He held up the ladle of excrement to the shop owner.

The shop owner closed his eyes and swallowed a mouthful. The terrible foul smell nauseated him and caused him to erupt and throw up.

Then Fool threw the ladle on the ground and shouted loudly, "Look! Look at the shop owner! He is eating shit!"

People crowded around. It was then that the shop owner realized that he had been had. He flew into a rage, with his face black and blue. He sat on the ground, puffing and blowing.

The Fool left, swaggering.

Once it happened that Liufa, owner of camels, sent for Fool. He said hypocritically, "Fool, I see that you are in a pitiful state. Will you graze my camels? I will give you meals instead of payment. Without that you will continue to suffer from hunger." Fool agreed, readily.

But already after two days of grazing the camels, Liufa asked Fool also to transport goods with the camels.

Fool went out with two camels for three days without carrying anything. He returned with the backs of the two animals empty, not loaded. Liufa asked him for the reason. The Fool—who still considered himself hired merely to graze the camels—slowly answered,

"Master, the camels are full [are fully loaded]. Just consider the forage they carry [in their stomachs] to be goods. Without those 'goods' they would surely have suffered hunger."

"Be gone! Go away!" Liufa was so angry that he could not get out a word.

The Fool took huge steps and went away without looking back.

Fool caused trouble here and there. He was reported to the county court. The magistrate ordered his men to take him to court. When the time for questioning came, the county magistrate, out of carelessness, broke a loud wind.

In order to cover for the embarrassment of his highness, the pen-knife [secretary] next to him rose and said, "Your Highness, I farted. Please pardon me."

The county magistrate nodded with pleasure: "It does not matter."

The pen-knife took his seat with satisfaction.

The county magistrate banged with his scary paddle and stared at Fool, shouting, "Why do you not abide by the law and behave yourself, but manage to create disturbances among the wealthy! As an official and your guardian I must put a stop to your mischief. You poor wretch! Do you confess your crime?"

Fool kneeled down on the ground and replied, "Yes, I do."

"What crime have you committed?"

"I farted too, please forgive me, Your Highness."

The county magistrate did not believe him and asked his men whether they had heard it or not. They all answered, "No."

Then he became angry and shouted, "How dare you deceive me, and interfere with the court?"

"No, I dare not," said seriously the Fool. "Just now Your Highness let go a loud fart, the kind which does not stink. But the one which I let go was of the stinking and silent variety!"

Thereupon the Fool was beaten with the big paddle, fifty times, and was driven out from the court.

14

Stories About Animals

The Tiger and the Hare

Place: Ningxia
Narrator and Recorder: Bao Xuecheng (Hui), 1982

Almighty Allah has created the Tiger and has let him prey on humankind and animals. So the Tiger told the animals that Allah permitted him to have all animals for food. The animals were not convinced by this, and on that account the Tiger had to put forth great efforts to eat his fill.

One day the Tiger thought, "How can I get the animals and eat without putting forth a great effort?"

He thought hard, until he had an idea. He would eat them in a specific sequence. Therefore, all the animals were called to a meeting.

"Allah lets me prey on all the animals," the Tiger said. "Because I can neither eat you all at once, nor eat the same thing day after day, my idea is that I will eat you taking turns, one each day. Whoever fails to come voluntarily, I will kill, along with his kind. Now you may discuss among yourselves who will be the first one to come."

The clever Hare was the first to speak: "Your Majesty, I have a good idea. Why not come in a sequence from the largest to the smallest?"

"That is settled!" The Tiger was delighted. He announced that the meeting was over. All the other animals could do nothing but obey.

431

The day came at last when it was the Hare's turn to be breakfast. It was long after sunrise, but the Hare did not show up. The Tiger felt a bit hungry. He waited and waited. At last he saw the Hare approach in a great hurry.

Before the Tiger had a chance to speak, the Hare said, out of breath, "Help me, Your Majesty! My wife has been taken away by a tiger. Please save her. Otherwise, what will you have for breakfast this day next year?"

The Tiger thought to himself, "How can I share this mountain with another tiger?"

He then asked the Hare, "Inasmuch as there is only one tiger on this mountain, and that is I, how can there be another?"

"If you do not believe me, please go and see for yourself. He is right there by the spring," said the Hare.

The Tiger believed it, more or less, and said, "Let us go and see. Lead the way for me!" He followed the Hare to the spring.

As they walked toward the spring, the Hare told the Tiger, "Your Majesty, I am rather afraid of that tiger. But if you were to hold me in your mouth, I would not be afraid at all." And so the Tiger continued walking with the Hare in its mouth.

Upon reaching the pond, the Tiger was surprised to see there, in the water, in fact, another tiger. It was just as big as he himself—and it also had a hare in its mouth.

Letting go his Hare, and not minding the consequences, the Tiger leaped into the pond. The Hare stood by the water, rejoicing. His face broadened into a grin. Before long the Tiger drowned. The Hare returned home and lived happily ever after with his wife and his children.

The Hare and the Dog

Place: Ningxia
Narrator and Recorder: Ma Jifu (Hui), 1981

Hare was feeding at a hillside when Dog caught sight of him. The Dog started off in hot pursuit of the Hare.

Hare ran around the hill. After a while he turned and saw that the Dog was left far behind. Hare changed direction and began to run down the hill. Because his forelegs were shorter than his hind legs he ran much slower than before. The Dog soon caught up with him. Now the Hare became very scared.

"Grandpa Dog, Grandpa Dog, have mercy on me! Have mercy on me!" So he begged while running as fast as his legs would carry him.

Upon hearing these words the Dog relaxed his efforts. But meanwhile the Hare did not stop running and rolling. He rushed down the hillside and headed for another mountain. This time the Dog was left even farther behind. Halfway up the mountain the Hare looked over his shoulder and saw the Dog still at the foot of the mountain. He plucked up his courage and shouted, "Dog, Dog, you are like my grandson! Now just see how fast your Grandpa Hare can run!" and with these words Hare continued running up the mountain.

The Dog could do nothing but listen to that talk. The Hare ran and ran, and he was soon out of sight.

Why Dogs Bark at Cats

Place: Longde county, Ningxia
Narrator: Li Guihua (Hui)
Recorder: Li Yinpan, 1981

Once a woman was kneading dough while her small son was relieving himself. When her son had finished, the woman tore off a piece of dough to clean his bottom. At that moment a dog was squatting at the door. When he saw the woman throw the dough into the fire under the heatable brick bed (*kang*), instead of giving it to him to eat, the dog got very angry. He immediately reported it to the god of grain.

The god came down to the world and found that there was too much grain wasted. He was so angered that he decided to strip all the kernels from their ears.

The god first stripped the ears of buckwheat. Unfortunately his hands were cut by the blade of a reed which grew among the buckwheat. The stem of the buckwheat was red with blood. The god flew into a rage. He made a hefty bite into the blade. That is why the stem of buckwheat is as red as blood and why there are three tooth-like breaches in the blade of a reed.

Fearing that all the diligent and kind people would suffer from hunger if the god stripped all kernels from their ears, the Dog pleaded, "I beg for your consideration. If you strip all the kernels from their ears I will die of hunger, because I am a big eater who can eat up to eight bowls and nine pots at a single meal. Moreover, those who do not waste grain will be starved to death as well. Please have mercy on us. Leave some grain for us to eat."

The Cat had been listening all that time, and now he cut in, "You better take away everything. Half a portion of food is enough for my meal."

The Dog flew into a rage when he heard the cat's words. He suddenly jumped at the cat, barking. The Cat whizzed past and was up a tree.

The god showed mercy as a result of the Dog's words. Some ears were left among the wheat and the buckwheat, and only a few ears of maize were left.

Because the dogs have rendered outstanding service to humankind, people today still keep dogs at their homes. When they have their meals they leave something for their dogs. But the dog and the cat have remained enemies ever since. Whenever they meet, the dog will give chase and bark at the cat. The cat will quickly climb up a tree, from fear.

The Monkey and the Turtle

Place: Tongxin, Ningxia
Narrator: Wang Weiguo (Hui, age 35)
Recorder: Wang Zhengwei (Hui), 1979

Long, long ago, there lived on Moon Mountain a small Monkey and a Turtle. They were on such intimate terms with one another that they became sworn brothers.

One day the little Monkey went to pick fruits on the mountain, leaving the Turtle at home. Turtle waited and waited and at last grew impatient; shortly after sunset he went for a walk in the village. He saw a notice posted at the gate of Squire Zhang's mansion. The notice read: "A handsome reward will be given to the person who can find the heart of a monkey to cure my daughter's illness."

The Turtle jumped with joy at this notice. "What an easy thing to do! Just give the heart of the Monkey to the squire, and I will make a fortune. With the money I will build me a new house by the river, and then hire another monkey to wait on me. From then on I will never have to worry about food or clothes. I will be able to live an easy life without having to work."

It was dark when Turtle returned home. He lay on the bed racking his brains: "The Monkey runs fast while I am rather slow. How can I obtain his heart?"

While he was thinking thus intensely, the Monkey bounced into the room and enticed him: "Look, I have brought you something good to eat."

The Turtle pretended to be worried. He said to the Monkey with a sigh, "Brother Monkey, I have something urgent to do. Can you help me?"

"What has caused you to be so worried—so that you do not even want to eat your supper? Speak out. I will do my best to help you, if I can."

The Turtle immediately got out of bed. "I am sure you can help me," he said. "The squire's daughter is confined to bed by illness. All the doctors that can be found have been tried, and still, they could do nothing for her. They say that only the heart of a monkey can cure her. I felt sorry for her and promised to give her your heart."

The Monkey gnashed his teeth with hatred when he understood what the Turtle meant. A brilliant idea came to him, and so, without showing his anger, he said, "That is easy! I can find ten monkey hearts easily. Do not worry. Each day several monkeys die on Moon Mountain. Let us go and take their hearts to the squire. There is no need to give him my heart."

When the Turtle heard that they could find even a greater number of monkey hearts, he agreed. And so, early the next morning they started out. The little Monkey thought while walking, "I treat the Turtle like a brother. But he is so heartless that he would sell my heart to the squire!"

The more he thought about it, the angrier he got. He began to walk faster and faster. The Turtle followed closely for fear that the Monkey would escape.

Finally they arrived at Moon Mountain and saw fruit hanging heavily on the trees. The little Monkey went up a tall tree. He saw plenty of fallen fruits under it. "Brother Turtle, come and look for yourself. There are many monkey hearts on the ground!" As the Turtle turned to look, the Monkey jumped and sat in the big tree. He was busy enjoying the fruit.

The sun had now risen from behind the mountain. It was so hot that the Turtle was sweating all over. He felt very thirsty. He begged the Monkey, "Brother Monkey, please come down. I am dying without water!"

The little Monkey answered, "Those under the tree are the hearts of dead monkeys; they are useless. Be patient and wait until I am full, then you can take away my heart."

The sun was rising higher and higher in the sky. It got hotter and hotter. At last the Turtle died in the scorching sun.

The Leaking Pot

Place: Guyuan, Ningxia
Narrator: Yang Shengjun (Hui, age 75)
Recorder: Yang Beizhi (Hui), 1981

Once upon a time there was a man who planned to sell his donkey, to obtain some money for a business undertaking.

One evening he asked his wife, "What are you afraid of most while I am away from home?"

His wife said, "I am not afraid of anything except a leaking pot."

It just so happened that at that moment Tiger had come with the intention of stealing their donkey, to eat, when he overheard the wife's words. The Tiger felt very much surprised, and he thought, "I am the king of all wild animals on the mountain. Can a leaking pot be more fierce than I?"

The more the Tiger thought about it, the more scared he became. He was about to run away when a thief came, from a nearby village, to steal the donkey. It was so dark that the thief could not see anything clearly. He climbed on the back of the Tiger because he had mistaken it for the donkey. The Tiger suddenly became very nervous. He thought it was "Leaking Pot" who was riding upon his back. He jumped over the fence and ran back toward the forest in a desperate hurry.

The thief also felt somewhat strange. As he bent over to look he found himself riding a Tiger. He was nearly scared to death. Luckily the Tiger slowed down when they reached the forest. The thief seized the chance to catch the end of a branch and climbed up a tall tree.

The Tiger, believing that he had gotten rid of the Leaking Pot continued running into the depth of the forest. He met Monkey along the way. And seeing the Tiger sweating all over, the Monkey asked, "Brother Tiger, what has happened to you?"

"Oh how dreadful! There is a Leaking Pot who is more fierce than I. He was on my back a moment ago. Now he is still on a tree at the foot of the mountain."

The Monkey was surprised to hear this. He asked the Tiger to go with him so he could see for himself. But the Tiger did not dare to go. The Monkey suggested, "Let us be tied to each other with a rope. When we reach the tree I will climb up to see, while you stay below. If there is really any danger I will wink to you and you can quickly run away, with me on your back."

The Tiger agreed. Together they arrived under the tall tree. Seeing that he was soon to be devoured by the Tiger, and thinking that his seventy-year-old mother would be left with no-one to look after her, the thief in the tree began to cry. Tears began running down his face. A few teardrops happened to fall into the Monkey's eyes.[1] The Monkey lowered his head and blinked his eyes. The Tiger thought the Monkey was winking at him. He therefore hastily started running for his life, without carrying the Monkey on his back. The Monkey was almost dead because he was dragged along by the Tiger, all the way.

---

[1]It seems obvious that tears, in this instance, indicate a polite refinement of the story plot—perhaps for the benefit of children. For the benefit of certain adult audiences some other bodily fluids were undoubtedly meant, and some of these make much more sense in the larger context—in a context where a thief is Leaking Pot riding the Tiger, and where a Leaking Pot happens to be a wife's greatest fear.

Why Swallows
Are Befriended with Humankind

Place: Yanchi, Ningxia
Narrator: Ma Youlin (Hui)
Recorder: Zhang Shulin, 1980

Once upon a time a wise man was reciting scripture in the mosque, when a big Snake came in. With its mouth wide open the Snake said to the wise man, "I would like to eat the most delicious flesh in the world. Please tell me which is the best."

"Wait a minute," answered the sage, "I will send Mosquito to taste first, then you can go and enjoy yourself." The sage told the blacksmith to fix a sharp and pointed iron mouth for the Mosquito. With that he sent him to taste all kinds of flesh.

It was getting dark, but the Mosquito still had not come back. The sage became impatient. Oh how he wished he could send the Snake away sooner! He therefore sent Swallow to go and to urge the Mosquito to come back as quickly as possible.

Swallow met the Mosquito halfway. The latter was still greedily tasting flesh.

"You have been tasting flesh a whole day. What do you find is the most delicious?" the Swallow asked.

"I have tasted all kinds of flesh. Human flesh is the most delicious," the Mosquito answered proudly.

The Swallow was worried and thought to herself, "If this villain reports this to the sage, it would be a disaster for innocent people." She suddenly jumped forward and snapped off the Mosquito's tongue.

The moment they returned, Snake eagerly asked: "What flesh is the most delicious to eat?"

The Mosquito, having lost its tongue, could only make a buzzing sound: "Hnn, hnn, hnn...." The Snake was puzzled.

Just then the Swallow cut in, "The Mosquito says *dong, dong, dong* (hole, hole, hole)...If you want to enjoy yourself, you must go into a mouse hole. The flesh of mice is the most delicious flesh of all."

Then the sage told the Snake, "You may live on mice from now on."

After the Snake had left, the sage said to the Swallow, "You are the most faithful friend of humankind. You have protected them. Go and live with them."

The nice swallows lived with humankind after that.

The Ahong Who Saved a Snake

Place: Guangxi
Narrator and Recorder: Bei Keyu (Hui), 1984

A Muslim once asked an ahong to accompany him on a visit to his ancestral grave, to honor the memory of the dead by reciting scripture. As the two entered the graveyard, a large spotted Snake suddenly appeared before them. The Muslim was about to kill the Snake when the ahong drew him aside, saying kindly, "Hold it! Do not strike it. Have you forgotten that the sage Muhammad has taught us 'You shall not kill any living creature without reason'? Let it go!"

The Snake ran away while the ahong was speaking. The next year, during Ramadan, the ahong went to visit the grave site alone. Just as he entered the graveyard, he saw again lying in his way the spotted Snake they had met the year before. It was facing him with its head erect and its tongue reaching out. The ahong was terribly frightened. Piteously he pleaded, "How ungrateful you are! Do you not remember me, who saved your life last year? Please let me pass!"

"That will not do," said the Snake. "Why did you save me? I will bite as long as I live." With these words the Snake struck and bit. The ahong died before he got back to his mosque.

Why People Do Not Understand Animals

Place: Ningxia
Narrator and Recorder: Wang Xueli (Hui), 1981

Long ago lived a man named Suha. He heard that Sulaiman, the sage, could understand the language of animals. He himself made up his mind to also learn this skill. He went to Sulaiman's house, one day, and asked to be accepted as an apprentice.

Sulaiman told him, "The skill was bestowed on me by Allah. No one can teach you but Allah."

Suha was not convinced. He said, "If what you said is true, will you pray to Allah for me? Please ask Allah to teach me this skill, too."

"All right. Let me try," said Sulaiman with a sigh. "But you must promise to keep it a secret. You cannot reveal what the animals say, even if they are quite unimportant words. Or else you will lose your life."

"Why?" asked the puzzled Suha.

"People have their own secrets, and animals have theirs. They should not tell them one another." Then Sulaiman continued, "For example, gold, silver, and other treasures are of no use to animals, so Allah let them know the secrets of treasures. And then, domestic animals in general cannot interfere with human life; Allah therefore lets them understand human language. But because men can interfere with animal life, Allah allows them neither to understand animal language nor to know the secrets of animal existence. If this were not so, the animals could never rest in peace. Do you see my point?"

"I see," Suha nodded.

"Can you promise to keep these secrets?" asked Sulaiman.

"Yes, I promise."

Sulaiman prayed to Allah then and there. Allah agreed to bestow on Suha the skill to understand animal language. With his new skill Suha cheerfully went home.

Suha's wife was a pretty, clever, and able woman; but she never respected her husband. In the family she was in command. On top of that, she made Suha tell her what he had heard, seen, thought, and done in the course of a day. He was not permitted to hold back anything.

Suha kept more than twenty hens, a cock, a dog, an ox, and a donkey. One evening he added more grain to the feed and took it to the barn.

Just as he was entering the barn he was noticed by the Donkey. The Donkey blinked its eyes and with a cunning smile said to the Ox, "I hear the master is going to take me to carry coal for him tomorrow. You will be plowing. I have something to discuss with you: Will you let me have your share of feed this evening? If I eat twice as much, I will be able to carry more coal tomorrow. As for you, the master will not have you plow the field when he sees how weak you are. Maybe he will send for a veterinarian to give you some tonics, to build up your health. You may take the chance to have a rest. Of course, I will repay your kindness tomorrow evening. No matter how much fodder I am allotted, I will give it to you. Do you agree?"

"Please do as you have suggested," the Ox readily agreed, with a moo.

Hearing the conversation, Suha knew that the Donkey was playing a trick on the Ox, but he did not interfere with their covenant. He only burst out into laughter. After Suha had put the feed into the crib, he patted the Donkey's head, touched the Ox's back, and then he left the barn.

He did not expect his wife to have heard him laugh. But she asked somewhat surprised, "Why did you laugh?" Suha did not dare to tell the truth. He only spoke evasively.

The next day, to see whether or not the Donkey would keep his promise, Suha deliberately did not make the Ox plow the field. When evening came he again went to the barn, with some better feed. Having put it in the manger Suha lingered nearby to see what would happen. The Donkey kept silent for some time. Meanwhile the Ox began to speak: "Brother Donkey, I think it is my turn to have all the fodder this evening."

"What a foolish thing you are!" said the Donkey with a sneer. "They said you were foolish, and I did not believe it. But now I know that you are really stupid."

The Ox asked, full of surprise, "What is the matter?"

The Donkey said, "Do you not know, that when the master came back today he found you weak and exhausted? He thought you were ill. Reluctant to send for a veterinarian, he sent for a butcher instead.

Tomorrow you will be butchered. I will carry the beef to the market to sell. You are destined to die tomorrow, and yet, you vie with me for more feed. You are an idiot beyond cure."

Terribly frightened, the Ox begged the Donkey for help: "Moo, moo, moo—what can I do-oo?"

The Donkey acted pompously. He pretended not to pay any attention to the Ox. Only when the Ox stamped its feet with great anxiety did the Donkey say, smilingly, "As for what you can do—we cannot really say that we have no idea."

"What idea?" asked the Ox hastily.

After a deliberate pause the Donkey slowly said, "If you eat up all the feed this evening, I am sure tomorrow you will look strong, head high and chest out. Then, when the butcher comes, he certainly will pay a high price for you, because you will be so plump and sturdy. In my opinion, you better not have any feed tonight. In this manner you will appear very weak and lean. The butcher will not pay a good price for you because he is less likely to get much beef out of you. Then the master will be reluctant to sell you, because he cannot get much money for you. If you take my advice, you will be able to save yourself."

The Ox thought that what the Donkey had said was quite reasonable. He expressed his joy with a moo.

Suha, who had been listening all the time, could not help but laugh again. To prevent the Donkey from taking advantage of the Ox again, he moved the feed over to the Ox. He pulled the Donkey aside and patted its head, saying, "I am sorry to have to pull you aside. You may continue playing tricks."

Just then Suha's wife came in, and she asked, "Yesterday evening I heard you laughing here. Now you were laughing again. Why on earth are you laughing?"

Even though Suha was afraid of his wife, he still did not want to tell her the truth, lest he would die. His wife got angry. She grabbed him by his arm and dragged him out of the barn into their bedroom. There, throwing Suha before the brick bed (*kang*), she continued questioning him. Unable to stand this kind of torture, Suha pleaded, "Please forgive me. Do not torture me any more. To tell you the truth, it is Heaven's secret and I must keep it hidden from anyone, or else I will lose my life."

"What silly nonsense! Do you think a good-for-nothing like you is qualified to know Heaven's secret?" So his wife shouted at him angrily. "Stop talking nonsense! I do not care whether you die or not. If you do not tell me the truth I will not let you off easily."

Suha gave a sigh. He felt great hesitation in telling the secret. Yet, his wife was relentless in questioning. Suha had no alternative but to speak: "If you do not let me off, then bring me a pen and some paper. Let me write down my will before I die."

Thinking that Suha was talking nonsense again, his wife brought to him a pen and some paper.

Suha stared at the paper with a blank look. Finally, with a trembling hand he began to write his will. His wife left him alone to write. She went out to let out the cock from its roost. Then she gave to the cock some wheat to eat, and to the dog a piece of bread.

Before the Dog realized it, the Cock had run off with the bread, into his roost. Instantly the Cock swaggered back out.

Suha heard the Dog speak to the Cock, barking, "The wheat is for you and the bread is for me. It has always been that way. Why did you snatch away my bread just now?"

"Something strange has happened," said the Cock.

"What has happened? I do not know anything about it," said the Dog.

"The master can understand our language. The sage told him not to tell anyone, no matter what, or he would surely die. But he can hardly hold it back from his wife. He is on the verge of speaking out."

"This is really something new," said the Dog.

The Cock continued, "Good times do not last long."

"What do you mean?" asked the Dog.

"Our master is really a worthless wretch. He insisted on being taught animals' language, and yet, he cannot withstand his wife's questioning. He is going to reveal the truth, and he can never go to paradise after he dies. He will be fit only for hell's fire!"

The Dog agreed with a nod, "You are right, quite right."

Suha was startled by their words, and he stuck out his neck to listen.

The Dog kept silent for a while, then he said with a wag of his tail, "What does this have to do with my steamed bread?"

"This concerns us deeply," said the Cock. "If the master dies, many guests will come to mourn him. The mistress will shut us up all day long. Perhaps some day she will kill one of us to serve to her guests. We will be living in constant fear. Therefore let us eat, drink, and be merry while we are still alive."

The Dog nodded his agreement, "If that is the case, I will not insist on you returning my bread. The master ought to have explained his reasons more clearly to his wife."

"Explain his reasons?" said the Cock resentfully. "This woman does not even care for her husband's life. How can he explain to her the reasons more clearly?"

The Dog could say no more. He lay down with his stomach empty.

Suha grew very angry. He picked up a stick and went to look for his wife. He would give her a good beating. When his wife saw him with a stick in hand, she said, "I will not let you off if you refuse to tell me your secret. What? You want to beat me? Try it if you dare."

Suha put the stick aside. He thought to himself, "It is very difficult not to tell the secret. It is even harder not to get involved in animals' quarrels. It is better to live a peaceful life without this skill."

Suha went straight to the sage Sulaiman's place and asked him to pray to Allah, once more, to have him take back this ability. Allah granted the sage Sulaiman's prayer. He took back Suha's skill of understanding animal language. And he never has bestowed this skill on any other man again.

A Soldier Understood the Skylarks

Place: Changji, Xinjiang
Narrator: Lou Fang (Hui)
Recorder: Yao Jinhai (Hui), 1984

Long, long ago, a young Hui prince was leading his troops home from a battle. When he came near a huge mountain he heard birds crying. They sounded so sorrowful that even stones would shed tears. The prince immediately ordered his troops to stop marching.

Then he ordered a search among his troops for someone who understood the language of birds. Finally, before they had checked nine thousand nine hundred and ninety-nine persons, they found a soldier named Gama who acknowledged that he could understand the language of birds.

Gama went to the entrance of the valley and listened attentively. Then he told the prince, "Your brave and kind Highness, the crying birds are skylarks. They did not know your troops would be marching through this valley and so they built their nests all over. At the present time their newly hatched chicks are still too weak to make way for your troops. The old skylarks are crying for fear that their nests may be damaged."

Hearing Gama's report, the prince said to him, "Please tell the skylarks that we would rather make a detour than harm their little birdies. Pass on my order, that instead of entering the valley all troops shall march the longer way around."

When, from the fluent language of Gama, the skylarks learned that thousands upon thousands of horses and soldiers had changed their route for their sake, they all hopped about with great joy. They preened their feathers and sang songs in the most beautiful voices of the world, praising the young Hui prince and his men. Their songs even caused the rocks to grow blossoms.

From then on the Hui people took great care of the skylarks, and on that account the skylarks were no longer afraid of them. When skylarks meet Hui farmers in the fields, or along the roadside, they merrily sing along with them.

If you do not believe me, just go to a Hui village and see for yourself. You will see that the skylarks are not at all afraid of people as they come and go. They know very well that all Hui people are well befriended with the skylarks.

Bibliography

Chinese sources of stories, as far as they were available, have been cited in the text. They are not included in this Bibliography.

Abu Saud, Mahmoud. *Concept of Islam.* Indianapolis: American Trust Publications, 1983.

Ali, Abdallah Yousuf, trans. *The Holy Qur'an,* in Arabic and English. United States: American Trust Publications, 1977.

Bai Shouyi. *Hui zu jian shi (A Brief History of the Hui Nationality).* Yinchuan: Ningxia People's Press, 1978.

Barfield, Thomas J. *The Central Asian Arabs of Afghanistan.* Austin: University of Texas Press, 1981.

————. *The Perilous Frontier—Nomadic Empires and China.* Cambridge, Mass.: Basil Blackwell Inc., 1989.

Bary, Wm. Theodore de, Wing-sit Chan, and Burton Watson, eds. *Sources of Chinese Tradition.* 2 vols. New York: Columbia University Press, 1960.

Brent, Peter. *Ghengis Khan: The Rise, Authority and Decline of Mongol Power.* New York: McGraw-Hill, 1976.

Brockelmann, Carl. *History of the Islamic Peoples.* Translated by Joel Carmichael and Moshe Perlmann. New York: Capricorn Books, 1960.

Chang Yusuf Hajji. "Ming Empire: Patron of Islam in China and Southeast-West-Asia." In *Journal of the Malaysian Branch of the Royal Asiatic Society,* Kuala Lumpur: Royal Asiatic Society, 1988, vol. 61, part 2.

Chen Huan. "Hui hui jiao ru zhong guo shi lue" ("The Coming of Hui Religion to China, an Outline"). In *Zhong guo yi si lan jiao shi can kao zi liao xuan bian, 1911–1949,* vol. 1. Yinchuan: Ningxia People's Press, 1985.

Dioszegi, Vilmos. *Tracing Shamans in Siberia: The Story of an Ethnographical Research Expedition.* Translated by Anita Rajkay Babo. Oosterhout: Anthropological Publications, 1986.

Dreyer, June Teufel. *China's Forty Millions.* Cambridge: Harvard University Press, 1976.

Eliade, Mircea. *Shamanism: Archaic Techniques of Ecstacy.* Translated by Willard R. Trask. New York: Bollingen Foundation–Random House, 1964.

———. *A History of Religious Ideas.* 3 vols. Translated by Willard R. Trask, Alf Hiltebeitel, and Diane Apostolos-Cappadona. Chicago: University of Chicago Press, 1978–1985.

Esposito, John L., ed. *Islam in Asia: Religion, Politics, and Society.* New York: Oxford University Press, 1987.

Fairbank, John King, ed. *The Cambridge History of China,* vol. 10, part 1, *Late Ch'ing 1800–1911.* Cambridge: Cambridge University Press, 1978.

Fan Wenlan. *Zhong guo tong shi jian bian (A General History of China),* vol. 3. Beijing: The People's Publishing House, 1965.

Faruqi, al- Ismail R. and Lois Lamya'l. *The Cultural Atlas of Islam.* New York: MacMillan, 1986.

Fei Xiaotong, ed. *Toward a People's Anthropology*. Beijing: New World Press, 1981.

Fletcher, Joseph F. "Central Asian Sufism and Ma Ming-hsin's New Teaching," *Proceedings of the Fourth East Asian Altaistic Conference,* edited by Ch'en Chieh-hsien. Taibei: National Taiwan University, 1975.

———. "The Naqshbandiyya and the Dhikr-i Arra," *Journal of Turkish Studies* 1:113–119 (1977).

———. "A Brief History of the Chinese Northwestern Frontier, China Proper's Northwest Frontier: Meeting Place of Four Cultures." In *China's Inner Asian Frontier,* edited by Mary Ellen Alonso. Cambridge: Peabody Museum, 1979.

Forbes, Andrew D. W. "Survey Article: The Muslim National Minorities of China," *Religion* 6 (2): 67–87 (1976).

———. *Warlords and Muslims in Chinese Central Asia.* Cambridge: Cambridge University Press, 1986.

Fu Loushu. *A Documentary Chronicle of Sino-Western Relations (1644–1820).* 2 vols. Tucson: The University of Arizona Press, 1966.

Fung Yulan. *A Short History of Chinese Philosophy.* Edited by Derk Bodde. New York: The Macmillan Company, 1960.

Geldner, Karl F. *Der Rigveda.* Harvard Oriental Series, vols. 33–36. Cambridge: Harvard University Press, 1951.

Geng Shimin. "On the Fusion of Nationalities in the Tarim Basin and the Formation of the Modern Uighur Nationality." In *Materialia Turcica.* Bochum: Studienverlag Brockmeyer, 1983.

Gibb, H. A. R. and J. H. Kramers. *Shorter Encyclopaedia of Islam.* Leiden: E. J. Brill, 1974 (1953).

Ginzberg, Louis. *Legends of the Jews.* New York: Simon and Schuster, 1961 (1909).

Gladney, Dru C. "Ch'ing Inner Asia c. 1800." In *The Cambridge History of China,* vol. 10, part 1, *Late Ch'ing 1800–1911.* Edited by John King Fairbank. Cambridge: Cambridge University Press, 1978.

———. "Muslim Tombs and Ethnic Folklore: Charters for Hui Identity," *The Journal of Asian Studies* 46 (3): 495–532 (1987).

———, ed. *The Legacy of Islam in China: An International Symposium in Memory of Joseph F. Fletcher.* Conference volume. Harvard University, 14–16 April 1989.

———. "The Peoples of the People's Republic: Finally in the Vanguard?" *The Fletcher Forum of World Affairs* 12 (1): 6276 (1990).

———. "The Ethnogenesis of the Uighur," *Central Asian Studies,* 9 (1): 1–28 (1990).

———. *Muslim Chinese—Ethnic Nationalism in the People's Republic.* Cambridge, Mass. and London: Harvard University Press, 1991.

Gladney, Dru C. and Ma Shouqian. "Interpretations of Islam in China: A Hui Scholar's Perspective," *Journal, Institute for Muslim Minority Affairs,* 10 (2): 475–486 (1989).

Goldziher, Ignaz. *Introduction to Islamic Theology and Law.* Translated by Andras and Ruth Mamori. Princeton: Princeton University Press, 1981.

Gulya, Janos. *Sibirische Märchen—Wogulen and Ostjaken.* Düsseldorf: Diedrichs Verlag, 1968.

Harrison, John A. *China Since 1800.* New York: Harcourt, Brace and World, 1967.

Jensen, Adolf E. *Myth and Cult Among Primitive Peoples.* Chicago: University of Chicago Press, 1963.

Jochim, Christian. *Chinese Religions.* Englewood Cliffs, N.J.: Prentice Hall, 1986.

Kao, Ting Tsz. *The Chinese Frontiers.* Palatine, Ill: Chinese Scholarly Publishing Co., 1980.

Kitagawa, Joseph M. *Religions of the East.* Philadelphia: The Westminster Press, 1976 (1960).

Leslie, Donald D. *Islamic Literature in Chinese, Late Ming and Early Ch'ing: Books, Authors and Associates.* Canberra, Australia: Canberra College of Advanced Education, 1981.

——. *Islam in Traditional China.* Canberra, Australia: Canberra College of Advanced Education, 1986.

Levy, Reuben. *The Social Structure of Islam.* Cambridge: Cambridge University Press, 1962.

Li Shujiang. *Hui zu min jian gu shi xuan (Selected Hui Nationality Folk Stories).* In *Zhong guo min jian gu shi da quan* (Chinese Minorities Folk Stories Series). Shanghai: Shanghai Arts and Literature Press, 1983.

——. *Hui zu min jian gu shi ji (A Collection of Hui Nationality Stories).* Yinchuan: Ningxia People's Press, 1988.

———. *Hui Zu Wen Xue Shi Gang (A Brief History of Hui Literature)*. Yinchuan: Ningxia People's Press, 1989.

———. *Hui Zu Wen Hua Da Ci Dian (Encyclopedia of Chinese Hui Culture)*. Shanghai: Shanghai Dictionary (and Reference Books) Press. In Press.

Lipman, Jonathan N. "Patchwork Society, Network Society: A Study of Sino-Muslim Communities." In *Islam in Asia,* edited by Raphael Israeli and Anthony H. Johns, vol. 2. Boulder: Westview Press, 1984.

———. "Hui Hui: An Ethnohistory of the Chinese-speaking Muslims." *Journal of South Asian and Middle Eastern Studies* 11 (1), 2: 112–130 (1987).

———. "Sufi Muslim Lineages and Elite Formation in Modern China: The *Menhuan* of the Northwest." In *The Legacy of Islam in China: An International Symposium in Memory of Joseph F. Fletcher,* edited by Dru C. Gladney. Conference volume, Harvard University, 14–16 April 1989.

Lörincz, Laszlo. *Mongolische Märchentypen.* Bibiotheca Orientalis Hungaria 24. Budapest: Akademiai Kiado, 1979.

Luckert, Karl W. *The Navajo Hunter Tradition.* Tucson: University of Arizona Press, 1975.

———. *Olmec Religion: A Key to Middle America and Beyond.* Norman: University of Oklahoma Press, 1976.

———. *"Cong jing hua lun de guan dian kan hui zu min jian wen xue"* *("Chinese Hui Muslim Traditions in Evolutionary Perspective").* Translated by Yu Fenglan. In *Hui zu wen hua lun cong* (Hui Culture Research Series), 4. Yinchuan: Ningxia People's Publishing House, 1991.

———. *Egyptian Light and Hebrew Fire: Theological and Philosophical Roots of Christendom in Evolutionary Perspective.* Albany: SUNY Press, 1991.

MacInnis, Donald E. *Religion in China Today: Policy and Practice.* Maryknoll: Orbis Books, 1989.

Mackerras, Colin, ed. and trans. *The Uighur Empire According to the T'ang Dynastic Histories—a Study in Sino-Uighur Relations 744–840.* Columbia, S. C.: University of South Carolina Press, 1972.

McNeill, William H. and Marilyn Robinson Waldman, eds. *The Islamic World.* Chicago: University of Chicago Press, 1973.

Ma Qicheng. "A Brief Account of the Early Spread of Islam in China," *Social Sciences in China* 4: 97–113 (1983).

Ma Tong. *Zhongguo Yisilan jiaopai yu menhuan zhidu shilue (A History of Muslim Factions and the Menhuan System in China).* Yinchuan: Ningxia People's Publishing House, 1983.

Martin, Richard C. *Islam.* Englewood Cliffs, N. J.: Prentice Hall, 1982.

Mayer, Reinhold. *Der Babylonische Talmud.* München: Wilhelm Goldmann Verlag, 1963.

Pillsbury, Barbara L. K. "Being Female in a Muslim Minority in China." In *Women in the Muslim World*, edited by Lois Beck and Nikki Keddi. Cambridge: Harvard University Press, 1978.

———. "Muslim History in China: A 1300-Year Chronology."*Journal, Institute for Muslim Minority Affairs* 3 (2): 10–29 (1981).

Rahman, Fazlur. *Islam.* Chicago: University of Chicago Press, 1979.

Riencourt, Amaury de. *The Soul of China: An Interpretation of Chinese History.* New York: Harper and Row, 1965.

Robinson, Francis. *Atlas of the Islamic World, Since 1500.* New York: Facts on File Inc., 1982.

Savory, R. M., ed. *Introduction to Islamic Civilization.* Cambridge: Cambridge University Press, 1976.

Sen, Makhan Lal, trans. *The Ramayana of Valmiki.* New Delhi: Munshiram Manoharlal Publishers, 1978.

Thompson, Laurence G. *The Chinese Way in Religion.* Encino: Dickenson Publishing Co., 1973.

Vasil'ev, Vasilij Pavlovich. "Islam in China." Translated by Rudolph Loewenthal. In *Central Asian Collectanea* 3: 1–37 (1963 [1900]).

Wei Cuiyi, "The Turkic-Speaking Minorities in China." In *Materialia Turcica.* Bochum: Studienverlag Brockmeyer, 1985.

———. "Ancient Chinese Historical Records about Central Asia." In *Central Asian Survey* 5 (2): 81–89 (1986).

Yang, C. K. *Religion in Chinese Society: A Study of Contemporary Social Functions of Religion and Some of Their Historical Factors.* Berkeley: University of California Press, 1967.

Index